FPC
STUDY TEXT

Paper 1

Financial Services and their Regulation

NEW IN THIS MAY 2000 EDITION

- New format, with added **Exam focus points** and **Key terms** identified: see inside front cover.

- Full coverage of **ISAs**; interaction between ISAs and **existing TESSAs and PEPs**; new rules on **dividend tax credits**.

- Full coverage of other April 2000 tax changes, for **exams from July 2000 to April 2001.**

UPDATES ARE AVAILABLE ON OUR WEBSITE at:
www.bpp.com
(see page (v) for more details)

BPP Publishing
May 2000

First edition 1995
Sixth edition May 2000

ISBN 0 7517 9935 1 (previous edition 0 7517 9950 5)

British Library Cataloguing-in-Publication Data
A catalogue record for this book
is available from the British Library

Published by

BPP Publishing Limited
Aldine House, Aldine Place
London W12 8AW

www.bpp.com

Printed in Great Britain by W M Print
Frederick Street
Walsall
West Midlands WS2 9NE

We are grateful to the Chartered Insurance Institute for permission to reproduce in this text the syllabus of which the Institute holds the copyright.

We acknowledge the major contribution of Bryan Potter, ACII, MSFA to earlier editions of this Study Text.

Page

(iii)

INTRODUCTION TO THIS STUDY TEXT

This Study Text has been designed to help you get to grips as effectively as possible with the content and scope of Paper 1: *Financial Services and their Regulation.*

Each *chapter* of the Study Text is divided into *sections* and contains:

- a list of topics covered, cross-referenced to the syllabus
- an introduction to put the chapter in context
- clear, concise topic-by-topic coverage
- examples and questions to reinforce learning, confirm understanding and stimulate thought, with answers at the end of the chapter
- exam focus points with hints on how to approach the exam
- a roundup of the key points in the chapter
- a quiz (with answers at the end of the Study Text)

Practice examinations

At the end of the Study Text, you will find two full practice examinations. You should attempt both of these before you sit the real examination.

A note on pronouns

On occasions in this Study Text, 'he' is used for 'he or she', 'him' for 'him or her' and so on. No prejudice or stereotyping according to gender is intended or assumed.

Updates to this Study Text

To cover changes occurring in the twelve months after the publication of this Study Text, we provide free **Updates**.

Possible changes to be covered in Updates are:

- syllabus changes, which normally take effect from January. (Look out for an Update in November or December.)

- changes in legislation, which for FPC may be examined eight weeks after they become legally effective, or 3 months in the case of AFPC papers. The main legislative changes are likely to be those following the 2001 Budget. (Look out for an Update in April.)

To obtain and print out your free Updates, go to our website at **www.bpp.com**. *You are advised to check this page when you begin your studies, and again during the run-up to your exam.*

Firms whose employees use BPP's Study Texts for FPC and AFPC can download the free Updates from our website for adding to their Intranet or other internal systems.

If you do not have Internet access and your firm does not make copies of our Updates available internally, please telephone our Customer Service Team on 020 8740 2211 to request a printed copy of Updates.

BPP PUBLISHING

CII SYLLABUS

Aims

The aims of the syllabus for Paper 1 are:

- to develop in the candidate a knowledge and understanding of the background to the financial services sector and its regulation;

- to develop an ability to apply investment knowledge to investment planning situations for clients, so that the candidate can advise clients on the implications of the knowledge covered by the paper.

Structure

The subject content for this paper is divided into three units:

Unit A   Regulation and compliance
Unit B   Financial services background
Unit C   Financial services providers and products

Each unit is divided into elements, which are further broken down into a series of learning objectives.

Each learning objective begins with either *know*, *understand* or *be able to apply*. These words indicate the different levels of skill which will be tested. Where the word *understand* is used, an adequate level of underpinning knowledge is assumed. Where *be able to apply* is used, a suitable level of both knowledge and understanding is assumed. These definitions apply to Paper 1 only.

Detailed syllabus

Notes

1   Each learning objective should be read in conjunction with the description of the corresponding element.

2   The syllabus is examined on the basis of English law and practice.

3   The syllabus applies from the January 2000 sitting.

**Covered in
Chapter**

Unit A Regulation and compliance

Element A1

The need for and scope of the Financial Services Act 1986, and the types of investment vehicle, transaction and activity regulated under the Act.   1

On completion of this element, the candidate should

A1.1   *understand* reasons for the government review of investor protection in 1981;

A1.2   *know* types of investment subject to the provisions of the Financial Services Act 1986 (FSA) and the types of investment business and investment activities covered by the FSA;

A1.3   *understand* the purpose of the components of the FSA regulatory system: authorisation, body of rules, complaints investigation, monitoring, enforcement, compensation;

(vi)

A1.4   *know* the main objectives of the Financial Services and Markets Bill.

Element A2

The regulatory framework within the financial services sector; the concept of polarisation and its effects.

2

On completion of this element, the candidate should

A2.1   *understand* the regulatory hierarchy of the Financial Services Authority;

A2.2   *know* the scope and powers of the Financial Services Authority;

A2.3   *know* which government departments are charged with supervision of the financial services sector;

A2.4   understand the principle of polarisation;

A2.5   *know* the difference between 'tied' and 'independent' financial advisers;

A2.6   *understand* the main responsibilities, under the FSA, of independent advisers;

A2.7   *know* who has the statutory responsibility for the financial advice given by different types of financial adviser.

Element A3

'Statements of principle' and 'Conduct of business rules'; the regulators' conduct of business rules/codes of conduct.

3

On completion of this element, the candidate should

A3.1   *understand* the statements of principles adopted by the Financial Services Authority;

A3.2   *understand* the purpose of the regulators' conduct of business rules/codes of conduct;

A3.3   *know* the regulator's rules concerning individual registration of an adviser and authorisation of a firm to undertake business regulated under the Financial Services Act 1986;

A3.4   *know* the requirements in respect of the advertising of investment products and services, and the content of business cards and business stationery;

A3.5   *know* the main criteria concerning unsolicited calls on a client or a potential client by an adviser;

A3.6   *know* the information that must be given by an adviser when first contacting a potential client in person or by telephone;

A3.7   *know* the range of products covered by the Product and Commission Disclosure Rules;

A3.8   *know* in detail the information which must be disclosed to clients when recommending a policy/product, in particular a written client-specific statement of key features, including surrender value, maturity value and the effect of charges and commission, and the stage in the transaction at which this statement must be supplied;

A3.9   *know* the circumstances under which an adviser must give or send to the client documentation including a terms of business letter and 'reason why' letter, and the circumstances under which this is not necessary;

A3.10 *know* the post-sale information that must be supplied by the issuer of the policy/product, including commission and benefits, as required by the disclosure rules;

A3.11 *know* the information which must be given by an adviser regarding cancellation periods when recommending a protection policy/ investment product

Element A4

Regulators' compliance rules: best execution and execution only, know your client, best advice, suitability, complaints, compensation.

4

On completion of this element, the candidate should

A4.1 *know* the principle of 'best execution';

A4.2 *know* the definition of 'execution only' and what should be obtained from the client when transacting 'execution only' business;

A4.3 *know* how to take all responsible steps to gather as much relevant knowledge about the client's circumstances as possible in order to know your client;

A4.4 *understand* how the adviser ensures that the client understands any risks;

A4.5 *know* the guidelines that should be followed in arriving at a suitable recommendation;

A4.6 *know* the sources of information which an independent adviser may use when selecting the most suitable provider of an investment product;

A4.7 *know* the actions required when a tied adviser does not have a product that would meet the needs of a client;

A4.8 *know* what steps should be taken when a client who has been offered 'best/suitable advice' instructs the adviser to effect a transaction which the adviser believes to be unsuitable;

A4.9 *know* the tasks that the adviser should ask the client to carry out when the adviser has completed an application form;

A4.10 *understand* the circumstances that the adviser should take into account when advising the client in respect of an existing investment contract, including the consequences of improper advice;

A4.11 *know* to whom clients should complain in different circumstances;

A4.12 *understand* the way in which, on receipt, client complaints are dealt with - by telephone, face-to-face and in writing - and the procedures for recording and dealing with complaints;

A4.13 *know* the compensation regulations that apply for clients who suffer financial loss.

Element A5

Purpose and scope of enforcement/inspection visits made by Regulators', and internal compliance arrangements of firms.

5

On completion of this element, the candidate should

A5.1 *know* the purpose of compliance monitoring by regulators;

A5.2 *know* how the monitoring of compliance by regulators and their members is carried out;

A5.3   *know* the arrangements for complying with the regulations by regulated members;

A5.4   *know* the scope and powers of regulators' enforcement/compliance officers;

A5.5   *know* in outline what steps must be taken to establish and maintain internal compliance procedures, including monitoring and compliance with regulators' rules;

A5.6   *know* the general responsibilities of the officer or department responsible for compliance within an organisation regulated under the Financial Services Act 1986;

A5.7   *understand* the application of Training and Competence rules on an adviser with particular reference to key performance indicators (KPIs) such as persistency rates;

A5.8   *know* the requirements for advisers undertaking specialist roles;

A5.9   *know* the requirements placed on advisers in relation to CPD.

Unit B Financial services background

Element B1

Legal requirements and economic conditions.   6

On completion of this element, the candidate should

B1.1   *know* advisers' duties under the Money Laundering Regulations 1993 and Joint Money Laundering Steering Groups' Guidance Notes;

B1.2   *know* individuals' rights under the Data Protection Act 1984 and Consumer Credit Act 1974 and Access to Medical Reports Act 1988;

B1.3   *know* the essentials of a valid contact, utmost good faith and insurable interest;

B1.4   *understand* how assignment of a policy in connection with a mortgage would affect the disposal of the proceeds;

B1.5   *know* the principles within the laws of intestacy/succession, and what constitutes a valid will;

B1.6   *understand* the terms 'own life' and 'life of another';

B1.7   *be able to apply* principles concerning the disposal of the proceeds of life assurance policies on death depending on how the policy has been written;

B1.8   *understand* the influence of the UK taxation system on protection and investment needs;

B1.9   *know* the definitions of inflation and (in outline) the ways in which the rates are calculated;

B1.10   *be able to apply* the effect of current and future levels of inflation to the returns on various types of saving, investing, spending and borrowing;

B1.11   *be able to apply* the effects of current and future levels of interest rates to the returns on various types of saving, investing, spending and borrowing.

Covered in Chapter

Element B2

The different taxes, their effect on individuals and their impact on financial planning.

7

On completion of this element, the candidate should

B2.1 *know* the circumstances in which income tax is payable;

B2.2 *know* the income covered by schedules A, D, E and F;

B2.3 *be able to apply* the main income tax allowances and the effect that they have on the individual's taxable income;

B2.4 *understand* the income tax treatment of sole traders and partnerships;

B2.5 *be able to apply* the principles concerning the tax treatment of benefits in kind;

B2.6 *understand* the methods used to assess and collect income tax; including self-assessment;

B2.7 *understand* in relation to inheritance tax (IHT) the term 'taxable estate', and the circumstances in which such tax is payable;

B2.8 *understand* the main exemptions to IHT liability, including potentially exempt transfers;

B2.9 *be able to apply* the basic principles of IHT and how it is collected;

B2.10 *understand* in relation to capital gains tax (CGT) the term 'taxable gain', with particular reference to indexation of acquisition price;

B2.11 *understand* how taper relief can reduce capital gains tax liability;

B2.12 *understand* the main exemptions to CGT liability;

B2.13 *be able to apply* the principles of who is liable to pay CGT and how it is collected;

B2.14 *know* how different financial services and financial products are treated in relation to VAT, IPT and stamp duty;

B2.15 *be able to apply* principles concerning the use of financial planning vehicles to mitigate tax liability.

Element B3

How national insurance contributions are made and the impact of the main social security benefits on financial planning.

8

On completion of this element, the candidate should

B3.1 *know* how the classes of national insurance (NI) apply to individuals;

B3.2 *know* those social security benefits which are dependent on the payment of NI contributions and those that are not;

B3.3 *understand* how the non-payment of NI contributions affects an individual's eligibility for benefits;

B3.4 *know* the definition of the term 'means tested', and which benefits are means tested either on income or capital;

B3.5 *be able to apply* principles concerning the circumstances in which the main types of social security benefit become payable;

B3.6 *be able to apply* principles concerning how the main types of social security benefit are treated for tax purposes;

B3.7 *understand* how the provision of social security benefits affects financial planning and how private financial planning provision affects eligibility for social security benefits.

Element B4

Financial needs throughout the life cycle.   9

On completion of this element, the candidate should

B4.1   *be able to apply* financial planning criteria to potential needs arising in future life stages;

B4.2   *understand* the need to protect the financial stability of individuals/families from the detrimental effects of certain events (eg death, illness, redundancy);

B4.3   *understand* the need to make pension provision to enjoy a reasonable standard of retirement;

B4.4   *understand* the need for individuals to supplement their state benefits;

B4.5   *understand* the need for individuals/families to make provision for future financial needs;

B4.6   *be able to apply* financial planning principles to meet the needs of employed individuals;

B4.7   *be able to apply* financial planning principles to the financial needs of the self-employed;

B4.8   *understand* how the standard of living and desire to pass on wealth affect the need for protection and investment related products.

Element B5

Gathering and analysing client information.   10

On completion of this element, the candidate should

B5.1   *know* the essential information required by a financial adviser, eg personal details, financial details, clients' attitudes and objectives;

B5.2   *understand* the importance of accurately recording clients' details;

B5.3   *understand* how to analyse clients' present and future circumstances;

B5.4   *be able to apply* methods of identifying, exploring, quantifying and prioritising clients' present and future needs;

B5.5   *be able to apply* the major factors to be taken into account when formulating a recommendation, eg regulation and compliance, economic conditions, taxation, state benefits, savings and investments, protection, clients' attitude to and understanding of risk.

Unit C Financial services providers and products

Element C1

The financial services sector and the services provided.   11

On completion of this element, the candidate should

C1.1   *know* in broad terms the influence of state provision on financial planning, eg through social security, national savings, the issue of gilts;

C1.2   *know* the services of banks and building societies which are relevant to financial planning;

C1.3   *know* the services of life offices and friendly societies which are relevant to financial planning;

C1.4   *understand* the nature of tied relationships involving banks, building societies and life offices;

C1.5   *understand* the services offered by unit trust and investment trust managers, stockbrokers and investment managers;

C1.6   *understand* why different risks attach to different types of investment products.

Element C2

Protection products in the market place which are suitable for satisfying the financial needs of clients.   12

On completion of this element, the candidate should

C2.1   *be able to apply* the different types of term assurance, eg level, decreasing and convertible, to satisfy clients' needs;

C2.2   *be able to apply* the provisions of different types of whole of life assurance to satisfy clients' needs;

C2.3   *be able to apply* the provisions of permanent health insurance (PHI) to satisfy clients' needs (excluding group PHI);

C2.4   *be able to apply* the provisions of critical illness cover to satisfy clients' needs;

C2.5   *know* the factors taken into account by the protection policy underwriter in deciding on the terms to be offered;

C2.6   *understand* the effect of charges on premium levels.

Element C3

Pension products in the market place which are suitable for satisfying the financial needs of clients.   13

On completion of this element, the candidate should

C3.1   *know* the broad tax advantages of pension arrangements in financial planning;

C3.2   *be able to apply* the main Inland Revenue rules regarding approval and taxation of occupational and personal pensions schemes;

C3.3   *know* the basic Inland Revenue rules regarding maximum contributions, maximum benefits and lump sum payments;

C3.4   *understand* the make-up of state pensions, including the role of SERPS, the difference between 'contracted-in' and 'contracted-out', and the effect of an individual's age on the decision whether to contract out;

C3.5   *know* the different types of occupational pension schemes, ie money purchase, final salary;

C3.6   *be able to apply* the provisions of occupational pension schemes, including death in service benefits and dependants' benefits, to satisfy clients' needs;

C3.7   *be able to apply* the provisions of additional voluntary contributions and free standing additional voluntary contributions, to satisfy clients' needs;

C3.8   *be able to apply* the provisions of personal pension schemes, including how tax relief is obtained on contributions, to satisfy clients' needs;

C3.9   *know* the basic methods of comparing the respective costs and benefits of occupational and personal pension schemes;

C3.10 *know* the issues involved in the portability of pension rights, including transfers from occupational pension schemes to personal pension schemes and 'Section 32' buy-out policies;

C3.11 *know* the choices available at retirement including open market options, pension fund withdrawals and staggered vesting;

C3.12 *understand* the provisions of executive pensions;

C3.13 *understand* the uses of unit trusts and investment trusts in pension provision;

C3.14 *understand* the risk implications of choosing different types of investment funds and their effect on the pension payable;

C3.15 *know* the objectives of introducing stakeholder pensions and their impact on financial planning.

Element C4

Mortgage products in the market place which are suitable for satisfying the financial needs of clients.   14

On completion of this element, the candidate should

C4.1 *know* the main types of mortgage-related products;

C4.2 *be able to apply* principles to evaluate the methods of repayment, both investment and non-investment, of mortgage capital and interest, to satisfy clients' needs;

C4.3 understand the tax treatment of mortgages;

C4.4 *be able to apply* principles to evaluate the advantages and disadvantages of the various types of investment products used in conjunction with mortgages;

C4.5 *understand* the risk implications in connection with the different types of investment-related mortgages;

C4.6 *understand* the ways of protecting mortgage repayments in the event of sickness, redundancy or death;

C4.7 *understand* the provisions of pension mortgages;

C4.8 *know* the methods of releasing equity from property.

Element C5

Savings and investment products in the market place which are suitable for satisfying the financial needs of clients.   15

On completion of this element, the candidate should

C5.1 *be able to apply* the provisions of the various savings accounts offered by banks and building societies to satisfy clients' needs;

C5.2 *be able to apply* the provisions of the various national savings products to satisfy clients' needs;

C5.3 *know* the provisions of the range of savings and investment vehicles available in the form of central and local government securities;

C5.4 *know* the types of savings plans offered by friendly societies, their tax treatment and the legal limits to contributions and benefits;

C5.5 *understand* the investment principles underlying life assurance contracts, eg unit-linked, with profit;

C5.6   *be able to apply* the provisions of different types of endowment assurance to satisfy clients' needs;

C5.7   *understand* the provisions of the main types of annuities;

C5.8   *be able to apply* principles concerning the advantages and disadvantages for taxpayers and non-taxpayers of insurance-based investments including the tax treatment of life/unit-linked funds;

C5.9   *know* the provisions of collective investments, eg unit trusts, investment trusts, open-ended investment companies, onshore and offshore insurance bonds;

C5.10   *know* the tax liability, charges, costs, risks and returns on collective investments;

C5.11   *know* the provisions and tax treatment of individual savings accounts (ISAs);

C5.12   *know* the provisions and tax treatment of existing tax exempt special savings accounts (TESSAs) and personal equity plans (PEPs), and the effect on these products of the introduction of ISAs;

C5.13   *understand* the different charging structures applied to with profit/unit-linked life policies, and to regular savings contracts through unit trusts and investment trusts;

C5.14   *understand* the relationship between investment risks and investment returns;

C5.15   *understand* the consequences of early encashment or surrender of an investment;

C5.16   *know* the criteria for assessing the investment record of the organisation offering the vehicle for investment.

THE EXAMINATION PAPER

The assessment based on the content of the three units will test candidates on their knowledge and understanding of the syllabus, and also their ability to apply this knowledge and understanding to investment planning situations to satisfy clients' needs.

The assessment will be by means of a **multiplc-choice test of 100 items**. The examination will be two hours long and the pass mark will be in the region of 70%. This figure will vary slightly from test to test to ensure that the tests are of a comparable standard.

Example of a multiple choice item to be used in the paper

Susan is in her employer's superannuation scheme and has death in service benefit of 1.5 times her salary. What is the maximum lump sum life cover she may have under a free-standing additional voluntary contribution scheme:

A   1.5 times her salary.
B   2.5 times her salary.
C   There is no limit.
D   The amount of cover that 5% of her pensionable salary will buy.

The correct answer is B.

Candidates can bring into the exam room and use a calculator, which must be silent and non-programmable. No reference material is allowed, but the exam paper includes **tax tables** giving rates of tax, tax bands, allowances and exemptions for income tax, IHT and CGT.

Legislation

The general rule is that the FPC examinations are based on the English legislative position **eight weeks** before the date for the examination. This means that changes are tested eight weeks after they become legally effective. Tax changes announced in the Budget usually take legal effect from the start of the next tax year, 6 April, and so they would be tested eight weeks after that date even if the Finance Bill had not been passed by that date.

Where legislation for a change has already been enacted, but does not take effect until an already announced future date, knowledge of the change will be tested eight weeks after the enactment of the legislation. (An example is the changes to tax credits on ISAs and PEPs taking place in 2004.)

So how up-to-date is your BPP study material?

This Study Text is up-to-date as at 1 May 2000. In particular, it has been updated for relevant changes announced in the 2000 Budget. Legislation which affects FPC from May 2000 up to the time of publication of the next (May 2001) edition of this Study Text will be covered by our free Updates, available on our website at **www.bpp.com** (see page (v) for further details). Provided that you obtain our free Updates, you will be able to use this Study Text for exams up to and including July 2001.

Part A
Regulation and compliance

Chapter 1

THE FINANCIAL SERVICES ACT

Chapter topic list	Syllabus reference
1 Why was investor protection reviewed?	A 1.1
2 Investments	A 1.2
3 Authorised investment business	A 1.2
4 Investment activities	A 1.2
5 Purpose of the regulatory components	A 1.3
6 The Financial Services and Markets Bill (FSMB)	A 1.4

Introduction

In this chapter we will look at why investment business is regulated, and at the scope of regulation.

1 WHY WAS INVESTOR PROTECTION REVIEWED?

1.1 In the 1960s and 1970s a number of financial scandals shook the financial world and **rattled the confidence of investors**. There was an Act of Parliament - The Prevention of Frauds (Investments) Act 1958 - which was supposed to prevent these sorts of problems from happening. However, it did not, and the government of the day decided to set up a review of the methods of regulating investments, advice and advisers.

1.2 The review was commissioned in July 1981 and was chaired by Professor Jim Gower. His job was to find a way of **ensuring that these problems could not recur**; his specific brief was to consider:

(a) the level of statutory protection for investors;
(b) the methods of control over investment advice and management;
(c) the need (if any) to change the law to make improvements.

1.3 His report resulted in the passing of the **Financial Services Act** in 1986 (from now on, we will mostly refer to the Act simply as 'the Act'). This main regulatory body is the Financial Services Authority (FSA).

Consumer protection

1.4 The exam covers the topic of **investor protection** and the Act is the only statute mentioned in Unit A, the Regulation and Compliance part of the syllabus. However, there are three other statutes which are concerned with **consumer** protection and we will now take a brief look at them.

BPP PUBLISHING

Policyholders Protection Act 1975

1.5 In the 1970s, a number of **insurance companies failed**, leaving their policyholders severely out of pocket or without cover or both. As a result, the Policyholders' Protection Act was passed.

> **KEY TERMS**
>
> - The **Policyholders Protection Act** aims to give some protection to UK holders of policies issued by authorised insurers that are or will be insolvent. In the case of long term business this includes:
>
>   o meeting 90% of a failed company's long term business liability, and
>
>   o arranging for the business of the failed company to be transferred to another insurer.
>
> - A **failed company** is one which is being wound up either compulsorily or voluntarily.

1.6 The **benefits** protected must be reasonable and will be scaled down if they are excessive.

1.7 The **costs** are met by a levy on insurance companies up to a maximum of 1% of their UK long-term premium income. The levy can also be applied to intermediaries.

1.8 The Act is applied by the **Policyholders' Protection Board**, a body appointed by the government to collect, administer and apply the levy and arrange for transfer of insurance business.

Insurance Brokers (Registration) Act 1977

> **KEY TERMS**
>
> **Insurance brokers** arrange insurance business. They have two special characteristics.
>
> (a) They are **independent of any insurance company**. They are able to select not only the most appropriate product for a client's needs but to select that product from a wide range of products marketed by insurers.
>
> (b) Insurance brokers act as **agents of their clients** (whereas an employee of an insurance company is the **agent** of the insurance company).

1.9 The **Insurance Brokers (Registration) Act 1977** required every company and individual using the title 'insurance broker' to obtain authorisation from the Insurance Brokers Registration Council. The Act does *not* regulate insurance brokers as such, but only those insurance brokers that choose to use the title 'insurance broker'. They must now obtain authorisation from the appropriate regulatory body in order to undertake investment business (normally the Personal Investment Authority).

Insurance Companies Act 1982

1.10 Insurance companies had been subject to regulation for many decades before the **Insurance Companies Act 1982** was passed, but the Act produced two new rules:

(a) Any insurer wishing to commence business, or to commence a new class of insurance business, has to be **authorised by the Treasury.** It was previously the Department for Trade and Industry. It is intended that this authorisation will in time be granted by the FSA once the Financial Service Bill is passed.

(b) A number of aspects of the way an insurer conducts business have to be overseen by the government.

Solvency margins

1.11 An **insurance company must be able to meet its liabilities,** so its assets must exceed its liabilities. The excess of assets over liabilities is known as the 'solvency margin'.

Conduct of insurance business

1.12 The people who control insurance companies, its directors and managers, must be suitable people to do so. This requirement is expressed by saying that such people must be '**fit and proper persons**'.

Accounting procedures

1.13 Insurance companies must keep **accounting records** which reflect their income and expenditure, and the position as to their assets and liabilities, at any time.

Control and intervention

1.14 The Act gives considerable general powers to the government to exercise **control** over a business and intervene if it feels that the business does not give the policyholders the security that they require.

1.15 Much of the motivation for the passing of these two Acts stemmed from malpractice in **general insurance** as opposed to the giving of investment advice, other than the fact that life assurance is one of a number of different types of insurance provided by insurers.

Investment protection: the Financial Services Act 1986

1.16 Investment business is currently governed by the **Financial Service Act 1986.** A new **Financial Services and Markets Bill** will be enacted during 2000. The Bill will change the manner by which the main powers of the 1986 Act is enforced, but will make few changes to the scope of the 1986 Act.

1.17 The requirements of the Act are quite simple.

> **Key point**
> If a business wants to carry on investment business in the UK, it must either be authorised, or exempt from obtaining authorisation. A business might be a company, a partnership or an individual.

1.18 The **objective** of all this regulation is to protect investors against the consequences of fraud and/or incompetence by **investment advisers,** by requiring them to display competence and experience which is adequate for the advice they are giving.

1.19 The description '**investment advisers**' is a little confusing. We will see later that many of the 'investments' that are regulated by the Act are in fact life assurance policies whose prime objective is to provide financial protection in case of death. These are products which are not normally thought of as investments. We must accept the official terminology but in practice the majority of people who are regulated by the Act are normally described as **financial advisers**. This is a more generic term and more accurately describes the intentions of the Act.

2 INVESTMENTS

2.1 The Act lists the **types of investment** which it is intended to regulate. It also goes on to explain what is meant by 'investment business' and 'investment activities'.

Types of investment regulated by the Act

KEY TERMS

- **Shares** represent the equity - share capital - of a company. They include permanent interest bearing shares (PIBS) which are issued by building societies even though the building societies themselves are not regulated by the Act. They exclude open ended investment companies (OEICs).

- **Debentures** are loans to companies. They include loan stock, bonds and certificates of deposit.

- **Government and public securities** consist of loans to the government, local authorities and any other public authority. They take the form of loan stock and bonds.

- A **warrant** is a document entitling you to subscribe for an investment if you want to.

- **Certificates representing securities** give you the right to buy or sell investments, to convert them to a different kind of investment or to underwrite an investment.

- **Units in collective investment schemes are** units in a unit trust or shares in an open ended investment company (OEIC).

- **Options** are financial instruments which give you the *right* to buy or sell investments, currency or commodities.

- **Futures** are *agreements* to buy or sell investments, currency or commodities at a future date at a price which has been agreed at the outset.

- **Contracts for differences** are contracts in which you hope to make a profit (but may sometimes make a loss) through changes in the value of property or an index. Currency and interest rate swaps are included.

- **Long term insurance contracts** are contracts such as life assurance and pensions which are officially classified as 'long term business'. Most long term insurance business is linked to an investment contract, but even when it is not, such contracts fall under the definition of investment.

- **Rights and interests in investment** is the 'sweep up' section which covers rights and interests in investments which have not been specified elsewhere in more detail.

2.2　Notice that although **National Savings** are loans to the government, they are specifically excluded from being classed as an investment for the purposes of the Financial Services Act.

What is a long term insurance contract, and what is not?

2.3　The Act is intended to provide investor protection. We are therefore concerned with contracts that provide some form of investment. This will include the majority of long term business such as **whole life** and **endowment policies**, whether regular premium or single premium, and **personal pensions contracts**.

2.4　It may seem strange that whole life should be included in a category which is defined as 'investments'. After all regular premium whole life assurance is associated with protection on death. Whole life policies are included because they have **surrender values**.

2.5　**Term insurance** and **permanent health insurance** with surrender values are similarly subject to the regulation.

2.6　**Long term insurance contracts**

Regulated by FSA	Not regulated by FSA
Whole life policies	Other form of term insurance and permanent health insurance which satisfy all these four conditions:
Endowment policies	
Personal pension contracts	
Unit-linked term insurance	(a)　benefits are payable only on death or as a result of incapacity due to injury, sickness or infirmity; and
Unit-linked permanent health insurance	
Term insurance for 10 years or more	(b)　no benefits are payable unless death occurs within 10 years or before age 70; and
Term insurance expiring when the life assured reaches age 70 or later	
	(c)　the contract has no surrender value or consists of a single premium with a surrender value less than the premium; and
	(d)　the contract cannot be converted to an investment contract.

2.7　If you have found all the details so far a little mind-numbing, try this mnemonic for remembering what investments are covered by FSA:

FLOWS D DRUGS

>　　**F**utures
>　　**L**ong term insurance
>　　**O**ptions
>　　**W**arrants
>　　**S**hares
>　　**D**ebentures
>　　**D**ifferences contracts
>　　**R**ights and interests in investments
>　　**U**nits in collective securities
>　　**G**overnment securities
>　　**S**ecurities certificates

2.8 Alternatively you may wish to use the following **three questions** as a check to identify whether the financial instrument in question is classified as an investment under the Act.

(a) Is it a **contract, certificate** or **entry on an electronic register?**

(b) Is the **capital invested at risk?**

(c) Was the purpose of entering the transaction to **make a gain** (ie earn a return in excess of your deposit, premiums, contributions)?

2.9 If the answer to these three questions is **yes, it is probably an investment**. For example, a bank account is not an investment since your capital is not at risk (question (b)). A house (even if bought for investment purposes) is not an investment since it is real, tangible property (question (a)), whereas a share in a property company is an investment because it satisfies the three characteristics above.

Question 1

(a) Regulatory powers are given to the Treasury by the Insurance Companies Act 1982 on what aspects of insurance companies' business?

(b) Briefly list the investments regulated by the Financial Services Act.

3 AUTHORISED INVESTMENT BUSINESS

KEY TERM

Investment business means the 'business of engaging in an investment activity'. This is not terribly helpful until you know what is meant by an investment activity. We will cover that in the next section.

3.1 Investment advisers who maintain **business premises in the UK** will be regarded as **carrying on investment business**. They will have to apply for and obtain '**authorisation**' under FSA if they meet the following criteria.

(a) They carry on a **business**, which
(b) consists of one or more specific **activities**, which
(c) relate to **investments**, and which
(d) are not **excluded activities**.

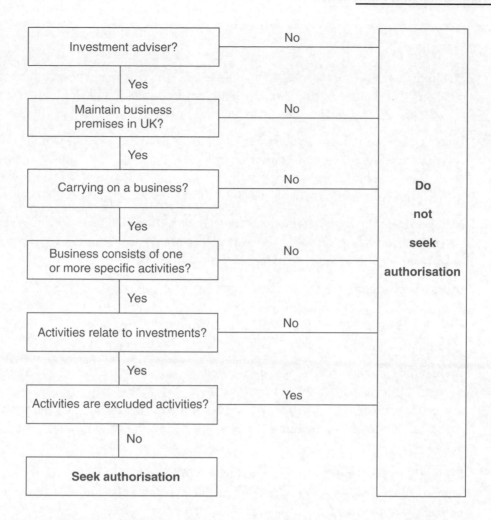

3.2 **Examples of investment businesses** include the following.

(a) Life assurance companies
(b) Investment managers
(c) Stockbrokers
(d) Dealers in futures and options

(e) Managers of unit trusts
(f) Advisers on collective investments
(g) Pensions advisers

4 INVESTMENT ACTIVITIES

What can you do with investments?

4.1 There are five activities which are '**investment activities**'. Before we look at each one individually it would help to remember that you can do various things with investments.

What you can do with investments:	Defined in Act as investment activities:
Buy and sell investments	Dealing in investments
Arrange for other people to buy and sell investments	Arranging deals in investments
Manage investments	Investment management, custody services
Give other people advice on what do with their investments	Investment advice
Organise schemes which invest for other people	Collective investment schemes

KEY TERMS

- **Dealing in investments** means buying, selling, subscribing for or underwriting investments whether as principal or agent. An example of a dealer in investments is a **stockbroker** whose business is to buy and sell shares on behalf of clients.

- You act as **principal** when you sell shares which belong to you but which you have bought from someone else with the specific objective of reselling them as a business. You should not confuse selling your own shares as a private individual with selling your firm's shares as part of your business activities.

- **Arranging deals in investments** means making arrangements with a view to someone else buying or selling investments. This could include referring a client to an insurance company for advice.

- **Investment management** covers the managing or offering or agreeing to manage assets belonging to someone else. An example would be a stockbroker who manages a private portfolio of shares under a discretionary management agreement. Custody services are also treated as investment activity.

- **Investment advice** covers advising investors or potential investors on buying, selling, subscribing for or underwriting an investment or on exercising any investment rights. This includes advice by a stockbroker on the purchase or sale of shares or advice by a financial adviser on effecting life assurance or pensions business.

- **Collective investment schemes** involve establishing, operating or winding up a scheme which invests money for other people. An example would be someone who manages a unit trust.

Categories not covered by the Act

4.2 The following categories are **not** covered by the Act.

(a) **Current, deposit and savings accounts** managed by banks or building societies

(b) **National Savings** accounts and investments

(c) **Mortgages** and other loans

(d) Commercial dealings in **commodities and futures**

(e) Commercial dealings in **land and buildings**

(f) Commercial dealings in '**alternative investments**', such an antiques, manuscripts and works of art

(g) **Investing your own money and assets**

(h) Dealings between **companies in the same group**

(i) Operating **employee share schemes**

(j) Giving advice or dealing in company shares carrying **75% or more of the voting rights**

(k) Dealings in **trust investments by trustees** unless they are offering investment services

(l) Dealings by **legal personal representatives** in investments of an estate of a deceased person

(m) Non-investment related business such as **legal or tax advice**

(n) Generic advice in **journals, magazines and newspapers** provided the principal purpose of the publication is not to encourage people to invest in a particular investment

(o) **General insurance**

Question 2

(a) Investment advisers must apply for authorisation if they meet certain criteria. List the criteria.

(b) Give examples of people carrying on investment business.

---

5 PURPOSE OF THE REGULATORY COMPONENTS

Authorisation

5.1 The objective of requiring investment advisers, or **financial advisers** as they are more generally known, to be authorised is to ensure that they have **enough knowledge and experience for the range of advice that they give.**

5.2 The general rule is that in order to give investment advice an individual must be as a **fit and proper person**.

> **KEY TERM**
>
> A **fit and proper person** is one that is honest, competent, financially sound and qualified.

Authorisation or exemption

5.3 The requirement to be *either* authorised *or* exempt is very specific. **If you are not one of those categories that is specifically exempted from the need for authorisation then you must be authorised.** Otherwise, you could face a **fine** and/or **imprisonment.**

Exemptions from authorisation

5.4 The **exemptions** specifically mentioned by the Act include both **bodies** and **individuals**. They are as follows.

(a) Appointed representatives of an authorised person
(b) The Bank of England
(c) Clearing Houses
(d) Court officials
(e) Investment Exchanges
(f) Listed Money Market Institutions
(g) Lloyds Underwriters
(h) Official Receivers of the DTI
(i) Public Trustees

5.5 The surprise amongst this group are the **appointed representatives** who can carry on investment business without being authorised.

> **KEY TERM**
>
> An **appointed representative** is any person or firm who is employed by an authorised person under a contract *for services* (as compared with an employment contract which is a contract *of service*).

5.6   The exemption of authorised representatives does not mean that they are not subject to the Act - they are. The reason is that the **principal** on whose behalf they are acting accepts written responsibility for their activities, and the **principal must be an authorised person**. Appointed representatives are therefore effectively regulated even though they do not need separate authorisation.

Body of rules

5.7   The **prime function** of all the FSA rules is to impose on financial advisers certain requirements which are meant to ensure:

(a)   that they act with **integrity** and **deal fairly with their clients**;

(b)   that they observe certain **standards of skill, care and diligence** in dealing with their clients;

(c)   that the advice they give to clients is **professional in quality** and **appropriate** for the clients' needs.

5.8   The Act has some **general rules**. Under it you must:

(a)   not make statements or indeed say anything **misleading** or **untrue,** or conceal any material fact;

(b)   not say anything which might **persuade** someone to take an investment decision which they would not otherwise take;

(c)   report to the firm's regulator any **significant matter** which could indicate a possible breach of the Act and its regulations if you are a firm's external auditor. Normally an auditor is under a duty of confidentiality to a client, but that duty is waived for this purpose.

5.9   The Act also sets down **principles** and authorises certain regulatory bodies to set out separate rules which are appropriate for each type of investment and each type of investment advice (we shall see these regulatory bodies in Chapter 2).

Question 3

(a)   List eight of the categories of financial activity which are outside the scope of the Financial Services Act.

(b)   Who and what are specifically exempt under the Financial Services Act from the need to be authorised?

(c)   What are the requirements for a person to be classified as fit and proper?

(d)   The requirements imposed on financial advisers by the regulatory rules are intended to achieve what purpose?

Complaints investigation

5.10 Whenever anyone is dissatisfied with the purchase of either a product or a service they can **complain** to the provider. In some businesses and with some manufacturers this will get them nowhere. The Act's regulatory system endeavours to ensure that the clients of financial services - people who rely on the financial advice of others - are not left in the lurch in this way.

5.11 Rules have been created to ensure that a client who has a complaint is given a **fair hearing**, that the complaint is **properly and promptly investigated** and if necessary the **appropriate action** is taken.

5.12 The rules require that any complaint must be dealt with by a **director** or employee of the financial adviser who is sufficiently **senior** to have authority to take corrective action if necessary, and who is more senior than the person against whom the complaint has been brought.

5.13 Complainants must also know that, if they are not satisfied with the way that their complaint has been handled by the firm, they can go direct to the firm's **regulator** and ask for the regulator to investigate their complaint.

Monitoring

5.14 Any system of regulation would be incomplete if there were no system whereby its **efficiency could be checked**.

5.15 All authorised persons must have rules and **compliance procedures** which must be followed. They must be reviewed at least annually and the review must cover the records, compliance procedures, supervision procedures and customers' accounts.

5.16 The regulatory bodies therefore have the **authority** to ensure that those rules are being observed. This means that they can take whatever reasonable steps they think fit to check that every financial adviser is observing all the requirements set out by the regulatory body.

5.17 To do this the regulatory bodies must be able to **examine evidence** that the rules have been observed. Such evidence will take the form of:

(a) records which set out the **compliance procedures** which have been instituted by a financial adviser;

(b) records kept at each stage of the adviser's activities to show that those compliance procedures are being **observed**.

Records must be kept for at least **six years**, and the compliance procedures must be **in writing** if there are ten or more authorised advisers in the company.

5.18 The regulatory bodies can ask for **information** from financial advisers and can pay **visits** to those advisers to make the appropriate checks.

Enforcement

5.19 The regulatory bodies have the right not only to check that their rules are being enforced but also to **take action if they are not**. They can:

(a) withdraw authorisation;

(b) impose fines;

(c) prohibit a particular kind of business from being carried out;

(d) prohibit a particular person from carrying out any kind of investment business;

(e) regulate the way in which advisers represent themselves as carrying on investment business.

Compensation

5.20 When a client makes a complaint it may be relatively easy to take **corrective action**. This will usually be intended to put the client back in the same position that he or she was in before the error occurred.

5.21 In some cases clients suffer financial loss as a result of defective advice. There is therefore a scheme which aims to provide compensation for clients who have suffered financial loss as a result of either poor advice, mismanagement or fraud on the part of an adviser. This scheme is known at the **Investors' Compensation Scheme** (ICS).

5.22 The ICS is used only when a firm has **ceased** or is **about to cease** trading and is unable to meet its liabilities. While the firm is trading, its **professional indemnity insurance** is the first protection for dealing with clients' losses arising from defective advice.

Question 4

(a) You are a company representative, and one of your clients - a stockbroker - has written to advise you that the investment bond you recommended has fallen in value. He complains that he was not advised of the possibility that the value of the bond could fall. What action must be taken by your company?

(b) How frequently must the compliance procedure of an authorised firm be reviewed?

(c) What are the objectives of the rules relating to client complaints?

6 THE FINANCIAL SERVICES AND MARKETS BILL (FSMB)

6.1 The Financial Services and Markets Bill was published in July 1998 and is expected to become law at some time in 2000. When introduced, the new act will place the Financial Services Authority on a statutory footing and abolish the need for the existing self-regulatory bodies, including the PIA.

6.2 The Bill sets out a number of statutory objectives for financial regulation:

(a) maintaining confidence in the financial system;

(b) promoting public understanding of the financial system, including awareness of the risks and benefits of different kinds of investment;

(c) securing the appropriate degree of protection for consumers. The Financial Services Authority will consider the differing degrees of expertise of consumers and recognise that consumers should be required to take responsibility for their decisions, ie there will be an element of caveat emptor - 'let the buyer beware';

(d) the reducing of financial crime.

6.3 The scope of regulation (in other words, what is within the scope of the definition of 'Investment Business') is similar to that in the existing Financial Services Act. However, the Bill makes provision for the FSA to regulate and supervise a wider range of products and services, including the giving of advice on mortgages and the selling/marketing of mortgages.

Extending the legislation to cover mortgages will, however, be dependent on a decision by the Treasury and the prior approval of Parliament. As at the time of the Budget in April 2000, there were no plans for the FSA to regulate mortgages (although this situation could change in the future).

6.4 Provisions in the FSMB relating to mortgage regulation (but which will require a Treasury initiative to be made into law) would allow the FSA to:

(a) authorise mortgage firms (banks, building societies etc) and individual mortgage advisers;

(b) regulate the advertising of mortgage products;

(c) regulate financial advice relating to the choice of a mortgage;

(d) require disclosure of mortgage terms and conditions at the point of sale;

(e) empower an ombudsman to deal with customer complaints about bad advice or bad service;

(f) require authorised firms to provide remedies to badly-treated borrowers;

(g) provide a compensation scheme for borrowers suffering loss as a result of bad advice.

BPP PUBLISHING

Chapter roundup

- *Reasons for review of investor protection*
  - Financial scandals
  - Investors lose money through mismanagement or fraud
  - Gower Commission report leads to Financial Services Act 1986
- *Other consumer protection legislation*
  - Policyholders' Protection Act 1975
    - Protects policyholders against failed insurer
    - Covers 90% of long term liabilities
    - Cost met by maximum 1% levy
  - Insurance Brokers Registration Act: regulates use of title 'insurance broker'
  - Insurance Companies Act 1982
    - Insurer must be authorised for new business
    - Regulates: solvency; conduct; accounting and intervention
- Financial Services Act 1986
  - Scope
    - Authorised or exempt
    - Defines investments (FLOWS D DRUGS), investment business and investment activities
    - Regulates marketing of various investments
- *Long-term insurance contracts:* contracts that contain investment element
  - Whole of life
  - Endowments
  - Personal pensions
  - Policies with surrender value - unit linked term assurance and unit linked PHI
- *Investment business:* carry on business consisting of investment activities which are not excluded
- *Investment activities*
  - *Cover:* advising on investments; dealing in investments; arranging deals in investments; managing investments; establishing and operating collective investments
  - *Excludes* several investment activities including: deposit accounts; mortgages; National Savings; general insurance
- *Purpose of regulatory components*
  - *Authorisation.* Advisers must be authorised or exempt. Authorised means demonstrating honesty, competence, knowledge and financial soundness. Appointed representatives exempt because authorised by principal.
  - *Body of rules.* Objective of rules to ensure: integrity; fair dealing; skill; care; diligence and professionalism.
  - *Complaints investigation.* Objective of complaints rules: to ensure client has fair hearing; complaint is promptly investigated; action taken. Complaint must be dealt with by senior officer with authority. Complainants must be told alternatives.
- *Monitoring.* Rules and procedures must exist and be comprehensively reviewed at least annually. Regulatory bodies will inspect records regularly.
- *Enforcement.* Regulators can:
  - enforce rules
  - withdraw authorisation
  - impose fines
  - prohibit business
  - debar individual
- *Compensation.* Loss must be recompensed by firm backed by Professional Indemnity Insurance PII or (if firm insolvent) Investors' Compensation Scheme.
- The Financial Services and Markets Bill will give statutory recognition to the Financial Services Authority and includes a provision for the possible extension of FSA regulation and supervision to mortgages.

Quick quiz

1 Why are some term insurance contracts included in the investments covered by the Financial Services Act?

    A A surrender value is included in the benefits.
    B They have a term longer than five years.
    C The sum assured is greater than 75% of the premiums payable.
    D They provide a sum payable on the diagnosis of a critical illness.

2 Authorisation to conduct insurance business is granted by which of the following bodies?

    A Treasury.
    B FSA.
    C DTI.
    D PIA.

3 In which of the following circumstances may the Policyholders' Protection Act 1975 provide protection?

    A For clients of insurance brokers that are insolvent.
    B For investors who have lost capital through bad advice.
    C For motorists with a claim against an uninsured third party.
    D For insured persons whose insurance company is insolvent.

4 Subscribing for investments as a principal falls into which category of investment activity?

    A Advising.
    B Arranging.
    C Dealing.
    D Managing.

5 Which one of the following categories of financial activity is not covered by the Financial Services Act?

    A Building society deposit accounts.
    B Contracts for differences.
    C Term assurance with a term in excess of ten years.
    D Unit-linked permanent health insurance.

6 In which of the following circumstances will a client of an IFA be able to make a valid claim against the Investors Compensation Scheme?

    A The IFA has failed to renew its professional indemnity insurance.

    B The IFA has been declared bankrupt and has ceased to trade.

    C The PIA is currently conducting an investigation into the firm's trading activities

    D The IFA has breached a client agreement which has caused the client to suffer a financial loss.

The solutions to the questions in the quiz can be found at the end of this text. Before checking your answers against those solutions, you should look back at this chapter and use the information in it to correct your answers.

Answers to questions

1   (a)   Authorisation to commence business; solvency margins; conduct of insurance business; accounting procedures; protection of policyholders' security.

    (b)   Futures: agreements to buy/sell commodities   F
          Long-term insurance: contracts for life assurance, pensions and disability insurance   L
          Options: give right to buy or sell investments, currency, commodities   O
          Warrants: rights to subscribe for investments   W
          Shares: the equity capital of a company   S
          Debentures: asset-backed loans to companies   D
          Differences contracts: currency and interest-rate swaps   D
          Rights and interests in investments   R
          Units in collective securities: unit trusts, shares in open-ended investment companies   U
          Government securities: loans to government and to local authorities   G
          Securities certificates: give right to buy or sell investments   S

2   (a)   Carry on a business with business premises in the UK which consists of specific activities relating to investments which are not excluded activities.

    (b)   Pensions advisers; life assurance companies; advisers on collective investments; dealers in futures and options; investment managers; stockbrokers; managers of unit trusts.

3   (a)   Deposit/current accounts; National Savings; loans; commercial dealings in commodities, futures, land, buildings and alternative investments; own assets; employee share schemes; advice on 75% of a company's shares; dealings by trustees and legal personal representatives; legal or tax advice; published generic advice; general insurance.

    (b)   Who: Lloyds underwriters, official receivers, court officials, appointed representatives, public trustees. What: Bank of England, clearing houses, investment exchanges, listed money market institutions.

    (c)   Honesty, competence, financial soundness and qualifications.

    (d)   To ensure that they act with integrity, fair dealing, skill, care and diligence, and that they act professionally and appropriately.

4   (a)   The complaint must be investigated by a director or employee more senior than you.
    (b)   Annually.
    (c)   To ensure a fair hearing, full investigation and corrective action.

Chapter 2

FINANCIAL SERVICES REGULATION

Chapter topic list	Syllabus reference
1 The regulatory hierarchy	A 2.1
2 The Financial Services Authority's enforcement powers (FSMB)	A 2.2
3 Government departments and supervision of financial services	A 2.3
4 Polarisation	A 2.4
5 Designated, tied and independent financial advisers and introducers	A 2.5
6 The main responsibilities of independent advisers	A 2.6
7 Statutory responsibility for financial advisers	A 2.7

1   THE REGULATORY HIERARCHY

1.1   The Act's regulations clearly define how financial advisers can be either authorised or exempted; all others are **unauthorised** and are committing a criminal offence. It then establishes a fairly complex regulatory hierarchy by which authorisation is given.

Authorised, exempt or unauthorised persons

1.2   There are three different types of financial services organisation.

(a)   **Authorised:** these are individuals or firms who are required to be authorised under the Act and who have been granted such authorisation.

(b)   **Exempt:** these are firms or individuals who are not required to be authorised and are specifically mentioned in the Act as exempt persons.

(c)   **Unauthorised:** these are firms who are required to be authorised but who are giving investment advice without having either sought or obtained such authorisation, or who have had authorisation suspended or withdrawn. They are **lawbreakers**.

The regulatory hierarchy

1.3   The **regulatory hierarchy** can be shown by a diagram. This will be explained in the paragraphs which follow.

Exam focus point

You do not need to learn the hierarchy, but you must understand its purpose and structure.

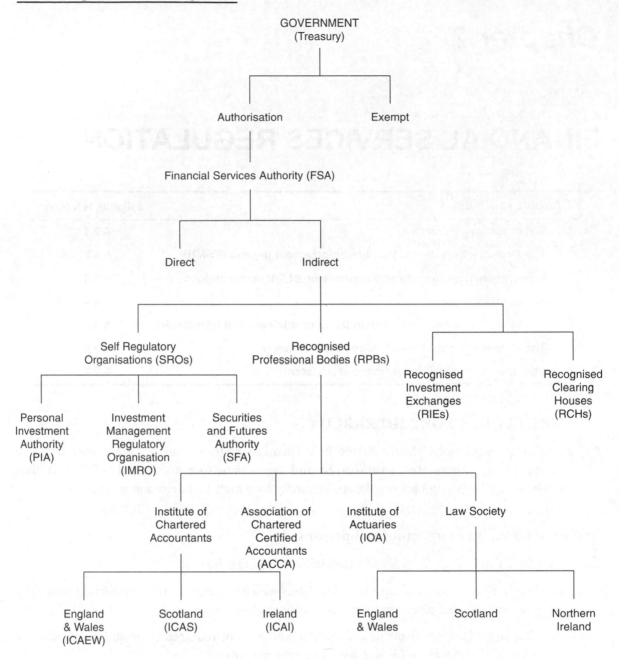

1.4   In order to set the appropriate standards for authorisation, the regulatory bodies have laid down **specific rules** which must be observed by authorised advisers, whether firms or individuals.

Breaches of the rules

Penalties or withdrawal of authorisation

1.5   The regulatory bodies can impose **penalties** on authorised firms for **breach of the rules.** Those penalties may take the form of fines. In more extreme cases, advisers are prohibited from conducting a certain kind of business, or authorisation is totally withdrawn.

Civil sanctions

1.6   A breach of the rules may lead to various **civil sanctions against the firm** (whether that firm is authorised or unauthorised). A contract for example may be unenforceable against the investor although the contract itself will not automatically be made illegal by a breach of the rules. The investor may therefore be able to enforce the contract against the adviser (or a product provider) even though the adviser cannot enforce it against the investor.

1.7 In addition the investor may be entitled to **recover property lost** as a result of the advice and perhaps obtain **compensation** from the adviser.

Criminal sanctions

1.8 An unauthorised firm is committing a **criminal offence** simply by giving investment advice without being authorised to do so. Every single activity which is part of giving unauthorised investment advice is a criminal offence.

Financial Services Authority

1.9 The basic principles behind the Act are **investor protection** and **self-regulation - the financial services industry regulates itself**. Consequently the responsibility for granting authorisation is delegated by the Treasury to a body known as the **Financial Services Authority (FSA).** This is the 'designated agency' under the Act.

1.10 The **FSA's role is changing** and the eventual aim is for the FSA to incorporate the functions of:

- The SROs
- The Insurance Directorate of the DTI
- The RPBs

The FSA will become the **one-stop regulator** of the financial services industry by the end of 2000, when the Financial Services and Markets Bill is enacted.

1.11 **In the overwhelming majority of cases authorisation is granted by the bodies to whom FSA has delegated that responsibility**. Those bodies are each responsible for a very specific section of financial services and usually the name of the body gives some idea of the area of financial services which that body regulates.

1.12 FSA will delegate its regulatory powers only to bodies whose rules and powers give **adequate protection** to investors. In extreme cases it has granted authorisation directly. In some cases it also acts as a lead regulator if the authorised firm has activities across the range of investment business.

1.13 Regulatory bodies are divided broadly into **three groups**: self-regulatory organisations, recognised professional bodies, and investment exchanges and clearing houses.

Self Regulatory Organisations (SROs)

1.14 SROs currently regulate individuals and firms that are likely to be engaged in giving financial advice full time. There are three SROs.

(a) The **Personal Investment Authority (PIA)** which authorises retail investment businesses.

(b) The **Investment Management Regulatory Organisation (IMRO)** which authorises investment managers.

(c) The **Securities and Futures Authority (SFA)** which authorises stockbrokers and dealers.

Recognised professional bodies (RPBs)

1.15 RPBs are professional bodies who can **authorise their members** to give investment advice. The investment advice must be **incidental** to their main business. It is intended that by the end of 2000 RPBs will transfer their right to grant authority to give investment advice to FSA.

Chartered accountants

1.16 There are three **Institutes of Chartered Accountants**: one for England and Wales (ICAEW); another for Scotland (ICAS); and another for Ireland (ICAI). Although the institute in Ireland is known as 'The Institute of Chartered Accountants in Ireland' it authorises accountants only for *Northern* Ireland, because the Financial Services Act does not apply in Eire.

Chartered certified accountants

1.17 There is one association - the **Association of Chartered Certified Accountants**.

Lawyers

1.18 There are **three Law Societies**: one for England and Wales; another for Scotland; and another for Northern Ireland. The one for England and Wales is known simply as the Law Society, whereas the other two are more specifically identified as 'The Law Society of Scotland' and 'The Law Society of Northern Ireland'.

Actuaries

1.19 There is one body for actuaries in England known as the **Institute of Actuaries**. Note that there is also Faculty of Actuaries for Scotland which is a professional body but **not** a *recognised* professional body.

Investment exchanges and clearing houses

1.20 Recognised Investment Exchanges (RIEs) and Recognised Clearing Houses (RCHs) are different from SROs and RPBs. Membership of one of these bodies does not of itself confer authorisation. **It is the Exchange which is recognised and exempted from authorisation – not the members.**

Question 1

(a) What two kinds of approval for financial organisations are allowed by the Financial Services Act?

(b) What is the basic principle behind the Financial Services Act?

(c) In what circumstances might a financial adviser be unable to enforce a contract even though a client may be able to enforce it against the financial adviser?

(d) Which regulatory body is directly accountable to the Treasury?

The powers of FSA

1.21 The FSA can:

(a) **Recognise** SROs and RPBs

(b) **Authorise advisers directly**

(c) **Monitor** and enforce compliance of directly authorised advisers

(d) **Make rules** for everybody

(e) **Investigate complaints** against directly authorised advisers and authorised authorisers

(f) **Disqualify** from authorisation anyone considered not to be a fit and proper person

(g) **Intervene** in the activities of any authorised person

(h) Maintain a **register of disqualified persons.** Someone on the register will be unemployable by any authorised person

(i) Establish a **compensation scheme**

1.22 FSA can exercise its powers of intervention if it considers that:

(a) the authorised person has **contravened a provision** of the Act or rules or regulations; or

(b) it is **desirable** for the protection of investors; or

(c) the authorised person is **not fit to carry on investment business**.

1.23 FSA can take steps to **protect the assets of investors**. It can prohibit an authorised person from entering into **transactions of a specific kind** or carrying on business in a specific manner. It keeps a **register of prohibited persons**; someone on the register will be unemployable by any authorised person.

1.24 Under provisions included in the Financial Services and Markets Bill (FSMB) the FSA will be given a broad range of powers and responsibilities, including:

(a) The power to force firms and individuals to co-operate with investigations, and
(b) The power to impose unlimited civil penalties on offenders, eg for insider dealing.

To provide some balance against the huge power of the FSA, the FSMB provides for an appeals tribunal, to which appeals can be made by those dissatisfied with decisions or actions of the FSA. The appeals tribunal will be administered by the Lord Chancellor's department (ie the judiciary) and not the Treasury.

PIA

1.25 The **PIA** regulates most of the investment business which is conducted between private investors (the '**retail market**') and the member firms of the PIA. PIA investment business can be analysed as follows:

BPP PUBLISHING

Regulated by FSA	Not regulated by FSA
Life assurance (including savings and protection)	Mortgage terms and loans. (When a loan or mortgage is connected with an investment, the investment is regulated but the loan/mortgage itself is not.)
Personal pensions	
Guaranteed income bonds	
Unit trusts	Bank and building society deposit accounts
Individual savings accounts (ISAs)	
Investment trust savings schemes	General insurance - house and contents and motor insurance
Offshore funds, such as gilts funds and bond funds	
Advice on and arranging deals in shares	
Management of a portfolio of investment	
Broker funds	
Advice on arranging deals and trading options	

1.26 The PIA is the lead regulator in respect of the services listed as regulated. **Members of the PIA** include life assurance companies (including bancassurers), independent financial advisers, friendly societies and firms retailing and operating unit trust schemes.

1.27 These are the PIA's **essential factors** in ensuring adequate regulation of the retail market.

(a) **Clear information** for customers
(b) Fully **professional salespeople**
(c) Clear and enforceable **rules** within the system
(d) Efficient **monitoring** of the quality of transactions
(e) Efficient **supervision** of firms' organisation and financial resources
(f) **Sanctions** for non-compliance
(g) Robust **complaints** mechanisms
(h) **Redress** where necessary

Exam focus point
These factors are reflected in the rules and processes which are outlined in the remaining chapters of Part A of this Study Text.

1.28 There are four **categories of PIA membership**.

1 – Unrestricted	2 - Money holders	3 - Arrangers	4 - Others
Such members have the following authorisation: • To deal as principals with investors • To deal as agents for investors • To manage investments for investors • To arrange deals for investors • To give investment advice to investors • To hold clients' money and assets	These have the same authority as Category 1 members except that they are not entitled to deal as principals with investors.	These members are allowed to arrange deals and give investment advice. They have no authority to deal as principals with investors or to act as agents nor are they authorised to hold clients' monies or assets.	These will mostly be firms regulated by a European regulator.

All **sole traders** were debarred from providing discretionary portfolio management services and holding client monies or assets with effect from 18 July 1995.

IMRO

1.29 IMRO regulates firms which:

(a) provide **discretionary investment management services;**

(b) manage and operate **unit trusts, investment trusts and pension funds;**

(c) provide **investment advisory services** to institutional clients; and

(d) advise on and arrange **deals in investments** which are **incidental** to a firm's main investment management activity.

SFA

1.30 The SFA regulates a wide range of investment business including that relating to securities, **futures and options and contracts for differences.** Most of its members are members of the Stock Exchange.

2 THE FINANCIAL SERVICES AUTHORITY'S ENFORCEMENT POWERS (FSMB)

2.1 Under the Financial Services and Markets Bill the Financial Services Authority are charged with maintaining confidence in the financial system, promoting public awareness, reducing financial crime and protecting consumers.

2.2 The active supervision and monitoring of authorised firms is considered to be central to executing these statutory objectives, though the FSA aims to address problems, if possible, by way of dialogue with the firms concerned rather than resorting to formal enforcement action.

2.3 Firms are expected to respond promptly to regulatory concerns, though if firms fail to do so the FSMB gives the FSA a number of powers that it can use to secure compliance. These include the following.

     (a)   Intervening in the business of authorised firms

     (b)   Ensuring that the extent of consumer loss (or risk of loss) are fully investigated

     (c)   Securing restitution for customers

     (d)   Bringing criminal proceedings for certain offences

     (e)   Imposing civil fines for 'market abuse'

2.4   A consultation paper has been published setting out how the FSA proposes to use these powers. There are a number of principles that underpin the proposals in the paper.

     (a)   **An open and co-operative relationship between firms and the FSA**

        The effectiveness of the new regulatory regime depend to a significant extent on co-operation and a firm's openness and co-operation will be an important mitigating factor in any disciplinary proceedings.

     (b)   **Transparent, proportionate and consistent exercise of the FSA's powers**

        The FSA will exercise its powers in accordance with a publicly-stated policy and the paper sets out the criteria that the FSA proposes to adopt.

     (c)   **Fair treatment**

        The paper considers the information that should be given to a person subject to the FSA's compulsory investigation powers and to a person suspected of committing criminal offences. The FSA is concerned that its powers are not used in a manner that is 'oppressive'. There will be a clear separation between the persons who carry out investigations and those who determine whether the FSA should impose sanctions.

The individual sections of the consultation paper

2.5   The consultation paper contains six key areas, dealing with:

     (a)   Intervention

     (b)   Investigations

     (c)   Securing redress for consumers

     (d)   Discipline of authorised firms and approved persons

     (e)   Market misconduct

     (f)   The FSA's decision-making process

Intervention

2.6   Though the FSA expects that the majority of concerns will be addressed by firms on a voluntary basis, it will not hesitate to use its intervention powers where it considers it to be 'appropriate'.

Investigations

2.7   The FSMB gives the FSA a wide range of powers of investigation. Once again, 'where circumstances dictate' it will use these powers should the firm fail to co-operate voluntarily. The paper lists circumstances such as where a firm appears to have been used for the purposes of money laundering or has engaged in other financial crime as meriting the exercise of the FSA's powers.

     The FSA has many powers of investigation, including the power to require a firm to commission a report by accountants or other relevant professionals approved by the FSA.

Securing redress for consumers

2.8   The FSA will have power to ensure that such losses are made good. As discussed above, the FSA expects to use this power rarely and expects firms to establish the extent of losses and to provide redress accordingly, voluntarily.

Discipline of authorised firms and approved persons

2.9   The draft Bill provides the FSA with two main powers: to make public and to fine.

In some cases the misconduct will be so serious as to merit a withdrawal of authorisation, permission or approval and disqualification of individuals.

The FSA's general policy will be to make public the imposition of disciplinary sanctions.

Market misconduct

2.10   This section consolidates the FSA's powers in the draft FSMB Bill to:

- Conduct investigations
- Prosecute insider dealing and misleading statements and practices
- Impose civil fines for 'market abuse'
- Impose or seek restitution orders in cases of market misconduct

2.11   This section of the consultation paper considers a number of key issues including the way in which the FSA proposes to work with other prosecuting authorities when considering criminal proceedings, and the principles and criteria that the FSA proposes to follow in making a decision as to whether to commence criminal proceedings.

2.12   With regard to such a decision, there will be two tests: the 'evidential test' and the 'public interest test'.

The evidential test is to ensure that the FSA is satisfied that the evidence against the suspect is such that a jury is 'more likely than not to convict the defendant of the charge alleged'. The FSA will also consider whether the evidence is reliable.

The public interest test provides that the FSA must consider whether it is in the public interest to commence criminal proceedings in cases of market misconduct. The FSA will carefully balance factors for and against prosecution.

2.13   The paper also considers the interaction of the FSA's criminal prosecution power (eg for insider dealing and misleading statements and practices) and civil fining powers (eg for 'market abuse') and looks at the circumstances in which the FSA will apply to the courts for an injunction to prevent market abuse. In this regard, the FSA will seek injunctions if it is 'desirable for the purposes of maintaining the integrity of the investment markets'.

The FSA's decision making process

2.14   The FSMB provides for a three-stage process - warning notice, decision notice and appeal to a tribunal.

The FSA recognises that it has considerable powers in its hands and that the consequences for anyone subject to its decisions will often be very significant.

3 GOVERNMENT DEPARTMENTS AND SUPERVISION OF FINANCIAL SERVICES

The Treasury

3.1 The **Treasury** is responsible for the operation of the Financial Services Act and for the operation of the banking sector and the gilts market, and it has assumed responsibility for the supervision of activities regulated by:

- The Policyholders Protection Act 1975
- The Insurance Brokers (Registration) Act 1977
- The Insurance Companies Act 1982

The Treasury is now the lead regulator for the banking sector assuming responsibilities previously held by the Bank of England.

Question 2

(a) What are the main powers of FSA?
(b) What is a lead regulator?
(c) IMRO regulates firms which provide what services?
(d) Which government department supervises the banking sector?

4 POLARISATION

4.1 A **product provider,** such as an insurance company with a particular endowment product, or a fund manager with a unit trust, needs people to sell the product to the general public. How it does so, and how the general public is protected in the process, is a key area regulated by the Act.

4.2 Before the Financial Services Act became effective there were **three types of agent** used by product providers to sell their products.

(a) **Agents of insurance companies who worked solely for that company**. They might be salaried, they might be self employed full time agents or they might even have been the equivalent of appointed representatives (although the term did not exist in those days).

(b) **Insurance brokers,** whose function was to act on behalf of a client and obtain, on behalf of that client, the most suitable product from a range of providers. The post-FSA category of Independent Financial Advisers (IFA) again performs the same function.

(c) The third category of firms or individuals were paid commission for introducing business to a small number of providers. They were not tied to one company but they did not have access to a sufficient number of providers to enable them to be classed as independent. These agents included **solicitors, bank managers** and **estate agents**.

4.3 The FSA killed off the third group. The reason was the new requirement that **there must be a clear division between agents who were tied to a particular product provider and those who were independent.** An agent clearly has to be one or the other.

KEY TERMS

- A **tied adviser** is limited to advising on the products of only one provider. He is the **agent of the product provider**.

- **Independent advisers** must be able to recommend products from a wide range of providers and the regulatory process requires such independent advisers to demonstrate that they have a suitable spread of business. He is the **agent of his client**.

- **Polarisation** is the requirement for an adviser to be either tied or independent.

5 DESIGNATED, TIED AND INDEPENDENT FINANCIAL ADVISERS AND INTRODUCERS

Designated individuals and introducers

5.1 The Personal Investment Authority introduced the term **designated individual** for individuals who give financial advice, manage discretionary investments, and handle client money or other assets. They must go through a staged training process to achieve competence, but will still be subject to continuing supervision and continuing professional development. The term *designated individual* includes anyone who gives financial advice and is covered by the Training and Competence rules and requirements. The term therefore applies to both tied and independent advisers, and indeed to the principals of firms giving independent financial advice.

5.2 **'Introducers'** may introduce potential clients to a product provider without the need to be a designated individual. Their activities must be restricted to introductions and to distributing advertisements.

Tied advisers

5.3 The employees of a provider work **solely** for that provider. However, that does not necessarily mean that they give investment advice. Obviously there are many employees who do not give any form of advice to any client of the provider.

5.4 However, those individuals who do give investment advice must be authorised and are known as **company representatives** (CRs). A designated individual may be a salaried employee of the provider or may have a service contract with the provider, or may be a self-employed agent acting for the provider. However, for any **tied adviser** the obligation exists to give advice only on the products of the one provider.

5.5 A provider may also appoint an 'outside' organisation to advise on its products. Such an organisation may be a company, or a firm or a sole trader engaged in a quite different kind of business. An example is a firm of estate agents which is independent as far as the selling of property is concerned, but which is tied to one adviser when it comes to giving investment advice. Another example is a building society that might tie itself to recommending the life assurance produces of just one life office. Such organisations are known as **appointed representatives** (ARs) of an authorised person.

5.6 Whereas company representatives are individuals operating for and in the name of the product provider, an appointed representative carries on its own business, with a separate business identity, but is tied to the provider for the purpose of recommending investment products.

5.7 Appointed representatives may have **employees** who give advice to their clients. Those employees are also **designated individuals** in the same way as those individuals who are direct employees of the product provider. In both cases the names of those designated individuals must be on a register maintained by the provider's regulator.

5.8 The duty of company representatives and ARs to give investment advice on the provider's products applies **irrespective of the competitiveness of that product**. For example, tied advisers may be well aware that their provider's performance on its investment products is among the worst in the industry. Despite this fact they are not allowed to advise on the product of any other provider. The prime objective is that the product is **suitable for the client's needs even if it is not the most competitive**. However, they are allowed to refer a client to an independent adviser (and receive remuneration for that referral) if their own company has no suitable product for a client's needs.

Independent financial advisers

5.9 **IFAs are agents of their clients** and not of the providers whose products they may recommend. **The tied adviser is unquestionably the agent of the product provider.**

5.10 Both tied adviser and IFAs must take **reasonable steps to establish a client's needs and recommend a suitable product type**. However, the similarity ends when it comes to recommending the particular product which falls under the heading of that product type.

5.11 The tied adviser can select only from one provider's range whereas the IFA must select **the most suitable product from the range of appropriate product types** provided by a large number of different providers.

IFAs and appointed representation

5.12 Confusingly, the term 'appointed representative' has two different meanings. Appointed representatives as tied advisers of a product provider have been described already. In a different meaning, an appointed representative may be a firm, company or individual who is appointed to represent **an independent intermediary**. IFAs therefore can and do appoint their own firms or organisations to act as their appointed representatives. Such ARs have the same duties in the advice they give to clients as the IFAs.

5.13 This situation is most commonly seen when a number of IFAs combine together to pay someone else to be responsible for their compliance with the regulatory rules. This is known as a '**network**' and the network appoints the IFAs as its appointed representatives.

The network has the ultimate responsibility for authorisation and the conduct of individuals within the network. (However, registration of the individual IFAs is also required.)

5.14 Such appointed representatives have not lost their **independence** in any way. They are effectively saving themselves the time and the effort needed to meet the compliance requirements by making use of the facilities provided by another organisation which accepts responsibility for their compliance.

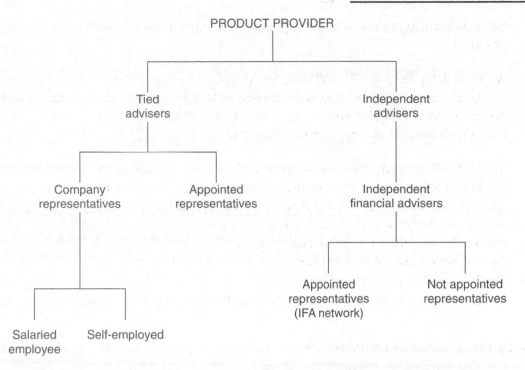

Question 3

(a) Define polarisation.

(b) What is the legal difference in the relationship of an investment adviser with a client between a tied adviser and an independent financial adviser (IFA)?

(c) What legal requirements regarding investment advice are common to both tied advisers and independent financial advisers?

---

6 THE MAIN RESPONSIBILITIES OF INDEPENDENT ADVISERS

6.1 IFAs have the same responsibilities under the Act as those of tied advisers. However, **additional requirements** apply to independent advisers.

> **KEY TERM**
>
> **Responsibilities of all financial advisers** are:
>
> (a) to comply with regulatory body rules;
>
> (b) to communicate clearly with clients; and
>
> (c) to have and be able to show competence in advising on products and services.

Choice of provider by IFAs

6.2 Once an independent adviser has established the needs of a client and decided on the type of product(s) most suitable, the IFA must:

(a) **select** the specific product from a wide range marketed by a large number of providers. The IFA's responsibility is to select from the products available the particular product which is suitable for the client and which will fulfil the client's needs. This does not mean that the IFA must select the 'best' product. It can be impossible to make such a judgment with the large number of **different factors** involved;

(b)   use his judgment regarding the factors which affect the product that he chooses, such as:

     (i)   the **financial strength** of the provider;

     (ii)   the **competence and efficiency** of the provider's administration and client servicing; and

     (iii)   (where appropriate) the provider's **investment performance**;

(c)   have sufficient knowledge and experience to apply **a high standard of competence in giving advice;**

(d)   understand the **law and tax regulations** and how they affect financial planning;

(e)   be able to **compare the products and services of different providers** and make a comparison (where appropriate) of different types of investments from different providers;

(f)   keep **up to date** in all the areas of knowledge required to give suitable financial planning advice;

(g)   keep **adequate records** on all their transactions in order to demonstrate that the advice they have given is suitable in each case.

Locum arrangements

6.3   There is a further responsibility on IFAs who are sole traders to make **locum arrangements**. If you are a sole trader and are going on holiday and one of your clients might want to make contact with you, you should not simply leave a message on your answering machine saying 'Back next week'. This would breach the regulatory requirements.

6.4   Clients must be able to **make contact** at reasonable times in order to discuss their financial requirements. Consequently, IFAs who are sole traders must show that they have adequate locum arrangements while they are on holiday or away sick so that any client can still obtain suitable advice in the absence of the IFA. The person who stands in for the IFA must obviously be suitably qualified and authorised to give investment advice.

Question 4

(a)   Give examples of the responsibilities under the Act of both tied and independent financial advisers.

(b)   What responsibility does an IFA have after selecting the most suitable type of product for a client?

(c)   Give examples of factors which an IFA must take into account when selecting a product provider.

---

7   STATUTORY RESPONSIBILITY FOR FINANCIAL ADVISERS

7.1   Any independent adviser who gives financial advice must be authorised as a **'fit and proper' person** to give that advice. It is giving of *advice* rather than the giving of *information* that matters.

7.2   The firm with which an adviser is connected will itself already have been authorised. *All* individual advisers must be authorised to give advice and all the advisers considered under this heading must be individually registered. The question is - who authorises and who must keep the register?

7.3 There are two routes for IFAs to take:

(a) to obtain authorisation direct by **FSA**. This is the least likely of the two. However, if it were chosen each individual adviser would need to be authorised and that adviser's name would need to be entered on the register kept by FSA; or

(b) to be both authorised and registered through the **PIA** (as SRO).

PIA authorisation

7.4 An investment adviser can obtain, through the PIA, authorisation to give advice which falls within the **appropriate PIA category**.

7.5 The PIA requires all IFAs to maintain **professional indemnity insurance** covering both regulated and unregulated business, and **certain levels of capital**. The level of capital differs depending on the size of the firm but will generally be the higher of £10,000, or £400 per registered adviser.

7.6 Each individual adviser must be authorised and registered as being **connected** with the named firm or company. This applies to all the categories of adviser.

Categories of adviser

7.7 **Proprietors of a registered firm**

Proprietors of a registered firm must be individually authorised and registered. Proprietors would include controllers, ie majority or substantial shareholders, partners or sole traders.

Advisers who work for a registered firm

All employees of a registered firm must be authorised and registered if they give investment advice. These advisers would include directors, managers and any other employees in the firm who give financial advice or who have contact with clients.

Appointed representatives of a independent network or other firm

Remember that an appointed representative can be appointed not only by a product provider (in which case they would be tied) but also by an IFA firm and by a independent network. In the latter case the appointed representatives will be as independent as the firm that appointed them and will have a responsibility to give independent advice to clients.

The appointed representatives of independent PIA members must be individually registered with the PIA even though the firm has already obtained authorisation.

7.8 **Networks** are organisations that are themselves PIA authorised registered firms. The purpose of a network is to provide services to IFAs which include accepting responsibility for the compliance of an IFA with the regulations. In return for providing these services the network is paid commission on business introduced by the IFA.

7.9 IFA firms are effectively **appointed representatives** of the network but individual advisers must still be registered with the PIA.

Tied advisers

7.10 All tied advisers must be authorised by the **product provider** to which they are tied. The provider accepts responsibility for the activities of all tied advisers whether they are company representatives or appointed representatives. Even the company representatives of appointed representatives must be authorised by the product provider.

7.11 Although tied advisers do not have to be authorised directly by any of the regulatory bodies, the **PIA** keeps a register of company representatives and appointed representatives. Each product provider must keep the PIA updated with any additions to or deletions from this list.

7.12 An employee of an insurance company or a friendly society who gives investment advice must be authorised as a **designated individual**.

7.13 If a tied adviser works for a company that is **directly authorised by FSA** the same requirement applies regarding authorisation and registration as for a company representative.

Question 5

(a) What are the three categories of independent financial adviser (not categories of membership)?

(b) Give examples of proprietors of a registered IFA who must be individually authorised and registered.

(c) What is the function of a network?

(d) Who is responsible for the advice given by a product provider's appointed representatives?

Chapter roundup

- The regulations distinguish between authorised, exempt and unauthorised investment advice.

    ° *Authorised*. Regulators create rules and impose penalties. Breach of rules can be civil wrong and criminal offence, and there may be civil sanctions. Investor may recover property and obtain compensation.

    ° *Unauthorised*. Criminal offence to give unauthorised investment advice.

- *Regulatory framework*. Basis of the Act is self regulation. Treasury delegates to FSA. FSA grants authorisation or delegates to SROs or RPBs. 3 × SROs: PIA, IMRO and SFA. RPBs are professional bodies with authorisation to authorise. RPB members are: accountants; actuaries; and solicitors.

- *Powers of FSA*. The main powers: recognise; authorise; monitor and enforce; investigate; disqualify; intervene; maintain register and compensate. Power to investigate against *direct* authorised firms and investigate complaints against other regulatory bodies. FSA can prohibit transactions or business practice and can protect assets.

- FSA as a direct regulator

    ° *Purpose*. Authorise fit and proper persons. Grant or withhold authorisation.

    ° *Scope*. Authorise firms needing more than one type of authorisation. Can be a lead regulator. Produces rules for directly authorised firms. Automatically regulates life companies not authorised by PIA.

- *PIA*. Regulates life assurance and unit trust providers and IFAs. Categories: (1) Unrestricted - can deal, arrange deals, advise and hold client assets; (2) money holders - as (1) but cannot deal as principals; (3) arrangers - can arrange deals and give advice: cannot deal as principals or hold clients' assets; (4) others - have European regulator.

- *IMRO*. Regulates firms of investment managers and institutional advisers.

- *SFA*. Regulates members of the Stock Exchange.

- *Government departments*. Treasury responsible for the FSA and now for PPA 75, IBRA 77 and ICA 82.

- *RPBs.* The purpose of a professional body is to regulate practice of a profession. A RPB - with the ability to grant authorisation will lose this authority by the end of 2000.

- *Polarisation:* requirement for investment adviser to be either tied or independent.

- *Designated individuals:* Designated by the PIA as being able to give financial advice and manage assets.

- *Introducers:* An individual who may introduce a client to a product provider, but may not give advice.

- *Tied advisers.* Company representatives (CRs) may be salaried or self employed but must be appointed representatives (ARs) of authorised providers may be company, firm or sole trader and are agents of provider. Tied representatives can select only from one product range.

- *Independent Financial Advisers (IFAs)* are agents of client. IFAs must select most suitable product from a range of providers' products. IFAs can appoint ARs who have same duties as IFAs. ARs of networks are IFAs.

- *Authorisation* required for firm/individuals giving investment advice (not information).

- Main *regulatory responsibilities of IFAs*: to comply with regulation; communicate clearly; demonstrate competence.

- Extra responsibilities. Select from wide range. Must judge provider's financial strength, competence and efficiency of admin and client servicing and (where relevant) investment performance. Must have adequate knowledge and experience. Must be able to compare products and services of providers. Must keep up to date and keep adequate records. Sole traders must have locum arrangements.

- Statutory responsibility for financial advisers. IFAs must be authorised to give advice and must be individually registered. Authorisation from FSA or PIA.

- PIA authorisation. Categories of adviser: proprietors of registered firm; advisers who work for registered firm; appointed representatives of network or other firm. Networks are PIA authorised firms.

- Tied advisers. Authorised by product provider.

Quick quiz

1 Regulatory bodies are unable to impose which of the following sanctions?

A Fines.
B Prohibition of a class of business.
C A suspended sentence.
D Withdrawal of authorisation.

2 Authorisation to give investment advice is automatically conferred by membership of which body?

A A listed money market institution.
B A recognised investment exchange.
C A recognised professional body.
D The Securities and Futures Authority.

3 Which of the following is an activity regulated by the Personal Investment Authority?

A The accountancy practices of pension companies.
B The authorisation of a class of life assurance business.
C The marketing of unit trusts.
D The solvency of insurance companies.

4   What business can be conducted by a Category 2 IFA under the PIA rules?

   A   All investment business except dealing as principal.
   B   All investment business without restriction.
   C   Investment advice but excluding handling clients' money.
   D   Arranging share transactions.

5   A firm which arranges investment deals as an incidental activity of its main investment management activity is regulated by which body?

   A   Personal Investment Authority.
   B   Investment Management Regulatory Organisation.
   C   Institute of Actuaries.
   D   Securities and Futures Authority.

6   The Treasury is responsible for the supervision of activities regulated by which of the following statutes?

   (1) Insurance Brokers (Registration) Act 1977.
   (2) Insurance Companies Act 1982.
   (3) Policyholders Protection Act 1975.
   (4) Financial Services Act 1986.

   A   (2), (3) and (4) only.
   B   (1) only.
   C   (1), (2) and (3) only.
   D   (1), (2), (3) and (4).

7   Augustus Conran is a company representative for the First Choice Life Assurance Company. During the course of a year he gives advice on the products listed below because his own company does not have any of those products in its range. Which product advice was an offence under the Financial Services Act?

   A   The Compensation Insurance Company's personal accident insurance contract.
   B   The medical expenses insurance policy from the Speedy Recovery Hospital Group.
   C   The Start-Out Company's deferred interest mortgage scheme.
   D   The unit trust marketed by Top Investment Management Group.

8   The term 'appointed representative' as understood under financial services regulations may be applied to an adviser who has been appointed by which of the following?

   A   A life assurance company.
   B   A Lloyd's underwriting syndicate.
   C   A private medical insurance group.
   D   An unrecognised professional body.

9   The section leader of an insurance company has received several telephone calls from clients or prospective clients asking for different kinds of information as shown below. Which question can the employee answer without the need to be authorised?

   A   Whether a policy can be effected on a joint life as well as a single life basis.

   B   Whether a number of endowments will meet the client's need for school fees capital.

   C   Whether a policy will be effective in meeting an inheritance tax liability on the client's partner.

   D   Whether a unit trust should be encashed when the price of units is at an historically high level.

The solutions to the questions in the quiz can be found at the end of this Study Text. Before checking your answers against those solutions, you should look back at this chapter and use the information in it to correct your answers.

Answers to questions

1   (a)   Authorised, exempt.

      (b)   Investor protection and self-regulation by the financial services industry.

      (c)   If the contract has been rendered unenforceable against an investor through a breach of the regulatory rules.

      (d)   FSA.

2   (a)   Recognise; directly authorise; rule; monitor and enforce; investigate; disqualify; register; compensate.

      (b)   The regulator which is responsible for the largest part of a firm's business.

      (c)   Investment management services.

      (d)   The Treasury.

3   (a)   The requirement for an adviser to be either tied or independent.

      (b)   The tied agent is the agent of the provider; the IFA is the agent of the client.

      (c)   They must both establish a client's need and recommend a suitable product type.

4   (a)   Comply with rules, communicate clearly, be competent.

      (b)   To select a specific product from a range of providers.

      (c)   Provider's financial strength, competence and efficiency of administration, client servicing and investment performance.

5   (a)   Proprietors of a registered firm; advisers who are employed by a registered firm; appointed representatives of an IFA or independent network.

      (b)   Sole traders; partners; majority or substantial shareholders (controller).

      (c)   To provide services to IFAs including accepting responsibility for compliance in return for commission on each IFA's business.

      (d)   The product provider. (However, individuals who give financial advice must be registered. Registration with the PIA imposes obligations on the individual.)

BPP PUBLISHING

Chapter 3

CONDUCT OF BUSINESS RULES

Chapter topic list	Syllabus reference
1 Statements of principle	A 3.1
2 Conduct of business rules	A 3.2
3 Authorisation of firms and registration of individuals	A 3.3
4 Advertisements	A 3.4
5 Unsolicited calling (cold calling)	A 3.5, A 3.6
6 Disclosure rules	A 3.7 - A 3.11
7 What information must be provided?	A 3.8 - A 3.11

Introduction

The regulatory framework includes both general principles and detailed rules interpreting those principles. In this chapter we will cover these principles and rules.

1   STATEMENTS OF PRINCIPLE

1.1   If the Financial Services Act contained all the rules and regulations which applied to investment advisers it would be massive. In fact, the Act deals with the **general principles** and the detail is filled in by the various regulatory bodies.

1.2   The first of these bodies is the **Financial Services Authority** - FSA (formerly SIB). In this chapter we are concerned with FSA's function as an **authoriser of authorisers** and **regulator of regulators**.

1.3   The various regulatory rules are divided into three tiers.

(a)   The **first tier** is embodied in the list of '**Statements of Principle**' originally issued by SIB, and subsequently adopted by the Financial Services Authority.

(b)   The **second tier** is a more specific list of '**designated' rules** which are designed to cover the following areas.

(i)   Conduct of business rules
(ii)   Financial resources rules
(iii)   Clients' money regulations
(iv)   Unsolicited calls rules

This second tier is more usually known as the '**Core Conduct of Business rules**'.

(c)   The **third tier** comprises the rules created by the **regulators themselves** (ie the PIA, IMRO and the SFA).

1.4 The **Core Conduct of Business Rules rules apply to all regulators** as if the regulators themselves had created them. They provide a common source of regulation which apply to all firms regulated by the regulators.

1.5 Note that these rules apply to the regulators only - **they do *not* apply to RPBs**. The reason for this is that the investment business of members of RPBs is already covered by RPB rules and codes of conduct.

> ### Exam focus point
> For the purposes of the syllabus we need only concern ourselves with the second and third tier rules of one regulator, the PIA.

FSA (formerly SIB) statements of principle

1.6 The **Statements of Principle**, of which there are ten, are the general rules which apply to all investment business.

Principle	Meaning
Integrity	Firm should observe high standards of integrity and fair dealing.
Skill, care and diligence	A firm should act with due skill, care and diligence.
Market practice	A firm should observe high standards of market conduct and comply with any code or standard in force from time to time.
Information about customers	A firm should seek from customers any information which might be relevant to its advice or recommendations to clients.
Information for customers	A firm should take reasonable steps to give its customers any information they need to enable them to make balanced and informed decisions.
Conflicts of interest	A firm should either avoid any conflicts of interest or, if one arises, should disclose it or - if necessary - decline to act. A firm should not unfairly place its interest above those of its customers.
Customer assets	A firm should arrange proper protection for customers' assets in its care, if necessary by segregation and separate identification.
Financial resources	A firm should maintain adequate financial resources to meet its investment business commitments.
Internal organisation	A firm should properly organise and control its internal affairs, keep proper records, have adequate compliance procedures and have adequate arrangements to ensure the suitability, training and supervision of staff.
Relations with regulators	A firm should deal with its regulator in an open and co-operative manner and keep the regulator informed of any relevant facts.

Proposed changes to the statements of principle

1.7   The CII intend to examine the principles that are in force at the time of the examination. Currently the FSA have adopted the original 10 principles established by the Securities and Investment Board, listed above.

        The FSA proposes to replace these ten principles with 11 principles 'after the FSA has received its rule-making powers under the Financial Services and Markets Bill.' Since the Bill is unlikely to be passed into law until late 2000, you should concentrate your studies on the existing ten principles if you are taking your examination before the FSMB becomes law.

Principles for businesses

1.8   The 11 Principles will be relevant to all firms, but their practical implications for firms' conduct, organisation and resources will depend on the size of the firm and the business it undertakes. The Principles do not require small firms to act or be treated as if they were large organisations.

Principle 1 - Integrity

A firm must conduct its business with integrity.

Principle 2 - Skill, care and diligence

A firm must conduct its business with due skill, care and diligence.

Principle 3 - Management and control

A firm must take reasonable care to organise and control its affairs responsibly and effectively, with adequate risk management systems.

Principle 4 - Financial prudence

A firm must maintain adequate financial resources.

Principle 5 - Market conduct

A firm must observe proper standards of market conduct.

Principle 6 - Customers' interests

A firm must pay due regard to the interests of its customers and treat them fairly.

Principle 7 - Communications with customers

A firm must pay due regard to the information needs of its customers, and communicate information to them in a way which is clear, fair and not misleading.

Principle 8 - Conflicts of interest

A firm must manage conflicts of interest fairly, both between itself and its customers, and between one customer and another.

Principle 9 - Customers: relationships of trust

A firm must take reasonable care to ensure the suitability of its advice and discretionary decisions for any customer who is entitled to rely upon its judgement.

Principle 10 - Customers' assets

A firm must arrange adequate protection for customers' assets when it is responsible for them.

Principle 11 - Relations with regulators

A firm must deal with its regulators in an open and co-operative way, and must tell the FSA promptly anything relating to the firm of which the FSA would reasonably expect prompt notice.

1.9 Senior management responsibilities will be covered by two distinct FSA regulatory regimes. Firstly, under the Principles for Business, firms will be responsible for organising themselves effectively and responsibly at senior management level. Secondly, under the 'Approved Persons' regime individual senior managers will have their own regulatory obligations.

The Principles will be formally made as Rules after the FSA receives its rule-making powers on implementation of the FSMB into law.

2 CONDUCT OF BUSINESS RULES

2.1 The second tier core conduct of business rules apply to **members of the regulators** and to advisers who are **regulated directly by the FSA**. These rules do *not* apply to RPBs who already have codes of conduct that must provide adequate investor protection.

2.2 The Conduct of Business rules - both those originally created by SIB (the 'second tier') and those created by the regulator - the PIA (substantially taken over from LAUTRO and FIMBRA) - are **developments of the ten principles**. They are drafted on the basis that different types of customer have different levels of knowledge and expertise regarding investments and are therefore either more or less capable of looking after their own investment affairs. The effect of this is that the adviser owes **different levels of duty of care to different customers**. The duty of care which the IFA owes to the mechanic is therefore far greater than that which is owed to the actuary. It is on this basis that customers are split into six categories.

Category of customer	Description
Private investor	Individual with the **least level of knowledge** of the investment business therefore the one to whom a financial adviser owes the **greatest duty of care**.
Ordinary business investor	Likely to have more knowledge of investments than a private investor although this will depend upon the nature of the business investor's activities. Could include individuals acting on behalf of a government or local authority, reasonably large companies, or trustees of a trust with a reasonable level of assets.
Professional investor	People whose profession is the carrying on of investment business, such as a manager of pension scheme assets. Services may be provided to such investors as part of their business but not as private individuals. The standard of care required to such investors is **low**.
Expert/experienced investor	May still be a private investor but is someone who is familiar with the types of investment transactions for which advice is being given. Such an investor understands the risks involved and therefore the level of care needed is **less than with the inexperienced private investor**.

Category of customer	Description
Market counterparty	Person who is effecting a transaction with the investment adviser and who is in the same kind of investment business as the adviser. A good example of such a person is one stockbroker specialising in equities who is giving advice on the purchase or sale of shares to another stockbroker who specialises in gilts. The duty of care required in such a situation is **very low**.
Execution only customers	People who have made it clear that they wish to take their own decisions regarding investments. Either they have clearly stated that they do not wish to receive advice or they have received advice but have chosen to ignore that advice completely and have selected investments, or none, for which they accept entire responsibility.

2.3 Where execution only customers instruct a financial adviser to put their requirements into effect the adviser is **no longer under a duty of care**, as such a duty should have been fulfilled in giving any advice in the first place. Financial advisers should obtain the **written signature** of customers (other than professional investors) to the effect that they are carrying out the customer's instructions regardless of the advice (if any) which has been given. Alternatively, where a life company accepts business on an execution only basis through its designated individuals, it must write to the customer confirming that the contract has been effected on this basis. As with the 'reasons why' letter (see later) this action is required for regular premium life assurance contracts, plus pensions and annuities. Although the adviser is no longer under a duty of care regarding the advice to the customer, he is still expected to carry out the customer's instructions in the customer's best interests and in the most efficient manner possible.

Customers' understanding

2.4 Financial advisers must take reasonable steps to ensure that **customers understand the nature of any risks** which are contained in any advice. Communications with customers must be accurate and understandable. This links with Statement of Principle No. 5 - Information for Customers.

2.5 Advisers must have **written terms of business** and, in addition, IFAs may need **customer agreements**. These will set out the terms on which advisers conduct business with their clients. This topic is one on which the regulations are rather more detailed. We need to look at the types of agreement between advisers and their customers as well as the methods by which this information is given to the customer.

2.6 Both IFAs and tied advisers must supply to clients (other than business investors) a **terms of business letter** or, if relevant, copies of a **client agreement** (see below).

Terms of business letter

> **KEY TERM**
>
> **A terms of business letter** is a letter which does not require the specific written agreement of the client. It is a statement of the terms on which the adviser does business and must be given by both IFAs and tied advisers to the customer at the beginning of a meeting or sent to the client. Alternatively it can be sent with any written material which is sent to the client (except for a direct offer advertisement) unless such a letter has already been sent or no financial advice will be given.

Question 1

(a)   What areas are covered by the second tier regulatory rules?

(b)   What are the subjects covered by the ten Principles?

(c)   What action should an investment adviser take when acting in an execution only capacity for a client?

2.7   The contents of the terms of business letter (which are additional to the rules for business stationery) are specified in the **regulatory requirements**. Statements must be included to the following effect by either tied advisers or IFAs, or both.

Statements	Tied advisers	IFAs
Advisers are either tied or independent	√	√
The category of the particular adviser	√	√
The effect of the category on the scope of the advice available	√	√
The name of the adviser's regulator in full, eg Personal Investment Authority, *not* PIA	√	√
The products or services provided by the adviser	√	√
The customer's rights to inspect records and the adviser's obligations to maintain records	√	√
The method of initiating a complaint, ie to whom complaints should be addressed and how and where to contact them	√	√
The responsibility accepted by the product provider for advice	√	X
Any material conflict of interest (note that the requirement is not that a conflict of interest should not exist, but that if it does it must be disclosed)	X	√
Whether regular reviews of a customer's investments will take place and, if so, how frequently	X	√
How customers can give instructions and how to end an adviser's authority	X	√

Statements	Tied advisers	IFAs
The basis of charges and fees (if any)	X	√
Whether commissions are receivable on packaged or other products and the adviser's liability to disclose those commissions	X	√
(**For sole traders**) Details of locum arrangements during the adviser's absence	X	√
Whether or not the adviser is authorised to handle the customer's money (this depends on the adviser's category) and other assets and, if so, the safe keeping of those assets and the client's rights of inspection of records (which must be kept for six years)	X	√
Whether a compensation scheme covers the business in question and, if so, what cover it provides	X	√

Customer agreement

> **KEY TERM**
>
> An IFA must issue a **customer agreement** in all cases where an IFA's services:
>
> (a) are **regular**;
>
> (b) include investments and transactions which are **more than** advice on life assurance, pensions or unit trusts.
>
> The agreement must state the relationship between the adviser and the customer, especially for the disclosure of fees and charges and the limits of the adviser's authority.

2.8 The arrangement must contain all the terms which are in the Terms of Business letter. **In addition** the following information regarding the terms on which the IFA does business must be included.

(a) An undertaking by the adviser to **limit** the customer's financial commitment to the value of any assets in the adviser's care.

(b) A statement of the customer's **investment objectives** and whether or not the customer is placing any restrictions on those objectives.

(c) The customer's permission for the adviser to hold the customer's money in an account **outside** the UK if the adviser considers this desirable and the customer allows it.

(d) How the adviser's **fees and other charges** are to be calculated and paid.

(e) Any **limits on the adviser's authority**.

(f) An undertaking by the adviser to advise the client of the **basis** for any investment advice (if this information is required by the customer).

(g) How the customer is to be **notified** of an adviser's recommendations.

(h) The terms on which an adviser may 'cold call' a client. This can be done at any time including during normally unsocial hours, or at the adviser's discretion if the client agrees in advance.

(i) The fact that, if cold calling is permitted, the **customer's rights following a cold call**, namely to treat any subsequent investment agreement as unenforceable, are unchanged for life and pensions contracts.

(j) **Cooling off rights** in respect of life policies, pensions and unit trust will be lost, and this must be stated.

(k) The terms on which the agreement can **be ended** without penalty.

(l) The **date** on which the agreement was signed.

(m) **Statements** that will be issued to clients.

Question 2

(a) List the topics to be covered by a terms of business letter.
(b) When must a customer agreement be issued?
(c) What are the required contents of a customer agreement?

Discretionary investment management agreement

KEY TERM

A **discretionary investment management agreement** is required whenever a customer has given a financial adviser the discretion to handle a portfolio of investments without prior reference to the customer. The type of advice for which it is required includes ISAs. As with the customer agreement a discretionary investment management agreement must be signed by both the adviser and the customer.

2.9 It must contain the information in the terms of business letter and in addition must cover the following points.

(a) The **limits of discretion** given to the adviser, for example types of investment which the client does not want to buy such as shares in tobacco or arms companies.

(b) Where services to be provided include **broker fund management**, details of the arrangements between the life office and the adviser.

(c) The basis of the **fees** which the adviser will charge.

(d) Any **commissions** or other benefits receivable (but not in quantified form).

(e) Any **financial benefits** which the adviser receives other than fees paid by the customer.

(f) The **date** the agreement was signed.

Best advice and best execution

KEY TERMS

- **Best advice.** The firm must take reasonable steps to ensure that its advice is suitable for a customer's needs. Customers must not be advised to switch products unless it is in their interests.

- **Churning.** Cancelling one product to earn commission by replacing it with another is prohibited.

- **Switching.** Changing products to earn higher commission is prohibited.

- **Best execution** means that an adviser acting for a client must obtain a best price either on buying or selling products. It excludes life policies and unit trusts and applies primarily to the purchase and sale of shares.

Information for customers about other packaged products

KEY TERM

'**Packaged products**' describe life assurance policies, pensions contracts and collective investment schemes, including OEICs, whether inside or outside an ISA.

2.10 An adviser must give clients **sufficient information** to enable them to make informed decisions. There are four forms of communication which fall within this category: **cancellation notice, with profits guide, key features statement** and a **reasons why letter**.

KEY TERM

Cancellation notice is a notice telling clients that they have 14 days to change their mind after they have received notification of acceptance of an application for investment or protection. This is a statutory right and must be put in such a form that no other information distracts the client's attention from the notice.

2.11 The cancellation notice must be given for all packaged products **except**:

(a) **Term assurance** for less than ten years with no conversion or extension options and expiring before age 70

(b) **Permanent health insurance**

(c) **Single premium policies** effected by: business investors, execution only investors or direct mail clients

(d) **Personal pensions** bought by **transfers** from occupational pension schemes

(e) **For non-life product sales conducted over the telephone**, when an oral summary of cooling-off rights must be provided

KEY TERMS

- A **with profits guide** is a document which explains how the bonus system of a life company works together with the basis of the profits calculation and how bonuses are allocated. It includes an explanation of the company's past performance and must be issued by all product providers who were previously members of LAUTRO.

- **Key features statement** is a statement which gives the key features of the specific packaged product which is being purchased by a client. The key features must be client-specific for all contracts. Subsequent substantial changes in a contract require revision of the key features statement.

2.12 **Product particulars** must be given to the client **before** he signs an application form for the product. In the unusual circumstance where a client does not complete a written application, key features must be sent to the client as soon as possible and in any event within three business days. The information which must be included is listed later in this chapter.

KEY TERM

Reasons why letter. An investor must be sent a written explanation as to **why** the recommendation for a long-term contract - life assurance, pensions and annuities - is suitable. This applies to recommendations to effect new contracts or to surrender or make paid-up existing contracts.

2.13 The **reasons why letter** must state why:

(a) A specific **new** investment contract is suitable for a client's circumstances

(b) An **existing contract should be changed,** eg surrendered, converted (if relevant)

(c) A transaction involving a pensions opt-out or transfer is a **suitable alternative** to membership of an occupational pension scheme

The letter must thus link the reason for the recommendation to the circumstances revealed in the factfind.

2.14 No letter is required for **execution-only transactions**.

2.15 A reasons why letter must be sent **as soon as practicable** or (where cancellation notice is required) not later than the sending of a cancellation notice.

2.16 In the case of **friendly society investment contracts** with premiums not exceeding £50 a year (or £1 a week), a 'reasons why' letter is not required. This applies to both societies and IFAs.

Independence

2.17 There are **two types of independence** under the Financial Services Act - independence of **status** and independence of **form**.

Status

2.18 We have already seen that a firm must be either **tied** or **independent** under the polarisation rule. There is an exception to this and that is for a firm that acts as **investment manager** for a customer. The firm can give advice on packaged products which include life policies, unit trusts and investment trust savings schemes.

Form

2.19 A firm must not accept inducements which conflicts with the interests of its customers. Its first obligation is to ensure fair treatment for a customer even if it has a **material interest** in a transaction. We have considered elsewhere the question of disclosure of such an interest.

2.20 Even if advisers have a material interest they are still under an obligation to ensure **fair treatment** for customers. If advisers intend to publish recommendations for customers, as often happens through the form of newsletters, then they must not enter into any transactions on their own account until the customers have had a reasonable period of time to consider and, if necessary, act on the recommendations. This rule matches the first of the ten principles regarding integrity and fair dealing.

2.21 Securities firms are allowed to enter into agreements to place business through particular persons or organisations in return for specific benefits or **soft commission**. Limits on these benefits are set by the regulators and the firms in question must not exceed those limits.

2.22 A number of firms issue newsletters or recommendations on products to all their customers. If they do so then they are prohibited from **dealing ahead of publication** on their own account in an investment for which they are about to make a recommendation or issue a favourable comment in a newsletter. However there is a time limit on this prohibition: once customers have had a reasonable time to be aware of the recommendation and to act on it, then the firm may subsequently deal on its own account.

Custody of customers' investments

2.23 If a firm is authorised to hold customers' investments then it is under a responsibility to ensure that those investments are kept **safe**. The fact that the assets are in the hands of the firm must be properly recorded.

2.24 **Authorisation** must be obtained to hold clients' assets and must be the subject of a written agreement (referred to earlier). The overwhelming majority of assets which are in the hands of an adviser are in the form of either money or documents representing money and this is reflected in the rules which must be observed. These rules are as follows.

(a) Any client monies must be **in trust in a client bank account at an approved bank.** A slightly different arrangement applies in Scotland.

(b) The account must be in the name of the **firm of advisers** but must include the word **'client'** in its title.

(c) The **bank must be told at the outset** and acknowledgement of that instruction obtained that the money is on trust and the bank cannot use it to offset against any other debts or liabilities of either the client or the adviser.

(d) Any **documents** must be kept in safe custody and a list sent to the client at least every six months which records the assets and the value of the assets.

Financial resources

2.25 A firm of financial advisers is required to have **£10,000 of its own funds** and also to meet a financial resources requirement which varies according to the category of the adviser.

Records

2.26 **Records** have three purposes in this context:

(a) to show that you have complied with all the requirements laid down under the **Financial Services Act**;

(b) to enable you to **run a business efficiently**; and

(c) to provide a source of information for future business.

For example, a fact find will give you information about your client's family and financial advisers who may themselves one day be a source of new business. For the purpose of this section we are concerned with the **compliance requirements**.

2.27 The records can be divided into **three parts** showing the following.

(a) Client dealings
(b) Accounting records
(c) Administrative compliance

Client dealings

2.28 The records which you must keep must show **compliance with the following rules**.

(a) Know your customer
(b) Suitability of investments
(c) Best execution

2.29 This means that the records must cover information relating to customers which includes the following.

(a) **Name and address**.

(b) Sufficient detail of the **client's circumstances** to demonstrate that any recommendations made and deals on his behalf were suitable, including details of any lapses or cancellations sufficient to demonstrate that the client was informed of any consequences and disadvantages as a result.

(c) The **date** of issue and form of any **Terms of Business** letter or a copy of any **Customer Agreement**.

(d) A copy of any **application** to purchase an investment.

(e) A copy of all **written communications** relating to advice given and each transaction arranged or effected.

(f) A copy of any **bank or registration mandate** or power of attorney granted.

(g) A copy of any **complaint** received together with the relevant record of the investigation and response.

2.30 **Records must be kept for at least six years** - indefinitely in the case of pension transfers and opt-outs. Clients have a right of inspection of their own records and any request for such access should be dealt with promptly. Fact-finds made by representatives of product providers need not be retained if the advice does not result in business.

Accounting records

2.31 A firm's **accounting records** should show the following information.

(a) All a firm's financial transactions

(b) A firm's solvency position

(c) A record of money received, including fees and commission

(d) Records of assets and liabilities

(e) Reconciliations of client accounts and broker funds (funds of different providers managed by brokers)

2.32 Accounting records must be available for **inspection by a regulator**. Annual accounts and **auditors' reports** must be submitted to the regulator.

2.33 Records relating specifically to a firm's **designated individuals** and **appointed representatives** are also required and must contain information relating to the following.

(a) The referencing and appointment

(b) The classification of each individual and identity of his supervisor

(c) Any training needs identified and all training undertaken, including any examinations or qualifications

(d) Any restrictions imposed on activity by the firm

(e) Details of any bank or registration mandate given by a customer

(f) Any complaint received

(g) Any disciplinary action taken including the reason for the action and whether any investor suffered loss or damage

(h) Details of any resignation or dismissal

(i) Persistency information (for product providers)

Question 3

(a) What are the required contents of the key features document?

(b) What are the rules relating to an adviser having a material interest in a transaction?

(c) What are the obligations on an adviser who is authorised to hold client's assets?

(d) An IFA firm is required to keep records relating to its dealings with clients. The records must show compliance with which rules?

(e) What information must be kept regarding investment advice given to clients?

(f) Why must details of cancellations of life policies be kept by an investment adviser?

(g) What information must be shown in a firm's accounting records?

Administrative compliance

2.34 Other records which must be kept include the following.

(a) **Advertisements (including newsletters)** - a copy of the advertisement, who approved it and what was the source of any facts specified in the advertisements.

(b) A copy of the firm's **compliance procedures**.

Compliance procedures

2.35 A **compliance action plan** must be formulated and must be reviewed at least every 12 months by an employee who is not involved in investment transactions. The plan must specify the action necessary in order to secure compliance in the following year and must include the following.

    (a) The scope of work undertaken at *all* sites

    (b) The staff assigned to conduct reviews, their qualifications and experience

    (c) A detailed monitoring programme and reporting systems

    (d) Supervision procedures which have been established

2.36 A firm must appoint a **compliance officer** who must either be or have access to a designated partner or director of the firm, and who must produce an annual compliance report.

2.37 Such **procedures should be in writing** although it is only firms with ten or more advisers who need to produce a formal written compliance manual.

2.38 **Notification requirements** (amongst others) include the need to give 28 days notice of changes which need PIA approval in advance, for example the appointment of a new director or partner or a change in membership category. The appointment and termination of appointed representatives and designated individuals must be notified to the regulator within ten business days after the event.

3 AUTHORISATION OF FIRMS AND REGISTRATION OF INDIVIDUALS

3.1 If any person or firm intends to give investment advice of any kind then first they must be **authorised** to do so. An authorised person can be a company, partnership or individual carrying out investment business.

    (a) The **firm** that is accepting responsibility for the advice given must be authorised; and

    (b) within that firm each **individual who gives advice** to clients might be authorised.

(An exemption from the requirement to obtain authorisation applies to appointed representatives of an authorised person. For example, a building society acting as appointed representative of a life office does not need to obtain authorisation under the FSA.)

Case examples

A client telephones an insurance company and asks for the surrender value on a life policy. An employee can give that information without the need to be authorised or registered. However, if the client then asks whether he ought to surrender a policy then the employee is not allowed to answer that question without being properly authorised to give investment advice.

Say an employee is asked to explain how an endowment works. Authorisation/registration is not required to give that information. However, authorisation would be required if the employee then commented on the endowment's suitability as a method of, for example, providing for school fees.

3.2 **Friendly society representatives** whose earnings are not more than £1,000 a year are exempt from the need to be registered and from the requirement to complete a training and competence programme.

3.3 Originally, the requirements for authorisation of individuals giving financial advice differed between IFAs and tied agents. Individuals acting as financial advisers for an IFA firm had to register with the appropriate SRO or RPB for personal authorisation. Tied agents, both company representatives and authorised representatives, did not have to obtain direct authorisation from their SRO: authorisation and compliance were the responsibility of the product provider to which they were tied.

If an IFA network, the network took on the responsibility for authorisation and compliance for the IFA member firms that became appointed representatives of the network.

The situation changed in 1998, with the introduction by the PIA of a requirement for individual registration.

Individual registration

3.4 Registration with the PIA is required for all individuals who are **principals** (including directors and partners) of regulated firms, all **managers** who are responsible for activities regulated by the PIA, and all **financial advisers**.

An individual providing financial advice may not require individual authorisation, but he does require to be individually registered with the PIA.

3.5 Individual registration is in effect a contract between the individual and the PIA. The effect of individual registration is that the PIA will be able to take **disciplinary action** against individuals as well as their firms for breaches of regulations.

3.6 This does *not* mean that every individual who has contact with the investing public must be authorised or registered. The requirement for authorisation or registration concerns the giving of **investment advice**. An employee who simply gives *information* as opposed to *advice* does not need to be authorised or registered, although companies may choose to go through an authorisation/registration procedure for such individuals in order to 'play safe'.

4 ADVERTISEMENTS

4.1 The regulations regarding **advertisements** apply to anything which can be used to advertise investment products or the services of an adviser. This will include newspapers, radio and television advertisements together with personalised letters and posters.

Standard of advertisement

4.2 All advertisements must be **fair, accurate and clear and not mislead either intentionally or unintentionally**. For example, it would not be fair to advertise a survey extract which compared a provider's product with five other providers' products which performed poorly in the survey. They should take account of the intelligence level of the audience at which the advertisements are aimed. Advertisements must clearly identify the advertiser and name the advertiser's regulator.

4.3 The **name of the regulator** must be shown in full, ie 'Regulated by the Personal Investment Authority' or 'Regulated by the Personal Investment Authority for Investment Business'. It is not sufficient to use the initials of the regulator. All advertisements must also observe the standards of both the regulator and the Advertising Standards Authority.

4.4 If an advertisement includes any reference to **past performance or future benefits** then the advertisement must include warnings that past performance is not a guide to future performance, and that the value of units can go down as well as up. Any facts stated in the advertisement must be provable and any tax implications or conditions must be made clear.

4.5   **Sales aids** should be treated in the same way as advertisements, with the contents going through an approval procedure to establish that they are fair, clear and not misleading.

4.6   All **tied advice** must be identified as such, and any advertisement by appointed representatives must show their status - their principal and the relationship between them and their principal.

4.7   An advertisement must be **approved by someone who is authorised** or someone who is exempt from authorisation and a record must be kept of the name of that person who checked and monitored the advertisement.

As with records of client dealings, advertising records must be kept for six years.

Business cards and stationery

4.8   **Business cards** must show the adviser's name and company, the business address and the telephone number of either the head office or the branch from which the adviser is working. They must include the name of the regulator, again in full.

5   UNSOLICITED (COLD) CALLING

5.1   If you as an IFA with a **customer agreement with a client** then **you can call on that client** at such time and in such circumstances and for such reasons as are laid down in the agreement (see Customer Agreements). If an agreement does not contain any provision for cold calling then the **normal rules for cold calling** on prospective clients will apply.

Prospective clients

5.2   When you contact a prospective client for the first time you must **identify yourself and your firm** and the nature of your business. This should take the form of handing to the client a business card at the start of the first meeting, unless the meeting takes place in the adviser's business premises.

5.3   If you wish to take advantage of a referral from an existing client or prospect then you must ask that person's **permission** to identify them to the new prospect. You must if requested give to the prospect the name of the person who gave you the reference. In an ideal world it would smooth the path to an introduction if your client who gave you the reference would contact your prospect before you made your first call, but this is not a regulatory requirement.

Cold calling on prospective clients

5.4   **Cold calling is permitted** for the purposes of marketing or introducing a service for life assurance, pensions and collective investments.

> **KEY TERM**
>
> A **cold call** is a contact made either by a personal visit or by a telephone call for the purposes of an interview without there being in existence any prior permission to do so.

5.5   The general rule is that such calls must be **reasonable** and must **not be made during unsocial hours**. These are generally considered to be between 9 pm and 9 am on a business day, although obviously there could be exceptions to this. An adviser, in making such a call, must check first with the prospect that it is convenient to continue with the call.

5.6 At the beginning of such a call you must **identify yourself,** your company and your status with the company. You must also state the service which you feel you can provide. This will mean giving at the outset the **genuine purpose of your call.** If you make an appointment with the client then you must provide (if you have not already done so) a telephone number or an address where your prospect can contact you to either change or cancel any such appointment.

6   DISCLOSURE RULES

6.1 There are many rules under the general heading of 'disclosure', covering both **information about investment products** and **details of advisers' remuneration.**

Objectives of disclosure rules

6.2 The rules are intended to **ensure that investors possess all the information they need** in order to take a decision on whether or not a particular product is suitable for their needs.

6.3 The information covers the following.

(a) **Details of the products**
(b) **Charges** made by the product provider
(c) **Commission** paid by the product provider to advisers
(d) The **effect on investment returns** of charges and commission
(e) The effect on benefits of **encashment** or **surrender** of a product

Topics covered by the disclosure rules

6.4 The rules cover the following topics.

(a) The **products** to which the rules apply
(b) The **key features** of those products
(c) **When** the information must be supplied
(d) The difference in the information which must be given by IFAs and tied advisers
(e) The **circumstances** when such information must be given to an investor
(f) The **remuneration** of an adviser
(g) Investors' rights to **cancel** contracts before committing themselves

6.5 Although it is not a requirement that **a copy of a client's application form** should be given to the client, it is good practice. The application should be completed by the client and also signed by the client. If it is completed by the adviser then the client's signature should be obtained with confirmation that the client has read the application form.

Products covered by the disclosure rules

6.6 The Product and Commission Disclosure Rules apply to a limited range of products. Those products are divided into the following two groups:

(a) **Life assurance products**

    (i)   Life policies - endowments or whole life - regular and single premium
    (ii) Pension policies - regular and single premium

(iii) Annuities

(iv) Second-hand life policies

(b) **Collective investments and ISAs**

(i) Collective investments - unit trusts and investment trusts

(ii) ISAs linked to unit trusts

6.7 **The rules do not apply to insurance policies** which are not generally regarded as investment contracts.

> **KEY TERM**
>
> An **investment contract** is one whose benefits depend entirely or in part on the performance of investments or which has a surrender value

6.8 **Non-investment products** include the following.

(a) Permanent health insurance (PHI) contracts which are not unit-linked

(b) Critical illness insurance

(c) Term assurance policies

7 WHAT INFORMATION MUST BE PROVIDED?

7.1 The information which **must** be given to an investor falls under the following headings.

(a) Details of the product (**the key features document**)

(b) An explanation of why the product is suitable (the **reasons why letter**) (see para 2.13)

(c) Further information when a sale is completed (**post-sale information**)

Key features document

Contents

7.2 A **key features document** must cover all of the following.

(a) The **nature of the contract**

(i) Its aims

(ii) The investor's commitment, including premiums payable, and their frequency and method of payment; the effect of non-payment of premiums

(iii) The risk factors (including a brief description of all factors which could adversely affect performance), including the basis of any unit-linked benefit and the funds into which premiums are placed

(b) **Details of the benefits**

(i) Whether any of them are guaranteed

(ii) When they are payable

(iii) Illustration of benefits where they are not guaranteed, using standard rates of return, and including the basis of any with profits bonuses

(iv) A statement that the illustrated figures are only examples

(v) A warning that benefits could be more or less than illustrated

(vi)   A statement that providers/insurance companies/friendly societies use the same rates of growth when illustrating benefits but that charges may vary

(vii)   A reminder that inflation would reduce benefits

(c) **Pension income (where relevant)**: a statement that it depends on performance up to retirement and interest rates at retirement

(d) A description of the **policy's principal terms in question and answer form**, including the tax treatment of benefits and of funds into which premiums are payable; this includes advising a client of the tax implications of purchase of a second-hand life policy.

(e) **Surrender values and deductions**

(i)   A statement that the surrender value may be less in early years than the amount paid in

(ii)   A table of **possible surrender values** (transfer values for personal pensions) in the **first five years**, the table to include:

- Deductions to date;
- The effect of the deductions;
- The total paid into the policy to date.

(iii)   A second table consisting of possible surrender values **in later years**.

- Every five years;
- In the final year of the term (where there is a term);
- Every ten years for whole of life policy up to age 75 (or after ten years if later);
- For single premium policies - a ten-year term should be assumed.

(iv)   Underneath the second table (the later years) the provider should insert:

(1) what the **deductions** are for;

(2) the fact that deductions include:

- **cost of life cover** and **sickness benefits**;

- **commission**, expenses, charges, any surrender penalties and other adjustments;

(3) the last line in the table shows the effect of **total deductions** over the full term of the policy could amount to £X;

(4) the **effect of the charges on the benefits** - the fact that if the cost of life cover and sickness benefits are omitted, the effect would be to reduce investment growth from x% a year to y% a year.

(v)   For a policy with no surrender value, the tables should be replaced by a statement: '**WARNING - this contract has no cash-in value at any time**'.

(vi)   When a policy is to be surrendered, the client should be advised of the possibility of a higher cash value through the **second-hand policy market**.

(f) **Commission/remuneration**

This topic should have a heading '**How much will the advice cost?**' and a statement as follows.

either

(i)   the adviser will give the investor details about the **cost of the specific product recommended** (the amount will depend on the premium size and the length of the policy term), and that the cost will be paid for out of deductions;

or (if the policy is a life policy)

(ii)   the adviser will set out the amount or value in cash terms of **commission** or **remuneration**:

(1)   in a manner which is fair, clear and not misleading;
(2)   showing the timing of payments;
(3)   the name of the adviser receiving the payments may be given.

(iii)   **charges borne by the investor** must be shown separately, eg if investment is reduced by a reduced allocation of units, the method and effect of the reduced investment must be shown.

(g) **Compensation etc**

A section of the document must contain any other key information not contained elsewhere in the document. It could include information about how to seek compensation in the event of the need arising.

Warnings

7.3   Where relevant the following **additional warnings** must also be included in key features documents.

Circumstance	Warning
A cancellation notice is required *and* the investor exercises the right to cancel *and* the value of the investments falls before the cancellation notice is received by the product provider.	The investor will not get a full refund as the fall in value will be deducted from the refund.
A fund has high volatility.	If the value of the investments falls, the effect could be substantial and may even result in no refund.
An investment is made in a property fund.	(1) A switch or surrender may be delayed in certain circumstances (2) The value of property funds is a matter of a valuer's opinion
Investment is made in a broker fund (a fund, managed by an IFA, which invests on the advice of the IFA in a number of product provider funds).	Investors must be advised: (1) whether or not they have any right to transfer to another fund; (2) whether or not they may have to transfer to another fund; (3) the terms on which any transfer will be made.

BPP PUBLISHING

Rules

7.4   The following rules apply to the key features document.

    (a)   It must be **separate** from any other material given to the investor.

    (b)   The **standard** must be the same as the member's other product material.

    (c)   It must be **specific** to the investor's circumstances.

    (d)   It must relate to the **investor's chosen policy**.

When the document must be provided

7.5   The key features document must be supplied to the investor **before** completing an application. When a material change takes place in a policy's terms or an adviser's remuneration, a written statement describing changes must be sent to the investor who must be offered a revised key features document.

Who supplies the key features document?

7.6   The document must be supplied **by the provider or IFA** who is making the recommendation.

Key features differences between IFAs and tied advisers

7.7   Both IFAs and tied advisers must make clear to a client their independent/tied status, and supply a key features document which discloses **commission as a monetary amount** as follows.

    (a)   For IFAs:

        (i)   Commission in cash terms received **by *the company***

        (ii)   Fees received for **acting as investment adviser** to a broker fund

    (b)   For tied agents:

        (i)   **Payments** made to designated individuals and appointed representatives

        (ii)   The value of **additional benefits in kind**

        (iii)   The value of the **life office's services**

Post-sale information

KEY TERM

Post-sale information is information which must be supplied after a sale has been completed but before a contract has been finalised. The information consists of:

(a)   a statement of the adviser's status; and

(b)   the information from the key features document described previously in paragraphs 7.2 (b), (c)(d) and (f)(ii);

or

if there have been significant changes made prior to completion of the contract, a revised key features document.

How must the information be supplied?

7.8 It must be sent by **post** (in the case of home service companies it can be given personally to the client).

When must the information be supplied?

7.9 Post-sale information must be sent to a **client not later than when the cancellation notice is sent.** If there is no notice, it must be supplied either **before** the contract is made or as soon as practicable afterwards.

Question 4

(a) What information must be maintained on a company's records in connection with disciplinary actions taken?

(b) Essex & Kent Independent Advisory Service is designing an advertisement to appear on the local television channel. What rules must the advertisement observe?

(c) William has been given the name of John Jones by a client as a possible prospect. What rules regarding the referral must William observe?

Chapter roundup

- *Conduct of business rules.* Three sets of rules: Statements of Principle; Core Conduct of Business Rules - apply to the regulators (ie. the SRO's) but not RPBs; regulators' rules for own members.

- *Statements of principle:* integrity; skill, care and diligence; market practice; information about customers; information for customers; conflicts of interest; customer assets; financial resources; internal organisation and relations with regulators.

- *Conduct of business rules* are based on different levels of consumer knowledge and expertise, and therefore different levels of care.

- *Categories of investor:* private (highest level of care); business; experienced; professional; market counterparty (lowest level of care).

- *Execution only:* accept customers' instructions without or regardless of advice.

- *Customers' understanding.* Customer must understand risk. Communications must be accurate and understandable. Advisers must have terms of business and (for IFAs) sometimes business agreements.

- *Terms of business letter* must normally be given to client at first meeting. Must contain: services; regulator; money authorisation; asset responsibility; remuneration; conflict of interest; locums; complaints addressee; ending authority; review frequency and charges basis.

- *Customer agreement* required when transactions are regular and/or beyond advice on packages. Must state relationship, fees/charges, limits of authority. Not necessary for execution only and market counterparties. Must contain: terms of business letter contents plus; commitment undertaking; customer's objectives and restrictions; non UK account authority; fee/charges basis; authority limits; advice basis undertaking; notification method; 'cold call' terms and effect on customer's rights; loss of cooling off rights; agreement termination; date of agreement and statement to clients.

- *Discretionary investment management agreement* required for portfolio discretion. Must contain terms of business letter contents plus: discretion limits; fees basis; commissions receivable; extra financial benefits and date of agreement.

- *Best advice.* Suitability of investments. Advice must be suitable. Churning and unnecessary switching prohibited.

- *Best execution.* Adviser must obtain best price. Excludes life policies and unit trusts.

- *Information for customers*. Packaged product clients (with specific exceptions) must receive:
  - cancellation notice - 14 days to change mind; exceptions: term assurance, PHI, single premium policies effected by specified clients; transfers to personal pensions;
  - with profits guide - explains bonus system and investment performance;
  - client specific particulars statement containing: premium; benefits; bonus basis; unit linked benefit and fund; risks; charges; tax treatment of policy and fund; effect of non payment of premiums and of early surrender; illustration of surrender values; illustration of effect of expenses.

- *Independence*. *Status*: tied or independent advisers. *Form*: material interest - no conflicting inducements; soft commission - limits and dealing ahead of publication - prohibited on own account.

- *Custody of customers' investments*. Responsible for safe keeping and keeping records. Authorisation required in writing. Moneys must be in trust. Account must be designated 'client'. No offset. Safe custody for documents and client advised every six months.

- *Financial resources*. £10,000 of own funds required.

- *Records*. Must show compliance and efficiency.

- *Client dealings*. Must show compliance with: know your customer; suitability of investments and best execution. Must cover: factfinds; recommendations; compliance with instructions; record of authority; instructions to third parties; lapses and cancellations; where documents kept; how they are accessible; date and time of action taken. Must be kept for six years. Clients have right of prompt access for inspection.

- *Accounting records*. Must show financial transactions: solvency; money received; assets and liabilities and annual accounts and reports required.

- *Administrative compliance*. Must keep: advertisements - copy, approval, source of facts; newsletters containing recommendations; register of CRs; disciplinary action taken and copy of compliance procedures.

- *Compliance procedures*. Action plan required and reviewed annually. Must include: scope of work; review staff details; monitoring and reporting programme and supervision procedures. Compliance officer required. Must be in writing - manual for 10 or more advisers. Must include notification requirements.

- *Advertisements* include: newspapers; radio; TV; personalised letters and posters.

- *Standards of advertisement*. Must be: accurate; fair; clear; not misleading and approved by authorised person. Should allow for audience. Must identify: advertiser and regulator; observe standards of regulator and ASA and show status of ARs. Warnings must accompany performance reference.

- *Business cards and stationery*. Show: adviser's name; address; telephone number and name of regulator. Restrictions on stationery produced by product provider for IFA.

- *Information for potential clients*. Identify self, firm and business. Referrals must be identifiable.

- *Criteria for unsolicited calls*. Existing clients - as agreed.

- *Prospective clients*. Cold call is personal visit or telephone call without permission. Must be reasonable and not during unsocial hours (9pm - 9am). Adviser must check if convenient and identify self, company, status and purpose and leave telephone number and/or address.

- *Information to clients*. Disclosure rules apply to most packaged products. To be supplied: key features document; terms of business letter; reasons why letter; post-sale information must be supplied with appropriate warnings.

Quick quiz

1   The Personal Investment Authority is responsible for the authorisation of financial advisers who previously were members of which body?

    A   Insurance Brokers Registration Council.
    B   Insurance Managers Regulatory Organisation.
    C   Institute of Chartered Accountants in Scotland.
    D   Law Society in Scotland.

2   In order to meet its investment commitments, a firm is under a specific obligation to:

    A   have adequate compliance arrangements;
    B   maintain adequate financial resources;
    C   provide its customers with regular financial reports;
    D   segregate customers' assets from its own business assets.

3   The document which explains how reversionary and terminal bonuses work is known as the:

    A   client agreement;
    B   key features document;
    C   terms of business letter;
    D   with profits guide.

4   A firm of financial advisers must have capital of not less than what amount?

    A   £10,000.
    B   £20,000.
    C   £25,000.
    D   £50,000.

5   For how many years must records of client dealings be kept?

    A   3
    B   5
    C   6
    D   10

6   An IFA's business card must contain what information?

    A   The name of an adviser's company.
    B   The principal product providers dealt with.
    C   A statement that business is fee-paying (if relevant).
    D   The name of the compliance officer.

The solutions to the questions in the quiz can be found at the end of this Study Text. Before checking your answers against those solutions, you should look back at this chapter and use the information in it to correct your answers.

Answers to questions

1   (a)   Conduct of business; financial resources; clients' money; unsolicited calls.

    (b)   Integrity; financial resources; information about customers; assets of customers; relations with regulators; information for customers; market practice; skill, care and diligence; conflicts of interest; internal organisation.

    (c)   Obtain the client's signature to a statement that the client's instructions are being carried out regardless of any advice given.

2   (a)   Services provided; adviser's regulator; care of client's money; client's right to inspect records; remuneration; material interest; locum arrangements; address for complaints; ending adviser's authority; review frequency; basis of charges.

(b) When services are regular and/or include investments which are more than life, pensions or unit trust advice.

(c) All the terms of the terms of business letter; relationship between client and adviser; undertaking to limit client's financial commitment; customer's objectives; permission to hold money in non-UK account; how charges are calculated and paid; limits to authority; basis for advice; method of notification; cold calling terms and consequences; how to end agreement; date of agreement; issue of statements.

3   (a) Premiums; benefits; bonuses; unit-linked basis; risks; charges; taxation; non-payment of premiums; surrender; surrender illustrations; expenses; projections; remuneration; complaints.

(b) A firm must not accept inducements, and must declare material interests.

(c) Written agreement must exist; keep assets safe; record their whereabouts; bank account must be in trust, have 'client' in title and be protected from bank offset; documents must be safe; client must be sent six-monthly list.

(d) Know your customer; suitability of investments; best execution.

(e) Details of recommendations, reasons, and reference material.

(f) To show that client was informed of disadvantages and consequences of cancellation.

(g) All financial transactions; solvency; money received including fees and commissions; assets and liabilities; reconciliation of client accounts and broker funds.

4   (a) Identity of adviser; details of offence; reason for loss; action taken regarding loss; action against adviser.

(b) Must be fair, accurate, clear; not mislead; match intelligence level of viewers; identify adviser and regulator; meet standards of regulator and Advertising Standards Authority; include warnings regarding performance (if mentioned); clarify tax implications.

(c) Obtain client's permission to identify him if requested; give John Jones the name of the client who gave the referral.

Chapter 4

REGULATORS' COMPLIANCE RULES

Chapter topic list	Syllabus reference
1 Best execution and execution only	A 4.2
2 Know your client	A 4.3
3 Know your client methods	A 4.3
4 Understanding risks	A 4.4
5 Best/suitable advice guidelines	A 4.5
6 Selecting providers	A 4.6
7 Products outside adviser's range	A 4.7
8 Unsuitable instructions	A 4.8
9 Adviser completed application	A 4.9
10 Advice on existing investments	A 4.10
11 Complaints procedures	A 4.11, 4.12
12 Compensation	A 4.13

Introduction

In this chapter, we will continue our study of the detailed rules affecting financial advisers.

1   BEST EXECUTION AND EXECUTION ONLY

1.1   'Best execution' and 'execution only' are two totally different concepts although they both have a direct bearing on the standard of care which an adviser owes to clients.

Best execution

> **KEY TERM**
>
> The rule of **best execution** is a requirement of the FSA and requires an adviser to obtain the best terms in any deal on behalf of a client. Such terms must take account of the charges involved in a transaction. The best example is of a stockbroker who, when instructed to sell equities on behalf of a client, is obliged to obtain the best possible price. It is in fact stockbrokers who are the ones normally affected by this rule.

1.2   There are very specific categories where **the rule does not apply**.

Products	Clients
Life policies	Business, experienced or professional
Pension contracts	investors where best execution is excluded
Collective investments	under a terms of business letter.

Execution only

KEY TERM

An adviser acts in an **execution only** capacity when he accepts the client's instructions to complete a transaction regardless of any advice.

1.3 Such circumstances arise where a client **does not seek advice** and where no advice has been given.

1.4 An adviser owes to the client only a duty to execute the transaction when he can reasonably assume that the client is **not** relying on the adviser for advice or assessment of any transaction.

1.5 If an adviser is acting in an execution only capacity for a client the adviser must **keep adequate records** to make it clear that advice was neither given nor sought. This means that written and signed confirmation must be obtained from the client making it clear that the transaction was conducted without regard to any advice either having been given or offered.

1.6 Additionally, where a designated individual of a **product provider** sells on an execution only basis, the product provider must write to the client confirming the basis of the sale (ie that advice was neither sought nor given in respect of the transaction).

2 KNOW YOUR CLIENT

Exam focus point

Before we proceed with this section we need to understand that there is no difference between a client and a customer. The syllabus refers to a client which is the expression normally used by financial advisers. However, the regulations use the words 'customer' or 'investor'. For the purposes of the examination, the three terms are interchangeable.

2.1 It is essential to take all steps to obtain **as much knowledge as possible about the client** simply in order to be able to give suitable advice which is relevant to the client's circumstances.

Information required

2.2 There is no specific rule stating exactly what information you must obtain from your client. The following list cannot be regarded as complete but is intended simply as a guide to the range of **desirable information** needed.

Personal	Financial
• Marital status (this must include partners living together) • Dependants (most likely to be spouse and children) • Occupation	• Income and expenses • Assets and liabilities • Tax situation - income and capital • Objectives, eg protection, savings, retirement provision • Future plans, eg career change or education for children • Debts, eg mortgage • Attitude to risk

2.3 The information must come **direct** from the client but, if the client refuses to give it, the adviser need not pursue the matter. However an adviser must keep a clear record signed by the client making it clear which information has been asked for but declined.

2.4 This sort of information is **not needed** for:

(a) business investors;
(b) experienced investors;
(c) professional investors;
(d) execution only clients;
(e) market counterparties.

3 KNOW YOUR CLIENT METHODS

3.1 The Act does not lay down any specific method of obtaining information regarding a client. However, the most practical way is to use a **prepared list of questions**. This is the procedure followed by nearly all advisers and has become known as the **fact find**.

> **KEY TERM**
>
> The **fact find** is simply an orderly method of obtaining information regarding a client. If a client does not wish to provide that information then, as we have seen in the previous section, the adviser is not debarred from conducting business with that client.

4 UNDERSTANDING RISKS

4.1 One of the problems faced by advisers is that, if an investment performs less well than the client expected, there is a potential for a **complaint** against the adviser.

4.2 In the past this situation may have arisen because the **risks** were not fully explained to the client but it may also have arisen because the client has forgotten the fact that the risks have been explained.

4.3 An adviser must therefore be totally satisfied that a client **understands** the nature of any risk which is associated with any transaction or explain the possibility of any future exposure to additional liability. This information must be given before recommending or entering into a transaction with a client. This applies especially to discretionary management of a client's assets.

4.4 The relevant information must be given to the client in the **format** required by the conduct of business rules. His will be in the **key features document** (see Chapter 3).

5 BEST/SUITABLE ADVICE GUIDELINES

5.1 The first consideration in giving advice to a client is the **best interests of the client**. This is one of the regulatory requirements.

5.2 In considering the client's best interests account must be taken of the client's **existing investments,** their distribution and the personal and financial situation of the client in addition to giving careful consideration to the type of investment being recommended.

5.3 The interpretation of the requirement to give best/suitable advice is to recommend a **suitable product**. It is not really feasible in many cases to recommend one product which can be said beyond any doubt to be better than any other comparable product. The requirement is to recommend the products or services which are suitable to a client's needs.

5.4 In doing so an adviser must exercise **due skill and care** in making recommendations or in exercising discretion on behalf of a client. The adviser must take into account all factors, not only regarding the client but regarding the product.

5.5 The adviser must possess **up to date knowledge** and **give well informed judgments**. If past performance tables are used in illustrations it must be made clear that they are no guarantee of the future performance and are produced for illustrative purposes only. Independent advisers are allowed to make recommendations from a short list of suitable products from different product providers.

Exam focus point

Different terminology is used in the industry. For examination purposes the expressions 'best advice' and 'suitable advice' must be regarded as interchangeable.

Connected person

5.6 If an independent adviser has a **vested interest** in a product then special care is needed in the recommendation. This situation can exist where there may be some common ownership between an IFA and a product provider.

5.7 In such a case the IFA must take extra special steps to be able to demonstrate that there is no other product which is better than the one that is being recommended. This is known as **'better than best advice'**.

5.8 For tied advisers suitable advice is made possible by recommending a product from the provider's own range. Under the rules of **polarisation** no alternative course of action is possible. Any packaged products must demonstrate their overall suitability to a client.

Question 1

(a) What is the difference between best execution and execution only?

(b) Why is it necessary to obtain all relevant information about a client before giving investment advice?

(c) What action must an adviser take if a client refuses to disclose information to the adviser?

(d) What is the realistic alternative to giving best advice?

6 SELECTING PROVIDERS

6.1 An IFA is under an obligation to **select the most suitable** *provider* of an investment product. This requirement is in addition to selecting the best *type* of product.

6.2 The factors that an IFA must take into account are as follows.

Product	Provider
• Suitability, including (where appropriate) investment performance	• Financial strength
• Premium rate	• Efficiency of service
• Underwriting considerations	• Speed of dealing with claims
• Product-specific charges	

6.3 For the purposes of the examination we do not need to deal with the detailed requirements regarding financial strength. It is sufficient to know that one of the prime considerations is the **excess of a provider's assets over liabilities** and, in the case of investment products, the consistency with which the provider has demonstrated investment performance over a period of years.

6.4 The **sources of information** that an independent adviser may use when selecting the most suitable provider of an investment product include:

Factor	Source of information
Financial strength	Company reports, DTI returns, independent reports produced by specialist agencies
Product benefits	Product providers, independent publications, professional bodies
Fund performance	Product providers, independent publications, the Stock Exchange

7 PRODUCTS OUTSIDE ADVISER'S RANGE

7.1 When a fact find shows that the needs of a client cannot be met by a tied adviser's provider, the adviser is **not at liberty to recommend any other product from the provider's range**. This does not mean that the product, to be suitable, must be the best on the market nor that it has to produce the best performance. If the investment performance of an adviser's product is not as good as that of other providers, he can still recommend the product on the grounds that it is a suitable solution to a client's problem.

7.2 If a tied adviser's company does not have a suitable product then the adviser is allowed to **introduce a client to an IFA and receive payment**. Remember however that while this is allowed under the regulations, the product provider may not be prepared to allow any of their agents to follow that course of action.

8 UNSUITABLE INSTRUCTIONS

8.1 A client may ask an adviser to effect a transaction which the adviser considers to be **unsuitable**. This may arise because the client does not agree with the adviser's recommendation.

8.2 This situation has become known as an **'insistent customer' sale**. Extreme care needs to be taken that a full record is made of both the advice given and, if it can be established, the reason why the client is disregarding the advice. In these circumstances you should use the rules relating to **execution only clients** as a guide.

9 ADVISER COMPLETED APPLICATION

9.1 One of the dangers of an adviser completing an application form in the case of life assurance and pensions business is that the client may consider that the **answers on the form do not match those given by that client**.

9.2 In order to avoid this sort of difficulty the adviser should:

   (a) **Read** to a client the contents of an application form

   (b) Obtain the confirmation from the client that they **understand** the contents of the form

   (c) Obtain the client's **signature**

9.3 If this procedure is not followed then there is scope for the client later to allege that the information on the form is not accurate and that this **invalidates the transaction** which was completed.

10 ADVICE ON EXISTING INVESTMENTS

10.1 One of the major problems that the industry has been faced with in previous years is accusations that clients have been recommended to cancel contracts in order to buy replacement products from the adviser's own provider (**churning**).

10.2 In doing so the client will almost certainly suffer a **financial loss,** often a substantial one, by cancelling a life assurance policy, in particular at an early stage.

10.3 The rule does *not* state that such advice must never be given. It does require however that **an adviser who is recommending the surrender of a life policy should explain clearly the reasons for the recommendation and the effect on the policy and its benefits**, and should keep careful record not only of the recommendations itself but of the reasons for it.

10.4 **The general presumption is that existing life assurance policies should be allowed to continue.** An example of the relatively rare circumstances in which an existing insurance can be replaced by a new one is in the case of **term assurance** where, if cover is obtainable at a lower premium, then this may be used to replace an existing contract. This is possible nowadays with progression in underwriting attitudes towards certain illnesses, particularly AIDS.

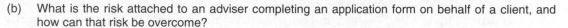

Question 2

(a) What factors must an IFA take into account in selecting a provider's product for a client?

(b) What is the risk attached to an adviser completing an application form on behalf of a client, and how can that risk be overcome?

(c) What rules apply when an adviser wants to recommend that a client cancels a life policy?

11 COMPLAINTS PROCEDURES

11.1 Under the Regulators' rules a client will have the **right of complaint** against an adviser in certain circumstances. Those circumstances include **negligence** by an adviser, or **breach** of a customer agreement, or **misrepresentation** by an adviser.

11.2 The client has the right to have a complaint **investigated** properly and thoroughly and appropriate action taken. The client may, if not satisfied with the way a complaint is handled, report the matter to the adviser's regulator and can ask the regulator to investigate.

11.3 Members of a regulator must have **written procedures** in place for handling complaints. They must also ensure that all staff, all appointed representatives and all the staff of appointed representatives are aware of the procedures.

11.4 A firm must **co-operate with its regulator** in any investigation.

11.5 When a complaint is received it must be **acknowledged** within seven business days of being received by the adviser.

11.6 If the complaint is an **oral** one, the firm's letter of acknowledgement of its receipt must state their **understanding of the complaint** and ask the complainant to confirm the accuracy of their understanding in writing.

11.7 The procedures must ensure that a complaint is handled by a person who was **not involved in giving the advice** that formed the source of the complaint. A sole trader, who is obviously in a difficult position regarding this requirement, must be able to demonstrate efficient handling of the complaint.

11.8 The adviser must handle a complaint **promptly** and must advise the client that the complaint will be investigated promptly and thoroughly and that action will be taken as appropriate by a responsible member of staff.

11.9 The client must be told of the procedures which can be followed if the client is not satisfied with the way the firm has handled the complaint. This will primarily be the right to complain to the firm's **regulator**.

11.10 The complaint must be **remedied** where possible, and a **written report** produced. The firm must explain to the complainant the outcome of the investigation, including terms of settlement or reasons for rejection as appropriate.

11.11 Investigation into a complaint should be completed within a **reasonable time**. If it is not completed within two months, a progress report must be sent to the client.

11.12 Within **seven days** of completing the investigation, the client must be sent a **letter** explaining the outcome and the terms of any settlement. Clients must also be advised that if they are not satisfied with the way the complaint has been handled they can refer to the **Regulator's Ombudsman**.

11.13 The Ombudsman can **make awards** up to £50,000, although there is scope for higher awards of up to £100,000 for non-regulated complaints which are referred voluntarily to the Ombudsman. The firm and adviser will be expected to **co-operate fully** with the Ombudsman, and to act promptly to implement any award.

11.14 **Records** must be kept for at least six years after the date a complaint has been received, although in view of the long-term nature of the business it may be advisable to keep them for rather longer.

12   COMPENSATION

12.1 If a client suffers a financial loss as a result of a breach of a regulatory requirement the client may seek **compensation** from the firm. If the firm is an IFA or a member of an RPB, adequate professional indemnity insurance (PII) should be in place to deal with this sort of situation.

12.2 However, a quite different situation arises if a firm is **insolvent** or is likely to become insolvent. The fact that a client may be able to demonstrate negligence or fraud on the part of a financial adviser will be of no financial help to the client if the company is going out of business. For this reason a compensation scheme known as the **Investors Compensation Scheme** (ICS) exists to provide compensation for valid claims. It operates by sharing the costs of compensation amongst the other members of a defaulting member's regulator by means of a levy. However such claims will be subject to the following limits.

   (a)   100% of the first £30,000 of any one loss
   (b)   90% of the next £20,000 will be covered

   Claims relating only to the first £50,000 of loss will be considered. If an individual who has suffered a loss of, say, £100,000 makes a claim, only the first £50,000 of the loss will be relevant with regard to compensation.

   This means that the largest sum that can be paid under the scheme is £48,000.

> **Exam focus point**
> For the purposes of examination questions there are two things to note.
> (a)   The claim must be a *valid* claim.
> (b)   The adviser must be either *insolvent* or *becoming insolvent*.

12.3 There is a cap on ICS payments of £100m for each regulator, and there are **no cross subsidies** between the members of the regulatory organisations. All firms subject to FSA rules must contribute with the exception of friendly societies and RPBs.

12.4 There is an investor protection scheme (IPS) for **building society share and deposit accounts**. The Scheme provides that, if a building society runs into financial difficulties, investors' money will be protected. The maximum level of protection is 90% of the total invested in share or deposit accounts in a society, with a deposit limit of £20,000 or (if higher) the sterling equivalent of €22,222.

12.5 A Depositors' Protection Scheme also exists for deposits in banks. Known as the **Deposit Protection Scheme** (DPS), the deposit limit is the same as for the Investor Protection Scheme, i.e. £20,000, the actual payment limit (90%) thus being £18,000.

Question 3

(a) What action must be taken by a firm when a complaint is received?

(b) What information must appear in a letter acknowledging an oral complaint?

(c) What information must be given to a client when an investigation is completed?

(d) In what circumstances may the regulator's Ombudsman Bureau make an award in excess of £50,000?

(e) Who must handle a complaint to a firm?

Chapter roundup

- *Best execution.* Adviser must obtain best terms taking account of charges. Does not apply to life/pensions policies and collective investments, nor to business or professional investors if excluded under terms.

- *Execution only and its requirements.* Adviser acts on instructions regardless of any advice given. Must keep adequate records to show advice not given nor (if appropriate) sought - signed confirmation required from client.

- *Know your client and methods.* All relevant information required. Must come from client who can refuse, but client should sign confirmation of refusal. Information not needed for: business/experienced/professional investors; execution only clients; market counterparties. No set method for obtaining facts, but factfind is practical.

- *Understanding risks.* Adviser must be satisfied client understands risks.

- *Best advice guidelines.* Adviser must consider client's existing investments and distribution, and personal and financial situation. Must give suitable advice exercising skill and care, taking all relevant factors into account. Adviser must be up to date and informed, and give warnings regarding investment performance. IFAs can recommend from short list.

- *Connected person.* Adviser with vested interest must give 'better than best' advice.

- *Selecting providers.* IFA must take account of: product (suitability, performance, premium, underwriting); provider (financial strength, efficiency of service, claims service).

- *Products outside adviser's range.* Product must be suitable but need not be best. Cannot recommend product outside own range, but can introduce client to IFA and receive payment.

- Insistent client disagrees with adviser's recommendations: adviser can act on execution only basis.

- *Adviser-completed application.* Adviser should ensure client reads contents and obtain signature.

- *Disclosure of referrals.* Adviser must obtain permission for referral and disclose source of referral on request, but not nature of transactions without client's permission.

- *Advice on existing investments.* Adviser must: explain reasons for recommendations to surrender; effect on policy and benefits; keep records of reasons. Term assurance may sometimes be suitable for replacement.

- *Complaints.* Complaints may be for negligence, breach or misrepresentation. Complaint must be investigated properly, promptly, thoroughly, and action taken. Client can contact regulator and ask to investigate. Complaints procedure involves: acknowledge in seven days; putting it in writing; action by responsible member of staff; telling client procedures if not satisfied. Written procedure must exist, staff must be aware of them, non-involved staff must handle complaint. Client must be told outcome, or two months later - progress report required. Members keep records for six years.

- *Compensation.* Adequate PII should be in place, ICS exists for insolvent firms. ICS limits: 100% first £30,000; 90% next £20,000; nothing over £50,000. Maximum payment £48,000. Claim must be valid and firm insolvent or nearly insolvent; Investor Protection Scheme limit for building societies is 90% × £20,000; the Deposit Protection Scheme limit for banks is also 90% × £20,000.

Quick quiz

1   The best execution rule applies to:

A   collective investments;
B   life policies;
C   pensions contracts;
D   share dealings.

2   In which of the following circumstances is a financial adviser not required to complete a fact find?

A   The client is an execution only client.
B   The client is purchasing equities.
C   The adviser's recommendations have been accepted.
D   The client has produced evidence of his income and expenditure.

3   Within how many days after receiving a complaint must a firm acknowledge it?

A   7
B   10
C   14
D   21

4   Advisers are required to give investment advice to clients which is considered:

A   adequate;
B   the best available;
C   better than best;
D   suitable.

The solutions to the questions in the quiz can be found at the end of this Study Text. Before checking your answers against those solutions, you should look back at this chapter and use the information in it to correct your answers.

Answers to questions

1   (a)   Best execution - adviser must obtain best terms for client; execution only - adviser acts on instructions given by client without receiving or accepting advice.

(b)   To ensure that the advice is suitable advice.

(c)   Keep a clear record (signed by the client) that the information has been declined.

(d)   To give suitable advice.

2   (a)   Suitability, performance, premium, underwriting, charges.

(b)   The client may eventually allege that the form was incorrectly completed and that the transaction is invalid. It is better if the client completes the form. Alternatively, if the adviser completes it, the contents should be read by the client, who should confirm that they are correct and then sign the form.

(c)   It must clearly be in the client's interest, and the reasons and the consequences must be explained to the client.

3   (a)   It must be promptly acknowledged.
(b)   The firm's understanding of the complaint, and does the client agree with it?
(c)   The outcome, or reason for rejection.
(d)   When the complaint is referred voluntarily to the Bureau.
(e)   Someone who was not involved in the source of the complaint.

BPP PUBLISHING

Chapter 5

ENFORCEMENT

Chapter topic list	Syllabus reference
1 Monitoring of compliance	A 5.1, A 5.2
2 The regulator's compliance visits	A 5.3, A 5.4
3 Compliance procedures by the firm	A 5.5, A 5.6
4 The Training and Competence rules	A 5.7
5 Knowledge requirements for advisers undertaking specialist roles	A 5.8
6 Requirements on advisers in relation to CPD	A 5.9

Introduction

This chapter concentrates on how the regulations are enforced. It will therefore cover the purpose and scope of the methods of enforcement.

Regular inspection visits are made by the staff of self regulatory organisations and recognised professional bodies. Their function is to check the effectiveness of the internal compliance arrangements of member firms.

1   MONITORING OF COMPLIANCE

The regulators

1.1   The extent to which regulatory bodies check the compliance of their members depends to a large extent on the **type of business** transacted by the member. For example, a large firm of independent financial advisers with branches throughout the country will be subject to a more stringent check than a friendly society which deals with all business by post and has one product in its range.

1.2   **Compliance visits** - known as **periodic inspection visits** or **PIVs** - will be made for one of three reasons.

(a)   As a part of the regulatory bodies' regular monitoring of their members.

(b)   As a result of a complaint which the body has been asked to investigate.

(c)   If the regulator has some reason to doubt the efficiency of the firm's compliance procedures.

1.3   **Regular compliance visits** will be made at least every 12 months for high risk firms, 24 months for the medium risk category, and 30 months for firms classified as low risk. A surprise visit will be made to 5% of the authorised firms. A firm can be in the high risk category simply because it is holding client moneys or assets, even if it is not in financial difficulties.

1.4 PIVs can be made without warning but it is more usual for a firm to be given typically **four weeks' notice** of an impending visit: previously two days' notice was normal for IFAs. Networks need to show the adequacy of their internal monitoring for appointed representatives, who must have a written contract.

Members

1.5 Each member of the PIA must have a **compliance officer** whose function is to monitor the compliance of the firm with the regulatory requirements.

1.6 This will involve the compliance officer ensuring that there are **regular checks** on the **keeping of records,** the **advice given** to clients and the contents of any **advertisements.**

2 THE REGULATOR'S COMPLIANCE VISITS

2.1 Regulatory bodies will want to know that their members are observing the **regulatory requirements** both of the Act in general and of their own regulatory body in particular. They will also wish to ensure that the members remain **fit and proper persons** to give investment advice.

2.2 The prime purpose of compliance visits or PIVs is to ensure that these requirements are met and, if they are not, to enable the regulator to take the **appropriate action**. The first step the regulator will take in the event of non-compliance will be to endeavour to ensure that the member **corrects any deficiency**. Ultimately however, in the event of failure to achieve this, **authorisation** to give investment advice may be **withdrawn**. In the most serious cases **court action** may finally result.

Powers of enforcement officers and scope of visits

2.3 The **enforcement officers** who are employed by regulatory bodies have the full authority of those bodies in their task of ensuring that member firms have complied with the regulatory requirements.

2.4 They can choose to **visit** any member or any appointed representative of a member at any time without warning although, as we saw earlier, four weeks' notice is normally given.

2.5 During their visits they have the authority to **inspect** any of the firm's records which will enable them to make a judgment on the compliance with the regulatory requirements and effectiveness of the firm's procedures. They may also institute such visits following the receipt of a complaint even if the client has not asked the regulatory body to investigate the complaint.

2.6 They are entitled to receive **full co-operation** from the staff of the member and/or any appointed representatives.

3 COMPLIANCE PROCEDURES BY THE FIRM

3.1 The basis for complying with regulations is the **keeping of adequate records**. These should cover all aspects of compliance, but the following will be examples of the principal categories of records that should be kept.

Area	Types of record
Dealing with clients	Copies of all fact finds
	Reasons for the recommendations made to clients
	The basis of those recommendations and the source of information
	Any agreements with clients
	Evidence that a transaction was on an execution only basis
	Evidence of any conflicts of interest and how they were handled
	Documentary evidence of transactions
Financial records	Daily record of income and expenditure, assets and liabilities
	Any other records to enable an auditor to satisfy the PIA requirements
	Members holding clients' money must observe additional special regulations
	All members must produce annual accounts but some may be required to produce information for the regulator more frequently depending on their category
	Any other records to enable an auditor to satisfy the PIA requirements
	Members holding clients' money must observe additional special regulations
	All members must produce annual accounts but some may be required to produce information for the regulator more frequently depending on their category
Personnel records	Records of the appointment and dismissal of advisers and appointed representatives
	Records showing that adequate references were taken up before appointment
Advertising records	Copies of each advertisement
	Records of who authorised each advertisement
	Date of last issue of an advertisement

3.2 The principle is that records must be **adequate for their purpose** and for the needs of the regulators. Ideally they should be in a standard format as this makes checking easier.

3.3 They should be maintained by advisers and their appointed representatives for at least **six years** and should be available for inspection by the regulator at any time. The firm itself may need instant access to records in the event of a complaint.

Compliance officer

3.4 The first responsibility of any firm in order to ensure compliance is that it must appoint a person to be responsible for ensuring that the company complies with regulations. That person - known as the **compliance officer** - must be an employee of the firm.

3.5 This principle applies to **all firms** whether they are insurance companies, banks, building societies, unit trust management companies or independent financial advisers.

3.6 The compliance officer, in the case of a larger firm, may need a separate **compliance department** in order to meet Act requirements. Although all the management of a company still retain legal liability for the company's activities, the prime responsibility for compliance rests with the board of a company or the partners. In practice the day to day compliance requirements are monitored by the compliance officer. If that officer is not a partner or a member of a board of directors then he must have direct access to a member of the board or the chief executive.

Compliance officer's responsibilities

3.7 The overall responsibility of a compliance officer is to supervise the **compliance procedures** of the firm and ensure that the **rules are enforced**. He must provide an **advisory service** to all business areas within the firm and ensure that all the firm's advisers continue to be **fit and proper** for the purpose of giving investment advice.

3.8 Compliance procedures must be kept **regularly under review**. Such regular review must take place annually if a firm has:

(a) ten or more advisers; or

(b) one or more appointed representatives.

3.9 The compliance officer must report **annually** to the board or partners and must liaise as required with the firm's regulator.

Written procedures

3.10 Where a firm has ten or more advisers the **compliance procedures must be in writing** as a **compliance action plan**. The plan must cover all dealings with clients. Examples of information which must be in the plan include fact finds and recommendations, complaints handling, personnel topics especially recruitment, and the issue of advertisements. They must also detail the records that must be kept in order to put into effect these procedures.

3.11 The written rules must be **available** to all employees and appointed representatives of the firm.

Question 1

(a) What is the objective of a periodic inspection visit?

(b) What are the reasons for which a periodic inspection visit may be made?

(c) Why may a firm be in a high risk category?

(d) What are the four principal headings which describe the types of records which a firm should keep?

(e) What is the function of a compliance officer?

(f) Who retains legal liability for the compliance of a company?

(g) If the compliance officer of a company is not a member of the board or a partner, to whom must he have access?

---

4   THE TRAINING AND COMPETENCE RULES

4.1 The PIA Training and Competence (T&C) scheme applies to all designated individuals.

All designated individuals who provide advice will be classified within the scheme under one of the following categories. This will determine their training status and the level of supervision they receive.

Category	Definition
New entrants	Someone with no appropriate industry experience.
Experienced new entrants	Someone with some relevant experience which allows the training process to be modified.
Competent designated individual	An individual who, being assessed competent at Stage 2 level, is continuing to trade satisfactorily and undertake Continuous Professional Development.

Minimum competence requirements for new and existing staff

4.2 T&C arrangements must aim to achieve a level of competence. This consists of the following components.

(a) Generic benchmark qualification, eg Financial Planning Certificate (FPC).

(b) Firm-specific knowledge, ie administration requirements, financial planning process, company products.

(c) The advisory process, ie gather and analyse client needs, present advice.

4.3 These standards must be demonstrated on an ongoing basis by all designated individuals and during off-job training by new entrants to the organisation.

Training arrangements

4.4 Training must be provided for any adviser who has not yet achieved the standard of competence required. For competent designated individuals, training will usually take the form of Continuing Professional Development (CPD, see below).

4.5 Training for any *new entrant* to an organisation will fall into two stages.

(a) Stage 1 - formal structured training provided for newcomers to the organisation which takes place 'off-job', ie not with clients.

(b) Stage 2 - structured training that takes place in the workplace usually under the control of the supervisor.

Training will consist of both knowledge and the development of practical experience and application skills.

Continuous Professional Development (CPD)

4.6 All competent designated individuals who have reached the required level of competence must then ensure that they maintain their competence. This may take the form of:

(a) Refreshing and updating technical knowledge of, for instance, products, regulation or taxation

(b) Developing knowledge and skills in new areas which support the requirements of the business such as a changed job role, or work in a new market etc

Supervision

4.7 Under the PIA requirements, all designated individuals must have a supervisor to ensure that standards are met and opportunities are taken to improve performance by the ongoing identification of training needs. The only exception to this requirement is for IFA principals. In this case, no supervisor is required because of the practical difficulties of arranging it. Principals should, however, apply the principles of supervision to their own job performance.

Key Performance Indicators (KPIs)

4.8 Sometimes also called performance or equality indicators, key performance indicators cover the areas which are deemed by the firm to be critical to the successful performance of an adviser. Examples suggested in the January 1998 PIA T&C Guidance include:

- Sales production/activity ratios
- Persistency rates
- Not taken up (NTUs)
- Quality of 'reason why letters'/fact finds
- Range of advice
- Complaints from investors

These measures allow the indirect monitoring of the designated individual's performance by the supervisor. They are also valuable as they allow trends in performance to be measured over time.

Persistency rates

4.9 If a product provider experiences a large number of **cancellations of policies** within a short period of time, it probably means that some of those cancelled policies should never have been sold in the first place.

This is particularly important with life assurance policies, where the penalties for cancelling a policy in the early part of its life can be severe, and result in policyholders losing all or a substantial part of their original outlay.

If, for example, only 1% of policies were cancelled within their first year, this would probably have no significance, as there can be all sorts of legitimate reasons for clients cancelling contracts, such as redundancy.

If, on the other hand, 25% of a company's policies were cancelled within their first year, it is highly unlikely that such a high proportion could have been cancelled for legitimate reasons.

KEY TERM

The proportion of contracts which remains in force is known as the **persistency rate**. A loss of only 1% means a good persistency rate. A loss of 25% would mean only 75% remained in force, and this is a poor persistency rate.

4.10 The PIA wants to know the proportion of policies which remain in force after specific periods of time so that **each provider's persistency rate can be monitored** and action taken if the rate is unacceptable. Persistency rates are a key performance indicator (KPI).

4.11 If 100 policies commence their existence, and after one year 99 are still in force, the persistency rate is 99%. This **simple formula** is the basis of the method of calculation of persistency.

Assume that the number of contracts which commence is CC and the number of contracts still in force after one year is CF.

In the above example, CC = 100 and CF = 99.

Persistency is thus calculated as $\dfrac{CF}{CC} = \dfrac{99}{100} \times 100 = 99\%$

The persistency formula is therefore $\dfrac{CF}{CC} \times 100$

Persistency records must be kept by **product providers** in respect of their own designated individuals and (where relevant) IFA business effected with the provider.

4.12 **All packaged investments** products must be monitored in the following groups.

(a) Endowments

(b) Whole life contracts

(c) Personal pensions (including group personal pensions business)

(d) Other pensions business (eg FSAVCs)

(e) Other life business (including investment-linked protection contracts such as PHI or term assurance)

4.13 **Product providers only** are required to submit persistency returns.

4.14 Returns must be made for policies covering every year of each policy up to and including **four years**. For persistency purposes, a policy is in force at the end of one year if the first premium in the second year is paid. A similar definition applies to each subsequent year.

4.15 Returns must be made **annually**.

5 KNOWLEDGE REQUIREMENTS FOR ADVISERS UNDERTAKING SPECIALIST ROLES

5.1 Stage 1 training: acceptable qualifications to meet the knowledge requirements are:

Examination	Offered by
Financial Planning Certificate (FPC) Paper 1	Chartered Insurance Institute
Certificate for Financial Advisers (CeFA) Paper 1	Chartered Institute of Bankers
Investment Advice Certificate (IAC) Paper 1	Securities Institute
Certificate in Investment Planning (CIP) Paper 1	Chartered Institute of Bankers in Scotland and the Institute of Bankers in Ireland

Those advisers who sell only tax-exempt friendly society policies or collect premiums under industrial life policies require only the Stage 1 knowledge qualification.

5.2 Stage 2 training - acceptable qualifications to meet the knowledge requirements are:

Examination	Offered by
Financial Planning Certificate (FPC) Papers 2 & 3	Chartered Insurance Institute
Certificate for Financial Advisers (CeFA) Papers 2 &	Chartered Institute of Bankers
Investment Advice Certificate (IAC) Papers 2 & 3	Securities Institute
Certificate in Investment Planning (CIP) Paper 2	Chartered Institute of Bankers in Scotland and the Institute of Bankers in Ireland

Specialist activities

5.3 A designated individual who undertakes certain specialist activities (shown below) must, usually in addition to the Stage 1 and 2 qualification, obtain a further qualification as shown. If he is involved only in the specialist activity, he need only obtain the qualification shown below.

Activity	Qualification
Discretionary portfolio management, or acting as a broker fund adviser	Investment Management Certificate (IMC) of the Institute of Investment Management and Research (IIMR)
Discretionary portfolio management	IMC as above; or
	Chartered Financial Analyst (USA) designation provided that, in addition, the individual has achieved a pass in the UK Regulation and Markets module of the Investment Management Certificate; or
	Associate or Fellow of the Securities Institute Diploma (including regulation and compliance, investment analysis and fund management papers)
Advising on, dealing or arranging deals in trading options	Futures and options representative examination of the Securities and Futures Authority
Managing investments with without discretion, or discretionary portfolio management, if the assets under management include or may include options or other derivatives or warrants	Securities and financial derivatives representative examination of the Securities and Futures Authority
Pension transfers and opt-outs where the individual is appointed as the member's pension transfer specialist	AFPC (G60), APMI (by examination), PIC (Pensions Paper), or certain higher level qualifications

6 REQUIREMENTS ON ADVISERS IN RELATION TO CPD

The purpose of CPD

6.1 All competent designated individuals are required to undertake CPD which is both appropriate in nature and sufficient in amount. There is no formal requirement for trainees undertaking Stage 2 training to also complete CPD but, in some respects (such as understanding changes in procedures, legislation and fund performance) some degree of CPD would seem sensible.

6.2 Some other professionals such as doctors, solicitors and accountants have recognised for some time the need for continuing professional development or CPE (Continuous Professional Education) as it is sometimes known. Its purpose is perhaps best remembered by looking more closely at the three words in its name.

(a) **Continuing** - it continues throughout an adviser's (and supervisor's) career once he or she is deemed competent, ie competence is a continuous process, not a destination in itself.

(b) **Professional** - it is intended to help individuals to develop and broaden their professionalism. At the very least, it must help them to retain credibility as professionals. For example, auditing procedures for accountants have changed over the years so an accountant who qualified 15 years ago would not be able, with having undertaken continuing development, to be able to act now in a competent manner.

(c) **Development** - this suggests a need not only to address the knowledge and skill required today, but also those skills or attributes required in the future.

6.3 The actual activities conducted as part of CPD will be unique to each individual as everyone's needs differ. For CPD to be effective, it is the individual who therefore needs to take responsibility for their own development, although under the T&C scheme the supervisor is also responsible for the identification of development needs, the appropriateness of the CPD and its transfer to the workplace.

Chapter roundup

- *Monitoring compliance.* The regulators. Larger firms - more checks. PIVs: regular checks; as result of complaint; if regulator doubts firm's compliance efficiency. Members must have compliance officer to monitor compliance. Adequate records must be kept on client dealings, plus financial, personnel and advertising records - kept for six years.

- *PIVs.* Monitor compliance of firms, remedy deficiencies or withdraw authorisation. Enforcement officers can: visit any member without warning (four weeks usual); inspect any records; make visit following complaint, even if not asked to do so.

- *Compliance procedures.* Employee compliance officer must be appointed who is or has access to partner or board of directors, must regularly review procedures. Ten or more advisers - written procedures must exist and be available to all employees and appointed representatives.

- *Training and Competence rules.* Rules apply to all designated individuals. Training arrangements for new entrants fall into two stages.

- *Key Performance Indicators.* The successful performance of an adviser can be judged according to a number of key performance ratios, such as persistency rates.

- *Specialist roles.* Designated individuals carrying out specialist roles require further qualifications.

- *CPD.* All competent designated individuals are required to undertake CPD.

Quick quiz

1   A self-regulatory organisation monitors the enforcement of its rules by:

    A   making annual checks with the Securities and Investments Board;
    B   making periodic visits to the member;
    C   requiring the completion each year of a business questionnaire;
    D   requiring members to have independent auditors.

2   For how many years should records be kept?

    A   3
    B   5
    C   6
    D   7

3   What specific action must be taken as a result of a firm having ten or more advisers?

    A   The compliance officer must supervise the compliance procedures of the firm.
    B   Compliance procedures must be reviewed regularly.
    C   A compliance action plan must be written.
    D   A record of all fact finds must be kept for three years.

The solutions to the questions in the quiz can be found at the end of this Study Text. Before checking your answers against those solutions, you should look back at this chapter and use the information in it to correct your answers.

Answer to questions

1   (a)   To ensure that Financial Services Act regulations are being enforced.
    (b)   Regular monitoring; following complaint; regulator doubts firm's compliance.
    (c)   In financial difficulties; holds clients' moneys or assets.
    (d)   Dealings with clients; financial; personnel; advertising.
    (e)   To ensure firm complies with regulatory requirements.
    (f)   The board of directors or the partners.
    (g)   A member of the board or the chief executive.

Part B
Financial services background

Chapter 6

LEGAL REQUIREMENTS AND ECONOMIC CONDITIONS

Chapter topic list	Syllabus reference
1 Money laundering	B 1.1
2 Consumer rights	B 1.2
3 Contracts, honesty and insurable interest	B 1.3
4 Intestacy, succession and wills	B 1.5
5 Ownership of policies and disposal of proceeds	B 1.4, B 1.6 B 1.7
6 Influence of taxation on protection and investment	B 1.8
7 Inflation: defining and calculating	B 1.9
8 The effect of inflation	B 1.10
9 Interest rates	B 1.11

Introduction

We will now turn from general rules, such as the requirement to give best advice, to the legal and economic factors which influence the advice actually given.

1   MONEY LAUNDERING

KEY TERM

Money laundering is the term given to attempts to make the proceeds of crime appear respectable. It involves the use of investments to hide the source of the funds.

1.1   An adviser's duties under the **Money Laundering Regulations 1993** are as follows.

(a)   **New clients must be required to prove their identity**. This is necessary when forming any business relationship, or when dealing with one-off transactions exceeding £10,000 or 15,000 euros or separate transactions that appear to be linked and in total exceed £10,000 or €15,000.

No check is required if funds come from an EU bank or building society account in the applicant's name. Checks are not required if the adviser is satisfied that:

(i)   Adequate checks have already been made

(ii)   The money is going into a pension scheme with neither surrender value nor facility for proceeds to be used as security for a loan

      (iii)   Money is being used for an insurance policy where the single premium is not more than €2,500 or the regular premium is not more than €1,000 a year

(b) **Adequate records must be kept**. Records must show evidence of a client's identity and details of transactions enacted by that person, and must be kept for five years. In the case of regular transactions, records should be kept until five years after the date of the last transaction.

(c) **Internal reporting procedures must be maintained**. One person must be nominated to receive from staff any reports involving suspicions regarding money laundering activities, and that person must be able to investigate such reports and, where appropriate, inform and co-operate with the police.

1.2 The requirements under the Joint Money Laundering Steering Groups' Guidance Notes are aimed at investment and insurance business. The principal requirements are outlined below.

(a) **New accounts for new clients**.

      (i)   Interview account holders personally (where possible)

      (ii)   Obtain identification documents (eg passport), verify address (eg from telephone directory or electoral register) and obtain date of birth.

(b) **Professional client accounts**. Advisers must be able to identify persons who open client accounts unless those persons are one of a small number of very specific exceptions such as an EU financial institution.

(c) **Corporate client accounts**. Advisers must obtain the certificate of incorporation and a directors' resolution to open an account, and make a search at Companies House.

(d) **Records** must be kept for five years.

2   CONSUMER RIGHTS

Data Protection Act 1998

2.1 The objective of this Act is to **regulate the use of information which is stored on a computer**. The rules do *not* apply to information which is kept manually. Some of the important features of the new legislation are as follows.

(a) Clarification of conditions under which data processing is lawful

(b) Right given to everyone to seek redress at court for breach of the Act

(c) Paper-based, microfilm and microfiche filing systems will in future be covered by the terms of the Act

2.2 The obligations on any organisation that keeps computerised personal information may be summarised as follows.

(a) Personal data must have been **obtained lawfully and fairly.**

(b) Data must be held and used only for **lawful purposes.**

(c) Data should be used only **for the purposes for which it was originally obtained.**

(d) The data must not exceed what is **necessary** for the purpose for which it was obtained.

(e) Data must be **accurate** and must be **updated regularly.**

(f) Data must **not be kept longer than is necessary** for its lawful purpose.

(g) The person whose data is on computer must have **access** to that information and have the right to correct it where appropriate.

(h) The data must be **protected** against unauthorised access.

(i) The data holder must **register** the fact with the Data Protection Register, listing the data, the purpose and source for which it is held, and who has the right to see it.

Consumer Credit Act 1974

2.3 One of the reasons for the passing of the Consumer Credit Act was because credit agreements were being signed without individuals properly reading them and without their understanding them. Such agreements could then be legally enforced even though they might have been **unfair or contain exorbitant terms**.

2.4 The Consumer Credit Act does not itself ensure that credit agreements are reasonable. It simply aims to ensure that anybody who signs a credit agreement **knows what they are doing**. They are thus free to sign an unreasonable agreement provided they have had the opportunity to find out that it is unreasonable.

Regulated business

2.5 Credit business is **regulated** where an agreement is in respect of credit of up to £25,000 (£15,000 before July 1998). Activities which are covered by the Act include the introducing of clients to sources of finance and advising on methods of repayment of loans. Mortgages and loans to limited companies are excluded.

Cooling off, disclosure and procedures

2.6 People entering into credit agreements must be given a **copy of the agreement** for their own records. They must be sent a copy of the agreement at least seven days before being sent the original agreement document for signing. In addition they must have a **cooling off period** in which to change their minds. That period is 14 days from the date when they were sent the first copy of the agreement.

2.7 The Act also regulates the procedures for the **enforcement** of an agreement and the requirement relating to the repayments of the credit given.

2.8 Any organisation giving credit needs a **licence** to do so. This includes not only life companies but also tied agents who need their own separate licences as they are not covered by the life company's licence.

2.9 The Act regulates how the **annual percentage rate** (APR) must be calculated in order to show the full effect of the rate of interest being charged.

Advertisements

2.10 The contents of **advertisements** for credit agreements are also regulated by the Act. The APR must be quoted prominently and if a house is to be used as security for a credit agreement the advertisement must include in capitals the words 'Your house is at risk if you do not keep up repayments on a mortgage or other loans secured on it'.

2.11 If a loan is in a **foreign currency** then an advertisement must include the words 'the sterling equivalent of your liability under a foreign currency mortgage may be increased by exchange rate movements'.

Access to Medical Reports Act 1988

2.12 Under the terms of this Act, a **medical report** by a doctor can be requested by a life office only after a proposer has been asked for his **consent**, and has been notified that he can withhold such consent. If consent is given, the proposer can have access to the report before it is sent to the life office or within six months of that date. He can request anything he considers to be incorrect to be changed. However, the doctor can withhold the report from the proposer if he considers that it would harm the proposer or reveal confidential information.

2.13 The proposer must also be asked for consent to the life office obtaining **any previous medical report**, and be given the right to see such report before it is sent to the life office.

3 CONTRACTS, HONESTY AND INSURABLE INTEREST

> **KEY TERM**
>
> A **contract** is a legally binding agreement between persons. In order to be binding, it must contain certain specific characteristics.

Offer and acceptance and intention to create legal relations

3.1 If you agree with a friend that the two of you will organise a sporting fixture and then, just before you are due to start the arrangements, you decide to pull out on the grounds that you do not have the time, you will incur the wrath of your friend but will probably **not suffer any legal consequences**.

3.2 A contract is a different matter. A contract is an agreement where both people (**the parties to the contract) intend to enter into a legal arrangement**. One of you must make an offer which, if accepted, will put legal obligations on you. Equally if it is accepted by the other party they also will have legal obligations placed on them.

3.3 In life assurance the **proposal form** makes up the offer which the life assurance company can either accept at standard rates or on special terms or reject. If the assurance company accepts on special terms, it is effectively rejecting the proposal and making a counteroffer, which the proposer then accepts or rejects.

Consideration

3.4 For the contract to become binding **consideration** must be given, which must be sufficient.

> **KEY TERM**
>
> **Consideration** is a technical term which basically means that you sacrifice something of value in return for receiving something else.

3.5 For example, if you buy **a car** you are sacrificing the **money** that you pay for it. Equally the person who is selling it to you is sacrificing the car in return for the money.

3.6 In the case of life assurance the consideration paid by the policyholder is the **premium** and the consideration paid by the insurer is the **promise to pay money** if and when a specified event occurs.

Capacity to contract

> **KEY TERM**
>
> **Capacity to contract** is the legal ability to enter into a contract. If, for example, you are insane, your capacity to contract may be limited by law.

3.7 In life assurance the question is most likely to occur with a proposal from someone under 18 (a **minor**). Minors do not have unrestricted capacity to enter into contracts.

Legality of object

3.8 If you enter into an agreement with an accomplice to steal property, such a contract would be **illegal** and the contract would **not be valid**.

Contractual agreement

3.9 If you are entering into a contract then both parties to the contract must be in **total agreement** on its terms. You may sometimes come across the expression *consensus ad idem* which is a Latin phrase meaning 'of the same mind'.

Utmost good faith

3.10 If you buy an old car and find that it falls apart soon after you bought it, that is **your problem**. Presumably you had the opportunity to look at the car and inspect it and try it out on a trial run before you bought it. Provided that the seller answered honestly any questions that you asked, they were not obliged to volunteer information which you did not seek.

3.11 **Life assurance is different**. If you propose for life assurance you are expected to give to the insurance company **all information** which will enable the company to assess whether you are a big (sub-standard) risk, eg you are seriously ill or in a dangerous occupation or have a risky lifestyle, or whether you are a normal risk for which the company would issue a contract on standard terms.

3.12 This requirement to be **more honest than honest** and **disclose all relevant information** is fundamental to a life contract. If the rule is not observed the policy can be treated by the insurer as **voidable**. The requirement is termed '**utmost good faith**' or *uberrimae fidei*.

Insurable interest

3.13 In 1774, it was decided that insuring the lives of people simply because you wanted to make a profit was unacceptable. The Life Assurance Act of that year introduced a rule that there must be **the risk of losing money** if you were to have the right to insure somebody else's life, and that rule has been unchanged ever since.

3.14 But there is a difference from the law on general insurance. If, for example, you own a house, you can insure it only for as long as you have **insurable interest**. That means that insurable interest must exist when you first effect an insurance, it must continue to exist throughout the time that the contract exists, and if damage occurs to the house you must still have insurable interest at the time the damage occurs.

3.15 **Life assurance is different in this respect. Insurable interest need exist only at the time that the policy is effected.** This means that if a married woman insures the life of her husband and they become divorced, she can continue the insurance after the divorce, even though she no longer has any insurable interest. However, she could not effect a *new* contract after the divorce has taken place unless she could show that her ex-husband's death would result in her suffering some kind of financial loss.

3.16 You can insure **your own life** and the life of your **spouse** for as much as you like. In all other cases the amount of insurable interest must, in principle, be **measurable** and the amount of the cover must match the amount of that interest.

Question 1

(a) What are the essential requirements for a contract?
(b) Who has limited capacity to enter into a contract?
(c) What is utmost good faith, and what is the consequence of its absence?
(d) What is insurable interest?

4 INTESTACY, SUCCESSION AND WILLS

KEY TERM

The **estate** of a person who has died represents their **total net assets**. These net assets consist of property owned by the deceased person plus amounts owed to them by other people, minus any debts owed by the deceased person to others (including mortgages).

4.1 When you die you must have done one of two things: either **you left instructions** on what you wanted to happen to your estate or **you did not bother**. The majority of people do not bother to leave instructions, not because they have taken a positive decision not to do so but simply as a result of inertia. The consequences can be quite different from those intended by the person who has died.

4.2 Writing down instructions - what is known as a **will** - on what you want to happen to your estate has a number of advantages. It is usually **cheaper** than not leaving instructions and the distribution of assets is certainly **faster**. It can also save a lot of **family argument**.

KEY TERMS

- In order to be valid, a **will** must be signed by the person who writes it - the testator - and witnessed by at least two people who are both present at the same time. The witnesses should not be beneficiaries as any gifts to them will be invalid.

- After death, the terms of a will are carried out by **executors**.

4.3 A will is **invalidated** if the testator tears it up with the intention of **destroying** it, or gets **married**.

4.4 Someone who dies without making a valid will is said to die **intestate**. The estate is then dealt with by **administrators**.

4.5 If you have not left a will behind you then **the law** will step in and decide what will happen to your estate. Not only will it then be too late for you to exercise any choice but the provisions of the law of succession may be completely different from what you would like to have happened.

4.6 The following is a summary of the distribution of an **intestate estate**.

Who is left behind	Who gets what
Surviving spouse, but no issue (ie children/grandchildren) and no other family.	Surviving spouse gets the lot.
Surviving spouse and issue.	Surviving spouse takes personal chattels plus remainder of the estate up to £125,000. What is left over will be held as follows. (a) Half on trust for the surviving spouse for life, thereafter to issue (b) The other half on trust for the issue
Surviving spouse with no issue but with other family.	Surviving spouse takes personal chattels plus remainder up to £200,000 plus half of what is left. The other half is taken by various members of the family.

Exam focus point

Be aware of the different amounts involved. You could easily be faced with a question on the amount which goes to the surviving spouse so notice the difference between the spouse with issue (£125,000) and the spouse without issue (£200,000).

4.7 It is most important that, where two people are living together but are **not married**, they should make wills. If they do not do so, the estate of the partner who has died will be distributed to his/her family members with no entitlement to the surviving partner.

4.8 There is one final point regarding **property that is held jointly**. You need to check the terms of the joint ownership. It will either be a joint tenancy or a tenancy in common.

(a) On the death of one of the owners the survivor will automatically inherit the property (a **joint tenancy**).

(b) The half owned by the person who has died goes to that person's estate and not to the survivor (a **tenancy in common**).

Question 2

(a) What are the obligations imposed by the Data Protection Act 1984?
(b) What are the obligations imposed by the Consumer Credit Act 1974?
(c) Who administers the estate of someone who has died?

5 OWNERSHIP OF POLICIES AND DISPOSAL OF PROCEEDS

5.1 There are a few **legal principles and practices** which you need to be familiar with before dealing with the mechanics of ownership of a life policy and what happens to the proceeds.

Title and assignment

> **KEY TERMS**
>
> - The word '**title**' in this context simply means ownership. Your ownership of a watch for example simply means that you are en*title*d to benefit from the watch, ie you possess the title to the watch.
>
> - **Assignment** means a transfer of ownership or title. Any transfer of the right to benefit from property is a transfer of ownership, ie assignment.

5.2 Assignment may be **temporary or permanent**. An example of a **temporary assignment** is found in the use of shares as security for a loan. You can transfer your shares to the lender, and he will transfer them back to you only when the loan is repaid.

5.3 On the other hand, transfer of ownership may be **permanent**. There are two ways of making such a transfer.

(a) Property may be permanently assigned by way of **sale**. For example, if you go into a jeweller's shop to buy a watch the chances are that when you have made your selection you will say 'I'll take it' and pay the price for it. You will not say to the shopkeeper 'I would like you to make a permanent assignment of that watch to me by way of sale' but technically that is what will have happened. You will have entered into a contract (see earlier for conditions of contract) for which you will have paid consideration (the price) and by the time you walk out of the shop the title to the watch will have been permanently assigned to you by way of sale. In other words, you have bought it.

(b) Property may be permanently assigned by way of **gift**. If, for example, you own a holiday home you may choose to give it to your sister. The gift will of course be permanent and you will have effected a permanent assignment by way of gift.

5.4 You can **permanently assign a life policy by way of sale or gift**, ie you can either sell it or give it away. A lot of life policies are sold either by auction or through intermediaries and when that happens the proceeds will be payable to the new owner. If it was originally your policy and you were the life assured then one thing has not changed - it is still your life that is insured.

5.5 This means that **the new owner benefits from your death**. The purchaser has no insurable interest in your life, but that does not matter because you had an insurable interest when you took out the policy.

5.6 A life policy can be used in connection with a **mortgage** for one or both of two purposes.

(a) To repay the loan on death
(b) To accumulate a fund to repay an interest-only loan on maturity

5.7 Where a policy - one of the varieties of **endowment policy** - is used to repay the loan at maturity, the lender may require assignment of the policy for the duration of the loan. The assignment will be **a temporary assignment**, with the policy being kept by the lender. The lender gives notice of the assignment to the life office.

5.8 At the maturity of the loan, the proceeds of the policy are **paid to the lender,** who retains an amount required to repay the loan. Any surplus will be paid to the borrower. If the borrower has repaid the loan with money from a source other than the policy, the lender will return the policy to the borrower who will then receive the full benefits of the contract. If the policy proceeds are not sufficient to repay the loan, the difference must be paid by the borrower.

5.9 Bear in mind that the above points apply only if the policy is assigned to the lender. Many lenders do not require the assignment of a repayment vehicle, in which case the proceeds will be **paid to the borrower** in their capacity as policyholder.

Trusts

KEY TERM

In a **trust,** one person (called the **settlor**) hands over assets to people he can trust (the **trustees**) to look after for the benefit of someone else (the **beneficiary**). The trustees become the legal owners of the assets but without the right to benefit from the ownership.

Case example: Trust for children

Let us look at an example which shows why trusts can be useful. Assume that you own a holiday home. If you leave it to say, your children, on your **death** then inheritance tax at 40% may be payable on the transfer.

One solution is to **give** the property now to your children. However, you may not want them to own it until after your death. (Perhaps they are too young to own property.) The solution therefore is to **put the property into trust**. That will take the property outside your estate for inheritance tax purposes which means that if you survive for seven years there will be no inheritance tax payable on it (see later section on inheritance tax).

The fact that your children cannot yet benefit from the property means that effectively the trust is a halfway stage between ownership by you (which you have now given up) and ownership by your children which will not happen until your death.

5.10 There is one problem which needs to be resolved. The property is going to be let and will therefore produce an income. **What will the trustees do with the income?** This will depend on what instructions you gave to the trustees at the outset. If, say, you have four children and you have told the trustees that they *must* distribute the income to one or more of those children then they must follow your instruction. When the income *must* be distributed, the trust is called an '**interest in possession**' trust (*not* a discretionary trust - see later).

5.11 You may have given the trustees discretion to decide which of your children will receive rent each year. The trustees can decide that in any one year one beneficiary will receive all the rent and in another year all four will each receive equal shares of the rent. The trustees will take the decision each year. It means effectively that the trustees can change the beneficiaries each year but only within the **list of beneficiaries,** ie your children, that you gave them at the outset. This discretion does *not* make the trust a 'discretionary' trust.

5.12 However, you might have told the trustees that they can distribute the rent to the beneficiaries if they so decide but that they have the right to retain the income of the trust and simply leave it invested in the trust. This is a **discretionary trust**.

> **KEY TERM**
>
> • An **interest in possession trust** is a trust where the trustees *must* distribute the income although they may have discretion on which beneficiary or beneficiaries receives the income
>
> • A **discretionary trust** is one where the trustees can decide not to distribute the income at all but to leave it invested in the trust.

5.13 For inheritance tax purposes, transfers into an **interest in possession trust** are **potentially exempt transfers**, and they will be tax free if the settlor survives for seven years. Transfers into a **discretionary trust** are **chargeable lifetime transfers** and such transfers are chargeable at half the death rate.

(*Note*. Inheritance tax is only chargeable if the nil rate (0%) threshold has been passed. For 2000/2001, the nil rate tax band applies to up to £234,000 of transfers.)

Question 3

(a) Distinguish between the two types of joint ownership.
(b) What kinds of assignment are there?
(c) What is a trust?
(d) What is the difference between an interest in possession (IIP) trust and a discretionary trust?
(e) What transfer is chargeable to inheritance tax as soon as it is made?

Life policies and trusts

5.14 You can effect a life assurance policy on your own life with the **proceeds payable into your estate**. The proceeds of the policy will then be distributed from the estate according to your will or, if you have not left one, according to the laws of intestacy.

5.15 If, after you have effected the policy, you then assign it - for example as security for a loan - then the proceeds will be paid by the life assurance company to the person to whom you have assigned a policy, ie the assignee. Any **surplus** in excess of the loan will then be paid into your estate.

5.16 If you have effected the policy on your own life and placed it in trust for other beneficiaries then the **proceeds of the policy will be payable to the trustees**. You may have decided to be one of those trustees yourself - there is nothing to stop you doing that and in fact it may serve to give you some control over the policy even though you will not benefit from it. On your death the proceeds will be paid to the surviving trustees.

5.17 If the beneficiary for example is your son and your son is also the other trustee, then on your death he will receive the proceeds as trustee. However, this procedure will have the advantage that the proceeds are paid **quickly** to the beneficiary, because the payee and the beneficiary are the same person.

5.18 The advantage of writing a life policy in this way is that the proceeds will not be payable into your estate and will therefore **not be subject to inheritance tax**.

5.19   A life assurance policy may have two owners and two lives assured. If you arrange a policy in this way then the proceeds may be payable either on the first of two deaths or on the second of two deaths. It should be payable on the **first of two deaths** if the reason for arranging the policy is to provide **security for a mortgage**. This will ensure that the mortgage will be repaid following the first death.

5.20   The policy will be arranged to pay the proceeds on the **second death** (of two spouses) if it is for **inheritance tax purposes**.

5.21   Such a policy will be known in the first case as a **joint life first death policy**, and in the second case as a joint life last survivor policy (or **a joint life second death policy**).

5.22   Another way of writing a life assurance policy is for you to **insure someone else's life**. As we have already seen, the insurable interest must exist and must be clear. In that case, on the death of the life assured the proceeds will be payable to you.

Question 4

What is the advantage of writing a life assurance policy in trust?

---

6   INFLUENCE OF TAXATION ON PROTECTION AND INVESTMENT

Protection

6.1   UK taxation affects the different forms of protection to such an extent that it can and does **influence** the way in which protection is planned.

6.2   In the case of protection on death the fact that the proceeds from a qualifying life assurance policy are tax free makes it tempting to consider such policies as essential for protection purposes. However, even though there is a potential higher rate tax liability on non-qualifying policies, the overwhelming majority of the population in the UK are **not higher rate taxpayers**. Thus most life assurances effected for protection purposes are tax free provided that, after taking account of life policy proceeds on a non-qualifying policy, the basic rate taxpayer is still a basic rate taxpayer in the tax year in which the policy proceeds are paid.

6.3   The effect of this is that the overwhelming majority of **non-qualifying contracts** are either those for basic rate taxpayers, or are investment contracts, such as investment bonds, which are of greatest benefit to higher rate taxpayers.

6.4   The inheritance tax treatment of **life assurance policy proceeds** means that if life policies are to avoid inheritance tax they need to be written in trust. The premium is treated as a gift and the proceeds of the policy accumulate outside the inheritance tax net.

6.5   In the case of **disability protection** the fact that the proceeds are tax free makes no difference to the way in which they are effected because there is no alternative. If the proceeds were taxable there would still be a need to protect clients against loss of earnings.

Investment

6.6   The fact that several types of investment have special tax advantages makes them attractive to basic rate or higher rate taxpayers. It puts such investment as **ISAs** (and existing TESSAs and PEPs) at the top of the priority list together with those **National Savings** investments that are tax free. (Individuals can invest in ISAs out of their after-tax income, but the income/capital gains from the ISA are tax free.)

6.7 The special tax treatment of **pensions** makes them also exceptionally attractive especially as not only is the fund subject to special tax treatment but a portion of the proceeds can be taken as tax-free cash. Add to that the tax relief on the contributions and we have an irresistible method of long term planning for retirement. (Contributions into a pension fund, up to a certain annual limit, are tax free. Most of the eventual proceeds - ie the eventual pension received - will be subject to income tax.)

6.8 For the **higher rate taxpayer** there will be less interest in investments that produce income and more in investments which produce **capital gains**. There is an annual exemption from tax on realised capital gains up to a certain amount. This annual exemption means that both basic rate taxpayers and even more effectively higher rate taxpayers can obtain an annual tax-free income by selling some part of their portfolio each year and keeping total gains within the annual exemption.

6.9 The amount of capital gain on an asset, when disposed of, was reduced by an indexation allowance, to allow for the effect of inflation on values and prices. Indexation allowances were ended from 6 April 1998.

6.10 Gains arising after 6 April 1998 will be tapered according to the length of time the asset has been held, and the effective rate of capital gains tax on the gain will also depend on whether the asset disposed of is a business asset (eg an employee's shares in his company, if it is a trading company) or a non-business asset.

7 INFLATION: DEFINING AND CALCULATING

7.1 **Inflation** affects almost every economic decision that we take and affects those that we do not take but which are unavoidable.

7.2 Inflation is measured by the general **index of retail prices** - generally known as the **Retail Prices Index** (RPI) but also called the **cost of living index**.

7.3 The RPI measures the **change in the average level of prices** of a wide range of goods and services which are purchased by households in the UK. There are in fact two measures on inflation: the one that includes mortgage interest is called the headline rate of inflation, and the one that excludes mortgage interest is known as the underlying rate of inflation.

7.4 Statistics to make up the RPI are collected every month by the government, but because short-term fluctuations can produce temporary distortions, it makes more sense to look at the **rate of inflation** on a year-by-year basis.

7.5 Inflation is measured by **comparing** the current average level of prices with the average level 12 months ago. If for example the level 12 months ago was 100 and the current level is 105, then the rate of inflation is 5%.

That was a fairly simple calculation but the way that it was measured is as follows.

$$\frac{105-100}{100} = 5\%$$

If in one year's time the index has gone up from 105 to 109.2 the calculation of inflation over that year would be as follows.

$$\frac{109.2 - 105}{105} = 4\%$$

8   THE EFFECT OF INFLATION

8.1   The overall effect of inflation is that it **reduces the value of the pound**. If you have £100 and intend to spend it on bars of chocolate each costing £1, you will able to buy 100 bars. If however, you have the same £100 but the price of bars of chocolate has gone up to £2 each you can buy only 50 bars with your money. The value of your money will have reduced as a result of the price increases.

8.2   The erosion of the value of the pound thus also **erodes the value of deposits** and also those investments whose value does not increase, such as National Savings certificates. It also erodes the value of interest received from fixed interest investments such as fixed interest gilts and fixed interest National Savings investments.

8.3   On the other hand, investments which do not carry the same level of security - **equities** - are more likely to show real rate of growth.

KEY TERM

A **real rate of growth** is one that exceeds the rate of inflation. For example if inflation over a period of time is 5% and the increase in the value of an investment is 6% then the real rate of growth will be about 1%.

8.4   Those savings and investments that are **index linked** such as some gilts and National Savings give protection against increases in the cost of living.

Spending

8.5   Inflation affects our **ability to spend,** as we have already seen with the bars of chocolate. If we want to buy the same number of bars of chocolate then we have got to spend twice as much money in order to get them. This is a typical effect of inflation. Inflation can lead to claims for pay increases which in turn can lead to higher costs which in turn can lead to higher prices which of course brings us back to higher inflation. Employees generally are better off in times of high inflation because pay rises often exceed the rate of inflation.

8.6   **Retired people** who are on fixed pensions are adversely affected by inflation. It reduces the value of the money that they have to spend without increasing the amount to spend. Those who are in a better position are, for instance, people whose retirement pensions are inflation linked. Those who receive pensions which are subject to discretionary increases may be protected but that will obviously depend upon the level of the increases.

8.7   If a pension increases by a fixed rate, ie it escalates, then whether or not the rate of escalation is greater than or less than the rate of inflation will be a matter of fortune - or misfortune. Many company pensions now have some form of **inflation linking**.

Borrowing

8.8 The principal effect of inflation on **borrowers** is that it reduces the capital value of their debt. If interest payments do not increase too much then borrowers will be in a fortunate position.

8.9 If anybody has **a fixed rate mortgage** at a rate which is less than the rate of inflation then they will be even more fortunate.

9 INTEREST RATES

9.1 **High interest rates** have a beneficial effect on savers who have savings in variable rate deposit accounts. A saver who is locked into a fixed rate investment such as National Savings Certificates is going to be immune from a fall in interest rates.

9.2 In the case of government securities, the fixed rate return on most **gilts** means that if interest rates generally fall then the price of fixed interest gilts will rise and vice versa.

9.3 High rates of interest can have an adverse effect on **businesses** that have a very high level of borrowing. This may force them to increase their prices which will have an adverse effect on sales.

9.4 People who **retire** when interest rates are high will tend to benefit in the form of higher returns for **annuities**.

9.5 Interest rate rises adversely affect **borrowers** where the loan is at a **variable rate**.

9.6 Interest rates are set by the Monetary Policy Committee of the **Bank of England**. New gilt-edged securities issued by the Treasury at a high rate of interest will put pressure on other borrowers to raise their rates of interest in order to compete with the new high rate gilts.

Question 5

(a) What types of protection and investment products receive special tax treatment?
(b) What is inflation?
(c) What is the effect of inflation?
(d) Who is adversely affected by inflation?

Chapter roundup

- *Money laundering*

  ○ Source of funds must be identified unless already checked
  ○ Keep adequate records
  ○ Maintain reporting procedures

- *Contracts.* A valid contract needs

  ○ Offer and acceptance
  ○ Consideration: money or a promise
  ○ Capacity to contract - the legal entitlement to enter into a contract
  ○ Legality of object - the purpose of the contract is legal
  ○ Contractual agreement - both parties agree on the contract terms

- *Honesty*

  ○ Ordinary commercial contract: you must answer questions honestly

  ○ Life assurance: you must disclose all relevant information whether or not you are asked for it

  ○ Consequences of non-disclosure: a voidable contract

  ○ Insurable interest: must exist in life assurance at inception - not subsequently; unlimited insurable interest on self or spouse (not on cohabiting partner)

- Data Protection Act 1984. Objective is to regulate use of information on computer. Obligations regarding data:

  ○ Obtained lawfully
  ○ Used for lawful purposes
  ○ Used only for original purpose
  ○ Must not be excessive
  ○ Must be accurate and updated
  ○ Must not be kept longer than necessary
  ○ Subject of data must have access and right to correct
  ○ Protected against unauthorised access
  ○ Holder registered

- Consumer Credit Act 1974

  ○ Ensures disclosure

  ○ Regulates agreements up to £25,000 (£15,000 prior to July 1998)

  ○ Individual must have: copy seven days before receiving agreement for signing; 14-day cooling off period

  ○ Credit organisation needs licence

  ○ Regulates calculation of APR

  ○ Advertisements regulated: must quote APR; warning regarding security of property; reference to foreign currency if relevant

- *Intestacy, succession and wills*

  ○ Intestacy - dying without leaving a will
  ○ Law governs distribution of assets on intestacy
  ○ A will leaves instructions for disposal of estate
  ○ Will must be signed and witnessed

- *Access to Medical Reports Act 1988*

  ◦ Access to report must be authorised by proposer, who has right to correct if relevant

- *Ownership of policies*

  ◦ Title means ownership
  ◦ Assignment means transfer of ownership
  ◦ Assignment may be temporary or permanent
  ◦ Permanent assignment may be by sale or gift

- *Trusts*

  ◦ Trust ensures individual has legal entitlement to property without owning it
  ◦ Interest in possession trust - income (if any) *must* be distributed
  ◦ Discretionary trust - income *may* be distributed or remain invested in trust
  ◦ Life policy proceeds paid to trustees
  ◦ Assigned policies - assignees receive proceeds and must pay surplus to assignor

- *Influence of taxation*

  ◦ Protection: qualifying life policies - proceeds tax free; non-qualifying policies - potential higher rate tax liability on proceeds; own life policies must be in trust to avoid inheritance tax; for IHT - premium is treated as a gift; disability income tax free

  ◦ Investment: ISAs (existing TESSAs, PEPs) and National Savings certificates have tax advantage for basic and higher rate taxpayers. Tax relief on pension contributions plus tax-free cash at retirement makes them attractive

- *Inflation*

  ◦ Inflation is an increase in the supply of money without an increase in the supply of goods and services

  ◦ Retail Prices Index measures the change in the average level of prices of goods and services: headline rate includes mortgage interest, underlying rate excludes it

  ◦ RPI statistics collected monthly

  ◦ Effect of inflation: reduces purchasing power of the pound; erodes value of fixed interest securities, deposits and fixed incomes; helps growth of equities; reduces capital value of debt

- *Interest rates*

  ◦ High rates benefit variable interest savings
  ◦ Fixed rate savings immune from interest rate falls
  ◦ High rates adversely affect businesses with high borrowing
  ◦ High rates benefit people buying annuities
  ◦ Gilt interest rates influence other interest rates

Quick quiz

1 Real growth for accumulated savings will be achieved if:

A a rate of return is higher than inflation;
B average earnings exceeds the rise in the Retail Prices Index;
C social security benefits are index linked;
D equities grow at a faster rate than average earnings.

2 The rules of insurable interest allow:

A a debtor to insure the life of a creditor up to the amount of the loan;
B a husband to insure his wife's life for an unlimited sum;
C business partners to insure each other without limit;
D a wife to insure her husband's life for no more than his annual salary.

3 The legal effect of non-disclosure of a material fact on a proposal form is that:

A it limits payment of a claim to a return of premiums without interest;
B it makes a life policy void from inception;
C it automatically terminates a life policy;
D it renders a life policy voidable.

4 The assignment of a life policy indicates that:

A any policy gain will be automatically taxable;
B a temporary or permanent transfer of ownership has occurred;
C the policy is no longer eligible to be used as security for a loan;
D the purchaser has become the life assured.

5 When a couple have been cohabiting but without marrying and one of them dies intestate, the survivor will automatically receive:

A nothing;
B the first £75,000;
C the first £125,000;
D half of the estate.

6 Under the Data Protection Act of 1984 one of the provisions is that:

A data can be retained on record indefinitely;
B manual information must be registered with the Data Protection Registrar;
C computerised data must be regularly updated;
D anyone who is the subject of manually recorded data has the right of access to it.

7 The distinguishing feature of a discretionary trust is that:

A the trustees must distribute the income but have the discretion to change beneficiaries;
B new beneficiaries can be added to the trust at the trustees' discretion;
C the settlor can change the terms of the trust without reference to the trustees;
D the trustees have the right to retain income within the trust.

8 The Consumer Credit Act 1974 applied to all credit agreements unless the credit exceeds:

A £5,000;
B £15,000;
C £12,500;
D £25,000.

The solutions to the questions in the quiz can be found at the end of this Study Text. Before checking your answers against those solutions, you should look back at this chapter and use the information in it to correct your answers.

Answers to questions

1 (a) Offer, acceptance, consideration, contractual capacity, legality, agreement.

   (b) Minors.

   (c) The requirement in insurance to disclose all material facts; without this, an insurance contract is voidable.

   (d) The risk of financial loss following death which can be insured.

2 (a) Data must be accurate and updated, obtained and used lawfully as originally intended and for no other purpose and for no longer than necessary; the person whose data is stored (and no unauthorised person) must have access to it; its existence must be registered.

   (b) Applies to £25,000 and less; persons must have copy, and time (14 days) to cool off; requires licence; advertisements must warn of risks.

   (c) Will - executor; no will - administrator.

3 (a) Joint tenancy: survivor inherits; tenancy in common: estate inherits.
   (b) Temporary; permanent by sale or gift.
   (c) Means of giving the beneficiary legal entitlement without ownership.
   (d) Income: must be distributed from IIP; option to retain income in discretionary trust.
   (e) Transfer into discretionary trust - at half death rate.

4 It mitigates inheritance tax.

5 (a) Qualifying life policy, disability insurance; ISAs (existing TESSAs, PEPs), some National Savings, pensions.
   (b) Change in the level of prices of goods and services over time.
   (c) It reduces the value of the pound.
   (d) People with fixed incomes.

Chapter 7

PERSONAL TAXATION

Introduction

We have already recognised that taxation affects the desirability of various investments. We will now look at the detailed rules of UK taxation.

1 BASIS FOR BEING TAXED

1.1 If you are physically present in the UK for six months in a tax year (a year from 6 April to 5 April) then you will be **resident** in the UK and taxable on your income and capital gains.

1.2 If you are in the UK for less than six months you may still be taxable. If you are abroad only temporarily, or if you spend an average of three months a year in the UK for four years, you will be treated as **ordinarily resident** and therefore taxable.

1.3 The next question is - do you regard the UK as your home? If you do then you will fall into another category and be classed as **UK domiciled**. You can be resident abroad but, if you consider the UK to be 'home' you will still be domiciled in the UK even if you have not set foot in the UK for years.

1.4 **Why does domicile matter?** As you will see when we come to inheritance tax later on, if someone dies while they are domiciled in the UK all of their assets anywhere in the world are chargeable to tax. If they are not domiciled in the UK then only their UK assets will be chargeable to tax. In addition, they are charged to UK tax only on remittances made to the UK of overseas investment income and capital gains.

1.5   You could therefore have someone domiciled in France but living and working in the UK. They would be subject to **income tax** and **capital gains tax,** but their assets outside the UK would not be taxable if they died while living in the UK.

1.6   However, the Inland Revenue treats people as **'deemed' UK domiciled** for inheritance tax purposes if they were one of the following.

   (a)   Resident for income tax purposes in the UK for not less than 17 of the 20 tax years up to the year of an inheritance-taxable event

   (b)   Actually domiciled in the UK within three years before an inheritance-taxable event

1.7   Domicile is something which we acquire at birth. It will usually be the domicile of our father but we can change it if we want. We can have only **one country of domicile** at a time whereas we can be resident or ordinarily resident in more than one country in any one tax year.

> **KEY TERM**
>
> • Being **resident** or **ordinarily resident** decides whether or not we are subject to income tax and capital gains tax.
>
> • Being **domiciled** or **deemed domiciled** decides whether all of our assets at death will be subject to inheritance tax, or only those that we own in the UK.

Income tax

1.8   **Income tax is payable by UK residents.** If we spend a period of time working abroad we will be taxed on our overseas earnings by the country in which we earn them. To prevent those earnings also being taxed in the UK there exists a number of agreements with most countries of the world that the earnings will be taxed *only* by the country in which they are earned. These agreements are known as double taxation agreements.

1.9   If we have **investment income from overseas** it will be taxed by the UK Inland Revenue at the time we become entitled to it. If tax is deducted in the overseas country it will be allowed as a credit against UK tax.

2   INCOME TAXING CIRCUMSTANCES

Individuals

2.1   Individuals are taxable on their **income for each tax year.** The tax year - or fiscal year - runs from 6 April in one year to 5 April in the following year.

2.2   Income for individuals comes from two sources: **earnings from employment or self-employment,** and **investment income.**

Employees

2.3 The **earnings of employees** will include salaries, bonuses, commissions, fees and benefits in kind such as a company car, cheap loans, mobile telephones and the cost of private medical insurance.

Sole traders/partners

2.4 These two groups will pay tax based on **profit in their accounting year**. The accounting year will be the one which ends in the current tax year (but see later for more detailed information on the tax treatment of sole traders and partners).

Question 1

(a) What is the difference between being resident and ordinarily resident?
(b) Why is residence important?
(c) What does 'deemed domicile' mean?

---

3 INCOME TAX SCHEDULES

Classification of taxable income

3.1 Income from different sources is not all treated for tax purposes in the same way. To make it easier to apply the various forms of tax treatment, income is divided into groups according to the **source** from which it comes.

3.2 The principal groups are called **schedules** (note there are no Schedules B or C). Some schedules are further sub-divided into sub-groups called **cases**.

Schedule	Case	Source of income
A		Income from land and buildings
D	I	Trades
	II	Professions or vocations
	III	Interest received (including gilt interest), annuities and other annual payments
	IV & V	Overseas income from certain investments, possessions and businesses
	VI	Miscellaneous profits not falling within any other schedule or case
E	-	Wages and salaries from employments (including directorships) and other benefits
	I	Employee resident in the UK and the work is done here
	II	Work done in the UK by a non-resident
	III	Work done wholly abroad by a UK resident whose salary is sent here during the course of the overseas employment; excluding income taxed under Cases I or II
F	-	Dividends paid by companies and certain other distributions that they make
	-	Building society interest
	-	Bank deposit interest

Income tax rates

3.3 A list of the current **income tax rates and allowances** can be found at the end of this Study Text. In some cases income tax must be deducted by the payer of income and the net amount paid to the individual.

3.4 The following list shows **the tax treatment of the different schedules**.

(LRT = lower rate income tax; PAYE = pay as you earn)

Schedule	Case	Source of income	Gross	Deducted at source
A		Property	Gross	
D	I & II	Trades/professions	Gross	
	III	Gilts	Gross	
		Other interest	Gross	
		Annuities		20%
	IV & V	Overseas income	Various	
	VI	Miscellaneous profits	Gross	
E	I & II	Wages/Salary in UK; pensions		PAYE
	III	Wages/Salary from overseas	Various	
F		Dividends		10/90^{ths} credit
		Building society/bank deposit interest		20%

Note 1 Dividends in respect of shares are now paid with an associated tax credit of 10/90^{ths} of the dividend received.

Non taxpayers may not reclaim this tax credit, although dividends in respect of shares held in PEPs and ISAs **will** be eligible for the reclamation of the tax credit until 5 April 2004.

Lower rate and basic rate taxpayers will pay no more tax on dividend income.

Higher rate taxpayers pay a special rate of 32.5% tax on dividends.

Note 2 All savings income, for example building society and bank deposit account interest, is subject to 20% tax for basic rate taxpayers, but higher rate taxpayers are liable for an additional 20% tax. A starting rate of tax of 10% applies to savings income (dividends and interest) as well as non-savings income.

Note 3 Building society and bank deposit interest can be paid gross to any investor who can show that he is likely to remain a non taxpayer. The same principle applies to any person in receipt of a purchased life annuity. Lower rate taxpayers must pay 10% tax on interest.

Note 4 Summary of tax treatment for different sources of income

Rate	Earned	Interest	Dividend
Lower	10%	10%	10%
Basic	22%	20%	10%
Higher	40%	40%	32.5%

Earned income includes income from employment, benefits in kind and profits for the self-employed.

Dividend income includes dividends from shares, investment trusts and equity unit trusts.

Interest income includes interest on bank accounts, building society accounts and cash unit trusts.

The 20% basic tax rate on interest income is known as the **savings tax rate**.

Dividend income and interest is treated as the top part of one's income. This means, for example, that if an individual has earned income and dividend income, the lower and basic rates of tax will apply to the earned income first. If earned income 'uses up' all the basic rate of tax (22%), the dividend income will be subject to tax at the higher rate.

4 INCOME TAX ALLOWANCES

KEY TERMS

- **Personal reliefs** and **allowances** are deductions from an individual's income before tax is calculated, or they reduce the tax on that income. They are available only to individuals.

- The term '**taxable income**' is used to describe income *after* allowances and other non-taxable items (such as pension contributions) have been deducted.

Personal allowance

4.1 Every UK resident is entitled to a **Personal Allowance** from the year of birth to the year of death.

4.2 If a couple are living together and one of them does not have sufficient income to use up a personal allowance, the other can transfer assets to that person so that the income from those assets - previously taxable - will now no longer be taxable because it falls within the personal allowance. Remember that in order to do this the **ownership** of assets must be totally transferred from one person to another: not everybody is willing to do that. These examples are for illustrative purposes only. You will not be examined in this much detail in the exam.

4.3 EXAMPLES: PERSONAL ALLOWANCES 2000/2001

Paul, single, self-employed

Example 1.A

	£
Building Society interest net	16,000
Plus tax deducted at source (20% of gross interest)	4,000
Statutory total income	20,000
Less personal allowance (2000/2001)	4,385
Taxable income	15,615

Tax			£
On	1st £1,520	10%	152
	On £(15,615 – 1,520)	20%	2,819
			2,971

	£
Tax liability	2,971
Less tax already paid (deducted at source)	4,000
Tax rebate due	1,029

Note that the interest was 'grossed up' (the tax credit was added back) and that taxable income is stated *after* the personal allowance. Paul benefits from the 10% lower rate tax band.

Example 1.B

	£	£
Earnings (none yet taxed)		34,395
Building society interest (net)	1,600	
Plus tax deducted at source (£1,600 × 20/80)	400	
		2,000
		36,395
Less pension contribution		1,000
Statutory total income		35,395
Less personal allowance (2000/2001)		4,385
Taxable income		31,010
Tax: £1,520		152
£(28,400 – 1,520) × 22%		5,914
£(31,010 – 28,400) × 40%		1,044
Tax liability		7,110
Less tax already paid (deducted at source)		400
Tax due		6,710

The interest income of £2,000 is treated as the top part of Paul's income. It falls in the higher rate band and is therefore taxed at 40%, with credit then given for the tax deducted at source at 20%.

Married couple's allowance (tax reducer)

4.4   Suppose Paul is married to Martha. Until 2000/2001, he would have been entitled to a **Married Couple's Allowance** (MCA). The allowance would have been deducted from the amount of tax payable. The MCA was abolished from 6 April 2000, although the right to claim MCA still remains for pensioners born before 6 April 1935. (The amount of the MCA depends on whether at least one of the couple is aged 75 or over.)

Age allowance

4.5   Once you reach age 65 you get a **Higher Personal Allowance**. When you reach the age of 75 you get an even higher allowance.

4.6   If someone entitled to an age allowance has income over an annual sum known as the **'income limit for age-related allowances'**, the allowance is reduced gradually. The income limit is £17,000 for 2000/2001. The rate is specifically £1 for every £2 of income in excess of the limit. The following example will show the effect of additional income for someone whose income exceeds the income limit. The reduction of £1 for every £2 excess will continue until the age allowance has fallen to the level of the ordinary allowance.

4.7   EXAMPLE: AGE ALLOWANCE

Mr Shuffle is aged 67 and single. The effect of the income limit is shown in the following examples.

	Example A	*Example B*
	£	£
Income (all pension)	17,000	17,200
Age allowance	5,790	5,690
Taxable income	11,210	11,510

Tax

	£	£		£	£
	$1,520 \times 10\%$	152.00		$1,520 \times 10\%$	152.00
	$9,690 \times 22\%$	2,131.80		$9,990 \times 22\%$	2,197.80
	11,210	2,283.80		11,510	2,349.80

Notice the difference in income and tax. Income of £200 in excess of the limit results in extra after-tax income of just £66!

	Income			*Tax*
	£			£
Example B	17,200			2,283.80
Example A	17,000			2,349.80
Additional income	200	Extra tax		66.00

Tax of £66 on £200 represents a rate of 33%, which is 1.5 times the normal basic rate of 22%. This is the effect of the loss of age allowance. The extra £200 of income meant a loss of £100 (£1 for every £2 excess) of allowances - is an effective (marginal) rate of tax of (1.5 × 22% basic rate) 33%.

Widow's bereavement allowance

4.8 When a man dies his widow will be entitled to an allowance in addition to the personal allowance. That additional allowance - the **widow's bereavement allowance** - is £2,000 for 2000/2001, for those widowed during 1999/2000 and who have not remarried before 6 April 2000. This relief has been abolished for those widowed from 6th April 2000.

Annual charges

4.9 An **annual charge** is an amount which a person is legally obliged to pay either as a result of an obligation voluntarily incurred or as a result of direction by a court.

4.10 Some annual charges may be deducted from income **before** tax is calculated. This means that the borrower is effectively relieved from paying tax on that part of his income which is used to meet the charge, ie he obtains tax relief. An example of such a charge is a pension contribution.

Other reliefs

4.11 **Termination of employment.** Payment to an employee on redundancy is exempt from tax up to a specified limit, currently £30,000 including statutory redundancy pay.

4.12 **Private medical insurance.** At one time, tax relief was available on private medical insurance premiums for people aged over 60. This relief is no longer available. Indeed these insurance premiums are now subject to insurance premium tax (IPT) at 5%.

Charitable covenants

4.13 A new scheme of tax relief on gifts to charities by individuals was introduced from 6 April 2000. The scheme applies to both 'Gift Aid' donations (one-off donations) and to annual donations by deeds of covenant. (A covenant is an agreement to pay someone, in this case a charity, a specific sum of money every year for a set number of years. A Gift Aid donation is a one-off payment, and the taxpayer claims tax relief by making a Gift Aid declaration.)

Under the scheme

BPP PUBLISHING

(a) There is no minimum limit for the size of donation.

(b) The individual makes the donation to the charity, and claims tax relief from the Inland Revenue. Higher rate tax relief is given where appropriate.

In addition, for charitable donations made by individuals through their employer's payroll, the government will pay a 10% supplement on the amounts donated, for three years from 6 April 2000.

Thus, if an individual who pays tax at the basic rate makes a charitable donation of £100 in 2000/2001, he can claim this donation against his taxable income, and so will pay (net) £78. If the payment is made through his payroll the government will make a further donation of £10.

Prior to 2000/2001, there was a maximum limit for payroll giving (£1,200 in 1999/2000). This limit has now been abolished.

There is also income tax relief for gifts to charity of shares in quoted companies.

Question 2

(a) Which income tax schedule deals with employment earnings?
(b) Which forms of income have 20% tax deducted at source?
(c) What is the effect of the loss of age allowance on a person's income tax rate?

5 SOLE TRADERS AND PARTNERSHIPS

KEY TERM

If you are a **sole trader** you are self employed running your own business. The number of employees that you yourself have is immaterial for this purpose.

5.1 As a sole trader you will be taxed on your **business income minus allowable expenses**. From that moment on the process will be the normal one of adding any other income to your earnings and deducting the personal allowance.

5.2 Even if you leave your profits in the firm and don't draw them out, they are nevertheless **taxable as earnings**. The fact that you have chosen not to draw and spend them does not change their status as earnings.

5.3 As a sole trader you will be taxed under **Schedule D Case I or II** (the difference is immaterial for the purposes of the examination).

5.4 Your tax for each tax year will be based on the **profits you made in the business year which ended in that same tax year**. For example, if your business year ends on 30 June then your tax for the fiscal year 2000/2001 will be based on the profit that you make in the business year ending on 30 June 2000. This is known as the **current year basis**.

5.5 Prior to 1997/98, businesses were taxed on a **preceding year basis**. Since 1997/98 everybody has been taxed on the 'current' year basis. There are special rules when someone commences or ceases trading, or when there are losses.

5.6 The taxation of **partnerships** is on the same basis, the only difference being that the partnership profits will be divided between the partners according to their partnership share in order to calculate their total individual liabilities.

5.7 Although individual partners may meet their **individual tax liability** it is customary for the firm to write the cheque in respect of the total tax due. In all other respects, ie when the profits are taxable and when the tax is payable, the position is the same as for a sole trader.

5.8 If any capital gains tax is payable that it treated in the same way as for **individuals**.

6 VAT

> **KEY TERM**
>
> **Value added tax (VAT)** is a sales tax which must be added by many businesses to the costs of their products and services.

6.1 EXAMPLE: VAT

A company manufactures furniture. It sells furniture valued at £8,000 to a shop. It must add to the price of the furniture VAT at the current rate of 17.5%, ie £1,400.

The shop thus pays to the manufacturer a total price of £9,400. If the shop adds 50% to the price of thc furniture when selling it to the customer, the selling price will then be £12,000. The shop must also add to this the VAT of £2,100, making a total retail price of £14,100.

The manufacturer will already have sent to Customs & Excise (who organise VAT) their VAT of £1,400. The shop now pays to Customs & Excise VAT of £2,100 less the sum of £1,400 for VAT which the shop has already paid to the manufacturer.

The **ultimate consumer** therefore bears the burden of the total VAT of £2,100. This is the intention of VAT.

6.2 For VAT purposes businesses are divided into two categories: **registered** and **unregistered**.

> **KEY TERMS**
>
> - A **registered business** must charge VAT on its products or services but, as we have already seen, it can recover VAT which it has paid to a supplier.
>
> - An **unregistered business** does not charge VAT. However, it is unable to recover VAT that it pays to suppliers.

6.3 There are **two principal rates of VAT** - 17.5% and 0%. A supply subject to VAT at 0% is described as being 'zero rated'. A third rate - 5% - applies to a few items, notably domestic fuel and power. Some supplies, such as insurance, are *exempt* from VAT. This is different from being zero rated, because someone making zero rated supplies can recover the VAT they pay to suppliers, but someone making exempt supplies cannot.

6.4 A business **does not have to register** for VAT if its annual non-exempt turnover is less than the annual income specified by the government: £52,000 in 2000/2001.

6.5 A business with turnover below the registration limit may register **voluntarily** for VAT. The advantage of doing this is that it can recover VAT on any of its purchases. If it supplies products or services to businesses which themselves are registered for VAT then those businesses themselves may recover the VAT that they have paid. However, if its customers are individuals, or are businesses that only make exempt supplies, then voluntary registration for VAT may be a disadvantage. In addition, even if there is an advantage in recovering VAT, unless the level of recovery is substantial it may not be worthwhile having to follow the compliance procedures required for the administration of VAT.

> **Exam focus point**
> For the purposes of the examination you need to know that **exempt supplies** include the **provision or arranging of insurance, banking and dealing in stocks and shares**. Although *supplying* insurance and the *arranging* of insurance contracts are exempt, this does not apply to the activity of giving *advice*. If you give advice on an investment contract then the **fees chargeable are subject to VAT**.

VAT return

6.6 VAT is calculated by a business under a '**self assessment**' **arrangement**. Customs & Excise, of course, have the right to come to inspect the books of any company to ensure that the figures supplied are correct.

6.7 Each **VAT return** must show the tax charged (output tax) and the VAT which has been paid to suppliers (input tax). The business must then either send a cheque or claim a refund according to which is the bigger figure. Returns must be made for quarterly periods and supplied to the Customs & Excise within one month of the end of the quarterly period.

7 INSURANCE PREMIUM TAX (IPT) AND STAMP DUTY

7.1 The standard rate of Insurance Premium Tax rose by 1% from 1 July 1999 to 5%. IPT applies to most general insurance but life insurance and most other long-term insurance is exempt. IPT is administered by HM Customs and Excise.

7.2 Stamp duty is an *ad valorem* tax charge on documents transferred in an asset transaction. Tax is borne by the purchaser of certain assets, including property and shares.

The rate of stamp duty applicable to the purchase of shares is 0.5% of the value of the transaction. The rate of stamp duty on the purchase of property depends on the price of the property.

Property: purchase consideration	Rate
£60,000 or less	0%
£60,001 - £250,000	1%
£250,001 - £500,000	3%
Over £500,000	4%

One rate applies to the full amount of the purchase consideration.

8 BENEFITS IN KIND

8.1 **Pay** is not the only benefit which can be provided by an employer for employees. One of the principal additional **benefits in kind** is the provision of a **company car**, most commonly provided for senior managers and sales representatives. The value of private use of the car is taxable.

8.2   In the case of **representatives** it is a necessary aid for them in their work. However they usually have the private use of a car when they are not using it on business and that private use is a benefit in kind.

8.3   For the senior managers of a company the car is less likely to be an essential part of their work and is more likely to be a **form of remuneration**. Other taxable benefits in kind are the value of **luncheon vouchers** in excess of 15p per day, company-provided **mobile telephones** and the cost of **private medical insurance**.

8.4   The position is complicated by the fact that different rules apply to employees in two **different groups**. The two groups are employees earning £8,500 per annum or more and those who are earning less than £8,500 per annum.

8.5   If an employee earns **£8,500 per annum or more** or is a **director of the company**, the employer must complete an Inland Revenue form giving details of all benefits and expenses payments. The form is numbered P11D and as a result such employees have become known as P11D employees.

8.6   **P11D employees** must pay tax on the value of benefits in kind whereas non-P11D employees are not liable for tax on many benefits. The deciding factor is whether or not an employee's pay and benefits in total reach the P11D level. Thus an employee whose pay is £8,400 a year and who has benefits in kind valued at £200 per year is classified as a P11D employee.

9   INCOME TAX ASSESSMENT AND COLLECTION

9.1   Income tax on employees' pay and benefits is calculated by the employer and deducted by the employer before paying the net income to the employee. This is known as **Pay As You Earn (PAYE)** but it makes no difference to the total tax liability of the employee. It is simply a convenient method of regular collection of tax.

9.2   As far as **benefits in kind** are concerned you would expect the Inland Revenue to add the value of those benefits to your pay in order to arrive at your total remuneration. In practice, the Revenue adopts a different approach which leads to the same result.

9.3   Let us say that your employer pays £300 a year of premiums into a private medical insurance scheme for your benefit. Instead of adding this sum to your income the amount of your personal allowance will be reduced by altering the **tax code**. It has exactly the same effect.

9.4   Inspectors of taxes issue **tax return forms** to certain taxpayers.

9.5   If a return is issued, it must be completed and submitted by the **filing date**. This is the later of:

(a)   31 January following the end of the tax year which the return covers
(b)   Three months after it was issued

9.6   Tax is only payable if there is an assessment. This is a **tax demand**. The normal system is **self assessment**, under which taxpayers write their own tax demands. However, the Revenue can also issue assessments.

9.7 Each return form includes a section for the taxpayer to compute his own tax payable (a **self assessment**), and this computation counts as an assessment to tax. The return and the balance of any tax payable are usually both due by 31 January following the end of the tax year. Payments on account of tax would have previously been made on 31 January in the tax year and on the following 31 July (ie 12 months and six months before the normal due date for the final payment). All CGT is payable on 31 January following the tax year, with no payments on account.

9.8 A taxpayer may choose not to complete the section of the return in which he works out his tax payable (the self assessment). The Revenue will then make the **computation** and prepare an assessment for him. This counts as a self assessment made by the taxpayer, so the rules in this section relating to self assessments still apply. However, the Revenue will not guarantee to have the work done in time for the taxpayer to pay the correct amount by the due date, unless the return is submitted by the later of:

(a) 30 September following the end of the tax year which the return covers
(b) Two months after it was issued

Question 3

(a)   In what circumstances can a business register voluntarily for VAT?
(b)   What additional tax liability is suffered by a P11D employee?

10   INHERITANCE TAX

> ### KEY TERM
>
> **Inheritance tax**, generally abbreviated to IHT, is charged when someone dies. It is based on the value of the person's possessions at death and will be a percentage of that value. However, in practice the tax is not quite so simple.

10.1 The first factor which makes IHT less simple is the ease with which it could be avoided by many people if **death** were the only event which gave rise to the tax. For example, if a wealthy elderly person knew that he would shortly die he could give his estate to his children prior to his death, thus avoiding tax.

10.2 To prevent this kind of tax avoidance, inheritance tax is chargeable not only on assets passing from one person to another on death but also on any assets which have been transferred during the **seven years before death**. Tax can still be avoided by transferring assets during a person's lifetime if that person, the donor, then survives for seven years after the transfer has taken place.

10.3 The second factor is that not all of a person's estate is taxed. Gifts to spouses or charities are exempt, and the **first £234,000 of taxable transfers are taxed at 0%.** This 'nil rate band' is adjusted annually in the Budget, and is £234,000 for 2000/2001.

Basis

10.4 Inheritance tax is based on **the value of assets which are transferred from one person to another**. Such transfers - **dispositions** - are added to the value of previous transfers.

10.5 EXAMPLE: IHT BASIS

If for example a transfer valued at £20,000 is made followed by another transfer of £30,000, the total transfer for IHT purposes is £50,000. Thus if that person died shortly after the second transfer was made and the value of his estate was £110,000, the total value of all dispositions for IHT purposes would be £160,000.

But now remember that only transfers within **the last seven years before death** are counted. Let us now assume that the dispositions were made as follows.

	Year	*Value* £	*Cumulative total* £
	1992	20,000	20,000
	1997	60,000	80,000
(Death)	2000	110,000	170,000

The reason for the cumulative total being £170,000 at the time of death, and not £190,000, is that the first disposition, £20,000, was made in 1992 which is more than seven years before death. That transfer has therefore dropped out of the calculation.

10.6 The assets which are included in the calculation comprise **everything to which the individual has a right or owns**. For example, you may own a house, a car and some furniture. All of that is part of your estate on your death. However, if you have lent money to someone and they still owe it to you then they are a debtor and the amount that they owe you is also part of your estate because you have a right to it.

10.7 On the other hand, if you owe money to other people as, for example, happens with a mortgage, then the mortgage will be deducted from the value of your estate because it is a **debt**.

10.8 Inheritance tax is payable on death or on some transfers of value made while you are alive (**lifetime transfers**). Notice that it is based on transfers by **individuals** and not companies.

Rates of inheritance tax

10.9 The rates of IHT are 0% on the first £234,000 (the nil rate band) and 40% above that. Thus for total transfers of £250,000, the first £234,000 will be taxed at 0% and the balance of £16,000 will be taxed at 40%: the total tax would therefore be £6,400.

10.10 Transfers during lifetime into **discretionary trusts** are taxed at **half the death rate**: 0% or 20%.

Gifts with reservation of benefit

10.11 Let us assume that you live in a house which you want to give to your children. You can give them the house that you live in, move into another one and, after seven years, the value of your first house will fall out of the cumulative total of transfers and will be **IHT free**.

10.12 But what if, having given the house away, you continue to live in it? You may have transferred the ownership to your children but you are continuing to benefit from the house simply by continuing to live in it. The gift you have made, therefore, is not unconditional. It is technically known as a **gift with reservation**.

10.13 Under the rules of inheritance tax even though you have transferred the ownership of the house to your children the 'seven year clock' does not start ticking until you **completely get rid of the benefit that you are reserving**. If the house is currently worth £50,000 and you continue to live in it until you die 30 years after you have given it away then, even though you have not owned the house for 30 years, its value (by then perhaps £2 million) will be included in your estate for inheritance tax purposes. This rule was reinforced by the 1999 Finance Act.

11   IHT EXEMPTIONS AND RELIEFS

11.1 There are some transfers that are not taxable. These are known as **exemptions**. Remember that the nil rate band is not an exemption.

11.2 One of them, and we deal with them all later, is an exemption from inheritance tax on **transfers between husbands and wives** - the spouse to spouse exemption. This of course means transfers from you to your spouse rather that to somebody else's spouse.

11.3 The significance is that such transfers **are exempt from inheritance tax**. Before we look at the other exemptions we must be clear on the difference between exemptions, reliefs and the nil rate band.

11.4 No tax is payable on an exempt transfer at any time - it is **tax free**.

11.5 However, some **transfers are entitled to reliefs**. A relief is a *reduction* in the value of a transfer for inheritance tax purposes. That is not the same as being tax free.

11.6 The reduction may even be **100%**. For example, if you own an unincorporated business and transfer the business to someone else, the value for inheritance tax purposes will be reduced by 100%. It is still a taxable transfer but the value has been reduced to nil for inheritance tax purposes.

11.7 Other reliefs exist but we deal with just one of them. If a donor made a **lifetime gift** and then died two weeks before the end of the seven years from the date of the gift, it would be tough if the full rate of IHT was charged when death two weeks later would have avoided IHT.

To soften the blow, the tax begins to reduce after the date of transfer plus **three years**, and continues to reduce at the rate of 20% a year until it is nil in year eight. This is known as tapering relief. Notice the differences from the other reliefs where the value of the **transfer** is reduced; with tapering relief it is the amount of the *tax* that is reduced.

11.8 Thus, if a donor dies within three years of making a lifetime gift, the tax payable on the gift will be at the full rate applicable (0% or 40%). If the donor dies in the fourth year, the tax payable will be at 80% of the full rate. If the donor dies in the fifth year, the tax payable will be at 60% of the full rate. If the donor dies in the eighth year or later, no tax will ever be payable on that lifetime gift.

11.9 There is another category of transfer. This arises because if you make a transfer during your lifetime and survive for seven years the transfer will not be subject to inheritance tax: transfers made more than seven years before death are exempt. **At the time you make the transfer** you do not know whether it will become an exempt transfer simply because you do not know whether or not you will survive for a further seven years. Thus at the time the transfer is made it is not an exempt transfer but it might be and this has led to its title **'potentially exempt transfer'** or PET.

Question 4

(a) A person who is resident in the UK but domiciled abroad dies. What effect will his domicile have on an inheritance tax charge?

(b) When is inheritance tax charged at half the death rates?

(c) What is a gift with reservation of benefit?

The main exemptions from IHT

Spouse to spouse

11.10 Transfers from **one spouse to another** can be made without limit and without risk of being subject to inheritance tax. The only exception to this is if a transfer is made to a spouse domiciled in another country, in which case there is a limit on the amount that will be exempt from tax.

Annual exemption

11.11 You can make gifts of up to **£3,000 a year** and they will be free from inheritance tax. This limit is a total of all your transfers and not an amount per gift. Thus, if you wanted to transfer £7,500 in one year to someone else or to other people, £3,000 of it would be exempt but the remaining £4,500 would be subject to the normal seven year rule.

11.12 This exemption can be **carried forward for one year** if it is not used. Thus, if you have made no previous transfers and want to transfer a total of £8,000 this year you can use this year's annual exemption plus last year's exemption and only £2,000 will be subject to the seven year rule.

11.13 Notice that **this year's exemption must be used first**. Thus if you wanted to transfer a total of £3,500 then that would mean using the current year's exemption of £3,000 and £500 from last year's exemption. As the exemption can be carried forward for only one year you will next year have lost the ability to use the unused £2,500 from last year's exemption.

Small gifts

11.14 You can give £250 to each of any number of friends, relations or enemies and all the gifts will all be **tax free**. If you give £251 to any one person in one tax year, the whole £251 is taxable (unless some other exemption applies).

Gifts in consideration of marriage

11.15 If you are getting married then you can receive **wedding gifts** without inheritance tax arising.

11.16 There are **limits**. Each parent can give £5,000 and each grandparent or remoter ancestor can give £2,500. Other people can each give £1,000.

Normal expenditure

11.17 The last exemption is a much more general one. It basically says that if you make gifts as part of your **normal expenditure** they will be exempt from inheritance tax.

11.18 The gifts must be **regular,** they must be made **out of income** and they must **not reduce your standard of living**.

Other gifts

11.19 Other transfers, including **gifts to charities and political parties**, may also be exempt from inheritance tax.

12 THE BASIS FOR INHERITANCE TAX

12.1 **How can you decide the value of an asset for tax purposes?** We do not need to go into detail about valuation. It is sufficient to say that it is the price for which an asset could be sold - the **market value** - which is used, no matter how difficult it might be sometimes to work it out.

12.2 More important, however, is the fact that the basis of the tax is not the value of the gift but the **reduction in the size of the donor's estate** which is caused by the transfer. This seems hard to understand. If you are giving away a watch worth £2,000 surely the reduction in the donor's estate must be exactly the same?

12.3 EXAMPLE: REDUCTION IN SIZE OF DONOR'S ESTATE

Usually it is, but there are circumstances when it is not. Imagine a pair of identical antique silver candelabra. Antiques which match have a value greater than the value of the total of the individual items. Thus, while each candelabrum might alone be worth say, £5,000, the pair might be worth £20,000. The value in the donor's estate is £20,000. If he gives one of them away the person receiving it will have an item worth £5,000. The donor will also now have one silver candelabrum worth £5,000. His estate will thus have reduced by £15,000 (£20,000 minus £5,000) and this will be the basis of the tax.

12.4 Remember what it is that makes a transfer chargeable to inheritance tax - it is a reduction in the value of a person's estate. In fact it is more than that because it is the **intention to reduce the value of your estate** that makes inheritance tax chargeable. For example if you want to give to a friend an antique table worth £16,000 it is no good charging them a nominal £5 in order to avoid inheritance tax. Your estate has reduced by £15,995 which is just what you intended to happen.

If on the other hand you sell the same table worth £16,000 to a friend for £10,000 because you haven't the faintest idea how much it is really worth, then inheritance tax does not come into play. You have simply struck a very bad bargain and your friend has got a very good deal, but it is not chargeable to IHT.

12.5 In the example just given, if you paid £25 for the table five years ago then the gain you have made may be subject to **capital gains tax** (see below).

12.6 We now return to the subject of the assets that are included in your estate for inheritance tax purposes. **All of your assets worldwide will be included in your estate.** Thus your country house in Oxfordshire, your apartment in New York, your chalet in Switzerland and the holiday cottage in France will all be valued and included in your estate for inheritance tax purposes.

12.7 However, there is an exception to this and that is if you are **not domiciled in the UK**. In such a case your estate would include only your UK assets and not those in other countries.

13 CAPITAL GAINS TAX

The basic rules

> **KEY TERM**
>
> When a person buys an asset and sells it at a profit the difference between the two is taxed as a **capital gain** by **capital gains tax (CGT)**.

13.1 If an asset was bought before 1982 the pre-1982 value will be ignored. Tax will be based on the difference between the sale price and the **value of the asset in 1982** (Ex 2) subject to other factors mentioned later.

13.2 It may be difficult to **establish the value** of an item in 1982 but this difficulty does not alter the principle which will be applied. Acquisition costs and subsequent improvement (but not maintenance) costs can be added to the purchase price or value. Equally disposal costs can be deducted from the sale proceeds.

13.3 There is another rule which will be applied next. The cost of the item when it was bought, or its value in 1982 if bought earlier, will be increased by an **allowance for inflation** from then until 5 April 1998. Obviously the actual cost or value cannot be changed: this step is purely part of the process for calculating CGT. This artificially increased sum will be deducted from the proceeds of the sale (Ex 3). This process is known as indexation.

Indexation is only allowed up to 5 April 1998 because different capital gains tax rules apply from that date.

13.4 Capital gains tax is based on the **taxable or chargeable gains** between 6 April one year and 5 April the following year, this period being known as the fiscal year. The next procedure is for all an individual's chargeable gains within that period to be added together.

13.5 However, not all sales lead to gains. A **loss** is obviously possible. All losses during a fiscal year will also be totalled. The total of the losses will then be deducted from the total of the gains to arrive at a net gain or loss during the fiscal year (Ex 4). Note that in working out a loss, we must ignore indexation: the allowance for inflation can reduce a gain, but it cannot be used to create or increase a loss.

13.6 Before the resulting gain (if there is one) is taxed there is an allowance which is deducted from the total before tax is calculated. This allowance is known as the **CGT exemption,** and it simply means that no tax will be payable on the total of the gains until the total exceeds the amount of the exemption. Even then only the excess above the exemption will be taxed (Ex 5). The annual exemption for 2000/2001 is £7,200.

13.7 Now we have the sum which will be taxed. To calculate the tax **the total is added to the income of the taxpayer in that same fiscal year**. The rate of tax applied will depend on the individual's income during that year. The higher the income the higher the rate of tax which may be applied to the gain (Ex 6).

The tax charged will still be called capital gains tax even though the rates of income tax are used in the calculation.

13.8 The minimum rate of capital gains tax which you will be charged is 10% as personal allowances cannot be used to reduce capital gains tax. Gains falling within the basic rate band will be charged at the **same rate as interest** - 20%, not 22%.

13.9 EXAMPLES: CAPITAL GAINS TAX

			Gain
		£	£
Ex 1	Proceeds of sale	12,500	
	Cost	4,500	8,000
Ex 2	Proceeds of sale	12,500	
	Cost (1977) - £4,500		
	Value 1982	6,500	6,000
Ex 3	Proceeds of sale	12,500	
	Value 1982 (£6,500 increased by inflation from 1982 to 5.4.98)	10,500	2,000

Ex 4		Gains	Losses
		£	£
	1	8,000	-
	2	6,000	-
	3	2,000	-
	4	-	4,000
	Total	16,000	4,000
	Deduct losses	4,000	
	Net gains	12,000	

Ex 5	Net gains	12,000
	Less exemption (for 2000/2001)	7,200
	Taxable gain	4,800

Ex 6	Taxable income		Tax on gain			
	Before adding net gain	After adding net gain				
(A)	£15,500	£20,300	£4,800	× 20%	=	£960
(B)	£26,400	£31,200	£2,000	× 20%	= £400	
			£2,800	× 40%	= £1,120	£1,520
(C)	£32,500	£37,300	£4,800	× 40%	=	£1,920

For periods from 6 April 1998

13.10 Indexation was ended as at 5 April 1998. It is being replaced by a **taper**. This means that a gain will be reduced according to how long the asset has been held. The objective is to encourage personal investors to keep assets as long as possible by reducing the tax payable.

13.11 The method will be to reduce the percentage of the gain that is taxable over a period of **ten years,** in the case of 'non-business assets' and **four years** in the case of 'business assets'. The taper does not start until an asset has been held for three complete years (see below for an exception). It works like this:

No. of complete years (after 5.4.98) for which an asset is held	Percentage of non-business asset gain chargeable %	Percentage of business asset gain chargeable %
0	100	100
1	100	87.5
2	100	75
3	95	50
4	90	25
5	85	25
6	80	25
7	75	25
8	70	25
9	65	25
10	60	25

13.12 For assets held as at 5 April 1998, the taper will reduce a gain on the eventual disposal of a **non-business asset** after 5 April 2001 and on **a business asset** after 5 April 1999. A gain is established in the normal way, except that indexation stops at 5.4.98. The gain is added to income in the normal way. The change shows itself in the **size** of the gain, which is reduced (or not) according to the length of time the asset has been held.

13.13 It should be stressed that **companies are not affected by these rules**.

13.14 Non-business assets acquired before **17 March 1998** qualify for an addition of one year to the period for which they are treated as held after 5 April 1998. So for example a non-business asset purchased on 1 January 1998 and disposed of on 1 July 2000 will be treated for the purposes of the taper as if it had been held for three years (two complete years after 5 April 1998 plus one additional year).

13.15 When looking at the period of ownership post 5 April 1998, if there has been a transfer of assets between **spouses** the combined period of ownership is considered.

13.16 One effect of the changes is to give a **maximum effective rate of CGT on non-business assets of 24%** for a higher rate taxpayer who has held the assets for ten years. For example, a gain of £100 would previously have been at 40%, ie tax of £40 would be payable. Under the new arrangement, after ten years only 60% of the gain will be taxed, ie £60 x 40% = £24.

13.17 The **maximum effective rate of CGT on business assets** for a higher rate taxpayer will be just 10% (40% or 25%) for assets held for four years or more. The distinction between business assets and non-business assets is therefore important, and a significant change was introduced in the Budget in 2000. This Budget extended the definition of business assets to:

(a) All shares in unquoted companies

(b) All shares held *by* **employees** in quoted trading companies

(c) Shares held by outside investors in quoted trading companies, for shareholdings above a 5% threshold.

13.18 Business assets therefore include all shares in unquoted companies held by entrepreneurs (and employees) and also all shares in quoted trading companies held by employees. Don't forget the annual exemption from CGT: the benefit of taper relief only applies to someone whose total capital gains on share disposals in any year are likely to exceed the exemption limit.

13.19 The extension of the definition of business assets to a wider range of shares in the 2000 Budget created an additional complexity. What happens to someone who held shares prior to 6 April 2000 that were classified as non-business assets originally, but are now classified as business assets?

13.20 For example, suppose that an employee held shares in his company from 1998, and the company is a public trading company? If he disposes of his shares after 6 April 2000, what taper relief applies, the taper for non-business assets or the taper for business assets?

13.21 The answer is not straightforward. A changeover period will apply, and will continue up to 6 April 2010. Between now and then, for shares held prior to 6 April 2000 that were originally classified as non-business assets but are now business assets, and that are disposed of at a chargeable gain, the effective rate of tax payable will be based on an averaging of taper reliefs. The following table is shown for illustrative purposes only.

Effective top rate of capital gains tax (higher rate taxpayer) for shares sold	*Shares acquired prior to 17 March 1998*	*Shares acquired in 2000/2001*	
2001/2002	30.7%	35%	(40% of 87.5%)
2002/2003	22.0%	30%	(40% of 75%)
2003/2004	18.8%	20%	(40% of 50%)
2004/2005	16.7%	10%	(40% of 25%)
...			
2010/2011	10%	10%	

Exempt assets

13.22 There are some items that are totally **exempt** from capital gains tax. For examination purposes you do not need to know all of them but the principal ones are your own home (principal private residence), a private motor car, National Savings certificates, gilts, betting winnings, chattels sold for £6,000 or less and life assurance policies (provided the latter are still owned by the original owner).

Who pays CGT and how is it collected?

13.23 You will be liable for capital gains tax if you are either **resident** or **ordinarily resident** in the UK. The tax is payable by partnerships as well as individuals.

13.24 Gains, and (if the taxpayer chooses to compute the tax) the CGT, are shown on **a tax return**. The taxpayer must pay that tax on 31 January following the tax year. There are no interim payments on account, as there are for income tax.

Question 5

(a) What are the main inheritance tax exemptions?
(b) What is the basis for inheritance tax?
(c) Name some assets that are exempt from capital gains tax.
(d) What is the objective of tapering capital gains?
(e) Why is the distinction between business assets and non-business assets significant?

---

14 MITIGATING TAX LIABILITY

14.1 Tax can be avoided by selecting **suitable investment vehicles**.

(a) **Income tax** can be avoided by placing money in an ISA instead of leaving it in a taxable deposit account.

(b) **Capital gains tax** can be avoided by investing in gilts instead of equities.

14.2 But remember that **tax is not the only consideration**. In practice, your advice to a client will take into account other factors such as investment performance and the client's risk profile.

14.3 Capital gains tax can also be avoided or reduced by selling assets to use up the **annual exemption** and then buying them back again to establish a higher base price.

14.4 Capital gains tax can be deferred by reinvesting the proceeds of a potentially CGT-liable sale into approved investments which entitle the seller to '**roll-over relief**' - the ability to defer tax to a later date.

14.5 **Inheritance tax** can be reduced by placing an investment bond **in trust for beneficiaries**, thus enabling investment growth to take place outside an estate.

14.6 The final step in inheritance tax planning is the use of **regular premium whole life assurance** as a means of funding for a liability which cannot otherwise be avoided.

BPP PUBLISHING

Chapter roundup

- *Basis for being taxed*

  ○ Resident: someone who normally lives in UK, or someone from abroad physically present in UK for six months in a tax year.

  ○ Ordinarily resident. Physically present in UK for average of three months a year for four years.

  ○ Domicile. The country you regard as home. Can be resident abroad but UK domiciled. Relevant for inheritance tax. Acquired at birth, usually from father, can be changed.

  ○ Deemed domiciled. Not domiciled, but treated as domiciled.

- Income tax paid by UK residents. If working abroad - earnings taxed in country of work. Overseas investment income - taxed in UK - overseas tax allowed as credit. Individuals taxed in fiscal year on earnings from employment or self employment and investment income. Employees taxed on employment benefits - including most benefits in kind. Sole traders/partners taxed on profits in accounting year. Income divided into schedules and cases for income tax purposes. Some tax deducted at source before being paid. Dividends have tax credit of $10/90^{ths}$: non taxpayer cannot recover it; basic rate taxpayer pays no more; higher rate taxpayer pays 32.5%. Deposit account interest and purchased life annuities can be paid gross to non taxpayers.

- *Income tax allowances.* Allowance is income which is tax free.

  ○ *Personal allowance.* For all UK residents. Cannot be transferred. Ownership of income producing assets can be transferred to spouse to use allowance.

  ○ *Age allowance.* For those over 65 - higher personal allowance. For over 75 - even higher allowance. Allowance reduced if gross income exceeds income limit: reduction of £1 for every £2 excess over income limit; entitlement to personal allowance remains.

  ○ *Widow's bereavement allowance.* Applies in year of husband's death and next year if not remarried. Widow can have this allowance in addition to MCA.

  ○ *Redundancy.* Up to £30,000 (including statutory payments) redundancy pay tax free.

- *Sole traders and partners.* Profits taxed even if not drawn. Basis: current year.

- *VAT.* Sales tax added to cost of products and services. Registered business charges and recovers VAT. Unregistered business does not charge and cannot recover. Zero rated supplies charged at 0%. Business must register when income reaches registration limit. VAT return must show tax charged and paid. Payment/Claim made quarterly within one month of quarter.

- *Benefits in kind.* Taxed on employees whose earnings (including value of benefits in kind) are £8,500 or more or who are directors of company - known as P11D employees.

- *Income tax assessment and collection.* Employees taxed under PAYE. Benefits in kind taxed by reducing personal allowance. Self employed taxed on gross profits and taxed in two instalments. Taxpayers can calculate own tax or rely on Revenue; tax payable on account 31 January, 31 July with balance on next 31 January.

- *Inheritance tax.* Basis, rates and gifts with reservation of benefit. Tax on cumulative transfer of assets on death or within seven years of death. Rates: 0% (nil rate band); 40%; half death rate (into discretionary trust). Gift with reservation of benefit not effective for IHT purposes.

- *Exemptions and reliefs*

  ○ *Exemptions not taxable.* Spouse to spouse (non domiciled spouse - limit £55,000). Annual - £3,000, can be carried forward for one year (using current year's exemption first). Small gifts - £250 to any number of people, but not exempt if same donee benefited from annual exemption. Marriage: £5,000 each parent; £2,500 each grandparent etc; £1,000 anyone else. Normal expenditure - regular, from income, standard of living maintained. PETs - may be exempt.

  ○ *Reliefs.* Business property - reduction in value of assets for IHT purposes. Tapering - relief in rate of tax (not in value of gift).

  ○ *Nil rate band.* Taxable transfers, but at 0%; not an exemption.

- *Value of transfers*. Reduction in value of estate. Intention to make a transfer of value. Could be affected by capital gains tax. UK assets only for non domiciled individual.

- *Capital gains tax*. Basis - Sale price less RPI indexed costs of purchase (or value in 1982) less annual exemption. Losses can be set against gains. Indexation cannot be used to create/increase loss. Tapering replaced indexation from 6 April 1998. Different rates of tapering relief apply to business assets and non-business assets. Exemptions include: home; car; National Savings certificates; gilts; winnings; some chattels; most life policies. CGT liability on UK resident taxpayers, companies and partnerships.

- *Mitigating tax liability*. Principles: avoid; reduce; defer; pay.

Quick quiz

1 The name given to the situation where an individual has made his permanent home in a country is:

    A deemed domicile;
    B domicile;
    C ordinarily resident;
    D resident.

2 Age allowance begins at ages:
    A 60 for men and 55 for women;
    B 60 for both men and women;
    C 65 for men and 60 for women;
    D 65 for both men and women.

3 If a single person with no dependants has taxable income of £17,000 in 2000/2001, his or her tax will be:

    A £3,558;
    B £3,740;
    C £2,593;
    D £3,400.

4 If an individual makes a lifetime transfer into a trust, no further inheritance tax will arise if, after making the transfer, the individual lives for at least a further:

    A 5 years;
    B 7 years;
    C 10 years;
    D 12 years.

5 On what value is inheritance tax chargeable?

    A A percentage of the total value of all transfers.
    B All transfers in excess of the nil rate band.
    C The reduction in a donor's estate.
    D The value of a gift in the hands of the donee.

6 Which of the following is subject to capital gains tax?

    A A profit on the sale of a principal private residence.
    B A profit from the sale of antique furniture.
    C Prizes from National Savings premium bonds.
    D A commuted lump sum from a personal pension fund.

The solutions to the questions in the quiz can be found at the end of this Study Text. Before checking your answers against those solutions, you should look back at this chapter and use the information in it to correct your answers.

BPP PUBLISHING

Part B: Financial services background

Answers to questions

1   (a)   Resident - in the UK for six months in one year; ordinarily resident - regularly in the UK an average of three months a year for four years.

    (b)   To establish liability to income tax and capital gains tax.

    (c)   Treated as domiciled for inheritance tax purposes.

2   (a)   E.
    (b)   Annuities; deposit account interest.
    (c)   It gives a marginal rate of 33% (1.5 times the basic rate of tax).

3   (a)   If its turnover is below the registration limit.
    (b)   Income tax on benefits in kind.

4   (a)   Non-UK property will not be taxed unless he was deemed UK domiciled.
    (b)   When a lifetime transfer into a discretionary trust is made.
    (c)   A transfer of assets by a donor who retains an interest in the assets.

5   (a)   Spouse to spouse, annual, small gifts, marriage, normal expenditure.

    (b)   A reduction in the value of a donor's estate.

    (c)   Home, private car, National Savings, gilts, ISAs, PEPs, betting winnings, chattels sold for £6,000 or less, life policies owned by the original owner.

    (d)   To encourage investors to retain assets as long as possible.

    (e)   Any chargeable gain on disposal of a business asset attracts higher taping relief than a non-business asset, and the tapering relief starts to apply within a shorter period of time.

BPP PUBLISHING

Chapter 8

NATIONAL INSURANCE CONTRIBUTIONS

Chapter topic list	Syllabus reference
1 National Insurance contributions	B 3.1
2 Benefits	B 3.2 - B 3.6,
3 Benefits and financial planning	B 3.7

Introduction

In addition to taxes, individuals have to pay National Insurance contributions. In return, they may be entitled to various benefits.

1 NATIONAL INSURANCE CONTRIBUTIONS

1.1 In the UK the state provides a number of different **social security benefits**. The benefits include a pension when we retire, an income if we become unemployed, an income if we are ill, and various other benefits such as maternity payments and income following an industrial injury.

1.2 In order to provide these benefits the state collects **contributions** from most employees, employers and the self employed. The contributions are paid into a pool known as the National Insurance Fund from which benefits are paid.

1.3 Although the word 'fund' is used to describe the collected cash, no attempt is made to accumulate an increasing pool of money from one year to the next. Contributions received by the fund during a year are all paid out in that same year in the form of benefits. This is known as a '**pay as you go**' **system**.

How contributions are organised

1.4 Payments must be made by employers, employees and the self employed to the state's social security system. These payments, known as **National Insurance contributions** (NICs), are used by the state to provide various benefits for individuals.

1.5 The state estimates how much it will need for the various benefits and fixes an appropriate **level of contributions** for the period from 6 April one year to 5 April the following year.

1.6 To obtain a full pension, contributions must be paid for **90% of an individual's working life**. If for any reason someone has not paid contributions to qualify for the maximum pension, extra contributions can be paid voluntarily to buy the extra benefit needed to bring

BPP
PUBLISHING

the total up to the maximum. Apart from these voluntary payments, contributions are normally compulsory for those who have earnings. Others who are not working through sickness or unemployment will be credited with contributions in order to preserve their benefits.

1.7　National Insurance contributions (NICs) are divided into **four groups** according to who pays them and their purpose.

Class 1 NICs

1.8　All employees whose earnings exceed a specific figure must pay **Class 1 contributions**. Their employers must also pay contributions. In both cases the amount is based on a percentage of the employee's earnings.

1.9　**The basic features of NIC**

(a)　If the employee's income is below a certain level, the **lower earnings limit** (LEL), neither the employee nor the employer pays NICs.

(b)　The amount of NICs payable is a percentage of the employee's income.

(c)　The employee pays NICs on a 'middle-band' of income. No NICs are payable by the employee on income:

(i)　Below a **primary threshold** (the primary threshold is higher than the LEL)
(ii)　Above an **upper earnings limit** (UEL)

(d)　The rates of NICs payable by the employer vary according to whether the employer has contracted out of the State Earnings Related Pension Scheme (SERPS) and, if so, what type of scheme the employer has established instead.

(e)　Whereas employees do not pay NICs above the UEL, there is no upper limit on earnings for which employer's NICs are payable. The top rate of employer's NICs is currently 12.2%.

1.10　The rules might seem complex. The following tables might help to clarify them.

Employee's NICs		
Weekly earnings	*Not contracted out*	*Contracted out*
Up to LEL (£67)	Nil	Nil
Between LEL and primary threshold (£67 - £76)	Nil	Rebate 1.6%
Between primary threshold and UEL (£76 - £535)	10%	8.4%
Above UEL (over £535)	Nil	Nil

	Employer's NICs		
Weekly earnings of employee	*Not contracted out*	*Contracted out*	
		COSR	*COMP*
Up to LEL (£67)	Nil	Nil	Nil
Between LEL and a secondary threshold (£67 - £84)	Nil	Rebate 3%	Rebate 0.6%
Between secondary threshold and UEL (£84 - £535)	12.2%	9.2%	11.6%
Above UEL (over £535)	12.2%	12.2%	12.2%

COSR = contracted out salary related scheme
COMP = contracted out money purchase scheme

Class 1A NICs

1.11 If employees receive benefits in kind, such as car and fuel benefits, NICs must be paid by the **employer** (but *not* the employee) based on the benefits. There are some exemptions - for small amounts of private use by an employee of assets owned by the employer, for qualifying beneficial loans, for general welfare counselling provided by the employer and for childcare in a workplace nursery or provided by vouchers.

Class 2

1.12 Contributions are payable by the **self employed** whose earnings exceed a stated figure. The amount payable is a flat rate, not a percentage of earnings.

Class 3

1.13 Individuals who have not paid enough to qualify for all the benefits can voluntarily pay extra to buy the balance of benefits (see earlier paragraph). Class 3 contributions are just that: **voluntary contributions** paid on a flat rate basis per week to make up for the shortfall.

Class 4

1.14 This is a further contribution from the **self employed**. In addition to the flat rate mentioned earlier, if the earnings of a self employed person exceed a specified figure, an extra compulsory contribution is payable.

1.15 The following table shows a **summary of the contributions payable**.

NATIONAL INSURANCE CONTRIBUTIONS

Class	Paid by	Based on	Compulsory/voluntary (C/V)
1 Primary	Employee	Employee's earnings (to limit)	C
Secondary	Employer	Employee's earnings	C
1A	Employer	Benefits in kind to P11D employee	C
2	Self employed	Flat rate	C
3	Employee	Flat rate	V
	Self employed	Flat rate	V
4	Self employed	Limited profits	C

Collection

1.16 Employers pay their own Class 1 and Class 1A contributions together with the contributions of their employees **monthly to the local collector of taxes**. The employees' contributions will have been deducted by the employer from the employees' pay. A collector of taxes passes on the relevant amount of contribution to the Department of Social Security (DSS).

1.17 The self employed pay Class 2 contributions either by **monthly direct debit** or by a **quarterly bill** sent to the Contributions Agency. Class 4 contributions are payable to the Inland Revenue **at the same time as payments of income tax** are made. Class 3 voluntary contributions are **payable direct** to the Contributions Agency.

Tax treatment of contributions

1.18 Contributions paid by employers in respect of their employees are **tax deductible** but the contributions paid by employees are not tax deductible. Consequently **there is no tax relief on employees' NICs.**

1.19 Self employed Class 2 and 4 contributions are **not tax deductible**. However, contributions paid by the self employed in their capacity as *employers* will be deductible.

2 BENEFITS

Exam focus point

It is important in this section *not* to make any attempt to learn the actual rates of State benefit which are payable. This is not a requirement of the syllabus and the examination paper should contain no questions requiring such knowledge.

2.1 State benefits are quite low. You should be aware of this so that you can judge just how important **private provision** for the financial welfare of clients is: the state benefits can be looked upon as an alternative to starvation but not as making adequate provision for individual needs.

2.2 The following sections have been divided according to the **broad grouping of benefits** as follows: family benefits, unemployment benefits, disability benefit, benefit for low incomes, retirement benefit, death benefits.

2.3 Within these categories you will notice that some payments will depend upon having made **adequate National Insurance contributions** and others will not.

Question 1

(a) For how long must a person pay or be credited with National Insurance contributions to be entitled to the full basic state pension?

(b) List the classes of National Insurance contribution and who pays them.

(c) Who is entitled to tax relief on National Insurance contributions?

Family benefits

2.4 Family benefits are divided into two: those related to **having children** (maternity pay and maternity allowance) and those related to **bringing up children** (child benefit and one parent families).

Statutory maternity pay

2.5 **Maternity pay** is a payment made by an employer to a woman who has been employed continuously by the same employer for at least six months. Some of the payment may be recoverable by employers depending on the size of the employing firm. The amount paid will depend upon length of service and earnings. The benefit is paid for a period of up to 18 weeks. The payment for the first six weeks will be 90% of her average earnings. A lower, fixed rate will be paid for the balance of 18 weeks. Although she is not working, the benefit is liable to National Insurance contributions and is taxable.

Maternity allowance

2.6 **Maternity allowance** is payable to a woman who is not entitled to statutory maternity pay but who has recently been employed or self-employed and on whose behalf Class 1 or Class 2 National Insurance contributions have been paid. She will receive a fixed rate for a period of 18 weeks.

Child benefit

2.7 **Child benefit** is payable to a mother who is legally responsible for a child up to the age of 16. This is extended to 19 for a child who is in full time education. The sum paid is a weekly amount for each child. The sum payable is less for second and subsequent children than for the eldest child. Only those claiming before 5th July 1998 may continue to claim this benefit

Child benefit (lone parent)

2.8 This is a weekly payment made to a person (not necessarily the child's parent) who is looking after one or more children. Payment is made in addition to child benefit but is made **only in respect of one child**. Only those claiming before 5 July 1998 may continue to claim this benefit.

Unemployment benefits

2.9 **Unemployment payments** are divided into two: payments on losing your job (redundancy payments) and payments after you have lost a job (Jobseeker's Allowance).

Redundancy payments

2.10 If you have worked for a firm for two years or more you will be entitled to receive a lump sum if you are made redundant. The sum will be payable by your employer.

2.11 The amount of the redundancy payment is determined by three factors: **age, length of continuous employment with the employer** and **weekly gross pay**.

- You must be at least 20 years old and under 65 years old to claim.
- You must have at least two years continuous employment. Service over 20 years is ignored.

You do not need to learn the detailed formula to compute the amount payable, and the following examples are for illustrative purposes only.

Employee age	Maximum payable
20	1 × one weeks pay
30	10 × one weeks pay
40	19 × one weeks pay

2.12 **Additional voluntary payments** may be made by an employer. A sum up to £30,000, including the statutory payments, will be **tax free**.

2.13 A client who has been made redundant needs advice on **what to do with redundancy payments**. The most sensible advice is likely to be to put it on deposit while a long term decision is being taken, but other questions come fairly soon, such as should debts be repaid or should the sum be used to boost retirement benefits?

Jobseeker's Allowance

2.14 When you have lost your job you will usually receive a **flat rate weekly payment** of Jobseeker's Allowance for your first six months of unemployment. A condition is that you are healthy and that you are actively job hunting at the time. After six months you may receive a sum similar to Income Support and subject to similar conditions.

2.15 The family should have **emergency funds** to cope with unexpected contingencies such as unemployment. The existence of an emergency fund does not affect the individual's unemployment benefit although it could have an effect on Income Support.

2.16 The **risk of unemployment** may make it desirable to improve pension provision or long term savings while earnings exist. No allowance is paid if you are in receipt of a company pension as a result of early retirement if the pension is greater than the allowance.

Disability benefits

2.17 The **state disability benefits** are not normally means tested so the existence of private provision such as permanent health insurance or critical illness cover should not adversely affect the level of state benefits. On the other hand, the existence of state benefits will affect the amount of payment made under a permanent health insurance contract.

Statutory Sick Pay

2.18 **Statutory Sick Pay** is a weekly sum paid by an employer for a period of up to 28 weeks excluding the first three days of disability. National Insurance contributions are payable on the benefit, which is taxable.

2.19 Some payments may be **recoverable** by employers. When statutory sick pay comes to an end, incapacity benefit may become payable.

Incapacity benefit

2.20 **Incapacity benefit** is a weekly benefit payable by the DSS. Two rates of benefit are payable.

- Short term incapacity benefit
- Long term incapacity benefit

Different rates apply for those under and over pension age.

The benefit is payable to employees who are not entitled to statutory sick pay, to the self employed and also to the unemployed.

Severe disablement allowance

2.21   This is a weekly payment made after a period of 28 weeks for people who do not qualify for incapacity benefit. There is no time limit for payment. A person must be **incapable of work** in order to qualify for the benefit.

Disabled person's tax credit (DPTC)

2.22   The DPTC was introduced in October 1999. It is intended to encourage people with disabilities to return to or take up work. The benefit is available to persons with a disability who work at least 16 hours a week. The benefit takes the form of a tax credit, administered through the employer's payroll system from 2000/2001. It is similar to working family tax credit in concept: WFTC is described later.

Low incomes

2.23   Benefit for those on **low incomes** falls into two categories: benefit for those working less than 16 hours a week (**Income Support**) and benefit for those working 16 hours per week or more but who also have family responsibilities (**Family Credit**).

Income support

2.24   **Income support** is a weekly payment made to those over 16 who have an inadequate income. A person receiving benefit must be actively trying to obtain work.

Family credit

2.25   As with income support, this is intended to help persons who are on low incomes but who also have **families** to look after. Family Credit is payable if at least one parent is working for 16 hours per week or more. It takes the form of a weekly cash payment to employees and also to the self employed for a period of 26 weeks, which may be extended if needed.

Working family tax credit (WFTC)

2.26   The WFTC was introduced in October 1999. It is intended to provide a **minimum income guarantee** for a family in full time work and ensure that no such family will pay tax unless income exceeds a certain minimum per week. To qualify for WFTC, the family must have at least one member working at least 16 hours a week, and there must be at least one child.

2.27   From 2000/2001, the tax credit is given to the individual through the employer's payroll system. The effect of the tax credit will be that the individual will pay less tax.

There are four possible elements to WFTC.

(a)   A basic tax credit
(b)   Tax credits for each child
(c)   A further tax credit if the claimant works more than 30 hours each week
(d)   A tax credit for families paying for registered child care

The total of tax credits receivable is reduced, however, by 55p for every £1 by which the family's net income exceeds £90.

Retirement benefits

2.28   **Retirement** is dealt with elsewhere in this Study Text.

Death benefits

2.29 Payments are made to **widows** whose husbands have died. Widow's benefits may take the form of either a lump sum (**widow's payment**) or an income. The income can be payable to either a widow with a child to support (**widowed mother's allowance**) or a widow over 45 who does not have a child to support (**widow's pension**).

Widow's Payment

2.30 A lump sum payment of £1,000 is payable to a **widow** on the death of her husband. This payment will not however be made if the widow and her husband were both over State pension age and the husband was receiving state pension.

Widowed Mother's Allowance

2.31 This is a weekly payment for a **widow who is looking after a child up to the age of 16** (19 if in full time education). It will cease when the child reaches the appropriate age.

Widow's Pension

2.32 This is a weekly payment made to a **widow who is over 45 but under 65** and whose widowed mother's allowance has come to an end.

Question 2

(a) For which family benefits is the DSS responsible?

(b) National Insurance contributions are payable on which social security benefits?

---

3 BENEFITS AND FINANCIAL PLANNING

Purpose of the welfare state

3.1 One of the purposes of the British welfare state has been to ensure that none of its citizens fall below **a minimum standard of living**. The method has been to provide each individual with income when it is needed or some other form of financial help in times of difficulty.

3.2 This has been achieved by making available National Insurance benefits which provide **protection against short term hardship** and which provide a **retirement pension** and a **National Health Service**.

3.3 An unintended result of this provision of state benefits has been the expression '**the state will provide**'. It represents a belief by many people that, no matter what misfortune comes their way, the state will rescue them.

3.4 On top of that, changes are taking place in the social security which **reduces** the level of benefits for which the state is responsible. This makes it all the more important for individuals to make provision for their own financial safety and security.

The effect of social security benefits on financial planning

3.5 The existence of social security benefits reduces the need for private provision but not by much. **The benefits are too small to live well on.**

3.6 Imagine that you have clients who are **self employed**. If they were unable to work what state benefits would they receive? What would happen to their business income? What private provision is available which would enable them to solve this problem?

3.7 You may have clients who are financially secure but what about their **children**? If they have children who are over 18 and out of work what benefit would they receive? If the children have partners and do not have enough to live on, what benefit would the state provide and for how long?

3.8 Imagine that you have two completely different clients. One is a company employee on high earnings but with **no pension scheme** and the other is self employed and paying regular contributions into a **personal pension**. Compare the benefits they will receive from the State at retirement. What effect would those state benefits have on their need to make their own financial provision? Think of other clients who have **families**. What benefits would their spouses receive from the state in the event of their death? What effect would those state benefits have on their need for private financial planning?

3.9 In probably all of these cases your conclusion will be that, while State benefits reduce the need for private financial planning, the reduction is not very much. In nearly every case you are likely to find that the **shortfall in their provision is considerable**.

How financial planning affects eligibility for State benefits

3.10 Social security benefits that depend upon the payment of National Insurance contributions are not affected by **private financial planning**. You will be entitled to those benefits as a result of the NI contributions, no matter what private provision you have made.

3.11 This applies also to some of the benefits which do not depend upon paying National Insurance contributions, for example, **child benefit** and **one parent benefit**.

3.12 The state benefits affected by private provision are those which are means tested. In the examples we have looked at there were two - **family credit** and **income support**. The problem with both of these is that even a very modest amount of savings may reduce the income benefit by a level out of all proportion to the value of the assets. State benefits which are means tested are normally lost to anyone who has £8,000 or more.

Retirement

3.13 The state pension may provide reasonably adequate earnings for low earners if it includes the **state earnings related pension scheme**. However, high earners will find that the state pension is much smaller than their final earnings and the drop in income after retirement will be substantial. The self employed, of course, will receive only the basic state pension.

3.14 The **dependants of employees and the self employed are not adequately provided for by the state** and again some form of private provision through a personal pension plan will be highly desirable. It could be worthwhile checking with the DSS what state benefits have been accumulated in order to establish whether Class 3 voluntary National Insurance contributions should be paid.

SOCIAL SECURITY BENEFITS: SUMMARY

Benefit	NI	Taxable	Means tested	Notes
Families				
Statutory maternity pay	Y	Y	N	Paid by employer
Maternity allowance	Y	N	N	
Child benefit	N	N	N	
One parent benefit	N	N	N	
Unemployment				
Jobseeker's Allowance	Y	Y	Y/N	Any increase for a child dependant is tax free
Redundancy payments	N	N	N	Paid by employer. A tax-free limit of £30,000 applies to redundancy payments by an employer, which often exceed the statutory redundancy pay amount.
Disability				
Statutory sick pay	Y	Y	N	Paid by employer
Incapacity benefit	Y	Y	N	Tax free if paid for less than 29 weeks
Severe disablement allowance	N	N	N	
Low income				
Family credit	N	N	Y	
Income support	N	N	Y	
Retirement				
Retirement pension	Y	Y	N	
Death				
Widow's benefits:				
Widow's payment	Y	N	N	
Widowed mother's allowance	Y	Y	N	
Widow's pension	Y	Y	N	

Notes

NI	Benefit depends on record of having paid adequate National Insurance contributions.
Taxable	Taxed as earned income.
Means tested	Benefit depends on level of income and capital. Benefit is reduced if capital exceeds £3,000, and entitlement ceases if capital exceeds £8,000.

The Jobseeker's Allowance is partly income-based (ie means tested) and partly dependent on NI contributions.

Question 3

(a) Which social security benefits are means-tested?
(b) On what conditions is Jobseeker's Allowance payable?
(c) For how long are the different incapacity benefit rates payable?

Chapter roundup

- *National insurance contributions* are paid by employers, employees and self employed.

- *State pension* depends on payment or crediting of contributions for 90% of working life - shortfall can be made up by voluntary contributions.

  ° Class 1 - paid by 'middle' employees (primary contributions) and employers (secondary contributions). Employee contributions based on 'middle' band earnings between primary threshold limit and UEL. Employer contributions depend on whether contracted in or out. There is no upper limit on employer's NICs

  ° Class 1A - paid by employers only on benefits in kind to employees.

  ° Class 2 - flat rate paid by self employed

  ° Class 3 - flat rate voluntary contributions payable by anyone

  ° Class 4 - percentage of profits payable by self employed

- *Employers* pay own and employees' NICs to DSS. Self employed pay Class 2 by direct debit monthly or quarterly to Contributions Agency. Class 3 payable to Contributions Agency. Class 4 payable to Inland Revenue. Employers' NICs are tax deductible. Employees' NICs are not deductible.

- Benefits

  ° *Statutory Maternity Pay.* Made by employer to employee of six months or more; some recoverable.

  ° *Maternity Allowance.* For woman not entitled to statutory maternity pay.

  ° *Child Benefit.* Payable to mother for each child up to 16 or in full time education.

  ° *Child benefit (lone parent).* Weekly payment to parent in addition to child benefit. One amount per parent - not per child.

  ° *Redundancy payments.* Statutory payment by employer based on age band and length of service.

  ° *Jobseeker's Allowance.* Flat rate paid to healthy job hunters for six months.

  ° *Statutory Sick Pay (SSP).* Paid weekly by employer for 28 weeks. NICs are payable on the benefit. Followed by incapacity benefit.

  ° *Incapacity Benefit.* Different rates paid for weeks 1-28, 29-52, and 53 onwards. Payable to employees not entitled to SSP, to self employed and also to unemployed.

  ° *Severe Disablement Allowance.* Weekly payment after 28 weeks to those who do not qualify for incapacity benefit.

  ° *Disabled Person's Tax Credit (DPTC).* Provides tax credits to disabled persons working at least 16 hours a week. Administered through employer's payroll.

  ° *Income Support.* For job hunters over 16 with inadequate income.

  ° *Family Credit.* For low income families with one person working 16 hours or more per week. For employees and self employed.

  ° *Working Family Tax Credit (WFTC).* Provides tax credits to families on low incomes, where at least one of the family is in full-time work. Administered through the payroll of the claimant's employer.

  ° *Widow's Payment.* £1,000 on death of husband. Not payable if both over state pension age and husband receiving pension.

  ° *Widowed Mother's Allowance.* Weekly payment to widow for child up to 16 (or 19 if in full time education).

  ° *Widow's Pension.* Weekly payment to widow between 45 and 65 whose widowed mother's allowance has ended.

- Social security benefits and financial planning

  ° *Purpose of welfare state:* ensure minimum standard of living.

  ° *Effects of social security benefits on financial planning:* reduces need for private provision by minimum amount. Effect of disability on business income of self employed - limited state provision. Unemployed with/without spouse/partners - minimal state benefits. Limited state provision in almost every financial situation.

  ° *Effect of financial planning on eligibility for state benefits.* Means tested benefits - family credit and income support. Check with DSS the entitlement of clients to state pension.

Quick quiz

1   In order to qualify for a statutory redundancy payment, an employee must have been employed by an employer for a period of at least:

   A   12 months;
   B   15 months;
   C   18 months;
   D   24 months.

2   Employees pay income tax and National Insurance contributions (NI) as follows.

   A   Income tax under schedule D and NI under Class I.
   B   Income tax under schedule D and NI under Class IV.
   C   Income tax under schedule E and NI under Class I.
   D   Income tax under schedule E and NI under Class II.

3   An employee who pays Class 1 National Insurance contributions and who is unable because of sickness to work for more than three consecutive days will receive:

   A   Disability benefit
   B   Invalidity allowance
   C   Incapacity benefit
   D   Statutory sick pay

4   Class 2 National Insurance contributions are payable by:

   A   The self employed as a percentage of their profits;
   B   Employees as a percentage of their band earnings;
   C   Employees and the self employed voluntarily;
   D   The self employed at a flat rate.

5   What is the highest lump sum paid by the state on the death of a member of a family?

   A   £500
   B   £1,000
   C   £2,500
   D   £10,000

6   Which of the following statements most accurately describes Class 4 National Insurance contributions?

   A   They are totally deductible for income tax purposes.
   B   The amount is based on all taxable profits.
   C   None of the contribution is tax deductible.
   D   A fixed amount is paid each week.

The solutions to the questions in the quiz can be found at the end of this Study Text. Before checking your answers against those solutions, you should look back at this chapter and use the information in it to correct your answers.

Answers to questions

1   (a)   90% of working life.

      (b)   1 - employers and employees; 1A - employers; 2 - self-employed; 3 - anyone; 4 - self-employed.

      (c)   Employers on Class 1.

2   (a)   Statutory maternity pay, maternity allowance, child benefit, one parent benefit.

      (b)   Statutory maternity pay, statutory sick pay.

3   (a)   Family credit, income support (working families tax credit after October 1999).

      (b)   The individual is healthy and job-hunting.

      (c)   Lower rate: weeks 1-28; middle rate: weeks 29-52; higher rate: after one year.

Chapter 9

FINANCIAL NEEDS

Chapter topic list	Syllabus reference
1 The life stages	B 4.1
2 The requirements and constraints of investment and protection	B 4.1, B 4.2
3 Applying planning criteria to potential needs	B 4.1
4 The need for protection	B 4.2
5 The need for pension provision	B 4.3
6 The need to supplement the state benefits	B 4.4
7 The need to make future provision	B 4.5
8 Employees' remuneration packages	B 4.6
9 The state treatment of the self employed	B 4.7
10 Applying planning principles to the self employed	B 4.7
11 Factors affecting planning needs	B 4.8

Introduction

We have looked in detail at the environment which the financial adviser works in. We will now start to look at how to analyse a client's needs in order to meet those needs. Notice that some of the products referred to in this chapter are explained later in the text.

1 THE LIFE STAGES

1.1 We can identify various **life stages,** with differing financial needs, but remember that there can be infinite variations on them. Two of the **assumptions** made are **not** necessarily valid.

(a) When your client sets up home and has children, he will have married first.
(b) He does not remain single for the whole of his life.

The only reason we make some assumptions in this section is to keep the number of life stages to manageable proportions.

Minors

1.2 If your client is **under 18** he may have very little in the way of financial needs. He is likely to be dependent on one or two parents and nobody is going to suffer financially if his bank balance runs out.

BPP
PUBLISHING

Single and still young

1.3   If your client is in his **early or mid twenties** he will probably not have any dependants. Although there are quite a number of exceptions to this, this is still the situation in most cases.

1.4   He will now be **financially independent** of his parents even if he is still living at home. Alternatively, your client may be renting a flat or possibly even buying a house.

1.5   Your client will probably **not have accumulated any capital** as he would be spending everything that he earns. He is also more likely to be an employee than to be self employed.

Married or cohabiting

1.6   He will have ceased to be dependent on parents at this stage and will be **earning** and either **renting or buying a house**.

Both working but no dependants

1.7   This is the time when a couple will be **building up their income** at the fastest possible rate before the expenses of looking after children begin.

One working with no dependants

1.8   This client's financial life will be a little bit more **fragile**. Dependence upon the earnings of one of the couple increases the possibility of difficulties if there is a fall in the earnings of the one person working.

One working and with dependants

1.9   With all the earnings concentrated in the hands of one of the couple and with there being both a partner and at least one dependant to look after, the **burden of dependency** has now begun to reach its maximum with the welfare of an entire family.

Married or cohabiting with older children

1.10   This is the point when the **expenses are probably at their highest** even without school fees. Higher education costs can increase the burden especially if it takes the form of university. Post-graduate education normally has to be paid for entirely privately.

1.11   The couple may again have **two incomes** and possibly even have a higher net income despite the higher level of expenses.

After children

1.12   When children have left home, their parents have a **higher net income** as a result of lower maintenance expenses.

Retired

1.13   This is the stage when your clients, if they have not planned properly, will once again become **dependent upon others**. Their income will have reduced and although their expenses will have reduced, there is a strong possibility that they will once again be hard up.

1.14 If investments can be cashed at this stage or endowments are maturing, this will certainly reduce the financial difficulties but will not eliminate them unless **adequate advance planning** has taken place.

Employment status

1.15 Your clients at different times throughout their lives may have gone through one or more of three stages of employment - as **employees,** as **self employed** and as **unemployed.** Each category has features which we will examine later.

2 THE REQUIREMENTS AND CONSTRAINTS OF INVESTMENT AND PROTECTION

Minority

2.1 There's not much in the way of financial planning you can do directly for those under 18. Nevertheless, one of their principal assets is their entitlement to the **personal allowance,** and you can demonstrate the use that can be made of this.

Single with no dependants

2.2 Skipping over the stage of being at university where again clients are likely to have little or no resources that require planning, we move to the stage where clients are **in work.**

2.3 If they are earning and are **spending everything they earn** then advice on how to make a long term tax efficient use of their excess income is not likely to be well received.

2.4 Nevertheless, they are beginning to have assets which could benefit from planning, and the first one is a need for cash which is easily accessible in order to handle **financial emergencies.** If they are willing to consider long term investment then they are certainly at an age where a modest level of saving started now can build up to a reasonable amount over many years.

2.5 They must nevertheless be careful **not to make too great a long term commitment** in case they have a greater need for funds later on. This is likely to happen if they want to buy a house.

2.6 It would be beneficial to start making plans at this age for **retirement**; nevertheless it is not a priority. **Disability protection** could be considered but probably the top priority is beginning **to build up a capital base.**

Married or cohabiting

Both working but no dependants

2.7 If both clients are renting property and intend to stay that way there is probably little need for life assurance. If they are intending to purchase a property later on the prime need is likely to be **to build up sufficient for a deposit.**

2.8 They will probably have some need for **life assurance** especially to repay the loan in the case of the death of one of them.

2.9   **Disability cover** becomes more important because even if they are renting and not intending to buy a property a secure income during long term disability will remove the pressure for them to move to a lower cost property.

One working but no dependants

2.10   In this situation whilst the **couple** have no joint dependants the one who is earning certainly does. They may now be facing constraints on their income but at the same time they will also face a real need to consider some form of **protection for disability or death**. If they have not already made **wills** they should certainly do so in view of the consequences of dying intestate.

2.11   They may also be able to make use of the **personal allowance of the partner who is not working** by transferring income earning investments. Having said that, the reality is that very early in a relationship may be too early to share assets for tax purposes. Even much later in their lives, couples may not wish to hand over assets to the other for tax purposes.

One working with dependants

2.12   The requirements of each of the previous stages still apply here but have increased. There is a greater need for **protection following disability or death** and, if the couple are considering sending their children to fee-paying schools, it is never too soon to start working out the consequences of that objective. The possibility of two incomes again would be a plus factor but the high expenses of having older children may wipe out the advantage of the extra income. In fact it is always possible that one partner could return to work specifically in order to pay for the costs of education for older children. In particular, **grandparents** could pass income to a minor who would not be liable to tax if the income was within the personal allowance.

2.13   If they have begun to acquire sufficient resources in order to invest then this could be the time to **assess their attitude to risk** and their need for accessibility together with their **long term investment objectives**.

After children

2.14   This group will have opportunities for **investment** which may not have existed until they have reached this stage. They will also be in a position to consider whether or not their **retirement provision** is adequate and whether they should be considering action to pass on some of their wealth to their children.

2.15   They should be able to take the maximum advantage of **tax efficient investments** and review the portfolio of existing investments. This may be particularly necessary if they have accumulated a large number of small shareholdings, particularly privatisation issues.

Retired

2.16   The rules now change considerably. The years of earning an income will be over and the need now will be to obtain the **maximum income from existing resources**. The income producing capacity will be limited by the investments that they already have or those to which they can switch.

Question 1

(a) What are the possible financial needs of a married or cohabiting couple with dependants, where only one of the couple is earning?

(b) What tax factor can enable grandparents to pass income tax-free to a minor?

3   APPLYING PLANNING CRITERIA TO POTENTIAL NEEDS

3.1   The two questions which you could usefully put to your clients are

- If you take no action what will be the consequences?
- How can you best plan and protect for your future financial planning needs?

3.2   The prime financial planning objective is to **make recommendations which suit a client's needs**. Strictly speaking needs may not always mean that the client is conscious of some financial disability unless the need is catered for. It can simply mean that even if clients do not have pressing requirements, you can nevertheless improve their financial position.

Minority

3.3   The entitlement of a minor to the **personal allowance** can enable parents and grandparents to divert taxable income to the minor in order to use up the tax allowance. This is achieved by gifting income earning assets to minors. However, income arising from assets given by a *parent* to minor children is still taxed as the parent's income if it exceeds £100 a year.

Single with no dependants

3.4   Your single clients who are earning will certainly be paying tax. Their need for accessible assets can be met by putting some of their **surplus cash on deposit** with banks or building societies. They can **minimise their tax by using ISAs**. If they need to withdraw the cash they will lose the tax advantage but this may be a risk worth taking, even if the interest rate on an ISA is lower than on an ordinary deposit account.

3.5   Their prime need will be for income, and the possibility of its stopping through long term disability can be substantially provided for by **permanent health insurance**.

3.6   The need for resources to fall back on in the event of **redundancy** can be catered for by the deposit account referred to earlier.

Married or cohabiting

3.7   The need for an **emergency fund** to handle such financial threats as redundancy is increased by the need also to maintain income during and following disability. Loss of earnings through illness can again be catered for by **permanent health insurance**.

3.8   If they are getting married or are planning to at some time in the future, this gives an opportunity for parents and grandparents to take advantage of one of the **inheritance tax exemptions** and make gifts in consideration of marriage up to the current limits.

Both working with no dependants

3.9 The prime need is for **disability cover** but now **life assurance** also becomes important. If resources are limited then term assurance will provide cheap life cover and convertible term assurance will preserve future insurability.

3.10 The loss of income will be the major problem in the event of **death** of one of the partners and this can be resolved by **family income benefit**.

3.11 **Long term retirement needs** should now start coming to the fore and clients should take account of their existing pension arrangements and review their likely retirement needs.

One working with dependants

3.12 All the considerations of the previous groups still apply but there is now an increased need to consider the effect on their financial position in the event of the **disability or death of the non earning partner**. Again family income benefit may be a suitable contract in addition to cover to protect a mortgage.

Married or cohabiting with older children

3.13 **Higher education** may be playing havoc with finances at this stage. The chances are your clients will be helping their children financially if they are going through university and if any post graduate education becomes necessary, the costs of that will probably defer any sensible financial planning until it is all over.

3.14 Nevertheless, if there is surplus income and the maximum advantage has not already been taken of **tax free investments** such as ISAs then now is the time to do so.

3.15 They will probably be paying tax at a fairly high level, possibly at higher rates, and the need to **minimise tax** must be balanced with the need at this stage to have **access to income**. However, it may be possible to make long term planning for retirement through **additional pension provision**.

After children

3.16 At this stage the constraints on financial planning are beginning to fall away and the only limitation may be that of **time**.

3.17 They will now want to make the maximum provision for **building up capital**, from which some of their future retirement income may come. A unit trust portfolio should be considered, as asset based investments will act as a greater protection against inflation. If they have sufficient resources then a balanced direct share portfolio could be considered. They will probably have unearned income available to divert into the building up of capital.

3.18 If one of the partners is a higher rate taxpayer while the other is taxed at the basic rate consideration should be given to **transferring income** producing assets from the higher rate taxpayer to the basic rate taxpayer.

Retired

3.19 Under normal circumstances they will now suffer a drop in income because they will have suffered a drop in earnings. **Investment income** will of course continue through retirement.

3.20 Their mortgage will under normal circumstances have been repaid and if it was on an endowment basis there may well be **maturing endowments** which provide a surplus which can now be invested to produce retirement income.

3.21 Their need for income could be partly met by the purchase of **purchased life annuities** but, in view of the irreversible commitment that these involve, the long term effect on income must be very carefully considered before recommending this step.

3.22 They will increasingly be looking for **security in investments** and a review of the portfolio would be useful, probably moving the emphasis towards more secure investments such as National Savings or gilts.

3.23 They will certainly be more likely to **need medical help** and may need to make use of medical insurance cover.

3.24 If they are eligible for **age allowance** they must take care to avoid the higher marginal rate which can result from a reducing age allowance. Placing funds in non income producing assets may be useful for this purpose.

3.25 The topic of **employment status** is being treated separately as it applies to **all the stages of life** except that of minority and the retired.

Employees

3.26 An employee whose employer provides no pension has an obvious need to consider the best way of making **long term provision for retirement**. If the employer also makes no provision for **life cover** or **disability insurance** then these too need to be considered. If the employer does not pay salary for a period (usually not more than six months) of disability then the need arises immediately the disability begins.

Employee in occupational pension scheme

3.27 An employee who is a member of an **occupational pension scheme** still needs to consider whether or not the scheme is adequate. If it provides less than maximum permitted benefits then additional voluntary contributions could be considered to make up for the shortfall.

3.28 An employee who has **changed jobs frequently** needs to look at the effect on retirement income.

Self-employed (sole traders and partner)

3.29 Sole traders **or partners** in a partnership have no long term provision made for them other than through the basic state pension as the self-employed have no entitlement to SERPS. Disability protection provided by the state incapacity benefit is also limited. They therefore need to consider the best way of **accumulating retirement income** and of **protecting their income** in the event of long term disability.

3.30 If a self employed person has a business in which the spouse can be employed then, on the assumption that the spouse would not otherwise be employed, this will enable the **spouse** to take advantage of the personal allowance. Remember that an occupational pension can be provided for a spouse employee even though the employer is either self employed or a partnership.

Question 2

(a) What are the most likely financial needs of a single person with no dependants?
(b) What financial planning opportunities may apply to a couple whose children are independent?
(c) What particular planning opportunities are available to employees?

Summary of financial planning criteria

3.31 The following is a summary of the principal criteria to be used when advising on a client's future needs.

(a) Are there any **anticipated future expenses**, for example:

 (i) School fees
 (ii) The need to save for a deposit on a house purchase?

(b) Has a **will** been made?

(c) Have all **available tax factor**s been taken into account, for example:

 (i) Using personal or married couple's allowance

 (ii) Transferring income-producing assets to a lower rate tax payer

 (iii) Can marriage gifts be made by parents and grandparents

 (iv) Can tax advantage be taken of ISAs and National Savings

 (v) Might a client face higher marginal rate tax through losing age allowance

 (vi) Has advantage been taken of tax treatment of pensions and medical insurance for the over 60s?

(d) Has maximum **use been made of available capital** such as:

 (i) Tax free lump sum from a pension scheme
 (ii) Free equity in a house?

(e) Have other factors been taken into account, such as the following?

 (i) Is there maximum **flexibility in investments**, including accessibility?

 (ii) How **efficient** are the investments? For example does the client have both a large mortgage and even larger sums on deposit making loan repayment worth considering?

 (iii) If the client wants **growth**: are the investments primarily in assets rather than on deposit as long term asset backed investments produce more capital growth than deposits?

 (iv) Does the client want **investment growth or income**?

 (v) Are the investments producing a **real rate of return**?

 (vi) Is the client concerned with **protecting capital or income**?

 (vii) Is the client a **cautious or adventurous investor**?

 (viii) Is the client obtaining the **maximum benefits from employment**?

 (ix) What is the client's **level of affordability**?

 (x) In prioritising needs, does the client need to consider whether to **reduce one expense in order to fund another**?

BPP
PUBLISHING

4 THE NEED FOR PROTECTION

4.1 In understanding the need for protection the prime question is 'what will be the consequences of no action?'

Death

4.2 The inevitable consequence of death will be a **loss of earnings**. If there are dependants then the survivors may have difficulty in making ends meet. This applies particularly to a person who is bringing up children.

4.3 If there are outstanding debts such as a mortgage it may no longer be possible to continue paying the interest on the mortgage and ultimately this could mean a **forced sale of a house**.

4.4 If the person who dies is the non-earner then there could be a substantial increase in expenses for the survivor in **paying for services previously performed by the person who has died**.

Disability

4.5 When a person becomes disabled then, if the disability is severe enough, there will be a **loss of earnings** from employment or, for the self employed, a loss of profits and possibly even the **total loss of a business**. The effect of looking after dependants will be the same as on death except that the disabled person might themselves have become dependent.

4.6 **Additional expenses** could be incurred in looking after such a person on either a part time or full time basis and costs may be incurred on restructuring a house if the disability is severe enough.

4.7 There will be **no disability benefit** normally payable under a life policy unless the limited cover of critical illness has been included or waiver of premium has been insured. State benefits offer little more than survival.

Redundancy

4.8 The loss of earnings which follows redundancy will be only partially replaced by **state benefits**, which again represent little more than survival. There will be no payment under life assurance policies nor on disability contracts. The only payments are likely to be those under a short term mortgage related redundancy protection contract.

5 THE NEED FOR PENSION PROVISION

5.1 Once again, the question which has to be asked is 'what are the consequences of taking no action?' People who have no private pension provision are likely to have a fairly miserable retirement. Although you occasionally come across someone who is receiving only the state pension and who is able to live quite happily on it, there are very often other factors that are helping and which have to be taken into account, such as help that they receive from relatives or that they are living in subsidised accommodation.

5.2 Retired people need to consider not only their level of income when they first retire but what their needs will be when, over the years, **inflation** has progressively eaten into the value of the pound.

5.3   People sometimes say that they cannot put money on one side for retirement as they cannot **afford** it. On the basis that at retirement their income will go down well below what it is at the present moment, they will then be even less able to exist.

5.4   There will be a need for house owners to meet the costs of **maintaining and repairing their property**. Furnishings will wear out and they may need to spend every penny of their income simply in attempting to exist.

5.5   The problem is solved with **advance planning**, through increasing contributions to provide occupational pension scheme benefits, paying personal pension contributions, or accumulating capital through investments such as ISAs for use in buying annuities.

6   THE NEED TO SUPPLEMENT THE STATE BENEFITS

6.1   We have already seen that the state benefits are at little more than **survival level**. Those who will suffer principally from this fact fall mostly into three categories.

People with no plans

6.2   The first category comprises those who have made **no plans at all for pension provision** and who have **not been in any company pension scheme**. They are the ones who, perhaps, could have done some planning and will eventually pay the costs of not doing so.

Job changers

6.3   Job changers will not necessarily realise the effect that **frequent changing of jobs** can have on their occupational pension scheme entitlement. Consequently at retirement the fall in their income could be much greater than they realise.

High earners

6.4   The state pension will provide only a tiny fraction of the pre-retirement income of somebody who previously was receiving high earnings. If such a person has no pension provision, especially a self employed person who has not considered retirement income, then they will receive a **fairly devastating shock at retirement**.

7   THE NEED TO MAKE FUTURE PROVISION

7.1   If your clients have made no provision whatever for their future financial needs then in many cases the inevitable consequence will be a **severe restriction on their choice of action**.

7.2   If they are unable to meet their living expenses because they have incurred debts and consequently are paying **interest on loans**, they will have little choice but to restrict themselves very severely on their personal expenses.

7.3   If they have not planned in advance for the private education of their children, then when the time comes for sending the children to fee-paying schools they will be faced with a choice. The choice will be either **not sending them at all**, **paying out of income** or **borrowing** in order to pay fees. Once again, borrowing will incur interest charges which may place a restriction on the family's other activities.

7.4 If you want to buy a house you will normally have to pay some money as a **deposit**. If you do not have that deposit and money for solicitors' fees, etc. you cannot normally buy a house. Consequently some form of **savings** is necessary in order to get on to the 'first rung' of the property owning ladder.

7.5 It makes sense to put money into an **emergency fund** in order to cope with unexpected expenses such as the need to make repairs to a house. If there is a substantial repair such as a new roof then it can be very expensive indeed. Failure to make such repairs can lead to longer term damage to a house.

7.6 If an employee wishes to become **self employed** then capital will be necessary in order to take that step. This will mean that the employee should be saving money over a period of time in order to provide for a base for beginning a period of being self employed.

8 EMPLOYEES' REMUNERATION PACKAGES

8.1 Not many employees have the opportunity to choose their **remuneration package**. Some employers have introduced a 'pick and mix' arrangement whereby a 'cafeteria menu' contains a list of benefits and employees may select the benefits they prefer within well defined limits.

8.2 Thus, an employee may have the option **in addition to salary** to benefit from pension contributions, private medical insurance, permanent health insurance, luncheon costs, a company car and other benefits.

8.3 The total value of the benefits will be **limited**.

8.4 For employees who do not have such a choice of remuneration package there can still, nevertheless, be considerable scope for planning. Pensions can be increased by means of **additional voluntary contributions**, and **share options** or **profit sharing schemes** may be available giving employees an interest in the company for which they work.

8.5 If an employee works for a company that provides no pension then the employee may be able to persuade the employer to reduce the employee's salary in return for paying into an occupational pension scheme an amount equal to the salary reduction - a **salary sacrifice scheme**.

9 THE STATE TREATMENT OF THE SELF EMPLOYED

9.1 The state treatment of the **self employed** is very limited.

9.2 The self employed are entitled to the **basic state pension** and to **incapacity benefit**.

9.3 Self employed people pay **Class 4 National Insurance contributions** even though they have already earned their state pension and incapacity entitlement by the payment of **Class 2 contributions**. Thus the Class 4 contributions represent an additional tax which produces no additional benefit.

10 APPLYING PLANNING PRINCIPLES TO THE SELF EMPLOYED

10.1 Many of the financial planning principles which apply to the self employed have already been dealt with earlier in this chapter. Contributions to pension plans are not paid on their behalf: **they must themselves pay such contributions**.

10.2 In the same way that an employee should build up a fund to prepare for redundancy should it occur, so a self employed person should build up a fund in order to prepare for the effects of a **recession** or simply a **drop in demand** for the products or services provided.

10.3 The self employed can take advantage of the **tax shelter** available through personal pensions and, where appropriate, by employing a spouse in their business. The tax shelter of a personal pension can of course be increased by taking advantage of the carry forward and carry back rules.

11 FACTORS AFFECTING PLANNING NEEDS

11.1 One of the biggest factors which affects planning needs is **inflation**. The cost of living is going up all the time.

11.2 Inflation therefore means that our clients' needs must be **continually reviewed** as, quite apart from any other reason, the continuing fall in the value of the pound reduces the value of provision which has already been made. It does not, of course, nullify the arrangements but simply makes it necessary for them to be continually reviewed.

11.3 The constant desire of everybody to increase their standard of living in itself impacts upon their need for higher earnings, higher investment income and greater capital from which to obtain that investment income. This makes it all the more important to ensure that clients are using the most **tax efficient route** to achieve most of their financial needs.

11.4 The desire to pass on wealth to the following generations can have an effect on the **form of investments**. It is virtually impossible to plan to pass wealth in a tax efficient way for a couple whose only substantial asset is the house that they live in. However, other assets may be disposed of annually in a way which not only makes full use of the capital gains tax exemption but which also makes use of the annual exemption for inheritance tax purposes.

11.5 Investments which are placed in **trust** on behalf of children and grandchildren will be tax free after seven years and all growth will take place outside the estate.

11.6 In the event that inheritance tax cannot be avoided altogether then some form of financial provision via **life assurance** will be necessary to fund the residual liability.

Question 3

(a) List the principal financial planning criteria.
(b) What are the main financial effects of death?
(c) What are the main financial problems of retirement?
(d) What items might be included in an employee remuneration package in addition to salary?

BPP PUBLISHING

Chapter roundup

- Life stages

  ° *Minority*. Few financial needs under 18.

  ° *Single and still young*. Independent but no dependants. Perhaps renting flat, probably not house buying.

  ° *Married or cohabiting*. Earning, and buying or renting home. Both working but no dependants - building up income at fastest rate. One working with no dependants - any financial set back serious through dependence on one set of earnings. One working and with dependants - dependency beginning to reach maximum. With older children - expenses at highest, two incomes possible. After children - higher net income and lower expenses. Retired - could be dependent upon others.

- Requirement and constraints of investment and protection

  ° *Minority*. Parents can maximise children's use of personal allowance.

  ° *Single with no dependants.* May need state unemployment benefits. Need for emergency fund. Can begin saving for house purchase or long term savings. Retirement savings beneficial but not a priority.

  ° *Married or cohabiting.* Both working but no dependants: savings for house purchase; life cover to repay mortgage; disability protection. One working but no dependants; protection for death/disability needed; make will; consider transfer of income producing investments to maximise allowances. One working with dependants; need for protection on disability/death; consider school fees objective; assess attitude to risk for investments plus need for accessibility and long-term objectives. After children: opportunities for investment; consider adequacy of retirement income; consider tax efficiency of investments; review portfolio of investments. Retired - maximise income from capital.

- Applying planning criteria to potential needs

  ° *Minority*. Use personal allowance. Parents/Grandparents divert income to minor. Care regarding tax effect of income from parent donated assets.

  ° *Single with no dependants*. Emergency fund on deposit. Minimise tax with ISAs. PHI for disability protection.

  ° *Married or cohabiting*. One or both working with no dependants: emergency fund for redundancy; IHT exemptions for marriage gifts; need for disability and life cover - possible at minimum cost; long term retirement needs - review existing pension arrangements. One working with dependants: consider need for death/disability protection. Married or cohabiting with older children: higher education costs may limit spare resources; make maximum use of ISAs; consider balance of need to minimise tax with need for access to income; consider retirement planning. After children: build up capital for retirement income; unit trust portfolio and direct share portfolio; consider transfer of assets to maximise allowances and/or transfer of MCA. Retired: mortgage repaid; consider purchased life annuities; adjustment of investments towards greater security; consider medical insurance; take care over loss of age allowance.

- Employment status

  ° *Employees*. No occupational pension: consider retirement provision; consider death and disability benefits. Occupational pension: is it adequate? consider AVCs; consider effect of frequent job changing.

  ° *Sole traders/partners*. No long term provision other than basic state pension. Consider retirement provision. Consider disability and death protection. Can spouse be employed in business to use allowance?

- *Financial planning criteria*. Check for all clients.

- Understanding need for protection

  ° *Death.* Loss of earnings. Outstanding debts. Loss of services of non-earning spouse/partner. Purchase of share(s) in partnership/company.

  ° *Disability.* Loss of earnings/profits/business. Additional care expenses.

  ° *Redundancy.* Loss of earnings. Possible short term payments under mortgagee related redundancy protection contract.

- Understanding need to supplement state benefits

  ° *No plans.* Only limited income.
  ° *Job changers.* Effect on retirement income - large fall.
  ° *High earners.* Substantial fall in retirement income.

- *Need to make future provision.* Restriction on choice of expenditure: difficulty in meeting school fees without planning - no school or loan; no house deposit - no house; no emergency fund - no solutions; no capital - limited choice of action.

- *Employees' remuneration packages.* Some employees can choose package. Pension can be increased by AVCs. Capital increase by share options. Salary sacrifice scheme can be considered.

- *Understand the state treatment of the self employed.* Entitled to basic state pension and incapacity benefit. Self employed Class 4 NICs do not increase state benefits.

- *Apply planning principles to the self employed.* No benefits unless self organised. Build up capital for recession or fall in demand. Tax shelter through personal pensions using carry forward/carry back.

- *Factors affecting planning needs.* Inflation. Wish to increase standard of living. Pass on wealth.

Quick quiz

1   Arabella is 21 years of age, single and works as an assistant in a supermarket. Which of the following financial needs is she most likely to have?

   A   A deferred guaranteed annuity to provide a retirement income.
   B   An investment bond to provide tax efficient long term savings.
   C   A level term assurance to provide cheap life cover.
   D   An emergency fund for unexpected expenses.

2   Ian is aged 27, single, living in a flat, and employed in clerical work with a local company. One of his principal financial needs is likely to be for:

   A   whole life assurance to pay inheritance tax on his death;
   B   an emergency fund to cope with unexpected expenses;
   C   convertible term assurance to provide a sum for his parents;
   D   National Savings guaranteed income bonds for secure income.

3   Brian and Christine are cohabiting in a rented house so that they can move easily to another part of the country, as their work requires them to move frequently. They are both working for the same company. They have no children. Which of the following is likely to be their most important need?

   A   Transferring the married couple's allowance to reduce their tax.

   B   Joint life unit-linked endowment to save for future house purchase.

   C   Building up a capital base to provide future security.

   D   Regular premium with-profits endowments to save for possible school fees if they have children.

BPP
PUBLISHING

4   Edward and Glenda are a retired couple in their early 70s. Edward's gross income in 2000/01 from pensions and investments is expected to be £15,900. He has just won a substantial sum on the National Lottery, and is considering investing most of it in gilts bought at a post office. Why should he consider an alternative investment?

A   There is a risk that maturity values may fall short of the sums promised.
B   The interest rate will depend on continuing tax revenue to be maintained at its initial level.
C   Basic rate income tax will be deducted from the coupon before it is paid.
D   The coupon could effectively be taxed in part at 33% instead of 20%.

5   George and Elsie are married. Elsie is unemployed, but George is employed and a member of his company's money purchase occupational pension scheme. The fund's performance is not good, and George has asked you what he should do. Ignoring charges, you could advise him to:

A   contribute to the company's in-house AVC scheme;
B   contribute to a free-standing AVC scheme;
C   make regular contributions to a personal pension plan;
D   ask the employer to agree to a salary sacrifice scheme to boost his benefits.

6   Why is it important to make a will?

A   To reduce inheritance tax by stating who should benefit from your estate.
B   To avoid legal costs which only arise on intestacy.
C   To ensure that tax-exempt investments such as PEPs and ISAs are inherited by taxpayers.
D   To ensure your estate is distributed as you wish on death.

The solutions to the questions in the quiz can be found at the end of this Study Text. Before checking your answers against those solutions, you should look back at this chapter and use the information in it to correct your answers.

Answers to questions

1   (a)   Protection on death or disability of either or both of the couple; possible fees for school; possibility of resources for saving or investment.

      (b)   The personal allowance.

2   (a)   Emergency fund for redundancy; protection of income through disability insurance.

      (b)   Build up capital; invest lump sums in collective investments and possibly directly in equities; prepare for retirement; transfer assets to transfer income; transfer married couple's allowance.

      (c)   AVCs; personal pensions (if no occupational scheme); employing spouse if employee is director/owner of company.

3   (a)   Future expenses; will; tax factors; free capital; flexibility/efficiency of investments; growth or income objectives; rate of investment return; protection of capital/income; client's risk profile; employment benefits; priorities.

      (b)   Loss of earnings; paying debts; additional expenses.

      (c)   Continuing expenses - house maintenance, wear and tear on furnishings, inflation.

      (d)   Pension contributions, private medical insurance, permanent health insurance, luncheon costs, company car, profit sharing.

Chapter 10

GATHERING AND ANALYSING CLIENT INFORMATION

Chapter topic list	Syllabus reference
1 Gathering and analysing information	B 5.1
2 Recording details	B 5.2
3 The analysis of circumstances	B 5.3
4 Practice in advising a client	B 5.4
5 Applying the major factors	B 5.5

Introduction

We have now looked at clients' needs in general terms. In this chapter we will move on to obtaining the information which will enable us to identify a particular client's needs.

1 GATHERING AND ANALYSING INFORMATION

1.1 You will be well aware of the need to possess a lot of information about your client before you can give them advice. This need is of course reflected in one of the basic requirements of the Financial Services Act to '**know your customer**'.

1.2 The process of obtaining this information is not only essential in ensuring that you give suitable advice; it can also reveal areas where you can help your clients. The first stage is to know the *essential* **information**. What is essential may sometimes seem to be limitless but even the most obvious of information can have benefits.

1.3 For example, the client's **address** - obviously necessary for the purposes of correspondence - may be useful in revealing a different country of residence or domicile, although it is more likely that this information will be revealed through a specific question.

1.4 Details of a client's **children** may produce contacts which could lead to further business. Information regarding a client's **financial advisers**, such as accountant and stockbroker, can help you to establish contacts which will widen the circle of people who are aware of your services.

1.5 Information regarding whether or not your client is a **controlling director** may open up the possibility of providing a service for the client's co-directors or for the staff of the company.

1.6 Initially, however, the job is simply to obtain **all relevant information**. Although the question of what is relevant may be subjective it is unlikely that you can safely omit any of the information which follows. You may well think of other items which should be included but the following will be a guide.

Personal details

(a) Name, address and age of client. Age is useful knowledge for some investments, eg PEPs, ISAs and National Savings and also for tax purposes, eg entitlement to age allowance, but mostly it is valuable for life assurance purposes and pension provision.

(b) National Insurance number and tax office. Useful for establishing the source of official information.

(c) Marital status - useful for establishing protection needs and for tax purposes.

(d) Health - useful for protection needs, for life and disability cover.

Family details

Dependants - age and, for adult children, marital status

Employment details

(a) Occupation
(b) Controlling director
(c) Employed by whom?
(d) Self employed

Financial advisers

(a) Bank manager
(b) Accountant
(c) Stockbroker
(d) Solicitor

Financial details

(a) **Assets**

   (i) Cash (liquid assets, eg bank accounts, deposit accounts)

   (ii) *Used*

      (1) House
      (2) Furniture
      (3) Personal belongings
      (4) Car

   (iii) *Invested*

      (1) Equities (revealing whether client is cautious or adventurous or has short term or long term needs or an active or passive investment approach)

      (2) How tax efficient are the investments?

      (3) Building society accounts

      (4) National Savings

      (5) Unit trusts and bonds

(b) **Liabilities**

   (i) Mortgage: details and repayment method. (Details can reveal whether a re-mortgage can be arranged more cheaply, but the client needs to take care regarding any penalties on re-mortgage.)

   (ii) Other liabilities

The asset and liabilities information will now enable you to assess your client's net worth.

(c) **Income**

   (i) *Earnings*

      (1) Employee - salary plus other remuneration package

      (2) Self employed - profits

   (ii) *Investment income*

      (1) Interest

      (2) Dividends

      (3) Rents

   (iii) *Pensions*

      (1) State

      (2) Occupational

      (3) Personal

      (4) Annuities

(d) **Expenditure**

   (i) Living expenses (these should be itemised so that nothing is missed)

   (ii) Mortgage interest

   (iii) School fees

   (iv) Regular savings

   (v) Expenditure on life assurance

(This will enable you to establish whether there is a surplus or a shortfall on income.)

(e) **Protection.** Full details of life cover and disability insurance

(f) **Pensions**

   (i) Details of any occupational pension scheme including life/sickness/medical cover

   (ii) Any personal pensions

   (iii) Any preserved pensions

   (iv) Any transferred pensions

(g) **Existing arrangements**

   (i) Has a will been made?

   (ii) What are its main provisions?

   (iii) When was it last reviewed?

   (iv) Have any gifts been made in the last seven years?

   (v) Are there any anticipated legacies?

Client's attitudes

1.7 (a) What is the client's **attitude to existing savings**/investment/protection?

   (b) Are they **sufficient**?

   (c) Are they **suitable**?

   (d) Have they been **reviewed recently**?

   (e) Is the level of **investment risk acceptable** to a client?

(f)   Is the client prepared to accept **more or less risk**?

(g)   Are there any **constraints** on investment, eg ethical investments?

(h)   Does the client consider that the **existing investments meet current needs**?

(i)   **Do you consider that they meet current and existing needs?** (Remember that with long term contracts such as life policies, surrender is not precluded but it must be recommended only when such a course is obviously suitable. This is likely to happen in very few cases except perhaps with term assurance where better terms may be obtained if premium rates have fallen.)

Client's objectives

1.8   The **client's objectives and expected liabilities** should be considered under headings such as:

(a)   Is the client expecting to buy **property** or move house or incur expenses for school fees or change jobs or buy a car or face major repairs?

(b)   What is the client's **timespan** for investments, ie short term or long term or both?

(c)   How **accessible** must the client's funds be?

(d)   What is the client's **current and future tax position**?

(e)   Are the client's needs for **income or growth** or both?

(f)   Does the client want any **personal involvement** in the direction of investment?

Question 1

What are the principal areas of information you are likely to need before advising a client?

---

2   RECORDING DETAILS

2.1   It is essential that the information given in the previous section should be **recorded carefully and meticulously**. The standard method of doing this is the use of a questionnaire designed to ensure that all relevant information is sought. This questionnaire has become known as the **fact find**.

2.2   All advisers should make use of a **comprehensive fact find**. As stated earlier this can be used as a means of expanding business but it is also important from the compliance point of view. It ensures that a proper record is kept, that information was sought from a client, that it was either given or refused and, combined with documents recording recommendations made to a client, can confirm that the advice given to the client was sound and suitable.

2.3   An exception to the requirement to complete a fact find applies to **friendly society investment contracts** with premium levels of not more than £50 a year (£1 a week) for which fact finds are not required. This applies both to friendly societies and IFAs.

3   THE ANALYSIS OF CIRCUMSTANCES

Present circumstances

3.1   The analysis of a client's current circumstances begins with a form of **accounts**. These should show a list of the client's assets and liabilities, and reveal whether there is a surplus or a deficit. It should include an income and expenditure account to reveal whether there is surplus income or a shortfall. If there is a surplus it will enable the client to put into effect at least some of any recommendations which involve an additional outlay. If it shows a shortfall it reveals the need for the client to take action not to increase liabilities and perhaps to reduce existing liabilities.

3.2   **Current income** needs should be measured and this will enable you to check whether or not the protection against death and disability is adequate to meet those needs.

Future circumstances

3.3   You must also analyse the client's possible **changing circumstances**. What are the consequences, for example, of moving to another house or a prospective job change or children approaching fee paying school age? If the client is employed and is planning to become self employed, are any arrangements in hand for replacing company group life and disability cover with personal life and disability cover? Are arrangements in hand to ensure that finance is available to enable the move to take place?

4   PRACTICE IN ADVISING A CLIENT

4.1   When the fact find has been completed, the method by which current and future needs can be **evaluated** is made much easier. You have all the information necessary regarding the client and you can quantify a client's protection needs against the existing provision and compare future income needs against expectations.

4.2   You can also assess the client's current and future **tax position** and evaluate the tax efficiency of existing investments.

4.3   After all this has been done, the chances are that **most clients will not be able to achieve all their objectives**. This will mean prioritising their objectives according to their resources.

5   APPLYING THE MAJOR FACTORS

5.1   For the purpose of applying the major factors which are relevant to formulating recommendations, we will use a **summary of the financial planning process** which needs to be followed from the time of the initial contact with the client to the point when a recommendation is made.

5.2   The six stages in the financial planning process are as follows.

(a)   Obtaining relevant information, ie completion of a **fact find.**
(b)   Establishing and agreeing the client's **financial objectives.**
(c)   **Processing and analysing the data** produced on the fact find.
(d)   **Formulating recommendations** in a comprehensive plan with objectives.
(e)   **Implementing the recommendations** as agreed with the client.
(f)   **Reviewing and regularly updating** the plan.

BPP PUBLISHING

Fact find

5.3 An adviser must take into account all the **regulatory compliance requirements** which apply before dealing with the client (such as giving a business card and terms of business letter) through the process to the stage where recommendations are given, when the reasons for those recommendations are required.

Objectives

5.4 The next stage is to establish with the client what are the client's **financial objectives**. This should cover all the possibilities which have been discussed earlier in this chapter.

Processing and analysing information

5.5 This covers the process discussed earlier of drawing up **statements of a client's financial position including assets and liabilities and cash flow**, and coming to conclusions based on that information.

Constructing a comprehensive plan

5.6 The prime objective of the plan is to make **recommendations** regarding the action needed to meet the client's stated and agreed objectives.

5.7 The plan must **take account of economic conditions** which could affect the client such as the possibility of redundancy, the prospects for a self employed person's business and the effect of inflation.

5.8 It should take account of a client's **current financial position**. Is there a surplus of assets over liabilities? If so, is the surplus in a form where it can be better used? For example, if you have a house valued at £80,000 with a mortgage of £50,000 the surplus of assets over liability, namely £30,000, is not in a form where it can be reinvested more efficiently. It may be possible to use the surplus as a method of borrowing but it cannot be reinvested directly.

5.9 If liabilities exceed assets then can **liabilities be rearranged**? For example if part of the reason is an expensive loan, can the loan be repaid (provided any repayment charges are acceptable) and replaced by a more effective loan such as borrowing on the security of a with profits policy where interest rates tend to be below average.

5.10 Such an action would reduce the client's total outlay by reducing the **total interest payable**.

5.11 **How liquid are the client's assets**? How much of the client's assets is in a format where it can be turned into cash quickly, if necessary? Liquid assets would include bank and building society current and deposit accounts and National Savings investments. On some National Savings investments there may be a loss of interest on quick encashment but the need for liquidity may outweigh the loss of interest.

5.12 Is the client expecting any **future inheritance**? If so, is there any way in which it can be arranged so as to eliminate or minimise inheritance tax?

5.13 The client's current **tax position** is of prime importance. Ordinary building society accounts can be changed into ISAs. The interest rate might be slightly lower but the tax advantages will outweigh the loss of interest.

5.14 The client's protection requirements will be affected not only by current needs but by **changing economic conditions**. Inflation could reduce the value of life cover with a fixed sum assured, whether the policy be for the purpose of protection against disability or death.

5.15 State benefits may provide some protection against **disability and death** but, as we have already seen, they are very limited and the client's changing circumstances may reduce the importance of state benefits.

5.16 In view of the fact that the state disability benefit is at a fixed rate and is not earnings related, the **higher earning clients** will suffer all the more from a drop in earnings through disability.

5.17 Similar factors apply to **retirement planning** where even the state earnings related scheme is not sufficient to protect higher earning clients from a substantial drop in income at retirement in the absence of adequate pension arrangements.

5.18 **Fixed interest investments** will be considerably affected by inflation and also by the client's tax position. From the tax point of view a tax exempt investment is of less value to the non taxpayer than to the higher rate taxpayer and the two factors need to be taken into account together in order to produce a suitable recommendation.

5.19 **Inheritance tax liabilities** will make it necessary to make the maximum use of exemptions such as the annual exemption or the normal expenditure exemption. Remember that making transfers to avoid inheritance tax may have the effect of reducing the client's income and that fact also must be taken into account.

5.20 Finally full account must be taken of the **client's attitude and understanding of risk** when it comes to arranging investments. Widows with small capital sum and whose only income is the state pension should not be investing in futures and options. Equally high net worth individuals with substantial excess of income over expenditure can spread their investments in a way which provides a careful mix of caution, medium risk and high risk.

Question 2

(a) What are the stages in the financial planning process?

(b) What are some of the factors that make it important to construct a comprehensive financial plan for a client?

BPP PUBLISHING

Chapter roundup

- *Gathering and analysing client information.* First stage - know the essential information - both necessary and useful. May produce valuable contacts for future business.

  o *Necessary information:* personal details; employment details; financial advisers; financial details - Liquid/used/invested assets and liabilities; income - earnings/investment income and pensions; expenditure; protection; pensions; existing arrangements.

  o *Client's attitude.* Existing arrangements: suitable/reviewed; acceptable risk. Investment constraints. Client's view of suitability of current arrangements.

  o *Client's objectives.* Property purchase. Incur costs for school fees/car purchase/major repairs. Change jobs. Timespan for investments. Accessibility of funds. Current and future tax position. Need for income or growth. Personal involvement in investment decisions.

- *Understanding the analysis of circumstances.* Accounts - surplus or deficit on assets. Adequacy of protection arrangements. Changes in circumstances - house, job, children, employment.

- *Practice and major factors.* Quantify needs against provision. Assess present and future tax position. Prioritise objectives. Stages in planning process: fact find; objectives; process and analyse; recommend; implement; review. Fact find - account for regulatory requirements. Objectives - cover all possibilities. Process and analyse - financial accounts. Constructing plan: economic conditions; current financial position; reducing liabilities; asset liquidity; future inheritance; tax mitigation; inflation and protection; state benefits; retirement planning; inflation and fixed interest investment; inheritance tax liabilities; client's attitude to risk.

Quick quiz

1   Which of the following investments would you put into the 'liquid' category?

   A   Deposit accounts.
   B   Equities.
   C   National Savings certificates.
   D   Personal belongings.

2   What is the next stage of the financial planning process after handing to a client a business card?

   A   Establishing a client's objectives.
   B   Obtaining referrals from a prospective client.
   C   Obtaining all relevant information about a client.
   D   Identifying the company of the adviser.

3   How can you establish whether or not a client's property is sufficient to cover all his debts?

   A   Calculate his net income and net liabilities.
   B   Complete a balance sheet of his assets and liabilities.
   C   Compare his gross income with his after-tax income.
   D   Compare his net asset value with his monthly outlay.

4   At what stage during the financial planning process should you consider the effect of economic conditions on a client's financial affairs?

   A   When formulating the recommendations you intend to make to him.
   B   At the opening interview when you are obtaining his financial data.
   C   When you agree his financial objectives with him.
   D   When you implement the recommendations you have made.

---

5   If you advise a client to encash National Savings investments, what warning should you give to him?

    A He may lose some of his capital for encashment before a maturity date.

    B The price will depend on the price ruling on the day of the encashment.

    C He may have to refund part of any tax relief he has obtained.

    D There might be some loss of interest for early encashment.

The solutions to the questions in the quiz can be found at the end of this Study Text. Before checking your answers against those solutions, you should look back at this chapter and use the information in it to correct your answers.

Answers to questions

1   Personal, family, employment, financial advisers, financial details - assets, liabilities, income (earnings and investment), pensions, expenditure, protection, retirement plans, client's attitudes and objectives.

2   (a) Fact find, objectives, data management, recommending, implementing, updating.

    (b) Meet objectives, allow for economic conditions - prospects of redundancy/business development, inflation; surplus/deficiency of assets; scope for improvement in use of assets - equity release; liquidity of assets; future inheritance; tax efficiency; protection needs; state benefits; retirement planning; inheritance tax liabilities; client's risk profile.

Part C
Financial services providers and products

Chapter 11

THE SECTOR AND SERVICES

Chapter topic list	Syllabus reference
1 The influence of state provision	C 1.1
2 Services of banks and building societies	C 1.2
3 Life office services and marketing	C 1.3
4 Tied relationships	C 1.4
5 Friendly societies	C 1.3
6 Management services	C 1.5
7 Investment risks	C 1.6
8 Associations	

Introduction

Once we have worked out a client's needs, we must identify providers of suitable products. In this part of the Study Text we will survey what is available.

1   THE INFLUENCE OF STATE PROVISION

1.1   You cannot give any of your clients any form of financial planning advice unless you are fully familiar with the **influence of the state on financial planning**. This influence falls broadly into two areas: the social security system and government investments. The second one of these - government investments - itself can be subdivided into two further categories, namely National Savings and securities.

Social security system

1.2   The social security system in the UK has had two major influences on financial planning. The first is that the **state makes some provision**, albeit limited, for the financial welfare of its citizens. The second influence is that the **cost of making this provision** can in itself restrict the ability of individuals to make provision for their own security and welfare.

1.3   The provision of state pensions provides **fallback income** for individuals so that at least they are not at starvation level. For employees the existence of SERPS increases the amount of retirement provision.

1.4   However, the **total state pension is not going to be adequate for a high earner** and the fact that there is no lump sum paid on retirement means that individuals will be reliant upon their own efforts in order to be able to supplement their income through investment or the purchase of annuities.

BPP PUBLISHING

Contracting out of SERPS

1.5 For employees occupational pensions can and do supplement quite considerably the amount of total income that they will receive in their retirement, but the state pensions create further questions. The first is - should an occupational scheme be **contracted out of SERPS**?

1.6 The contracting out decision in itself must be supplemented by one of two further decisions - to replace SERPS by an **earnings related pension** or by a **contribution based method**. The first has the advantage for the employee that it will provide a pension equivalent to SERPS.

1.7 From the employer's point of view that fact is a disadvantage because it creates an **open ended cost**. For the employer the best method is through a money purchase scheme where the cost is controlled at a level which the employer considers acceptable. The disadvantage falls on the employee whose occupational pension will then depend upon the amount of the contribution, the performance of the fund into which the contributions are put, and the annuity rates at the date of retirement.

1.8 The **state pension retirement ages** have a considerable influence upon the retirement ages for occupational schemes. Although many schemes provide a normal retirement age of 60, nevertheless male employees and, by 2020, female employees have to wait until they are 65 in order to receive the state pension. This leaves a gap from 60 to 65 when their earnings have stopped and they are receiving only part of their pension. There can sometimes be a need to provide bridging income for that five year period.

Self employed people

1.9 In the case of the **self employed** their entitlement is only to the basic state pension. If they have been running a successful business then their drop in income when they retire will be considerable if their only income in retirement is the state pension.

1.10 While a self employed person may be able to sell a business, nevertheless this is a **high risk strategy** as there may be no potential buyers at the time that the self employed person wants to sell.

1.11 This makes it essential to make provision for retirement income through **personal pensions**. For the self employed there is no such thing as an earnings related pension and they have no choice but to rely on a money purchase basis. However, this will go a considerable way to providing them with some form of security in retirement.

Incapacity

1.12 The existence of the state **incapacity benefit** goes some way towards providing both employees and the self employed with income following disability. However, that income is extremely limited and some form of private provision is necessary.

1.13 For the employee, **statutory sick pay** is compulsory for a very limited period. The costs of statutory sick pay for employees whose employers are entitled to only a limited recovery from the state is going to influence the amount which employers are willing to pay in order to provide employees with voluntary disability benefits.

Question 1

(a) What pension options are available to an employer who contracts employees out of SERPS?

(b) For what reason might male employees need a bridging income immediately after they have retired?

(c) What risk might be faced by a self-employed person relying on the sale of his business to provide him with a retirement pension?

National Savings

1.14 The influence of National Savings on financial planning cannot be underestimated. A number of the **National Savings products** have advantages over private provision.

1.15 There are **five principal benefits** of National Savings investments. The benefits do not apply to all the investments but each benefit is found in at least one investment.

(a) Tax free growth
(b) Taxable interest paid gross
(c) Security of capital
(d) Redeemable at any time
(e) Easily bought through post offices

1.16 More details of the various National Savings investments are contained later in the Study Text. The two banking accounts offer variable interest which is relatively low. The **ordinary account** provides instant access and no tax on the first £70 of interest. The **investment account** is more suitable for a child with income below the personal allowance as the interest is payable gross.

1.17 **National Savings certificates** are tax free and are particularly suitable for higher rate taxpayers. The same applies to **index linked certificates** which provide for inflation proofed redemption. The interest which is inflation proofed gives a real rate of growth. These are primarily of interest to higher rate taxpayers at times when there is an anticipated increase in the level of inflation.

1.18 **Income bonds** produce an income regularly and the interest, albeit taxable, is paid gross. This makes them suitable for non taxpayers such as children or for the elderly whose tax position may either be nil or lower rate only.

1.19 **Capital bonds** are suitable only for taxpayers whose income is below the level of the personal allowance. This is because the interest is not receivable until the bonds are cashed but it is taxed every year when it is allocated to a bond. Obvious beneficiaries of this situation are children with no income.

1.20 The FIRST option bond has been replaced with the **Fixed Rate Savings Bond**. This bond offers a choice of Income or Capital Growth. The rate of interest paid on the bond is determined at the outset of the bond term and will depend on the initial investment amount and the term selected. There are four terms available either 6, 12, 18 or 36 months. Interest is paid with 20% tax deducted at source. The minimum purchase is £500 per bond and the maximum investment is £1 million per person in all bonds held either solely or jointly. It is available to those aged over 16. If the bond is withdrawn before the end of the term there is a 90 day interest penalty.

1.21 Finally, the **pensioners' guaranteed income bond** which is specifically for the over 60s provides a guaranteed rate of interest which, although taxable, is payable gross. This has the attraction of providing secure income together with security of growth. (There is a two and a five year term available).

1.22 National Savings investments must form part of the **portfolio** of most individuals on the grounds of the tax benefits, the security of capital which they give and their easy accessibility.

Gilt edged securities

1.23 For any client who wants a guaranteed return on their investment, **gilts** must form a major consideration. They provide security of capital over a period of time and, in most cases, the interest payable on them is fixed thus giving security of income. Their capital gains tax free status makes them attractive to higher rate taxpayers whose gains are already using up their annual exemption.

1.24 They can also have an indirect effect on financial planning because of their influence on the **general level of interest rates**. When the government issues a new gilt it will do so at a rate of interest which it considers sufficiently competitive to attract funds. If this level of interest is high then other borrowers may be forced to put up their interest rates in order to attract funds.

1.25 If the **general level of interest rates rises** then the interest rates on any existing gilts which are lower than the current rates will become uncompetitive. This will have the effect of reducing the value of those gilts which could in turn reduce the value of the portfolio of any client who has a number of gilts within the portfolio.

1.26 With effect from 6 April 1998, gilt holders can choose to receive interest gross regardless of the method of purchase of gilts, and **all new issues will pay interest gross**.

1.27 Again, the position is similar to some National Savings investments - also available from a post office. Dealing costs are low and the interest, albeit taxable, is payable gross which gives a **cash flow advantage** to a taxpayer.

1.28 **Local authority bonds** are rather less popular than gilts. No capital gains tax is payable on them but the interest is taxable.

Question 2

(a) Name five possible benefits of National Savings.
(b) Who particularly benefits from capital bonds?
(c) What might be the effect of the government issuing a highly competitive gilt?

2 SERVICES OF BANKS AND BUILDING SOCIETIES

Banks

2.1 The prime function of banks is **to provide non interest bearing current accounts** which are used as a repository for income and paying debts. The instant withdrawal facilities are usually augmented by the ability to withdraw cash from wall safes in public areas. In practice, some banks pay interest on current accounts.

2.2 Banks also provide **deposit accounts** on which variable interest is payable.

2.3 Most banks provide services as **trustees for trusts** which has the advantage of providing continuity of trustees. The same continuity also applies to another service provided by most banks, namely acting as executors for estates. This can resolve the problem of executors who have died before the person whose estate they are scheduled to administer.

2.4 In addition to providing overdraft facilities and **personal loans**, banks increasingly have become involved in providing **mortgages** for the purchase of homes.

2.5 They also provide **portfolio management services** for individuals either on a discretionary basis or as administrators executing the instructions of clients, and also the management of unit trusts.

2.6 In recent years they have become more and more involved in providing **wider financial planning services** including general insurance advice through subsidiaries, and also life assurance, pensions and ISAs.

Building societies

2.7 Building societies, like banks, are considered safe and provide similar current and deposit account facilities. In addition to deposit accounts a number of societies have issued **permanent interest bearing shares** (PIBS).

2.8 However, their prime business is and always has been the provision of **mortgages to buy private homes**. To this end their prime method of raising funds has been and still is interest-bearing share and deposit accounts.

2.9 The general principle on which building societies exist, namely **borrowing over a short period of time and lending for long periods**, seems a little insecure but in fact has worked successfully from the time building societies first came into existence.

2.10 Societies, some of which have now converted to banks, have also expanded their **financial planning services** in the same way as banks.

3   LIFE OFFICE SERVICES AND MARKETING

Life office services

3.1 The principal products dealt with by life assurance companies are covered elsewhere in this Study Text. The products that are available have the objective of **providing protection on death and disability, long term savings** and **lump sum investment**, together with the **provision of retirement income**. This is achieved through the issue of term assurances, whole life assurances, endowments, pensions, investment bonds and annuities.

3.2 Although it is not one of the principal services of life assurance companies, those that issue **with profits contracts** are normally willing to **lend money** on the security of an existing life policy up to a percentage of the surrender value of the contract.

Marketing

3.3 Life offices market their products in two ways - **personal advice** and **advertisements**.

3.4 **Personal advice** will be given either by independent financial advisers on the one hand or by company representatives or appointed representatives on the other, reflecting the requirements of the polarisation rule. Most companies deal through both channels but there are some who will deal only through IFAs and others who will deal only through their own company representatives.

3.5 A steady stream of business is obtained from the alternative method of marketing, namely by means of **advertisements** through newspapers, magazines, radio and television, through direct mail, and by telephone sales.

4 TIED RELATIONSHIPS

4.1 Banks and building societies give advice on life assurance products. However, they may do so in one of two capacities which reflect the **polarisation rule**.

4.2 A bank or building society may act as a **tied adviser** of a life assurance company in which case it can recommend the products of only that one life company. Alternatively the bank or building society can act as an **independent financial adviser**, in which case it must have access to a wide range of products and product providers.

4.3 A number of these financial institutions have their own life offices but also have a subsidiary company which acts as an independent financial adviser. These organisations have become known as **bancassurers**. Each arm of the institution, ie the tied arm and the independent arm, performs the same functions as any other organisation of a similar kind but they are all managed within the same group.

5 FRIENDLY SOCIETIES

KEY TERM

A **friendly society** may be either a mutual organisation or an incorporated body. Societies began as mutual self help organisations and this still tends to form the basis of the way a few of them work.

5.1 The prime purpose of friendly societies has changed to some extent over the years and some of them have marketed their products on the same basis as any other life assurance company. However, many of them still retain their original purpose of **self help** and have meetings of their policyholders (members) on a voluntary basis and there remains a very strong social bond between many of the policyholders and the representatives of the societies. However, the more recent development has been primarily in the marketing of tax exempt funds of which most are ten year endowments. As a result of the Friendly Societies Act 1992, societies can, amongst other things, become incorporated, manage unit trusts and ISAs (on approval from the Inland Revenue), establish residential homes for the elderly and nursing homes, administer estates and act as executors of wills.

6 MANAGEMENT SERVICES

6.1 The prime function of **stockbrokers** is to buy and sell equities on behalf of individual and corporate clients. They will also provide a service of giving advice on the choice of share purchase and sale.

6.2 Increasingly **investment managers** have been joined by stockbrokers in providing much wider investment services. They will provide a discretionary management service where the manager takes all the decisions to buy and sell equities within parameters which have been agreed with the client. They will also manage the administration required in a portfolio and produce regular reports - usually half yearly - for their clients, for which a fee will be charged.

6.3 Investment managers will provide **research and analysis of investment situations** in the form of reports which are not only for their own benefit but also for the benefit of fee paying clients.

6.4 **Management of unit trusts, investment trusts and ISAs** is a standard facility provided by a number of stockbrokers and some have initiated cheap share dealing services especially for privatisation issues.

7 INVESTMENT RISKS

7.1 Investment risks are divided into two categories - those relating to **capital** and those relating to **income**.

7.2 The greatest risk of all is the possibility of **losing all the capital** placed in an investment. This could happen in the case of equities if a company goes out of business.

7.3 The likelihood of total loss of capital is reduced with those **collective investments** which involve a **wide spread of risk**. These are principally unit trusts and investment trusts.

7.4 **Unit trusts** and **investment trusts** cannot avoid totally the risk of loss of some capital. Bearing in mind the fact that they invest in assets which can rise or fall in value, this is inevitable. The risk varies according to the type of investment but unit trusts and investment trusts may for example invest in fixed interest gilts where the risk of loss of capital is minimal. Alternatively, investment in exploration companies carries with it a high risk of loss as well as the prospect of substantial capital growth.

7.5 **Income risks** attach rather more to investments which carry variable rates of interest. These tend to be deposit accounts where the risk of loss of capital is virtually nil.

7.6 A further form of risk exists with **long term investments**, some of which carry no guarantee. For example, with profits bonds and plans depend on growth over a long term and they can produce a useful growth over an adequate number of years. However, if they are encashed within a relatively short period of time there may be penalties which will produce a loss. With any unit linked product there is a risk of falling prices but, once again, good growth is likely to occur over the long term.

8 ASSOCIATIONS

8.1 A number of **associations** exist which represent the interests of various parts of the life assurance industry. They include the Association of British Insurers (ABI) which represents insurance companies (both life and general companies), the British Insurance and Investment Brokers Association (BIIBA) which represents those insurance and investment brokers who have chosen to join it, and the Independent Financial Advisers Association (IFAA) representing those intermediary companies in its membership.

Question 3

(a) What is the main difference between the principal services provided by banks and building societies?

(b) List the principal products marketed by life assurance companies.

(c) What are bancassurers?

(d) What has been the prime purpose of friendly societies?

(e) Who provides fund management services?

Chapter roundup

- Influence of state provision

  - *Social security*. Makes limited provision. Pensions are fallback but inadequate for high earners, no lump sum. Occupational schemes: contracted out; final salary or money purchase; minimum pension or performance related. Male NRA 60 - State NRA 65 - bridging income? Self employed: basic state provision only; drop in income or unable to sell business; personal pension essential for standard of living; limited state disability benefit; incapacity benefit inadequate. Employees - statutory sick pay plus incapacity benefit limited.

  - *National Savings*. Benefits: tax; gross interest; security; redeemable; accessible. Banking accounts: gross interest plus some tax free. Variable treatment of other National Savings investments.

  - *Gilts*. Mostly fixed interest paid gross. Mostly CGT free - useful if exemption used. Influence general interest rate levels. Post office purchases cheaper plus gross interest. Local authority bonds - CGT free and interest taxable.

- Services of banks and building societies

  - *Banks*. Current accounts (sometimes interest bearing): accessible cash; overdrafts and personal loans; interest bearing deposits; trustees and executors; portfolio management services; manage unit trusts; provide financial services.

  - *Building societies*. Current and deposit accounts. Permanent interest bearing shares. Long-term loans for house purchase - borrow short and lend long. Provide financial services.

- *Life office services and marketing*. Protection on death and disability. Long term savings. Retirement planning. Some lending. Marketing by personal advice and advertisements: personal advice via IFAs or designated individuals or ARs. Banks and building societies may have IFA organisation and/or be tied to life office - increasingly their own. Friendly societies are life offices with mutual help tradition, tax exempt funds.

- *Management services*. Stockbrokers buy/sell equities and give advice. Available services: discretionary management; investment administration; research and analysis; management of unit trusts, investment trusts and ISAs.

- *Investment risks*. Relate to capital and income. Total loss of capital. Spread of risk in collective investments. Income risks - uncompetitive, penalties.

Quick quiz

1 Which one of the following types of organisation are product providers of life assurance?

   A Banks.
   B Building societies.
   C Friendly societies.
   D Unit trusts.

2 One of the advantages available to ten year qualifying life policies provided by a friendly society which is not available on qualifying policies from other life offices is that:

   A policy proceeds are free of all taxes when the policy reaches maturity;

   B unincorporated friendly society investments are not restricted to those authorised by the Trustee Investments Act 1961;

   C the life fund in which premiums are invested is exempt from some income tax and capital gains tax;

   D surrender values must always be not less than the total of premiums paid.

3 What is a disadvantage to a company of a final salary exempt-approved occupational pension scheme?

   A There is no provision for the employee to share some of the costs of the scheme.
   B There is an open-ended cost over which the employer has little control.
   C Directors of the company are not eligible to join the scheme.
   D The employee is taxed on the value of the employer's contributions.

4 What is the purpose of the state incapacity benefit?

   A To credit an employee with pension contributions during a period of illness.
   B To provide individuals with income to replace earnings lost through disability.
   C To reimburse an employer's payments to an employee absent through disability.
   D To relate a self-employed person's sickness benefit to the number of dependants.

The solutions to the questions in the quiz can be found at the end of this Study Text. Before checking your answers against those solutions, you should look back at this chapter and use the information in it to correct your answers.

Answers to questions

1   (a) Final salary or money purchase scheme.
   (b) To close the gap between retirement at 60 and commencement of the state pension at 65.
   (c) There might be no buyers at a satisfactory price.

2   (a) Tax-free growth, gross interest, security, redeemable, easily available.
   (b) Non-taxpayers, eg children.
   (c) A rise in the general level of interest rates.

3   (a) Banks mainly provide current accounts and overdrafts; building societies mainly finance home purchase by borrowing.

   (b) Life assurance, pensions, disability insurance, savings, investment.

   (c) Banks or building societies who have tied subsidiaries and independent subsidiaries.

   (d) Self-help.

   (e) Stockbrokers and investment managers.

Chapter 12

PROTECTION

Chapter topic list	Syllabus reference
1 Financial insecurity	
2 Life assurance	C 2.1, C 2.2
3 Permanent health insurance (individual contracts)	C 2.3
4 Critical illness insurance	C 2.4
5 Underwriting	C 2.5
6 Premiums and expenses	C 2.6

Introduction

Before thinking about investments to improve their financial position, clients should consider whether their present position is adequately protected. In this chapter we will consider forms of protection.

1 FINANCIAL INSECURITY

1.1 When a person dies or is taken seriously ill some sort of **financial problem** will usually result. On death, for example, the costs of a funeral will have to be met. If the person who dies is a married man with a young family, his dependants will still have the problem of finding the money for food, light, heat, clothes - in fact all of the normal living expenses. On top of that, if the husband and wife were buying a house with the help of a mortgage, the widow will be faced with an outstanding loan.

1.2 Similar problems will apply to couples who are not married but who are nevertheless bringing up a family in the normal way. The **death of a mother** creates some financial dilemmas and in those cases where a mother is earning more than the father financial difficulties are reversed but the principle is still the same.

1.3 For the sake of simplicity in this section we will refer mostly to the consequences of the **death of a male partner**. However, you will not need much imagination to work out that whenever anyone dies some sort of financial problem will be left behind.

1.4 Sometimes the financial difficulties which follow **long term disability** are even worse as ultimately you can lose your job if you are too ill to carry on working. The state may give some help, but it will not be enough.

Financial protection on death

1.5 There are three principal **financial consequences** of death.

178

(a) Loss of income
(b) The existence of debts
(c) Tax liabilities created by death

1.6 This creates a need for two different types of life cover, one providing a **replacement income**, the other a **lump sum to repay debts, pay taxes or meet one-off expenses** such as funeral costs.

1.7 In the case of the death of someone who does not have earnings - and the principal example of this is still a wife with young children - the husband will still be faced with financial problems: **who cares for the children while he goes to work**? The wife may have been a cook, domestic, gardener, nanny, chauffeur and nurse - all unpaid, but any professional replacement for these services will have to be found.

1.8 We are therefore looking for a method which will provide financial help at the time when it is needed in order to replace income, repay debts (eg mortgage), pay taxes and at least live without financial worry. **Life assurance** fulfils this function.

Disability

1.9 If you are disabled and unable to work you will ultimately **lose earnings** because your employer will not go on paying you. In addition you could be facing additional expenses such as structural alteration of your house in order to convert a downstairs room into a bedroom (if you cannot get upstairs), or widen doorways to take wheelchairs.

1.10 There may be some help from the state in the form of **income** but, rather like the payments on death, it will be little more than a minor solution to a major problem.

1.11 There are various forms of **disability insurance** which will help to solve these problems.

2 LIFE ASSURANCE

Who's who and what's what

2.1 The terminology used in life assurance can vary from one company to another so, right at the start, we will look at some of the most **fundamental terms**.

KEY TERMS
- Should it be **life assurance** or **life insurance**? It started hundreds of years ago as life assurance but in recent years life insurance has been growing in usage. For all practical purposes there is no longer any significant difference.
- This leads to the fact that the sum that is payable under a life assurance policy can be either the **sum assured** or the **sum insured**. We are sticking to 'life assurance' but don't feel offended if you work for a company that refers to it as life insurance.
- The person whose death triggers off a payment under the policy is the **life assured** or the **life insured**.
- The person who is initially the legal owner of the policy is known by one of the following names: **policyholder, assured, insured, grantee, policy owner**.
- When that person is applying for a life policy they are known as either the **proposer** or the **applicant**.

2.2   If you were applying for a policy on your own life then you would initially be the **proposer** and then, when the policy came into existence, you would become both the **policyholder** and the **life assured**.

2.3   The proceeds of a life policy will often be paid to the **legal personal representatives** of a person who has died. They will be either the **executors** or the **administrators** depending upon whether or not a will has been left by the deceased. If a policy has been temporarily transferred (assigned) to someone else (the assignee) then the assignee will receive the proceeds.

2.4   You can insure someone else's life provided you have an **insurable interest** in their life (see Part B).

Exam focus point
We now turn to the different types of policy which are covered by the examination.

Term assurance

KEY TERM

Term assurance, as the name implies, provides life assurance for a fixed term. The sum assured is payable only if the life assured dies within that period. There is no benefit payable on maturity or on cancellation. Premiums are payable throughout the term of the contract. The major advantage of term assurances is that they give very high life cover for low premiums.

2.5   There are basically two kinds of term assurance, those that pay a **lump sum on death** and those that pay an **income**.

Lump sum

2.6   Under a **level term contract** the sum assured payable will remain unchanged through the term of the contract. The term is usually a period of years.

2.7   **Convertible term assurance** is level term assurance with the option to convert the policy during the term. Conversion can be made into a whole life or an endowment policy.

2.8   The advantage of this is that when the policyholder wants to convert the contract he or she can do so quite **regardless of their state of health** at the time.

2.9   In addition, even if the policyholder's health has deteriorated the new contract cannot be subject to a **premium** increase on account of the policyholder's changed state of health. The premium rate used must be the same as for any other policyholder in good health effecting the same kind of contract at the same age and for the same amount. There will be no special terms applied to the contract. The exception to this is if the original term policy was the subject of a special condition, in which case that same special condition may be carried forward to the new contract.

2.10 The sum assured for the new policy can be no greater than that under the original convertible term contract. **Partial conversion** is often allowed.

2.11 Normally the term assurance sum assured cannot be increased but some contracts have a special provision that the **sum assured can be increased if a particular event takes place**. Such an event will usually include getting married, moving house or producing or adopting children.

2.12 **Decreasing term assurance** has a sum assured which reduces steadily throughout the term of the policy although the premiums will normally remain level throughout the term.

2.13 The most common use for this type of contract is to protect a **repayment mortgage** where the outstanding loan is reducing during the term. The capital outstanding on many repayment mortgages reduces at an uneven pace throughout the term and the sum assured will be adjusted to reflect this. When used for this purpose the decreasing term assurance is usually called a mortgage protection assurance.

2.14 Sometimes a decreasing term assurance will include an **option to convert**. In this case the maximum sum assured under the new policy will be the sum assured at the time of the conversion.

2.15 **Renewable term assurance** is a term assurance contract usually for a relatively short period - five years is common - and when the term expires the policy can be extended or renewed, usually for the same period of time as the original. This process can be continued at the end of each period until the life assured reaches retirement age. At each extension of the term the premium rate will increase to the standard rate appropriate at that time.

2.16 **Increasable term assurance** is a contract which starts with a fixed sum assured. Either this will be increased automatically at a fixed rate such as 10% a year, or it *can* be increased at the option of the policyholder. Premiums will increase at the same rate as the sum assured.

2.17 **Renewable increasable convertible term assurance** is a convertible term assurance which can be extended at the end of the term in the same way as renewable term assurance. The sum assured may be increased when the policy is extended.

2.18 The periods for the contract are most commonly **five years** and the most common increase allowed is 50% of the immediately preceding sum assured.

2.19 The number of benefits - sum assured payable on death plus the right to convert plus the right to extend or renew plus the right to increase the sum assured - means that this contract is **much more expensive** than a term assurance for a limited period. It is most suitable for people with young families whose need for life cover is high but who want the option to increase the sum assured at a later stage.

2.20 At each renewal point **no medical evidence of health** is required and the rate of premium charged will be the standard rate for the policyholder at the age at renewal.

Income

2.21 **Family income benefit contracts** - usually known by its initials FIB - provide an income from the date of death until the end of the policy term. It is most commonly used for people with young families who want to replace the earnings of the life assured who has died. The level of payments may escalate each year by a fixed regular amount from inception or from the time payment begins.

> ### Exam focus point
> Beware of a question on this topic that makes comparison with decreasing term assurance. A FIB policy is in fact exactly the same as a decreasing term assurance except that the sum assured is payable in equal instalments. Example: a FIB policy is effected to provide an income of £1,000 per month over a 20 year period. The benefit will be shown as follows.
>
> | Month | Sum assured | Monthly benefit | Payable for (months) |
> |-------|-------------|-----------------|----------------------|
> | | £ | £ | |
> | 1 | 240,000 | 1,000 | 240 |
> | 2 | 239,000 | 1,000 | 239 |
> | 3 | 238,000 | 1,000 | 238 |
>
> The sum assured will thus be described as £240,000 reducing by £1000 per month and payable in equal monthly instalments for the remainder of the term. Under current tax rules, this income is tax-free.

2.22 Many insurers will allow a **lump sum to be paid instead of an income**. This practice, known as **commutation,** will produce a lump sum which is lower than the total number of outstanding payments. This is because the payments are made in one sum and the life company has no opportunity to invest the outstanding balance.

Question 1

(a) How can financial insecurity arise when a person dies?

(b) What expenses could arise on disability?

(c) What are the advantages of convertible term assurance?

(d) Why is renewable increasable convertible term assurance more expensive than level term assurance for a given sum assured?

Endowments

2.23 Endowments are only worth a brief mention here as they are primarily **savings contracts,** so for the time being we simply note that they have **some protection value**.

Whole life policies

2.24 A whole life policy for which regular premiums are payable provides for the **payment of a lump sum on death**. There are three different ways for deciding how much that lump sum will be.

(a) The sum assured may be fixed at the same level throughout - a **non-profit policy.**
(b) The sum assured may be increased at regular intervals - a **with profits policy.**
(c) The sum assured is linked to the value of investments - a **unit linked contrac**t.

Non profit policy

2.25 Non profit policies are sometimes called **without profit** or **non participating policies**. The sum assured **is fixed** at the same level for the entire duration of the contract's existence. There is a relatively small demand for such contracts which tend to be confined to providing life assurance for people over the age of 50.

With profits policy

2.26 A with profits policy is often known as a **participating policy**. Both expressions mean the same thing - a policy which shares in the profits of the insurance company.

2.27 When the company calculates the premium rate it makes certain assumptions regarding future expenses and income (these are referred to later in this chapter). Every year the company values its assets and liabilities and this normally reveals a **surplus**.

2.28 A large part of the surplus is used to **increase the guaranteed sum assured** on with profits policies. These increases are known as reversionary bonuses and once they are added to the policy cannot be taken away.

2.29 Bonuses are normally based on either the **initial sum assured** or, more commonly, on the **sum assured including previously allocated bonuses**. Companies may either base their bonuses on a percentage of the total sum assured or alternatively apply one percentage to the basic sum assured and a different percentage to previously allocated bonuses.

2.30 There is **no guarantee** that bonuses will be allocated. Their objective is to provide a steady growth in the sum assured. In deciding how big a reversionary bonus will be, a life office will be cautious in its assumptions of the future growth rate of its investments.

2.31 If a life assured dies shortly before the next bonus is due to be added to the sum assured, an **interim bonus** is likely to be added even though it is not yet time for the annual bonus to be allocated.

2.32 When a with profit policy comes to an end it is the practice of most companies to add a **special bonus** at that time. This is called a terminal bonus, referring to the termination of the policy. These bonuses are **not guaranteed** in advance and are entirely dependent on the company's view on the amount of profit available for distribution.

2.33 If a with profit or non-profit policy is cancelled the policyholder may receive a payment from the insurance company. This is because the policy builds up a **cash value** after a period of time. This cash value, otherwise known as a **surrender value**, gradually increases over a period of time.

2.34 Cash values are **low in the early years of a policy** because the company incurs expenses such as underwriting and marketing costs which must be recovered from the policy's reserves.

Exam focus point

Sometimes **terminal bonuses** may be added to a with profit policy's surrender value when it is cancelled. However, this is not universal and an examination question may disregard that fact. The wording of the question needs to be very carefully noted.

2.35 It is often possible for a policyholder to have **a loan** from the insurance company which issued a policy. The loan will be limited by the cash value and will usually be a percentage of that cash value. The percentage is most commonly between 85% and 95% although different limits are available.

2.36 As the insurance company no longer has that money available to earn interest it **charges interest** to the policyholder. The policy will be treated as security for the loan and will be retained by the life company until the loan is repaid.

2.37 A policyholder may want to stop paying premiums and yet not want to cancel the policy. This can be done by arranging with the life company that the premiums will stop and the benefits thereafter will be based on premiums paid up to that time. The policy is then known as a **paid up policy**. As a result the sum assured will reduce to a new level. It may stay at that level with no further increase, or bonuses (possibly at a reduced rate) may be allocated.

Unit linked assurance

2.38 Unit linked assurance benefits depend directly on the **value of investments bought with the premiums,** although there is usually a minimum sum assured payable on death.

The sum assured

2.39 Under any regular premium whole life contract there will be a **guaranteed minimum sum payable on death**. This will be fixed at the outset and will be the minimum sum payable if death occurs while the policy is in force.

The premium

2.40 The premiums for a unit linked policy are divided into two very distinct parts. One part is retained by the life office to contribute towards the **cost of the guaranteed life cover**. The other part is used to **purchase investments** which will be the basis for calculating the policy benefits. The investments which are bought with each policyholder's premium form a fund and will be the basis of the sum payable on death.

2.41 There is thus a **fund for each policyholder** which is building up for two reasons.

   (a) Each time a premium is paid, more investments are bought.
   (b) The value of those investments should be increasing over a period of time.

2.42 In the early years of a policy, the value of these investments is obviously going to be very low, and not of much value if the policyholder dies during those early years. This is the reason why, as stated earlier, there is a minimum sum payable on death. However, if and when the value of the investments exceeds the guaranteed sum assured, **the value of the investments will be paid on death**.

2.43 The **sum assured payable on death** therefore is the guaranteed sum assured or, if greater, the value of the investments. If the investment value, having exceeded the guaranteed sum assured, falls below it subsequently then once again the guaranteed minimum sum will be the amount payable.

How the sum assured is decided

2.44 It seems fairly obvious that the higher the sum assured, the bigger will be the premium necessary to pay for it. In fact a unit linked policy is flexible and the premium does **not** always need to be bigger to pay for a higher sum assured.

2.45 The reason for this is the **division of the premium** between paying for life cover and buying investments. If the life cover is very low only a very small part of the premium will need to be retained by the life office to pay for it. If on the other hand the life cover is very high, a much bigger part of the premium will need to be retained to pay for the higher cover.

2.46 There has to come a point where **increases in the level of life cover** required will be too great for any further use of this method of allocating part of the premium for life cover and the total premium will have to be increased.

2.47 A **unit linked policy** will often have a fixed amount of life cover for a given level of premium and the only way for a policyholder to have higher life cover is to pay a bigger premium. However, there are many whole life policies which are flexible enough to allow for variations in life cover by varying the proportion of the premium devoted to pay for it. These are usually known as **flexible whole life policies**.

2.48 The portion of the premium used to buy investments is known by various names, the most common of which are the **investment content** and the **allocation percentage**.

The investments

2.49 You may have had the impression that each time a premium is paid the life company may buy some shares or equities with part of the premium. It is not quite as direct as that. If say, a **regular premium** was being paid of £50 per month of which £45 was intended to be used to buy equities, you would not be able to buy many equities for that amount of money and the administrative costs would be exorbitant. The method used is for the life company to create a pool or **fund of policyholders' money** and to buy investments in bulk with the fund. It is essential to keep track of each policyholder's share of the fund. In order to achieve this each fund is divided into units and each policyholder's investment content buys units in that fund.

2.50 EXAMPLE: INVESTMENTS

A fund may consist of a total amount of cash of £5m. If it is divided into five million units each unit will be worth £1. It will then be very easy for the £45 investment content referred to earlier to buy 45 units at £1 each. If the fund eventually doubled in value then each unit would be worth £2.

2.51 The **equity, property, fixed interest** and **cash funds** reflect the four principal types of investment which form the content of unit linked funds. There is a fifth fund - probably by far the largest - which usually buys units in each of the other four funds. This is known as a managed fund and gives a very wide spread of types of investment.

2.52 Many funds are even **more specialised** than those named above. Thus a fund may specialise in shares of companies trading in oil. Such a fund might be called an energy fund or an exploration fund, but it is nevertheless an equity fund which happens to concentrate on a very narrow range of investments. An agricultural fund is one which concentrates on buying and managing farmland but it is simply a specialised form of property fund.

Unitised with profits funds

2.53 A **unitised with profits fund** is divided into units like other unit-linked funds. An annual bonus is declared and then mostly used to increase unit prices. The bonus cannot be taken away although it may be reduced if funds are switched or surrendered. Terminal bonuses apply in the same way as a traditional with profits policy.

BPP PUBLISHING

Who chooses the fund?

2.54   The **policyholder** decides at the outset which fund's units should be bought with the investment allocation. From then on all the investment content will continue to be used to buy units in that same fund until the policyholder changes his mind.

Changing your mind (switching)

2.55   A policyholder may decide he would like to change the fund to which his premiums are allocated. Most insurers will allow this to take place and, subject to certain conditions, the policyholder can move his accumulated fund into another fund. This facility is known as **switching**.

2.56   The **conditions** are most likely to be related to the minimum value which can be switched and to the minimum amount which can remain in a fund from which a switch has taken place. It may be that only a total switch of a policyholder's fund value can take place but partial switches are often allowed.

2.57   Usually one or two **free switches** are allowed in each year, after which there is a charge for subsequent switching. There could be a problem for the fund if a large number of policyholders want to switch substantial sums out of a fund at the same time. If the company must sell investments to meet such switches this could cause a fall in the value of the assets, especially in the case of property which cannot usually be sold quickly.

2.58   To overcome this problem a life company will retain the **right to delay any switching** (or total withdrawal of funds) for a period of up to one month for most funds but six months for a property fund.

Unit prices

2.59   We have already seen that the investment content of a premium is used to **buy units** at a price which depends on:

(a)   The value of the fund
(b)   The number of units in the fund

Thus the lower the unit price the more units will be purchased. Conversely the higher the price the fewer units can be allocated.

2.60   When units are allocated a **charge** is made and is retained by the life company. This charge has already been taken into account when calculating the price of the units. The general level of charge is 5%. When units are cashed because, for example, the sum assured is payable, there is no extra charge at that encashment time.

2.61   There is thus a difference between the price at which units are allocated and the price at which they are encashed. The higher price, used when units are first allocated, is known as the **offer price**. The encashment - that is, lower - price is known as the **bid price**. The difference between the two is called the **bid/offer spread**.

Charges

2.62   A life company makes various **charges on a unit linked contract**. We have already looked at two of them. The first was that part of the **premium** which is used for life cover. The other was the **bid/offer spread**. There are potentially four others.

(a) **Annual management charge**

The life company makes an annual charge on each of its funds. The charge varies but is mostly either 0.75% or 1% of the value of the fund each year. In practice the charge is usually deducted in instalments at monthly intervals.

(b) **Additional management charge**

There may be an additional charge applied to units which are allocated during the first one or two years. This extra charge will be applied to those units usually over the duration of the policy.

Units which are subject to this additional charge are usually known as either capital units or initial units. All other units are normally called accumulation units.

(c) **Policy fee/allocation percentage**

A fixed charge may be made each year or month on each policy of, for example, £12 per year or £1 per month. The policy fee may be added to the premium or deducted from that part of the premium used for the allocation of units.

Some contracts instead of charging a policy fee allocate a larger percentage of the premium where the premium is above a specified level. Thus the higher the premium, the higher the percentage used to allocate units to the policy.

(d) **Cancellation fee**

If a regular premium policy is cancelled there may be a cash value payable to the policyholder depending on how long the policy has been in existence. If cancellation takes place within a given number of years, usually ten years, a deduction called a surrender charge is made from the cash value.

Question 2

(a) What is a benefit of with-profits assurance compared with unit-linked assurance?
(b) What benefit does a unit-linked assurance contract have that a with-profits assurance does not?
(c) What is a benefit of a paid-up policy?
(d) What are the principal unit-linked assurance funds?
(e) What is the benefit of switching under a unit-linked assurance policy?
(f) List the charges made under a unit-linked policy.

Flexible whole life policies

2.63 Policyholders can choose at the outset a sum assured from a range offered by an insurer. The insurer is at risk for the difference between the **cash value** of the policy and the **guaranteed sum assured (GSA)**. The cost of this life cover is met by the insurer making a monthly charge on the fund in which the premiums are invested. The charge is based on the policyholder's mortality profile.

2.64 The higher the level of life cover the bigger will be the **charge** which the insurer must make on the fund. As the policyholder gets older so the cost of the increased mortality risk will itself increase. If the investment performance of the fund is sufficient it will pay for the increasing cost of the life cover. This is unlikely when the highest level of life cover is chosen.

2.65 The **minimum** level of cover offered by an insurer is normally that which will enable the policy to be classified as a **qualifying policy** (see section on taxation). The level could of course be lower if the policy is non qualifying.

2.66 The plan will be **reviewed regularly**, the first review taking place normally on the tenth anniversary. Subsequent reviews will take place every five years until age 70 when they will be done annually. The sum assured or the premium will then be subject to change according to the amount at risk, the mortality of the insured and the income from the fund.

2.67 The higher the guaranteed level of protection, the **slower is the growth in the number of units**. The reason for this is simply that the monthly charge on the fund is achieved by cancelling units. The high cost of the guaranteed life cover means that a larger number of units will be cancelled each month than under either the medium level of cover or the minimum level of cover.

2.68 At the end of the first ten year period it is extremely likely that the **sum assured will have to be reduced or the premium increased**. The reason is a mixture of the low level of income being produced by the smaller number of units, the high guaranteed life cover and of course the fact that the policyholder is now ten years older and will be subject to a higher rate of premium.

2.69 The **medium level of sum assured** is set so that if the fund achieves a reasonable level of growth then at the end of each review period it should be possible to renew the contract without either a reduction in the sum assured or any increase in the premium.

2.70 There is no point in setting the sum assured at the outset at the minimum level as it becomes much more of an **investment contract** and will be expensive.

2.71 The aim of the plan is to provide **high life cover for young families**. The maximum sum can be reduced later when responsibilities reduce. Increases in the sum assured are likely to need fresh underwriting.

2.72 Sums assured may be increasable through a **guaranteed insurability** option such as automatic increases in line with RPI or by a set percentage each year. Some insurers offer the option for a special event such as marriage, becoming a parent or on moving house and increasing a mortgage.

2.73 Other benefits may be included such as **critical illness cover, waiver of premium protection, permanent health insurance** and **hospital cash payments**. Occasionally it is possible to substitute a life assured or add a life assured to the policy. Non qualifying contracts may allow for lump sum payments to be made for investment purposes or a premium holiday to be taken.

Personal accident and sickness insurance

2.74 **Personal accident and sickness insurance** is designed to provide benefits in the event of the death of or injury to the life insured resulting from an accident. It pays a lump sum on death or for serious disability. It also pays an income in the event of less serious disability, including temporary and partial disablement.

2.75 **Income payments** will be paid for a maximum period of 104 weeks. There will be a deferment period from the date of injury or commencement of illness during which no income will be payable. This period is usually between seven days and four weeks.

2.76 Unlike permanent health insurance, which is a long term contract, accident and sickness insurance policies have a term of **one year only**. At the end of each year both the insured and the insurer can choose not to renew the contract. This contrasts with permanent health insurance where, under most circumstances, the insurer cannot refuse to renew the policy.

2.77   This type of cover is often used by **sports clubs** and as part of **holiday insurance**.

3   PERMANENT HEALTH INSURANCE (INDIVIDUAL CONTRACTS)

Objective

3.1   The objective of **permanent health insurance** (PHI) is to replace earnings lost through long term disability. This means that the benefit is not a capital sum but an **income**.

Factors in PHI planning

3.2   The principal factors to take into account in assessing clients' needs are:

(a)   Their **level of earnings**
(b)   **Any other benefits** payable

3.3   The main source of other benefits is the **state incapacity benefit** and (for employees) initially **statutory sick pay**. For employees any continuing benefits from an employer must be taken into account.

Benefit

Replacement of earnings

3.4   An income will be payable during disability which aims to **replace at least some of the consequent loss of earnings**. The basis for the level of benefit is loss of earnings. If a person has no earnings, eg through unemployment or because he has sufficient investment income to live on, there cannot *normally* be payment under a PHI policy (but see 'Housepersons' later).

3.5   In the case of an employee who receives full salary for, say, six months from the time disability begins, there will be **no payment under a PHI contract** during that period of time. The reason is that a PHI income is intended to replace lost earnings and, in such a situation, no earnings have been lost.

3.6   The existence of PHI cover can ensure that clients **do not have to take retirement benefits early**. This would cause them to receive a lower pension than they would receive by delaying the pension's starting date.

Amount of income benefit

3.7   The income benefit for an employee will thus be **reduced by any continuing income** from the employer. However, other benefits may be received by the employee such as state benefits or income from another policy, all of which would help to reduce the employee's loss of earnings if the income benefit were not adjusted (see below) to take account of them.

3.8   Furthermore, an insurer will pay only a proportion of the pre-disability earnings. The proportion varies from one insurer to another. Most adopt a **percentage of between 50% and 66%**, the objective being to give the policyholder a financial incentive to return to work. It is not unknown for an insured to be able to receive a disability income equal to his pre-disability earnings, although this is unusual.

BPP PUBLISHING

3.9 The income paid to the policyholder **may not necessarily be level**. Many insurance companies will increase payments by a fixed percentage each year. This is known as escalation. A common escalation rate is 5% a year but annual increases between 3% and 10% a year exist. Some companies may limit the rate of escalation to increases in prices or earnings. An extra premium will be charged for this benefit. The same applies if benefits are indexed in line with the National Average Earnings Index.

3.10 To ensure that an employee is **not financially better off** following disability than when earning, PHI payments will be on the following basis.

   (a) Percentage of pre-disability earnings *minus*
   (b) Continuing income from employment or self employment *minus*
   (c) State benefits *minus*
   (d) Disability income from other insurance.

3.11 The percentage of pre-disability earnings payable as benefit may be subject to **further limits**. For example, if the insured's income exceeds a certain sum the percentage limit may be lower for earnings in excess of the sum. Benefit may be, say, 66% of earnings up to £40,000 salary but one-third or 50% of earnings in excess of £40,000, with an absolute limit of £90,000. Remember that this is only an example: actual limits vary according to the provider.

When income benefits begin

3.12 Payments will not usually begin immediately a policyholder becomes disabled. There will be a gap between the start of the disability and the first payment. That gap is usually known as the **deferment period**.

3.13 The longer the deferment period the smaller will be the potential liability of the insurance company to make payment. As a consequence, the longer the deferment period the lower will be the premium. **Typical deferment periods** are 4, 13, 26 and 52 weeks.

3.14 A policyholder may recover from his disability and return to work but subsequently become ill again due to the same medical condition. If this happens **payments under his policy can restart**. In such a case, because the cause of disability is the same, the new and the previous payments are classed as linked claims and the deferment period will not apply to the second claim. Cover applies on a worldwide basis. However, if the insured is outside a group of countries known as the 'free limits', claim payments will be limited to (mostly) 13 or 26 weeks. The 'free limit' countries are most commonly the UK, Republic of Ireland, Channel Islands and Isle of Man, Western Europe and North America, but the range depends on the insurer.

Partial loss of earnings

3.15 Someone who has been totally disabled for a time may make a **partial recovery** and be able to return to his original occupation in a reduced capacity. Alternatively, he may be able to take up another occupation less demanding than his original one.

3.16 In either case his earnings may be less than they were before he was disabled. A PHI policy will pay a **proportionate income** which will at least partly compensate for the continued loss of earnings.

Unemployment

3.17 PHI cover will not be obtainable for someone who is **unemployed**. This is because there is no occupation on which a premium rate can be based.

3.18 If a person with a PHI policy subsequently becomes unemployed many insurers will not pay benefit because **an unemployed person has no earnings**. Other insurers are willing to make payments subject to a monetary limit per month or per year. A standard condition will be that the policyholder must be confined to the house.

Housepersons

3.19 At one time a small number of companies offered limited PHI cover to housewives, recognising that their disability could lead to hefty additional expenses for a family. A standard condition required housewives to be confined to the house. That position is unchanged, but the replacement title for housewives - **housepersons** - recognises that an increasing number of men are taking over this role, sometimes because a man has retired and his partner is still working, and sometimes because her earnings are much higher than his would be and the arrangement is economically advantageous.

Escalation

3.20 Some policies will automatically increase the benefit by either a fixed percentage each year or in line with inflation or average earnings. The cost will be included in the standard premium rate. In other cases **escalation** is an extra benefit which will lead to an increased premium.

Increase option

3.21 Some insurers will allow the insured benefit to be **increased by up to a stated percentage** of the original benefit at specified intervals, eg every five years. The new premium rate may be the same as for the original cover or may be charged at the rates current at the time.

Definition of disability

> **KEY TERM**
>
> **Disability** will mean that an insured is unable to follow one of three categories of occupation:
>
> (a) His own
> (b) Any occupation for which he has had training and experience
> (c) Any occupation of any kind

3.22 In addition he must not be following **any occupation for profit or reward**. The third of the definitions above is the most stringent. It means that, in order to receive *any* benefit the insured must be unable to perform *any* occupation of *any* kind.

Taxation

3.23 Premiums for individual PHI contracts are not eligible for any kind of tax relief. **Benefit payments are tax-free.**

Question 3

(a) Briefly outline a flexible whole life policy.
(b) What type of disability insurance is annual rather than long term?
(c) What is the objective of permanent health insurance?
(d) Explain the deferment period under a permanent health insurance contract.
(e) What are the three categories of disability covered under permanent health insurance?

4 CRITICAL ILLNESS INSURANCE

The problem

4.1 **Serious illness** can cause **financial problems** which arise for a number of reasons.

- The cost of primary health care
- A person giving up work to care for a spouse
- The cost of home help
- The cost of a holiday needed for recovery or convalescence
- The cost of home alterations, including installing a chair lift
- The cost of equipment for treating kidney failure at home
- The cost of transport for the disabled, eg adapting a car
- Cash needed to supplement an early retirement pension

The cause

4.2 The cause of the problem lies in an illness or disability that may be serious enough **to alter a person's lifestyle**. The solution is the payment of a lump sum on the diagnosis of an illness specified in a policy and known as critical illness insurance. Its uses are to:

- Repay a mortgage

- Provide specialist care and equipment

- Modify a home or car

- Meet responsibilities of dependants

- Provide aid for older people (widows or widowers with no family to support them)

4.3 **Diagnosis *alone* of one of the specified illnesses is sufficient to justify payment**. There is no requirement for loss of earnings or even for special medical treatment, although in practice this usually follows.

Disabilities insurable

4.4 A **wide variety of illnesses** may be insured. They include the following.

- Alzheimer's disease
- Blindness
- Cancer
- Coronary artery disease
- Heart attack
- Kidney failure
- Major organ transplant
- Multiple sclerosis
- Paralysis
- Stroke
- Total permanent disability

Cover provided

4.5   Cover is based on diagnosis of a specified illness. It can be on a **stand alone basis** or linked with a whole life assurance policy.

> ### Exam focus point
> You sometimes need to use some commonsense on this topic in the exam. A question such as 'which one of the following is not normally a critical illness' is a difficult question to answer, as it is not easy to define 'normally'. Critical illnesses are those which are specified in a policy and this will vary from one insurer to another. However, if one of the options is 'obesity', the fact that this is often (albeit not always) self-inflicted by over-eating points to such an 'illness' as not being insurable.

5   UNDERWRITING

> ### KEY TERM
> The process by which an insurer decides whether or not to accept a proposal and, if so, what terms will be offered, is known as **underwriting**. The objective of underwriting is to classify each proposal according to the risk that it represents, either of **death** in the case of life assurance or of **disability** in the case of permanent health insurance, accident and sickness insurance or critical illness insurance.

5.1   The factors which have to be taken into account are therefore **anything which affects either of these risks**. The factors are the following.

   (a)   Age and sex
   (b)   Health
   (c)   The proposer's present and past health and the health of his/her family
   (d)   Occupation
   (e)   Hobbies, including sports
   (f)   Lifestyle (including smoking and drinking)

5.2   Other factors may be relevant such as **residence** and **aviation risks**. All this information will be requested on the proposal form. According to the information given an insurer may want further information from the proposer's own doctor and also a medical examination by a doctor appointed by the insurer.

5.3   Each insurer has certain levels of cover which, if not exceeded, may enable the proposer to be granted cover without any form of **medical examination**. These are known as the non medical limits. The effect is that for cover above those limits further medical information *will* be required. For cover within these limits the insurer is prepared to consider granting cover on the basis of the proposal alone. However, the insurer retains the right to seek further medical information if it is considered desirable.

5.4   The **type of policy** and the **term of the contract** will also have an effect on the underwriting decision.

5.5   Many underwriting decisions are taken by computers programmed to recognise information and react to it. The method of underwriting is known as the **numerical system of rating**. Standard risks are represented by a figure of 100 and this figure is increased on a points basis for the unfavourable features. Ordinary rates apply up to a cumulative total of points, after which special terms may be offered. The decision will be either to **decline** *or* to **accept**.

5.6 If the decision is to accept the risk, the **terms** may be:

- Standard
- Increased premium
- Subject to conditions

6 PREMIUMS AND EXPENSES

6.1 There are three factors which have to be taken into account in **calculating premiums**.

- Mortality (the risk of death) or morbidity (the risk of disability)
- Expenses for new business and management
- Investment income

6.2 The **mortality and morbidity risks** account for a substantial part of the premium in term assurance but less in investment contracts. If the risk is high because of adverse features relating, say, to health or occupation, this will be covered by additional premiums.

6.3 The **initial expenses** cover the costs of setting up a policy, including marketing and selling costs. Initial and continuing expenses involve management costs, including staff, equipment and routine administration costs.

6.4 To counterbalance this, **investment income** is received by the insurer in the form of interest, dividends, rent and capital gains.

6.5 The **charges** are **hidden in with profits contracts** but their effect is revealed ultimately in the **level of bonuses**. The charges are clear and specific in unit linked assurance taking the form of bid/offer spreads, premium allocation, annual management fees and type of units, eg capital units.

Question 4

(a) Under what circumstances will benefit be paid under critical illness insurance?
(b) What factors affect underwriting in life assurance?

Chapter roundup

- *Financial insecurity.* On death: funeral costs; living expenses for survivors; mortgage debt; cost of alternative services. On disability: loss of earnings; cost of house alterations.

- *Life assurance.* Cause of payment - death of life assured/life insured. Applicant for life assurance - applicant, proposer. Owner of policy - policyholder, assured, insured, grantee, policy owner.

- *Term assurance.* High cover for low cost for fixed term.

    ○ *Lump sum.* Level term - fixed sum assured. Convertible term - level term plus right to change to whole life/endowment regardless of health; standard rate of premium at conversion. Decreasing term - reducing sum assured; used for mortgage protection. Renewable term - fixed period plus right to extend for further period. Renewable increasable term - level term extendible and sum assured increasable at policyholder's option.

    ○ *Income.* Family income benefit - FIB – tax-free income from death to end of term, form of decreasing term.

- *Endowments.* Have some protection value in addition to savings.

- *Whole life.* Pays sum assured on death - non profit, with profits, unit linked.

    ○ *Non profit.* Sum assured level throughout existence of policy.

    ○ *With profits.* Participating in profits. Valuation leads to surplus, increases sum assured - reversionary bonuses - on original or total sum assured. Interim bonuses on death before next bonus. Terminal bonus on maturity/death. Cash value - surrender value - payment on cancellation nil, then increases slowly. Loans - 85% - 95% of cash value. Paid up policy - premiums stopped, reduced sum assured, may attract bonuses.

    ○ *Unit linked.* Depends directly on value of investments - minimum sum assured. Sum assured on death - guaranteed from outset, value of investments if higher. Premium - two parts; part retained by life office, part buys units. Premiums buy units in fund; amount retained can determine level of guaranteed sum assured. Investments classified into separate funds selected by policyholder, fund divided into units, units purchased by premiums. Unitised with profits fund - bonus added - reducible only if switched or surrendered. Switching funds allowed - subject to minimum value, free switches then charges; delay may be imposed. Unit prices depend on value of fund and number of units; units bought at higher (offer) price and cashed at lower (bid) price.

- *Charges.* Unallocated premium. Bid/Offer spread. Annual management - charge on fund - accumulation units. Capital/Initial units - additional management charge. Policy fee or allocation percentage. Cancellation fee.

- *Flexible whole life policies.* Flexible sum assured, usually low, medium, maximum. Costs met by monthly charge based on mortality. Reviews: first after ten years, then every five years, eventually annually. Options: to reduce sum assured; to increase sum assured on specific events; to include critical illness; waiver of premium; PHI. lump sum investment on non qualifying contract.

- *Personal accident and sickness insurance.* Lump sum on death or serious disability. Income for disability for 104 weeks. Annual contract.

- *Permanent health insurance*

    ○ *Objective.* To replace earnings lost through long term disability, taking account of state incapacity benefit and SSP.

    ○ *Benefits.* Replacement of earnings. No earnings - no insurable interest except for housewives. No loss of earnings (eg continued salary) - no payment.

    ○ *Income.* Benefit reduced by other payments: income payment = proportion of pre-disability earnings; proportion may differ for different levels of earnings; income may escalate. Deferment period applies: longer deferment = lower premium; repeat of same illness - deferment waived. Proportionate benefit paid for lower earnings resulting from disability. Income may escalate or be index linked. Unemployment - PHI not available. Unemployment while insured - cover may continue.

BPP PUBLISHING

    ° *Definition of disability.* Unable to follow: own occupation; any occupation with experience; any occupation.

    ° *Taxation.* Premiums not eligible for relief. Benefits are tax free.

- *Critical illness*

    ° *Problems.* Healthcare costs. Loss of earnings. Cost of earnings. Cost of help. Recovery costs. Cost of alterations. Cost of equipment. Transport costs. Retirement supplement.

    ° *Cause.* Diagnosis of specified illness.

- *Underwriting.* Underwriting is decision on level of risk of each proposal and acceptance terms or decline. Factors: age; sex; health - own present/past and family; occupation; hobbies; lifestyle; sometimes residence and aviation. Non medical limits may apply. Underwriting usually by numerical system of rating.

- *Premiums and expenses.* Factors: death or morbidity; expenses; investment income.

Quick quiz

1   The level of benefit being paid under a PHI contract is affected by all the following forms of income except:

    A   benefits payable under another PHI policy;
    B   continued earnings from an employer;
    C   an insured's continuing investment income;
    D   the state sickness benefit.

2   If the fund growth rate under a flexible whole life contract is less than the assumed rate, one of the possible consequences at the end of a review period is:

    A   an automatic premium loan facility will be activated;
    B   the premium may be reduced;
    C   the premium paying term may be extended;
    D   the sum assured may be reduced.

3   A businesswoman wants to provide an income for her children in the event of her death while they are still dependent. The most suitable contract is:

    A   a convertible increasable renewable term assurance;
    B   a decreasing term assurance payable in instalments;
    C   an index linked level term assurance;
    D   a limited payment whole life assurance.

4   A family income policy for 20 years has an income benefit level of £2,000 per month. The life assured dies ten years and ten months after the policy's inception. How much benefit will be paid in total?

    A   £110,000
    B   £220,000
    C   £240,000
    D   £480,000

5   Norman is aged 27, married with two young children. He wants a policy which provides high protection on his death, and which has the right to be turned into an investment plan when the children are independent. A contract which will meet all these requirements is:

    A   an increasable term assurance;
    B   an endowment with renewal options;
    C   a flexible whole life contract;
    D   a with profits whole life policy.

6   Who administers the estate of someone who has died, whether they have left a will or whether they are intestate?

     A   Administrators.
     B   Executors.
     C   Legal personal representatives.
     D   Trustees.

7   One of the principal uses of decreasing term assurance is:

     A   to provide an income during temporary disability;
     B   to pay a lump sum on diagnosis of a specified illness;
     C   to provide a flexible means of long-term savings;
     D   to repay a mortgage on death.

8   Which of the following features does decreasing term assurance have in common with family income benefit?

     A   They have an unlimited insurance period.
     B   They are both decreasing term assurances.
     C   They both pay a low surrender value on early encashment.
     D   They are both classified as investments under the Financial Services Act.

9   Under which type of life policy is it possible to take a percentage of the surrender value as a loan without undertaking to repay it on a specific date?

     A   Level term assurance.
     B   Personal pension.
     C   Unit-linked endowment.
     D   With profits endowment.

The solutions to the questions in the quiz can be found at the end of this Study Text. Before checking your answers against those solutions, you should look back at this chapter and use the information in it to correct your answers.

Answers to questions

1   (a)   Funeral costs, loss of income, need for living expenses, debts, tax liabilities.

     (b)   Structural alterations to house.

     (c)   High life cover, cheap, guaranteed insurability on conversion.

     (d)   Extra benefits: can be extended, sum assured can be increased, policy can be converted regardless of health.

2   (a)   The sum assured cannot reduce and usually increases.

     (b)   Direct link with investment performance.

     (c)   Protection continues without further premiums.

     (d)   Equity, property, fixed interest, cash, managed, unitised with-profits.

     (e)   Policyholder can change the nature of the investment, usually free for one/two switches a year.

     (f)   Unallocated premium, bid/offer spread, annual management charge, capital/initial units, policy fee, cancellation fee.

3   (a)   Sum assured can be chosen from range; reviewed after ten years then every five, eventually annually, to assess adequacy of premium; if premium inadequate, sum assured will be reduced or premium increased.

     (b)   Personal accident and sickness.

     (c)   To replace some of the earnings lost following long-term disability.

(d)   It is the period from beginning of disability to beginning of payment of benefit; the longer the deferment, the lower the premium.

(e)   Own, any for which trained and experienced, any occupation.

4   (a)   On diagnosis of illness specified in the policy.
    (b)   Age; health - own present and past, family health; occupation; hobbies; lifestyle.

Chapter 13

PENSIONS

Chapter topic list	Syllabus reference
1 Pension from employment and personal pensions	C 3.5
2 Tax advantages of pension schemes	C 3.1, C 3.2
3 State pensions	C 3.4
4 Occupational pension schemes	C 3.3, C 3.5 - C 3.7
5 Executive pension plans (EPPs)	C 3.12
6 Personal pensions	C 3.3, C 3.8, C 3.9
7 Contracting in and out of SERPS	C 3.4
8 Portability of occupational scheme benefits	C 3.10
9 Use of unit trusts and investment trusts	C 3.13
10 Fund risks	C 3.14
11 Retirement options	C 3.11
12 Objectives of stakeholder pensions	C 3.15

Introduction

Having looked at protection, we will now move on to one of the most important forms of financial provision - provision for an income in retirement.

1   PENSION FROM EMPLOYMENT AND PERSONAL PENSIONS

1.1   Imagine a small firm of architects with just two partners. They appointed an office manager who has now been with them for two years and is aged 40. She is responsible for the entire administration of the office and liaison with clients when the partners are absent. She is therefore a key employee for the firm and the partners have decided that they want to provide her with an **occupational pension** in addition to the pension she will receive from the state. Let us now ask a simple question: what decisions will they have to take between the time that their conscience tells them that they should provide her with a pension until the time when pension arrangements are in place?

1.2   They have to decide on **six factors**.

BPP PUBLISHING

Factor	Decision to be made
Eligibility	She is eligible to be provided by them with a pension simply because she is an employee of the firm.
Basis of pension	They can provide her with one of two pensions - **earnings-related** or **investment-related** (see Section 4 of this chapter).
Pension date	When will her pension begin? In practice this will be linked to her retirement age and will be known as the **Normal Retirement Age (NRA)**.
Other benefits	The most common benefit is likely to be some form of life assurance which pays on her death either a lump sum or an income or both. As this life assurance is payable if she dies while she is in the firm's service it is called **Death in Service Benefit** (DIS) and the income is normally referred to as a **dependant's pension**.
Who pays?	All these benefits will cost money. Will she contribute towards the cost (a **contributory scheme**) or will they pay the entire cost themselves and not require any contribution at all from her (a **non contributory scheme**)?
Who administers?	They can administer the scheme themselves and the fund which they will set up with the pension contributions (a **self administered scheme**). This is unlikely to make sense for a small firm and they are more likely to pay contributions to an insurance company (an **insured scheme**). The insurance company is then responsible for all the investment of the funds.

1.3 You can now **review the decisions** which they have had to take. Not once was there a mention of the word **tax** and the only reference to the state pension was that they wanted to provide her with a pension in addition to the state pension.

1.4 So far the decisions are quite simple. They get a bit more complicated later when we see how tax can affect her pension and how it can **interact with the state pension**.

Personal pensions

> **KEY TERM**
>
> A **personal pension** is a do-it-yourself scheme. In the overwhelming majority of cases personal pensions are for people who have no pension in respect of their earnings but who want to provide one. Anybody is eligible to contribute to a personal pension if they have earnings which are not already providing them with a pension.

1.5 Personal pensions are **investment-related only** (see later). The partners above could contribute to a personal pension, instead of an occupational pension, for the office manager. Alternatively, if they did not wish to set up a pension arrangement for her, she could provide one for herself.

2 TAX ADVANTAGES OF PENSION SCHEMES

2.1 A pension scheme is eligible for **special tax treatment** provided it meets certain rules (see later). In this chapter we look at the special tax treatment and the rules which have to be fulfilled in order to obtain that tax treatment.

Contributions

2.2 **Contributions** made to an approved pension scheme are eligible for **tax relief**. This applies to contributions made by an employer or an employee and to contributions made to either an occupational pension scheme or to a personal pension.

2.3 In the case of occupational pensions the employer's contributions might be seen as a **benefit in kind**. However, unlike other benefits in kind, pension contributions by an employer are not treated as taxable income in the hands of the employee if they are to an approved pension scheme.

Hancock annuities

2.4 One of the conditions for the tax treatment of the employer's contribution is that a pension scheme must be approved by the **Pension Schemes Office (PSO)**, a department of the Inland Revenue. This will normally be given only if the contributions are paid before an employee retires, the retirement age being not later than age 75.

2.5 Early this century an employer bought an immediate annuity for an elderly member of staff who had already retired. The employer then tried to claim tax relief on the contribution. The Inland Revenue, through one of its inspectors - Mr Hancock - refused the relief. The employer took the Revenue to court and won, and Mr Hancock went down in history through the name 'Hancock annuity'.

2.6 In principle, these annuities are like any other pension annuity, and the annuity income is **fully taxable**. They are *not* set up under trust (a normal Revenue requirement), and they are purchased by a lump sum contribution from an employer for an employee on or after retirement (at any age) or is an annuity purchased for someone over 75. A condition is that the annuity must begin at once, ie be an immediate annuity.

Fund

2.7 The fund into which the contributions are paid is **free from tax on its income** (other than dividend income) and **capital gains**. This means that, all other things being equal, it will grow faster than a fund which suffers tax.

Retirement benefits

2.8 There are two types of benefit available at retirement - a **pension** and a **lump sum**.

Pension

2.9 The retirement pension is **taxable as earned income**.

BPP
PUBLISHING

Lump sum

2.10   When a pension is due to begin the pensioner can take a reduced pension in return for receiving a **lump sum**. It is important to remember this point - with few exceptions the lump sum cannot be taken without forgoing some of the pension. This lump sum is **free from tax**.

Life cover

2.11   This is treated very similarly to a retirement pension. If a **dependant's pension income** is provided by life assurance then the pension will be **taxed as earned income**. Any **lump sum** paid from life assurance will be **tax free**.

Question 1

(a)   If you decide that you wish to provide an occupational pension for an employee, what are the first six factors you must consider?

(b)   What is a Hancock annuity?

Rules for approval

2.12   In order to obtain the special tax treatment a large number of **rules** must be fulfilled. We are concerned only with a relatively small number and at a relatively basic level.

2.13   The rules are divided into two kinds:

(a)   those which must be **fulfilled by the scheme from inception and which are part of the basic structure** of the scheme.

(b)   those which are related to various limits which must be observed and which relate primarily to the **benefits and contributions**.

We deal with the second kind of rules later in this chapter.

Rules on the structure

2.14   The fundamental rules which must be fulfilled are as follows.

(a)   The only benefits allowable must be a **pension or lump sum to be available at a specified age** and/or a **pension and a lump sum available on death**.

(b)   **Occupational schemes**

(i)   The **employer must contribute** to the scheme
(ii)   The **employer must be responsible for the administration** of the scheme
(iii)   The scheme must be **in trust**

(c)   **Personal pensions.** The scheme must be **in trust** (unless the provider is an insurer in which case it can be issued under deed poll).

(d)   **Assignment.** The pension benefit **cannot be assigned** under either an occupational or a personal pension.

3 STATE PENSIONS

3.1 The state pension is provided for the majority of UK citizens. It is based on the contributions which have been paid into the state social security fund via **National Insurance Contributions (NICs)**.

3.2 The pension will be a **fixed amount each week** which is usually increased each year. It is paid in full to individuals who have paid contributions for 90% of their working life beginning at age 16. People who are registered as unemployed or long term disabled or in full time education are credited with contributions in order to maintain the benefit.

3.3 The state pension becomes payable at 65 for men and 60 for women, although in the next century (by 2020) this will change to a **state retirement age** of 65 for both men and women. Thus, currently the 'working life' referred to in Paragraph 3.2 is 90% of 49 years for men (16 - 65) and 90% of 44 years for women (16 - 60).

3.4 The basic state pension is available for both employees and the self employed but **employees are eligible for an additional pension** known as the State Earnings Related Pension Scheme (SERPS). This is related to an individual's earnings that exceed a certain minimum level.

3.5 SERPS is not based on all of an employee's earnings. The State sets a lower **earnings limit**, and no entitlement to SERPS will be built up by employees whose earnings are below this level. There is also an upper earnings limit and earnings in excess of that limit are ignored when an employee's SERPS benefits are calculated. The amount of SERPS payable can therefore be stated as a percentage of this 'middle band' of income.

3.6 Both SERPs and pensions for spouses changed from 1999/2000, and there is a period of transition between 2000/2001 and 2009/2010 - ie for individuals contracted into SERPS retiring during those years. The current and proposed bases are as follows.

Old basis to 1998/99	New basis
State Earnings Related Pension Scheme (SERPS)	
1.25% of the average of the **best 20 years** of revalued band earnings for each year (maximum - **25%**)	1.25% becomes 1.0% (from 1/80th to 1/100th) 'Best 20 years' becomes 'lifetime earnings' 25% becomes 20% in 10 equal instalments from 1999/2000 - 2009/2010 (½% per year reduction).
Widow's/Widower's pension	
Basic pension plus spouse's SERPS pension plus (for widowers) wife's SERPS. Maximum allowed is the overall maximum for one person of 25%	SERPS spouse's pension entitlement reduced to 50%.

3.7 The State allows employees to withdraw from the SERPS part of the state pension. This process of withdrawal is known as **contracting out**. It is subject to conditions which we look at later on in this chapter.

4 OCCUPATIONAL PENSION SCHEMES

4.1 We have already seen that there are two kinds of pension scheme - earnings-related (**final salary schemes**) and investment-related (**money purchase schemes**).

Final salary schemes

> **KEY TERM**
>
> In a **final salary scheme** - also known as a **defined benefits scheme** - the pension can be based on employees' earnings at retirement and linked to the number of years they have worked for the firm.

4.2 For example, the basis might be a pension of 1/80th of earnings at retirement multiplied by the number of years they have been with the firm. If, therefore, earnings at retirement are £16,000 a year and they have worked for the firm for 20 years, the pension will be:

earnings (£16,000) × 1/80th (£200) × 20 years = £4,000 per annum.

The advantage of this type of pension is that it gives a **guarantee** of a pension linked to earnings at retirement.

4.3 The title given to this type of scheme is final salary, but this is a little misleading because the pension can be based not only on an employee's salary at retirement but upon any other remuneration such as overtime, commission and benefits in kind. The broad rule is that **if the benefit is taxable it's pensionable**.

4.4 As you will see later, a final salary scheme leaves the employer with a **commitment of which the cost is unknown,** and it is unlikely that a small firm would use this approach.

Money purchase schemes

> **KEY TERM**
>
> A **money purchase pension** - also known as a **defined contribution scheme** - does not provide any guarantee regarding the level of pension which will be available. It consists of two parts - **build up** and **pension**.

Build up

4.5 During the years that an individual is earning, contributions will be paid to a money purchase fund and the total fund will be **built up** by those contributions and the returns on the investment of the contributions. The fund can be built up in one of the following ways.

(a) **With profit**

A guaranteed minimum sum will be available at retirement which will be increased by reversionary bonuses and terminal bonus.

(b) **Unit linked**

A fund will be built up in the same way as a unit linked endowment with the same potential fluctuations being a feature of the plan.

(c) **Deposit**

Interest is added to contributions in the same way as any other bank or building society deposit account.

Pension

4.6   At retirement the fund will then be used to buy an annuity which will then be payable as a **pension** for the remainder of the individual's life.

Limits

4.7   Various **limits apply to the benefits and contributions** in respect of an occupational pension scheme. These limits apply to both final salary and money purchase schemes. Even though as you will see the basis of a final salary scheme bears a remarkable similarity to the limits for tax purposes, that does not alter the fact that the limits also apply to money purchase schemes.

Retirement benefits pension

4.8   There is a limit on the retirement pension of **two-thirds of an employee's remuneration at retirement**. Thus in the case of our office manager at the beginning of the chapter, if her final salary is £16,000 pa, she will be allowed to have a pension of two-thirds of £16,000, ie £10,667.

4.9   In order to achieve this, she must have worked for the firm for **20 years**. In her case, if her employment begins at the age of 40 and she retires at the age of 60 she will achieve this qualifying period. However, the employer must be willing to pay for a pension to be achieved after that length of time and it can be very expensive. Consequently, it is more usual for a pension to be built up over 40 years.

4.10 EXAMPLE: RETIREMENT BENEFITS

Peter Pan joined his employer at the age of 25 and retired at 65. His earnings at retirement were £24,000 a year and his pension is based on a fraction of 1/60th of final salary for each year of service.

His pension after 40 years will therefore be:

£24,000 × 1/60th (£400) × number of years service (40) = £16,000 a year

Had he worked for the firm for say, 25 years, the calculation would have been:

£24,000 × 1/60th × 25 = £10,000 a year

On the other hand, if Peter had joined the company at the age of 45 and the employer was willing to pay the extra cost, he could have a pension of:

£24,000 × 1/30th × 20 = £16,000 a year

In other words he would achieve a two-thirds pension after 20 years.

4.11   A pension which is built up at this fast rate is normally only available to senior executives of large companies or the directors of small companies. It is known as a **short service** or **uplifted pension**.

4.12 If Peter's earnings had been £240,000 a year instead of £24,000 we would not have been able to multiply every figure by 10. The reason is that there is a limit on the amount of earnings on which a pension can be based. This limit - known as **capped earnings** or the **earnings cap**- began in 1989 at the level of £60,000 a year and has been increased most years since.

Tax free cash

4.13 There is a limit on the tax free lump sum at retirement of **1½ times an employee's earnings**. Thus, in the case of Peter earning £24,000 a year he would be entitled to a tax free lump sum of £36,000. However, remember that in order to get it he must reduce his pension below the maximum pension to which he is entitled.

4.14 In addition, in the same way that pension benefits are reduced below the maximum for less than 20 years service, so the maximum tax free sum will be less than 1½ times final salary for anyone with **less than 20 years service**.

Death in service

Lump sum

4.15 The **maximum lump sum payable** on death is **four times an employee's remuneration at that time** or £5,000 if greater. If the employee has contributed to the scheme then the employee's contributions may be added to this lump sum together with interest on them at a reasonable rate. The beneficiary is selected by the trustees of a scheme, to whom an insured lump sum is payable by an insurer. The trustees will normally choose a beneficiary named by the employee, but are not compelled to do so.

Dependants' pensions

4.16 There are three limits applied to **dependants' pensions**:

(a) **Spouse**. The limit is two-thirds of the employee's pension entitlement.

(b) **Children**. The limit per child is one-third of the employee's pension entitlement.

(c) **Overall limit**. The total limit of all dependants' pensions payable to spouse and children is an amount equal to the employee's pension.

4.17 If Peter had built up a pension entitlement of £12,000 at the time of his death in service, his spouse could receive a pension of £8,000 per year and if he had one child that child could be paid £4,000 a year. If however Peter had more than one child the £4,000 a year would have to be divided between them so that the overall total payment was £12,000. If Peter had no children at all the limit for his spouse would still be £8,000 a year.

4.18 Employees' contributions are limited to **15% of their capped earnings**. In the case of a final salary scheme there is no specific limit on the employer's contributions. However the Inland Revenue applies the principle that contributions must not be so great that they appear likely to produce benefits in excess of the maximum which applies to occupational schemes. For this purpose the Revenue makes assumptions regarding the growth of earnings and investments.

Normal retirement age

4.19 Retirement ages for occupational pensions are divided into two kinds - **planned** and **unplanned**.

Planned

4.20 An occupational scheme can provide for a **planned retirement age** - the normal retirement age (NRA) - of an employee at any time between 60 and 75. In practice the overwhelming majority will choose retirement ages between 60 and 65.

Unplanned

4.21 An employee may retire earlier than the earliest NRA of 60 but it **cannot be planned in advance**. This is what is known as 'early retirement' and can take place from age 50 for any reason or at any age for reasons of serious ill health.

Additional voluntary contributions (AVCs)

4.22 An employee may be entitled under an occupational pension scheme to benefits which are **less than the maximum allowed by the Inland Revenue**. There will usually be one of two reasons for this: (a) the employee has **not worked for the employer for long enough**, or (b) the level of benefits provided by the employer is **less than allowed**.

4.23 An example of the first is where a pension scheme is based on 1/60th of final salary for each year of service and the employee will have worked for the firm for 25 years. This will be long enough for the Revenue to allow a **two-thirds pension** but if the employer is not willing to pay for that (and in most cases they are not) then the employee's pension will be less than the maximum allowed.

Alternatively the employer may provide a pension which is **mediocre**. If say, the pension was 1/120th of the employee's final salary, then even 40 years of service would not entitle the employee to the maximum of two-thirds.

4.24 In order to deal with these two situations an employee may make **voluntary contributions** (in addition to any compulsory contributions) in order to improve the benefits. There are two ways of doing this:

(a) via the employer (in-house)
(b) independently (FSAVCs)

In-house AVC schemes

4.25 **Employers must provide AVC schemes if employees wish to contribute voluntarily.** These schemes are sometimes known as additional voluntary contribution schemes, but this fails to distinguish them from the free standing AVC schemes which are described later. The expression 'in house' AVC scheme is a more accurate way of describing the employer's arrangements.

4.26 The employer's scheme may perform one of two functions. If the main pension scheme is a final salary scheme the employer can add years of service to the employee's total in order to improve the benefits. This method is often known as the **'added years' method**.

4.27 EXAMPLE: ADDED YEARS' METHOD

An employee paying AVCs to the employer's scheme may ultimately receive a pension of say, 28/60th of final salary even though the employee may have worked for only 25 years. The additional three years, not representing actual service, provide additional benefits.

4.28 The alternative is for an employer to arrange a **money purchase scheme**. This can be done whether the main pension scheme is final salary or money purchase. The employer's AVC scheme will build up a fund in the same way as any other money purchase scheme and that fund will be used to buy an annuity which will be added to the employee's main pension scheme benefit.

Free standing AVC schemes (FSAVCs)

4.29 An employee can arrange to pay voluntary contributions to a provider quite **independently of the employer**. This provider will usually be an insurance company although it may also be a bank, building society or unit trust.

4.30 FSAVCs are available only on a **money purchase basis**.

Tax treatment of AVCs

4.31 This is a useful place to remind ourselves of the limit on employee's contributions for occupational pensions. **The limit remains at 15%**. Thus if, for example, an employee was a member of a contributory scheme to which contributions of 4% were required and was voluntarily contributing an additional 5%, then the employee could contribute no more than 6% to a free standing AVC scheme to make up the total of 15%.

4.32 Notice that an employee may contribute to both an in house scheme and a free standing AVC scheme. Notice also that **the limit on the benefits does not change**. The benefits from the main scheme plus those from an in house AVC scheme plus those from an FSAVC scheme must still not exceed in total the limits set by the Revenue, ie two-thirds of final salary as a maximum pension.

4.33 In order to ensure that the total pension benefits from all schemes do not exceed the maximum permitted levels, the Inland Revenue require anyone contributing £2,400 or more a year (£200 a month) to any FSAVC to supply to the FSAVC provider **information about his current benefit entitlement**. The FSAVC provider will then do a calculation to test if the total benefits will exceed the Revenue limits.

This test - known as the **headroom test** - is not required if FSAVC contributions are less than £2,400 a year.

Comparison of in house AVCs and FSAVCs

4.34 Both schemes have their advantages and disadvantages. The **costs of administering** an in house scheme will usually be met by the employer whereas the employee must pay the charges which are appropriate for a free standing AVC scheme. On the other hand with an FSAVC the **employee chooses the provider** as well as the fund whereas under an in house scheme the employer will have made that choice.

4.35 FSAVCs are **not available to controlling directors** and only one is allowed per tax year. FSAVC benefits may be taken early (after age 50) if the link with the main scheme is broken.

Earnings cap

4.36 The contributions by employees for occupational pension schemes and the benefits in the form of lump sum and pension are subject to an **earnings cap** which is increased each year in line with inflation. For 2000/2001 the earnings cap is £91,800.

Thus the maximum contribution and maximum benefits for 2000/2001 are as follows.

Contribution	15% × £91,800	= £13,770
Lump sum	1.5 × £91,800	= £137,700
Pension	2/3 × £91,800	= £61,200

4.37 The earnings cap applies only to contributions for the purposes of **personal pension plans**.

5 EXECUTIVE PENSION PLANS (EPPs)

5.1 **Any employee can have an EPP**. An EPP could be provided, for example, for an office cleaner who may have no aspirations to become an executive of the company. The reason they have become known as executive pension plans or sometimes **directors' pensions plans** is the market at which they are aimed.

5.2 EPPs are subject to precisely the same rules as any other occupational pension scheme. They are in fact **occupational schemes for just one person** or perhaps for a small number of individuals. They have the advantage that they can provide different levels of benefits from those for employees in the main occupational scheme and those benefits may also be confidential to the employee concerned.

Question 2

(a) What are the tax advantages of an exempt approved occupational pension scheme?
(b) Outline the rules and limits for exempt approved occupational pension schemes.
(c) Who can be a provider of a free-standing AVC?
(d) What type of pension scheme is an executive pension plan?

6 PERSONAL PENSIONS

6.1 **Personal pensions** have existed since July 1988. Prior to that year pension plans which were remarkably similar existed but were under a different name - **retirement annuities**. Retirement annuities were subject to different tax rules but performed the same function as personal pensions. They were usually called by the section number of the Act of Parliament that created them, ie Section 226 schemes.

> ### KEY TERM
>
> **Personal pensions** are money purchase schemes and work on the same basis as any other money purchase scheme. They also have the same tax advantages as were outlined earlier in the chapter.

Eligibility

6.2 **Any individual** who has earnings which are not the basis of a pension can make contributions to a personal pension. The self employed have earnings for which only the self employed themselves can make pension arrangements. Any employee who is not in an occupational pension can also arrange for a personal pension. The principle applies to any employee who has a second source of non-pensionable earnings.

6.3 The basic principle is that anybody with **non-pensionable earnings** can contribute to a personal pension.

Limits

NRA

6.4 **Normal Retirement Age** can be at any time between 50 and 75. Unplanned retirement - early retirement - can take place before age 50 but only on the grounds of serious ill health. However, some occupations are allowed to have normal retirement ages earlier than 50.

Retirement limits

6.5 There are **no limits** on the amount of the pension allowable. At retirement the fund can be used to buy the highest annuity available at the time and there will be no restriction on the amounts.

6.6 There will be **no cash restriction** on the amount of tax-free cash but it is limited to 25% of the size of the fund at the time. The individual effectively takes a reduced pension in order to obtain the tax free cash simply because only the balance (75%) of the fund remains for an annuity purchase (ie buying an annual pension).

Contributions

6.7 Although benefits are not limited, there is a restriction placed on **contributions**. The limit is a percentage of the net relevant capped earnings of the individual concerned which, in the case of employees, will be total remuneration, and in the case of the self employed will be basically taxable profit. The percentage increases with age, from 17.5% (aged up to 35) to 40% (aged 61 or more). Up to 5% of net relevant capped earnings (deductible from the pension limit) can be paid for personal pension term assurance.

6.8 If contributions in any years are less than the maximum allowable then the **unused relief can be used up in future years on a cumulative basis**. This carrying forward - known as the **carry forward rule** - can continue for up to six years. In addition a contribution made in any tax year can be treated for tax purposes as though it had been paid in the previous year or, if there were no net relevant earnings in that year, then it can be carried back to the year before that - the **carry back rule**. To use carry forward the full current year contribution must be made and must relate only to employee contributions. Employer contributions are not allowed for either carry forward or carry back.

6.9 The **maximum contribution** allowable in any one year is equal to the net relevant earnings in that year.

Tax treatment of contributions

6.10 Although tax relief is available on the contributions, the method by which it is given varies according to whether the policyholder is an employee or is self-employed.

(a) **Employees**

An employee pays contributions net of basic rate income tax. An employee who is a higher rate taxpayer will obtain an adjustment in their tax code to give higher rate relief.

An employee who is a non-taxpayer will not lose the tax relief. This puts the contributions on the same level as mortgage interest relief at source where non-taxpayers still benefit from the relief.

(b) **Self-employed**

The self employed pay contributions gross and obtain relief by deducting the contributions from their taxable profits.

Comparison of occupational and personal pensions

Costs

6.11 Factors to be taken into account in comparing the **costs** of occupational and personal pensions are as follows.

(a) The **employer *must* pay some of the costs of an occupational pension**. In practice employers pay most or all of the costs.

(b) An **employee must normally pay the entire cost of a personal pension**, but sometimes an employer will contribute to personal pensions on a group basis.

(c) An occupational pension places a **percentage limit** on the contributions by the employees and an **'appropriate' limit** on the contributions of employers.

(d) Contributions to a personal pension are limited as a **percentage of earnings** although the limit varies according to the age of the contributor.

Benefits

6.12 The benefits provided from a personal pension are **not guaranteed**. Even a with profits personal pension guarantees a minimum level of lump sum available at retirement but does not guarantee the actual amount of pension payable. There is no relationship between pension and employee's salary.

6.13 If an occupational pension is on a **final salary basis** then there will be **a clear link between benefits and earnings at retirement**. Such guarantees will be lost if the employee chooses to withdraw from (opt out of) the employer's occupational pension or if the employee chooses not to join in the first case.

6.14 Note the use of the term **'opt out'**. Withdrawal from SERPS is 'contracting out' but withdrawing from an employer's occupational pension scheme is 'opting out'.

6.15 The fact that an employee can remain a member of an occupational scheme *and* contribute to a personal pension (but *only* for contracting out purposes) must be taken into account. Consideration should be given by an employee who has contracted out of SERPS to contracting back in at an appropriate age - known as the **'pivotal age'**.

6.16 A **comparison** should always be made between occupational and personal pensions and indeed between final salary and money purchase occupational pension schemes.

Question 3

(a) What type of pension was preceded by personal pensions?

(b) What is meant by the 'carry forward' rule?

(c) Who can contribute to a personal pension?

(d) What is the basis of the percentage contribution limits for personal pensions?

(e) What is the difference in the tax treatment of personal pension contributions for employees and the self-employed?

7 CONTRACTING IN AND OUT OF SERPS

7.1 We saw in the earlier section on state pensions that there is a basic state pension plus (for employees) SERPS. We also saw that employees could be contracted out of SERPS either by their employers or by the employees themselves. We now look in a little more detail at **the workings of SERPS**.

7.2 We already know that people receiving earnings pay National Insurance contributions (NICs). NICs are used as the basis of payments for various benefits of which **state pensions** is just one example.

7.3 When employees are contracted out of SERPS this **reduces the liability of the Department of Social Security (DSS)** - the government department responsible for administering social security benefits. As the liability is reduced so its need for income is reduced. The cost of SERPS has been carefully worked out and therefore the DSS can rebate the cost of the benefit which it is no longer required to supply.

7.4 The question is - **who gets the rebate?** This is where we briefly look at the practice.

Employer does contracting out

7.5 When an employer contracts employees out of SERPS the employer has one of two alternatives:

(a) to guarantee that the pension will meet **minimum requirements,** or
(b) to guarantee that **minimum contributions will be paid towards a pension.**

Minimum requirements

7.6 An employer, until 5 April 1997, used to be able to promise employees that their pension would be at least equivalent to the one they would have received had they remained in SERPS. This was the **Guaranteed Minimum Pension or GMP**. The principal condition on which this was based was that the employer set up a pension scheme which, like SERPS, was earnings related. This meant a final salary scheme. From April 1997, contracted-out salary related schemes (COSRs) must meet a kind of 'benchmark' test that they are 'broadly equivalent' to the benefits under a reference scheme. (The reference scheme offers higher pension payments than SERPS.) GMPs accrued before April 1997 must still be provided.

7.7 In return for the employer paying for a final salary pension scheme, the NIC rebates are used to **reduce both the employer's and the employee's NICs.** Thus where employees are members of a contracted out final salary scheme their NICs are less than they would be if they were not contracted out. The same applies to the employer's contributions.

Guaranteed minimum contribution

7.8 The expression '**guaranteed minimum contribution**' is not one that is officially used but describes the principle on which the employer's alternative is based. This is that the employer does not guarantee an earnings-related pension but instead pays the rebates - both the employer's and the employee's rebates - into a pension scheme which is not earnings

212

related. This inevitably means that a money purchase scheme is installed. A money purchase scheme which is used for contracting out purposes is know as a Contracted Out Money Purchase Scheme (COMPS).

7.9 The employee pays contributions through the employer who deducts the contributions from salary and then pays them into the pension scheme. The employer also pays into the pension scheme. The employer also pays into the pension scheme an amount equal to the employer's rebate. The DSS receives the balance of both contributions. Rebates are now related to the age of the employee and range from 2.2% to 9% per annum of middle band earnings.

7.10 The employer must pay an amount at least equal to the employer and employee rebates into the pension scheme, as pension contributions but can pay more. The employee's portion of the payments qualifies for tax relief.

7.11 The employer might decide, however, not to take any contribution from the employee, but to pay the total amount as an employer contribution.

Employee does contracting out

7.12 Where the employee does the contracting out then **full NICs are paid by both the employer and the employee**. The employee chooses a personal pension provider (insurance company, bank, building society or unit trust) and the DSS pays both NIC rebates directly to the pension provider. The pension is known as an appropriate personal pension scheme.

When to contract in/out

7.13 The benefit of contracting out with an appropriate personal pension scheme lies in the possibility that the fund that will be built up from the NIC rebates plus any incentive which may apply together with the value of the annuity purchased at retirement will produce a pension which **is greater** than would have been produced by SERPS.

7.14 You cannot know whether contracting out is worthwhile or not until it is too late to do anything about it. However, it is fairly obvious that the longer the period that contributions are paid into a contracted out personal pension (the appropriate personal pension scheme) the bigger the fund available at retirement is likely to be. The fund itself is known as **'protected rights benefit'**. The rebates are known as **'minimum contributions'**.

7.15 Equally it is obvious that if there are only **two or three years to go to retirement** there is no time in which to build up an adequate fund to produce a pension bigger than SERPS.

7.16 Consequently not only is the 'right age' somewhere between 25 and 60/65 but there are so many assumptions that have to be made regarding investment growth and earnings growth that it is impossible to set a specific age. This is one of those questions to which there is no fixed answer. You can only advise on the basis of **reasonable assumptions**. Each pension provider will recommend a **pivotal age** for their product and for each sex.

8 PORTABILITY OF OCCUPATIONAL SCHEME BENEFITS

8.1 When employees leave their employer after more than two years in a company pension scheme, they are entitled to do one of two things with their pension: **leave it where it is or take it somewhere else** (or, if they are over 50, take benefits from the scheme).

8.2 If they leave their pension entitlements with the old employer then they will simply collect a pension from that employer when they eventually retire. This is known as a **preserved pension**. It must be increased each year even though the employee is no longer working with the company (this is known as **statutory revaluation**).

8.3 If the employee chooses to take the pension elsewhere then the employer must calculate the lump sum (**transfer value**) which they will pay as an alternative to being saddled with the liability to pay a pension on the employee's ultimate retirement. The employee can then ask for the transfer value to be paid to one of three destinations: a new employer, a personal pension or an individual guaranteed plan.

A new employer

8.4 If the new employer has an occupational pension scheme then the transfer value can be paid into that scheme, provided that the new employer is **willing to accept it** (they don't have to).

8.5 If the new scheme is a **final salary scheme** then the transfer value will be used to **increase the number of years on which the employee's pension will be based** - the same 'added years' principle that was discussed earlier.

8.6 If on the other hand the new scheme is a **money purchase scheme** then the transfer value will simply be added to the **employee's share of the pension fund** and invested in the same way as the existing money in the fund. (Any GMP would convert to protected rights.)

Personal pension

8.7 **Transfer values can be paid to a personal pension**. The employee will then receive a pension which will depend on the value of the investments and the annuity rates at the time. If the previous employer's scheme was a money purchase scheme then the personal pension fund will be based on the same principles.

8.8 Remember that the personal pension fund can be built up on a **with profit**, **unit linked** or **deposit basis**.

Individual guaranteed plan

8.9 If an employee is leaving a contracted out final salary scheme and the new employer has a pension scheme which is not contracted out (often known as a **contracted in scheme**) then the employee will not be able to transfer to the new employer all of the transfer value from the old scheme.

8.10 If the employee likes the certainty of an earnings related pension and therefore is not happy with the insecurity of a personal pension, the employee can take advantage of a third alternative. This is an **individual occupational pension scheme** which contains an earnings related guarantee. That guarantee corresponds with the SERPS part of a contracted out scheme. (This scheme can accept the GMP. However, it cannot take COMPS Protected Rights.)

8.11 These individual pensions have the advantage that they provide an earnings related pension which obviously is not the case with a personal pension. The individual schemes are **single premium contracts issued by insurance companies**. They are usually known as **buy out bonds** although sometimes they are called **transfer plans**. They are also sometimes described by the section number of the Act of Parliament which brought them into existence, namely Section 32 schemes.

9   USE OF UNIT TRUSTS AND INVESTMENT TRUSTS

9.1   **Unit trusts** and **investment trusts** can both be used in order to fund for retirement income. However, their use is divided very clearly into two.

(a) **Pensions**

A pension fund can invest in a unit trust and buy shares in investment trusts. As such, such investments are precisely the same as any other investments by a pension fund. The fund itself will be subject to the normal pension rules regarding tax relief on contributions and tax reduced growth of the fund, but with the requirement to use a substantial part of the ultimate fund to buy a taxable pension.

(b) **Savings**

Individuals can buy units in unit trusts or shares in investment trusts and use either or both as a means of building up a fund.

Such investments will be totally unrelated to pensions and there will be no tax relief on the contributions. The funds themselves will be taxable unless they are part of a personal equity plan which will then be free from income tax and capital gains tax.

The advantages of buying investments in this way is that there will be no minimum age for drawing the benefits which will be entirely in the form of a lump sum. That lump sum can be used to buy a purchased life annuity but there is no requirement to do so.

Such savings should be held in a tax efficient package such as an ISA.

10   FUND RISKS

10.1   The main principle of pension fund investment is to ensure **security of assets plus good investment performance**. In order to achieve the former the fund will be invested amongst a wide range of assets.

10.2   If the fund is in respect of an **occupational pension scheme** providing final salary benefits, any **adverse performance risks will be borne by the fund**.

10.3   If however the scheme is a **money purchase scheme** or is a **personal pension** then the **risks will be borne by the individual employee** or policyholder. In the case of a with profit fund there will be no risk of the fund reducing but there could be a risk of it not increasing by as much as anticipated.

10.4   If the fund chosen is a **unit linked fund** then there will be same risks as with any other unit linked fund of a fall in the value of the investment.

10.5   A **deposit fund** will carry virtually no risk of loss of capital but will not produce very good performance over a long period of time.

Question 4

(a) What is the difference between contracting-out and opting-out?

(b) What is a COMPS?

215

(c) What options regarding a company pension entitlement are available to an employee on changing job?

---

11 RETIREMENT OPTIONS

11.1 Apart from the normal options at retirement of buying different kinds of annuity, eg level or increasing, single life or joint life, there are other options which give individuals a range of fundamentally **different choices of pension**.

Personal pensions

11.2 A person who has contributed to one or more personal pension plans can have the choice of **buying an annuity** from the insurance company which invested the contributions, or **exercising an option to buy an annuity from another insurance company** which is paying a better annuity rate.

11.3 This choice is known as the **open market option**. It is not in itself a pension. It is simply a right available to policyholders to exercise freedom of choice of pension provider.

Timing of personal pensions

Buying a lot of annuities

11.4 An individual can have **one or more personal pension plans** - there is no limit on the number, only on the total contributions which can be made to personal pensions. Each one of those pension plans can be converted into a pension at any age between 50 and 75. This means that a policyholder can **convert each one at a different time,** or convert several - but not all - at any one time. The effect is to have pensions beginning one after another rather than all starting at the same time.

11.5 The advantage of doing this is that, if **annuity rates** are low when the policyholder wants to begin receiving a pension, he can either defer taking all his pension entitlement or buy an annuity with just part of the total pension fund, leaving the rest to buy annuities at a later time when hopefully annuity rates have increased.

11.6 This possibility can be increased still further by making contributions to one pension plan which is split into a **large number of different policies**, each one of which can be converted to an annuity independently of the others.

11.7 This practice is known as **phased retirement**, even though it is not necessary to retire in order to begin receiving a pension. Alternatively such a practice is sometimes known as **staggered vesting**. Phased retirement, because of its costs, is not for those with small pension funds. A fund of around **£100,000** is usually needed to make the arrangement worthwhile.

11.8 The **advantages** of phased retirement are that it gives greater flexibility of retirement benefits, and defers the purchase of annuities until annuity rates increase at higher ages. The **disadvantages** include the possibility that annuity rates might not increase, but actually decrease. Worse still, if the remaining fund is unit-linked, the fund itself may fall in value. Also tax free cash is received piecemeal rather than in one lump sum.

Taking an income from your pension fund

11.9 If you have a personal pension fund, you can have an income from it without buying an annuity, if you so choose. You must withdraw some of your pension fund each year in order to give you an income. You do not have to buy an annuity until you reach age 75, although you may choose to do so earlier. Again this arrangement is not for small pension funds: a fund of around £100,000 is needed.

11.10 This arrangement is described as **income withdrawal**. Remember that an annuity has *not* been bought. As with phased retirement, the fund not yet withdrawn remains invested.

Occupational pension scheme

Open market option

11.11 An employee who is a member of an individual pension arrangement - usually known as an **executive pension plan** - will have the same choice as someone with a personal pension regarding where an annuity is bought. In other words, such employees have the choice of pension provider through the open market option.

Transfers to a personal pension

11.12 An employee is allowed to take an **occupational pension scheme transfer value to a personal pension scheme**. The benefits are subject to scrutiny to ensure that the transfer does not lead to any distortion of benefits.

The point of doing this is that it can enable the employee to take advantage of the benefits of phased retirement or income withdrawal.

Question 5
(a) What is the reason for using an open market option?
(b) What are the advantages of staggered vesting?
(c) What is an advantage of income drawdown?
(d) Why should someone with an executive pension plan transfer its value to a personal pension?

12 OBJECTIVES OF STAKEHOLDER PENSIONS

12.1 The government plans to introduce stakeholder pensions. The objectives of stakeholder pension arrangements are as follows.

(a) to encourage low-to-middle income individuals (usually those without access to an occupational scheme) to save for retirement via a regulated pension scheme;

(b) to ensure such regulated pension schemes have the following features:

(i) low charges
(ii) high flexibility
(iii) minimum regulatory requirements

12.2 Proposals issued in September 1999 aim to achieve these features.

(a) **Low charges**. Charges cannot be higher than 1% per annum, nor can there be hidden charges.

(b) **High flexibility**. The minimum contribution is to be £10 per annum. Contributions can continue to existing schemes whilst payments are made to the stakeholder pensions. If the contributions are less than £3,600 per annum, they can be made, regardless of the earnings position of a stakeholder, thereby allowing the unemployed, housepersons or those taking a sabbatical to continue.

(c) **Minimum regulatory requirements**. Only if contributions are above £3,600 will questions be asked regarding earnings.

12.3 Stakeholder pensions will impact upon financial planning in two key areas.

(a) If contributions are less than £3,600, stakeholder pensions will effectively be an extension of the range of tax efficient savings schemes currently available.

(b) Their impact on personal pension schemes may be significant, since their flexibility and low charges will make them very attractive. Personal pension plans will need to prove themselves as having superior investment features to compensate for the comparative weaknesses of their present format.

Chapter roundup

- *Pensions from employment*. Factors: eligibility - employee; basis of pension - final salary or money purchase; pension date - normal retirement age; other benefits - life cover; who pays - contributory or non contributory; who administers - employer or insurance company.

- *Personal pensions*. Eligibility - non pensionable earnings. Money purchase only.

- Tax advantages of pension schemes

  - *Contributions*. Tax relief for employers and employees and for personal pensions. Employer's contributions not taxed as employee benefit.

  - *Fund*. Free from tax on investment income other than for shares and gains.

  - *Retirement benefits*. Pension - taxable as earned income. Lump sum - tax free.

  - *Life cover*. Lump sum - tax free. Dependants' pension - taxable as earned income.

- *Rules for approval*. Structure: benefits must be pension or lump sum at specified age and/or pension/lump sum on death; occupational schemes - employer must contribute and administer scheme in trust; personal pensions - scheme must be in trust (insurer - under deed poll); assignment - pension benefit cannot be assigned.

- *State pensions*. Based on NICs; pension is flat rate each week based on contributions through 90% of working life. Long term unemployed or disabled or those in full time education credited with contributions. Basic pension for self employed plus (for employees only) SERPS; pension ages 65 for men and 60 women (65 for both in 21st century). SERPS based on band earnings between LEL and UEL; withdrawal from SERPS (contracting out) allowed.

- Occupational pension schemes

  - *Final salary*. Based on earnings and other remuneration at retirement and linked to number of years service. Cost is unknown.

  - *Money purchase*. Consists of build up of fund. Size of fund depends on performance. Basis of fund can be with profit, unit linked or deposit.

- *Occupational scheme limits*. Apply to final salary and money purchase schemes.

  - *Pension*. Maximum is two thirds of employee's remuneration after 20 years' service including pensions from previous employment (retained benefits) or after 40 years excluding retained benefits. Fast speed of build up of pension in less than 40 years normally for senior executives or directors.

  - *Tax-free lump sum*. Maximum 1.5 times employee's remuneration at retirement. Pension must be reduced to obtain lump sum.

- o *Death in service.* Lump sum: limited to 4 × remuneration plus employee's contributions (compulsory or voluntary); Dependant's pension: spouse: max is two thirds employee's pension entitlement; children - max per child is one third of employee's allowable pension; overall limit - total of dependants' pension must not exceed employee's pension.

- o *Revenue v Employers.* Above limits are what Revenue will allow, employer may not provide as much as those limits in benefits.

- o *Employees' contributions.* Limited to 15% of earnings, including compulsory, in house voluntary and free standing AVCs.

- o *Normal retirement age (NRA).* Planned - allowed between 60 and 75. Unplanned - Early retirement allowed: any time for ill health; from 50 for any other reason.

- *Additional voluntary contributions (AVCs).* Useful to increase benefits if less than Revenue limits

  - o *Via the employer.* In house AVCs: final salary scheme - can add years of service or arrange separate money purchase AVC scheme; money purchase main scheme - separate money purchase AVC.

  - o *Free standing AVC schemes (FSAVCs).* Employee contributes to independent provider on money purchase basis.

  - o *Limit.* Employee may make compulsory contributions and contribute to in house AVC scheme and FSAVC scheme provided: total contributions must not exceed 15%; ultimate benefits remain within Revenue limits.

  - o *Comparison.* Employer pays cost of in house AVC and chooses provider. Employee meets charges on FSAVC but also chooses provider.

- *Executive pension plans.* Anyone can have one if eligible. They are one person occupational schemes. Subject to same rules as any other scheme. Can provide different levels of benefit and be confidential.

- *Personal pensions.* Began in 1988, preceded by retirement annuities. All are money purchase schemes.

  - o *Eligibility.* Individuals with non pensionable earnings.

  - o *Limits.* Planned NRA - 50 - 75. Unplanned retirement - any age for ill health. Retirement pension: no limit; tax free cash: max 25% of fund.

  - o *Contributions.* Limit on contributions as percentage of (employees) total remuneration and (self employed) taxable profit. Unused relief can be carried forward and contribution can be carried back.

  - o *Tax treatment of contributions.* Employees: pay net of basic rate tax; relief is available to non taxpayers. Self employed: pay gross and obtain relief by reduction of taxable profit.

- *Comparison of occupational and personal pensions*

  - o *Costs.* Employer must pay some costs of occupational scheme. Employee normally pays entire cost of personal pension (employer may contribute). Occupational pension: specific limits on employee's contributions; benefit-related limit on employer's contribution. Personal pension - specific limit on contributions.

  - o *Benefits.* Personal pension benefits not guaranteed. With profits fund guarantees fund but not amount of pension. Final salary occupational scheme guarantees relationship between pension and pre-retirement earnings. Opt out will lose such guarantee.

- *State pensions* - contracting out of SERPS

  - o NIC rebates available for contracting out. Employer contracts out: equivalent pension with final salary scheme; rebates reduce NICs for employer and employee; Guaranteed minimum contribution with money purchase scheme - NIC rebates paid into scheme. Employee contracts out: rebates paid by DSS direct to provider.

  - o When to contract out/in. Contracting out builds up bigger fund over long term. Shorter period to retirement - contracting back in should be considered - no fixed age.

- Portability of occupational scheme benefit. Options: preserved pension with previous employers, take transfer value to: new employer if acceptable - either added years (final salary) or earmarked in new scheme (money purchase); personal pension; individual occupational pension - buy out bond/transfer plan.

- Unit trust and investment trust. Pension funds can invest in unit trust and buy shares in investment trust to build up fund. Individuals can also use unit trust and investment trust to build up fund: the tax advantages of pension fund are absent, but there is no specific age for taking benefits which are entirely in the form of a lump sum.

- Fund risks. Risk is reduced by spread of investment. Adverse performance borne by fund of final salary scheme and by scheme member in money purchase scheme. With profit and deposit funds do not decrease. Unit linked fund carries risk of volatility.

- Personal pensions: open market option available; phased retirement allowed; income withdrawal can be arranged.

- Occupational pensions: open market option available for executive pension plans; transfer values can be taken to personal pensions.

- *Stakeholder pensions.* Proposals for stakeholder pensions were issued in September 1999. The aim of these pensions is to encourage low-to-middle income families to save for retirement via a regulated pension scheme.

Quick quiz

1   One of the reasons that the self employed need pension planning is that:

A   they cannot contribute to a personal pension plan;
B   they are not eligible to receive the basic state pension;
C   they are not eligible to receive the State Earnings Related Pension Scheme;
D   they cannot receive any retirement pensions until they reach age 60.

2   The basic condition on which an employee can be contracted out of SERPS is:

A   the employer must contribute to a contracted out scheme;
B   the employee must be entitled to a guaranteed minimum pension;
C   he must make contributions under PAYE and based on his band earnings;
D   he must be a member of an alternative private pension scheme.

3   In the event of a member dying in service, to whom is the death in service benefit under a pension scheme policy payable in the first instance?

A   The beneficiaries named by the member.
B   The executor of the member's estate.
C   The trustees of the scheme.
D   The widow or widower.

4   The objective of a free standing additional voluntary contribution scheme is to enable an employee to:

A   increase his pension above the Revenue limits;
B   top up his pension scheme benefits;
C   share the cost of his employer's pension scheme;
D   create a segregated fund from which a tax free cash sum can be taken.

5   An appropriate personal pension scheme is a pension arrangement which is:

A   selected from an adviser's range of pension products as being the most suitable for a client's needs;

B   funded by an incentive from the Department of Social Security but is not eligible for National Insurance contribution rebates;

C   used to contract an employee out of the state earnings related pension scheme;

D   suitable for receiving free standing additional voluntary contributions from an employee.

6   If an individual is a member of his employer's exempt approved scheme and is also a member of a free standing additional voluntary contribution scheme, his total lump sum death benefit (excluding a refund of contributions) in 2000/2001 if his annual earnings are £50,000 cannot exceed:

A   £50,000;
B   £75,000;
C   £84,000;
D   £200,000.

7   The maximum tax free cash sum allowable from a personal pension is:

A   25% of the fund;
B   subject to an overall limit of £150,000;
C   three times the residual annual pension;
D   one and a half times final salary if the insured is an employee.

The solutions to the questions in the quiz can be found at the end of this Study Text. Before checking your answers against those solutions, you should look back at this chapter and use the information in it to correct your answers.

Answers to questions

1   (a)   Eligibility, final salary or money purchase, normal retirement age, other benefits, contributory or not, self-administered or insured.

     (b)   An immediate annuity bought with a single contribution by an employer for an employee who has already retired or is retiring after age 75.

2   (a)   Contributions deductible and not taxed on employee, limited tax on fund investments, lump sum death benefit tax-free, tax-free lump sum at retirement.

     (b)   Employer must contribute to and administer scheme in trust; pension cannot be assigned; maximum pension two-thirds final salary over minimum period of 20 years; retirement tax-free cash limit 1.5 × final capped salary; life cover maximum - lump sum 4 × capped salary, pension two-thirds × employee's entitlement; employee contributions 15% × capped earnings; normal retirement age 60 - 75; early retirement 50 (ill-health any age).

     (c)   Insurance company (including friendly society), unit trust, bank, building society.

     (d)   Occupational pension scheme.

3   (a)   Retirement annuities.
     (b)   Unused tax relief for one year can be used up to six years later.
     (c)   Anyone with non-pensionable earnings.
     (d)   Employees: total remuneration; self-employed - taxable profit.
     (e)   Employees pay net of basic rate tax; self-employed pay gross.

4   (a)   Contracting-out is withdrawal from SERPS; opting-out is withdrawal from or not joining an occupational pension scheme.

     (b)   A group money purchase occupational pension scheme contracted-out of SERPS.

     (c)   Leave it (preserved); transfer it to: new employer, personal pension, insurance policy with earnings-related pension.

5   (a)   To improve an annuity rate.
     (b)   Greater flexibility of retirement; allows annuity rates to rise.
     (c)   Undrawn pension remains invested.
     (d)   To obtain advantage of phased retirement or income drawdown.

Chapter 14

MORTGAGES

Chapter topic list	Syllabus reference
1 Mortgage related products	C 4.1
2 Tax treatment of mortgages	C 4.3
3 Evaluating repayment methods	C 4.2, C 4.4, C 4.5
4 Evaluating investment mortgages	C 4.2, C 4.4, C 4.5
5 Protecting mortgage repayments	C 4.6
6 Pension mortgages	C 4.7
7 Equity release	C 4.8

Introduction

Most clients will use mortgages to buy their homes. The loans must of course be repaid, but repayment can be achieved in several different ways. Some of the repayment methods can be linked with investment opportunities.

1 MORTGAGE RELATED PRODUCTS

1.1 Most people who buy a house need to **borrow** in order to finance the purchase and the majority of loans are obtained from building societies, banks or centralised lenders. The loans are normally repayable not later than the end of a fixed term which is agreed at the inception of the loan.

KEY TERM

A **mortgage** is a loan given on the **security** of a property, although in legal jargon it means the use of property as security. The purchaser pays a proportion of the purchase price of a property - a **mortgage deposit** - and the balance is lent by one of the three lenders mentioned above.

1.2 In return for the loan the borrower gives the lender **legal rights over the property** for the duration of the loan. While the loan is outstanding the property remains the lender's security that the loan will be repaid. During that time the borrower cannot sell the property.

1.3 If the borrower does not repay the loan - defaults - **the lender has the right to take possession of the property,** sell it, recover the amount of the loan (assuming the sale price is higher than the loan) and pay the balance to the borrower.

1.4 On the assumption that the loan is repaid according to the terms of the mortgage the legal rights over the property must be given back to the owner **at the end of the term**.

1.5 Sometimes **a life assurance policy** is part of the conditions of a mortgage as happens when the repayment of capital is made by means of an endowment assurance (see later). Such a life policy is described as collateral security and may be assigned to the lender. It ensures that the mortgage is repaid in the event of the death of the borrower. A personal pension cannot be assigned in this way.

Interest rates

1.6 The **interest rate** charged by a lender is variable with the exception of a few loans where the rate of interest is fixed for a specified period of time. The variable rate means that the rate of interest can be changed at any time by the lender. It is mostly suitable for the majority of people who accept that the rate of interest could either rise or fall or who, alternatively, believe that rates of interest will fall.

1.7 Some variable rates of interest are limited to a specified maximum but may rise or fall subject to that maximum. These are '**capped' mortgages**. Others are variable between both a maximum and a minimum rate - '**cap and collar mortgages**'. A number of mortgages are available at a rate of interest which is fixed for a specific period of time. The longer the fixed period the higher the rate of interest.

1.8 Other mortgages may allow a discount on the rate of interest for a specific period of time - **discounted mortgages**.

Methods of repaying capital

1.9 During the term of the mortgage the borrower must pay **interest** at the agreed rate. There are two methods of **repaying the capital**: during the term or at the end of it.

> **KEY TERM**
>
> If capital is repayable in instalments during the term it is a **repayment mortgage**. When the loan is entirely repayable at the end of the term it is an **interest only mortgage**.

Repayment mortgage

1.10 **Each time interest is paid to a lender, part of the capital is repaid at the same time**. Each time a regular payment is made, part of it is used to repay the capital. There are two kinds of repayment mortgage:

(a) the capital is repaid in equal monthly instalments throughout the life of the loan.

(b) payments made to a lender in the early years of the mortgage consist almost entirely of interest.

1.11 If you have this second kind of mortgage you will no doubt recall how you felt when you received your first statement telling you how little capital you had repaid in the first year. During the loan term the portion of the payment which consists of capital gradually increases until eventually the position is reversed and the majority of each payment is made up of capital repayments.

1.12 This type of mortgage **does not automatically include life assurance**, which needs to be arranged separately.

Interest only mortgage

1.13 These are mortgages where **the entire sum which has been borrowed is repaid on the last day of the mortgage**. Many lenders will want the borrower to take some action to accumulate during the term of the mortgage sufficient money to repay the loan at the end of the term, although some lenders will in certain circumstances allow a borrower to have an interest only mortgage without any provision to repay the loan. The basis for allowing this to happen is that, of course, the lender can sell the property if the borrower is unable to pay the loan.

1.14 There are a number of different methods of **accumulating the fund** with the objective of repaying the mortgage. Each one may lead to an interest only mortgage being called by a term which more specifically reflects the method of capital accumulation. Thus an interest only mortgage where a pension is used to accumulate the loan is usually known as a pension mortgage (see below).

1.15 One of the principal methods of accumulating the sum to repay the loan is by means of one of various forms of **endowment** and we now take a brief look at each one of them.

With profits endowment

1.16 A **with profits endowment** is effected for the same term as the loan and for a sum assured equal to the loan. There is therefore a guarantee from the beginning that, provided all the premiums are paid, there will be sufficient to repay the loan plus reversionary bonuses and terminal bonuses which will belong to the borrower. This is an expensive type of mortgage and is rarely used.

Non profit endowment

1.17 The **sum assured equals the loan** and again, effectively guarantees repayment of the loan. However there is no other benefit apart from life cover and as the policy is an inefficient method of repaying a mortgage this type of endowment is also rarely used.

Low cost endowment

1.18 This consists of a **with profits endowment with the sum assured fixed at a level well below the amount of the loan**. The level is such that, if reversionary bonuses continue at around 80% of past levels, the sum assured will become sufficient to repay the loan by the end of the mortgage term. There is thus no guarantee that the sum assured will be sufficient to repay the loan although the use of a conservative estimate of bonuses reduces the risk of this objective not being achieved.

1.19 The **shortfall** in the sum payable on death unless and until the bonuses take the sum assured above the level of the loan, is covered by means of a decreasing term assurance. Under this the sum payable on death is the difference between the amount of the loan and the sum payable under the endowment assurance. In this way the repayment of the mortgage on death within the term is guaranteed.

1.20 The **cheapness** of the term assurance results in a lower total premium than for a full with profits endowment. This leads to the title 'low cost endowment' although the titles 'low cost mortgage' and 'endowment mortgage' are still used.

1.21 In calculating the required level for the endowment sum assured **terminal bonuses are ignored**.

Low start low cost endowment

1.22 This is a **low cost endowment, but with lower premiums** for the endowment in the early years of a mortgage. The premiums begin at a lower level than those for an equivalent low cost endowment but increase each year for a period of years. The most common period is five years and the premiums in that case will increase by 20% a year. At the end of the five years they have reached twice the level of the premium at inception, the maximum increase which will allow the policy to remain a qualifying policy.

Unit linked endowment

1.23 With a **unit linked endowment** there is no guarantee that the cash value will be the same as, less than or more than the amount of the loan at maturity. In some cases some companies will guarantee repayment of the loan but this is subject to the policyholder following very strict conditions, and is unusual.

1.24 The **sum payable on death will be the amount of the loan**. Notice the different use of the term 'endowment sum assured' between the low cost endowment and the unit linked endowment. In the first case the term refers to both the death benefit and the maturity value, whereas with the unit linked contract it refers only to the death benefit.

Question 1

(a) Give an example of collateral security in connection with a mortgage.

(b) On the assumption that all payments are maintained, which method will guarantee from the outset that sufficient capital will be available to repay a mortgage?

(c) What type of mortgage repayment vehicle consists of a combination of a with-profits endowment and decreasing term assurance?

(d) Under a low-start low-cost endowment, what is the maximum premium allowable after all increases have taken place in order that the policy remains a qualifying policy?

ISA/PEP mortgages

1.25 **Individual savings accounts** and existing **personal equity plans** may be used to repay an interest only mortgage. The same principles apply as to the unit linked endowment except that there will be no life cover but the fund into which the contributions are paid will be tax free. The ISAs/PEPs will be used to repay the mortgage principal at the mortgage redemption date.

2 TAX TREATMENT OF MORTGAGES

2.1 Interest payments on a mortgage do not attract any tax relief. Arguably, there is an exception in the case of pension mortgages, which are described later. There is also an exception in the case of some home income plans, also described later.

2.2   Until 1999/2000, some tax relief was available. This was known as MIRAS, or mortgage interest relief at source. The value of the tax relief had been reduced in various ways over a number of years, and in 1999/2000, it was 10% of the interest on the first £30,000 of the mortgage. Thus, if interest of £7,000 was paid in 1999/2000 on a mortgage of £100,000, the taxpayer would obtain tax relief of (10% × 30/100 × £7,000) = £210. The relief was obtained by means of lower mortgage payments to the mortgage lender (eg building society). The mortgage lender then reclaimed the relief from the Revenue.

2.3   MIRAS was abolished from 6 April 2000.

2.4   With ISA mortgages (and PEP mortgages), the ISA or PEP funds will be tax free when they are used to repay the mortgage. However, there is no tax relief on the interest payments on the mortgage nor on payments into the ISA.

2.5   With endowment mortgages, there is no tax relief on either the mortgage interest payments or the endowment policy premiums.

3   EVALUATING REPAYMENT METHODS

3.1   There are several factors which have to be taken into account in considering which is the **most suitable method of repayment for any one client**.

Capital repayment

3.2   The advantage of the **repayment mortgage** is that the loan outstanding is reducing during the course of the term. This appeals to many people who like to feel that their outstanding liability is going down. At the end of the term the loan will have been completely repaid and the borrower will own the property. No other benefits will have accrued.

3.3   The **interest only mortgage** carries with it the disadvantage that no capital is repaid at all during the term and the full amount must be repaid in one lump sum on the maturity date of the mortgage. The various methods of repayment normally carry with them the risk that the accumulated capital sum may not be sufficient to repay the loan.

3.4   Depending upon the savings vehicle used with a non-repayment mortgage, such as an endowment, the borrower might hope for an **additional sum** to become available from the accumulated capital. This could be attractive if it is paid at the time of retirement and might be used to buy an annuity or pay for a major item of expenditure.

Evaluating repayment methods and investment risks

Cost

3.5   Cost is one of the most important factors in evaluating the repayment method.

   (a)   The cost of a mortgage depends on the interest rate obtainable from the mortgage provider. The mortgage market is very competitive, and lower rates are often offered to first-time/new borrowers.

   (b)   A borrower might prefer a repayment mortgage, since the size of the loan gets smaller over time, and so the interest payable will also fall over time. Repayment mortgages are currently much more popular than endowment mortgages, probably for this reason (and the absence of any tax relief on interest payments or endowment policy payments).

3.6 In the case of a **personal pension** (see later) the fact that there is tax relief on eligible pension contributions means, in effect, that there is tax relief on the repayment of the loan.

3.7 A **repayment mortgage without life cover** (although life cover is highly desirable) **is probably the cheapest form of mortgage.**

Flexibility of repayment

3.8 The following factors should be taken into account in evaluating the flexibility of repayment.

(a) The choice of **repayment term** available from the outset

(b) **Redemption penalties**

(c) **Increased or reduced payments** under a repayment mortgage will affect the term

(d) Increases or reductions in payment under interest only mortgages will affect the **outstanding loan but not the term**

(e) (i) The reducing capital under a repayment mortgage means **reducing interest portions**

(ii) If interest rates reduce and repayments remain the same the **repayment date is brought forward**

(f) If part of an interest only loan is repaid and the repayment method is an endowment the sum assured should not be reduced as this will result in loss of terminal bonuses. Leaving the sum assured unchanged will result in a **bigger surplus**

(g) (i) **Early repayment** of a personal pension mortgage is possible if the fund is adequate but only if the borrower is at least aged 50

(ii) The repayment date for a personal pension mortgage must coincide with the borrower's **expected retirement date.**

Question 2

What factors should be taken into account in assessing the flexibility of a repayment method?

Flexibility on redundancy

3.9 Redundancy has increased considerably in recent years and is probably going to remain a feature of economic life for some time to come. All borrowers should therefore take account of the lender's conditions in the event of a borrower **becoming redundant.**

3.10 The factors to be taken into account are as follows.

(a) Interest payments under a repayment mortgage can be **deferred** for long periods of time as the unpaid interest is simply added to the capital outstanding (capitalised). Capitalisation of interest increases debt and may ultimately reduce the borrower's ability to repay the loan.

(b) With an **interest only mortgage** the interest may be deferred but if an endowment has been used there will be less flexibility with regard to the payment of premiums.

(c) **Personal pensions** allow flexibility on the premium payments.

(d) **ISAs** allow a considerable amount of flexibility as a new plan is effected each year.

Problems with endowment mortgages

3.11 Endowment mortgages have come in for a considerable amount of criticism recently, and have become much less popular than in the past. The main concern has been that with falling rates of inflation, returns on investments have also fallen. As a result, there is a serious risk, with many endowment mortgages, that the amount of capital built up in a borrower's endowment fund will not be sufficient to repay the mortgage when the time to do so arrives.

3.12 In 1999, the FSA issued an endowment mortgage fact sheet. This attempted to:

(a) explain the facts about endowment mortgages and give a balanced view of their advantages and disadvantages;

(b) suggest how individuals can judge whether an endowment mortgage would be suitable for them;

(c) explain the courses of action available to individuals with an endowment mortgage, whose endowment policies might provide insufficient capital to repay the mortgage.

3.13 Also in 1999, the Institute of Actuaries issued a report stating that:

(a) *short-term* endowments are not suitable for mortgage repayments, because of the high cost;

(b) long-term endowments (25 years) were suitable, provided that the policyholder/ borrower understood the possible risks, and was not already in debt before taking out the mortgage;

(c) front-end loading of endowment premiums should be scrapped. With front-end loading, the early premium payments of the policyholder are used to pay commission and are not invested in a fund.

4 EVALUATING INVESTMENT MORTGAGES

4.1 In evaluating the different types of investment mortgage the prime factor to remember is the need to **accumulate a sufficient sum at maturity in order to repay a loan**. The risks of the different types of endowment must be viewed with this in mind.

With profits endowment

4.2 There is a **guarantee** from the outset that if premiums are paid the sum at maturity will be sufficient to repay the loan. However if the policy is cancelled in the early years a low surrender value could result in loss to the policyholder.

Low cost endowment

4.3 The **performance** of a low cost endowment is crucial to accumulating sufficient funds to repay the loan. Insurers may reduce their rates of reversionary bonuses although bonuses already in place cannot be removed. On the other hand there is the prospect of a surplus at the end of the term. The vital factor to consider is the investment performance of the life office which issues the endowment. Surrender values on such contracts are relatively low.

Low start low cost endowment

4.4 The same provisions apply as for low cost endowment except that, because of the exceptionally low premium in the early years, **surrender values** are likely to be even lower than for the low cost endowment.

Unit linked endowment

4.5 The **time** at which the endowment matures is all important as the maturity value depends on the price of the units at the time that the maturity is reached.

ISA/PEP mortgage

4.6 The same applies to ISA/PEP mortgages as applies to unit linked endowments. It is unwise to consider using an ISA/PEP for a very small number of companies. A **unit trust or investment trust ISA/PEP** gives a much better spread of risk.

5 PROTECTING MORTGAGE REPAYMENTS

5.1 There are primarily three factors which could **prejudice the borrower's ability to make continuing payments** under a mortgage or to repay the capital.

- Disability
- Redundancy
- Death

Disability

5.2 There are three methods of providing **disability protection**

(a) **Accident and sickness insurance**

The risk of losing earnings and therefore being unable to make continuing repayments can be protected after a deferred period has elapsed. That period is usually between one and four weeks. Payments will continue if a borrower is unable to work for up to one or two years.

(b) **Permanent health insurance**

This is usually separate from the mortgage and provides for a longer payment term than accident and sickness insurance. It also usually has a longer deferment period.

(c) **Critical illness insurance**

Protection can be provided against the most severe disabilities through critical illness insurance. This will pay a lump sum and, unlike accident and sickness and permanent health insurance, can enable a mortgage to be repaid instead of providing the method by which continuing interest payments may be met.

Redundancy

5.3 **Redundancy cover** may be available in conjunction with the mortgage itself, in which case the lender will arrange for the protection.

5.4 The most likely method is for the cost of the cover to be in the form of a **single premium** which is added to the loan and on which interest is therefore chargeable throughout the duration of the term.

5.5 The cover provided will be payment of the continuing interest for a period usually of **not more than two years**. There is an obvious risk to insurers of individual contracts which are likely to be effected only by individuals who have some reason to suspect redundancy in the near future. Such cover is available, but subject to strict conditions.

Death

5.6 The **endowment mortgage includes life cover** but that obviously does not apply to the repayment mortgage nor to ISA/PEP mortgages. For a repayment mortgage the most appropriate form of cover is normally decreasing term assurance which will undertake to repay the loan provided interest rates move within a specified band. The advantage of decreasing term assurance is that the mortgage will be totally repaid. An alternative, although unusual, is for a family income benefit to provide the ability to continue making interest payments.

5.7 When **personal pensions** are used to accumulate the fund, life cover will be limited usually to a return of the fund - which may be insignificant in the very early years - or possibly a return of contributions with interest.

5.8 It is therefore highly desirable for a borrower to effect **term assurance** which, in view of the fact that it is an interest only mortgage, should be on a level term basis.

5.9 If the term assurance is effected under the personal pension rules then tax relief will be available on the contributions. However this will restrict the amount which the borrower can contribute to **retirement income**.

5.10 In the case of occupational schemes the sum assured as opposed to the contributions will be limited. Remember that personal pension life assurance is assignable but an **occupational pension scheme life assurance is not**.

Mortgage payment protection insurance

5.11 Insurance is available for mortgage payment protection. In the event of an accident, sickness or unemployment, the insurer undertakes to make mortgage payments on behalf of the insured person.

5.12 In the past, the terms and conditions of these policies varied widely between different providers, and they have not been particularly popular. However, all policies issued after 1 July 1999 have been required to comply with certain minimum standards specified by the Association of British Insurers (ABI) and the Council of Mortgage Lenders (CML).

5.13 The effect of minimum standards might be to make these policies more popular - and so possibly cheaper. The minimum standards for mortgage payment protection policies include requirements for the policy to:

(a) provide all of accident, sickness and unemployment cover;

(b) start paying out after the insured has been off work for 60 days. (Some existing policies specify 90 or even 120 days);

    (c)   provide insurance cover for at least 12 months;

    (d)   in the case of a self-employed person, pay out provided the person has informed the Inland Revenue that he has stopped trading involuntarily, and has registered for incapacity benefit.

5.14   These policies protect mortgage payments, but can also be extended to protect the premiums on mortgage-related life policies.

5.15   Policies can be taken out by joint borrowers, not just individuals.

6   PENSION MORTGAGES

6.1   The advantage of using a personal pension to accumulate sufficient to repay a loan lies in the **tax relief on the pension contributions**. In addition, tax relief for payments for life assurance is available on contributions of up to 5% of earnings, which is likely to produce a more than adequate sum assured.

6.2   **The mortgage will be repaid from the tax free cash sum** which is available at retirement. The disadvantage of this type of arrangement is that, with a limit of tax free cash of 25% of the fund, a substantial fund has to be built up to provide sufficient capital to repay the mortgage out of the fund, and this means making substantial contributions.

6.3   **Executive pension plans** can be used for building up the tax free sum but their disadvantage is that the *sum assured* is subject to revenue limits whereas this is not the case with personal pension life assurance where *contributions* are limited.

6.4   You must also remember that even though **a free standing AVC** is an occupational pension, the fact that it cannot be used to provide tax free cash effectively rules it out as a means of repaying a mortgage.

7   EQUITY RELEASE

7.1   If you own a house and have a mortgage, the difference between the value of the house and the mortgage - the **equity** - is yours. This may not be very impressive if you have a large mortgage but it does enable you to borrow still more on the value of the property if you so wish.

    For example, if you own a property valued at £75,000 and you have a mortgage of £40,000 there is another £35,000 of value in your property which is known as **free equity**.

> **KEY TERM**
>
> The term **equity release** refers to your ability to use this free equity as security for further loans. Of course, if you own a house and have no mortgage at all then the entire property is yours to use as security for a loan.

7.2   The purpose for which you require a loan is not subject to too much scrutiny by the lenders. Provided it is for a legitimate purpose such as improving your home, paying for your children's education or buying a business, then there is a good chance that you will be allowed to borrow. The crucial factor will be **your ability to repay the loan** eventually and to maintain payment of interest in the meantime.

7.3 A **secured loan usually attracts a rather lower rate of interest** than an unsecured loan. This is because the lender of an unsecured loan is taking a greater risk and the higher rate of interest is a payment for taking that risk.

7.4 In view of the fact that mortgages are usually one of the cheapest forms of loan, the ideal method of raising more cash is usually to **increase your existing loan**. If this is not possible you may be able to re-mortgage your property to another lender although the chances are there will be higher costs in doing so. However, if it enables you to replace a high interest loan with a lower interest loan then it may be worthwhile.

Home income plans

7.5 It often happens that retired people have considerable value in their property but have insufficient income to live on. It is possible for them to borrow, using the equity in their house, and use the loan to buy an annuity. Such schemes are usually called either **home income plans** or **equity release schemes**.

7.7 Interest relief is given on home income plans that were already in existence on 9 March 1999. The relief is 22% on the interest for the first £30,000 of the loan, for the tax year 2000/2001.

7.8 These schemes can be useful for providing **additional income**. However, there have been schemes where the loan has been used to invest in a bond. The ability of the borrower to pay the interest on the loan will then depend on the performance of the bond. Relying on capital growth is not a suitable method of funding for regular expenses.

Question 3

(a) Compare the investment factors of different capital repayment vehicles.
(b) What are the three methods of providing disability mortgage protection?
(c) What benefit is provided by redundancy cover?
(d) Why is a free-standing AVC scheme not suitable for use as collateral security for a mortgage?
(e) What is the objective of a home income plan?

Chapter roundup

- *Mortgage-related products.* Loans on security of property for fixed term. Purchaser pays deposit - remainder borrowed. Borrower assigns legal rights to lender. If borrower defaults lender can sell property, recover loan and pay balance to borrower. Re-assignment takes place at end of term.

- *Interest rates.* Rates variable unless fixed for fixed period. Maximum rate - capped. Maximum and minimum rate - cap and collar. Discount on rate for period - discounted.

- There is no tax relief on mortgage interest payments. (An exception applies in the case of some home income plans.) Pension mortgage: outlay reduced by tax relief on pension contributions - effectively relief on capital repayment.

- *Repayment methods.* During term = repayment mortgage: capital repaid in instalments through term; capital steadily reduces. At end of term = interest only mortgage. Method of repayment: endowment - with profits, non profit, low cost, low start low cost, unit linked; ISA/PEP.

- *Evaluating repayment methods.* Capital repayment: loan steadily reduces; repaid by end of term. Interest only: no capital repaid until final day of term; repayment vehicles carry risk of being insufficient to repay loan, but advantage of producing spare capital.

  - *Flexibility of repayment.* Factors: choice of term; redemption penalties; repayment term flexible; repayment = reduced interest; redemption date advanced by reduced interest under repayment mortgage; part repayment under endowment mortgage; leave sum assured unchanged = bigger surplus; early repayment of pension mortgage depends on borrower's age.

  - *Flexibility on redundancy.* Factors: interest deferment opportunities; flexibility on payments.

- *Evaluating investment mortgages.* With profits endowment: guaranteed maturity; low surrender on early encashment. Low cost endowment: dependent on profits - surplus v risk of shortfall. Low start low cost endowment: as low cost endowment but with lower surrender values. Unit linked endowment: performance plus price at maturity crucial. ISA/PEP mortgage: as for unit linked endowment.

- Endowment mortgages have recently been subject to criticism, due to concern that policies might provide insufficient capital at maturity to pay off the mortgage loan.

- Protecting mortgage repayments

  - Disability. Accident and sickness: limited payments for 1-2 years. PHI: longer term protection than accident and sickness, helps to pay interest. Critical illness: lump sum can repay mortgage.

  - Redundancy. Cover can be joined with mortgage. Single premium added to loan. Benefit pays interest for up to two years.

  - Death. Protection exists with endowment mortgage. Repayment mortgage needs decreasing term. Personal pension mortgage needs level term, attracts tax relief on premiums but may restrict borrower's pension contributions.

  - Mortgage payment protection policies are available, but currently quite expensive. All policies issued after 1 July 1999 must conform to certain minimum standards.

- Pension mortgages. Tax relief on contributions. Mortgage repaid from tax free cash - 25% limit on cash means substantial total fund needed. EPPs - tax free cash subject to Revenue limits.

- Equity release. Free equity = difference between value and loan. Equity can be used for further loans. Important factor is ability to repay interest. Interest rate is lower on secured loan.

- Home income plans. For the over 65s. Equity is security for existing loan. Loan must be used to buy annuity - relying on capital growth through bond is not suitable.

BPP PUBLISHING

Quick quiz

1   The main purpose of redundancy insurance is to enable policyholders to:

   A   maintain their mortgage interest commitments;
   B   maintain their savings at a constant level;
   C   preserve their existing standard of living;
   D   repay their outstanding loans.

2   Which of the following is a feature of a capped mortgage?

   A   It is fixed for an unlimited period.
   B   It is limited to a maximum rate for a fixed period.
   C   It is directly linked to the London inter-bank offered rate.
   D   It is linked to the European currency unit for a fixed term.

3   Joan Appleyard, who is in pensionable employment, is buying a house and wants an interest only mortgage for the minimum outlay but with reasonable prospects of sufficient money being available to repay the loan. A possible method of accumulating the sum needed would be a:

   A   low cost endowment;
   B   personal pension;
   C   unit linked endowment;
   D   with profits endowment.

4   A lender provides an interest only mortgage, but is unable to take an assignment of the method of repaying the loan if it is a:

   A   low cost endowment;
   B   unit-linked endowment;
   C   personal pension;
   D   with profits endowment.

The solutions to the questions in the quiz can be found at the end of this Study Text. Before checking your answers against those solutions, you should look back at this chapter and use the information in it to correct your answers.

Answers to questions

1   (a)   An endowment policy.
   (b)   Non-profit and with-profit endowment where sum assured is same as loan; repayment mortgage.
   (c)   Low-cost endowment.
   (d)   Twice the lowest annual premium.

2   Choice of term, penalties, effect of changed payments, effect of capital repayments, effect of interest rate changes and part capital repayment, restrictions on maturity date.

3   (a)   With-profits endowment: guaranteed maturity value, low surrender value, expensive; low-cost endowment: guaranteed death benefit, proceeds adequacy depends on performance, cheaper than with-profits, surrender values lower in early years; low-start low-cost endowment: as low-cost but starts cheaper, surrender values even lower in early years; unit-linked endowment: no maturity guarantee; ISA/PEP: no guarantee; higher risk for small number of companies.

   (b)   Accident and sickness, PHI, critical illness.

   (c)   Continuation of interest payments.

   (d)   It cannot be assigned; the pension cannot be commuted.

   (e)   To increase the income of someone in retirement.

Chapter 15

SAVINGS AND INVESTMENT

Introduction

In this final chapter we will look at a wide range of savings and investment products. Most clients will want a portfolio, built up using several products.

1 DEGREES OF RISK

1.1 Probably most people think of financial risk as being the possibility of **losing money** following the failure of an investment. However, the possibility that you may receive a **poor return** on your investment as a result of low interest or low dividends is also a risk.

1.2 The general assumption is that 'savings' can be regarded as low risk and 'investments' can be regarded as higher risk.

KEY TERM

Savings may be regarded as the regular putting on one side of income in order to accumulate capital or the capital itself which has been built up in that way.

1.3   **Low risk savings** will mostly take the form of deposit accounts with either a bank or a building society and National Savings on the grounds that under normal circumstances the capital can be regarded as safe.

1.4   **Gilt edged securities** will follow closely behind because, although the price can fluctuate between the time of issue and the time of redemption, there is nevertheless a guarantee that at redemption the promised sum will be paid.

1.5   **High risk investments** where there is the possibility of losing all capital or, in most cases more likely, facing a fall in the value of capital, would include **unit trusts, investment trusts and investment bonds**. Regular saving schemes do not carry the same risk but only because the amount invested is spread over a long period of time.

1.6   Investments where it is possible to lose everything would include the **financing of new companies or buying futures and options**.

1.7   A kind of half way stage is reflected in **permanent interest bearing shares or PIBS**. These are shares issued by building societies which pay a fixed rate of interest. They have no maturity date and as such are equivalent to undated gilts. They rank behind the ordinary accounts for insolvency purposes and they can be bought and sold only through the stock exchange. This means that there will be price fluctuations depending on supply and demand. Interest is paid twice yearly net of tax and any gains are free from capital gains tax. They are mostly suitable for people who require a secure rate of interest and who have already used their capital gains tax exemptions.

1.8   The other risk is in the possibility of a **poor rate of return of income**. National Savings for example will produce a fixed rate of interest and provide the best of both worlds, namely secure capital and fixed interest. However even National Savings may produce a poor rate of return.

1.9   This can happen if **interest rates** rise after an investor has bought National Savings and competitive interest rates rise above the rate of return available on National Savings.

1.10   The effect is even more noticeable on **gilts** that have a fixed coupon. If competitive interest rates rise, making the gilt coupon uncompetitive, then the price of the gilt will fall. There is therefore an inverse relationship between interest rates and gilt prices.

1.11   **Principal factors which affect the degree of risk**

- A possible change in markets
- Inflation
- Exchange rate variations
- Government decisions
- Interest rate fluctuations
- A fall in demand

2   SAVINGS ACCOUNTS

Banks

2.1   The prime function of a bank is the provision of a **current account** - (often) a non interest bearing repository for cash giving instant access to funds. This includes the installation of cashpoints to enable account holders to withdraw funds either within or outside normal business hours from publicly placed safes. The capital can be regarded as safe and cannot fall in value as it is not asset linked.

2.2 Such accounts are suitable for those who want **convenience** of cash handling with **easy access** to their funds plus **safety** of capital.

2.3 **Deposit accounts** are again repositories for funds which pay interest (normally variable) on capital. Higher rates of interest will usually be paid for longer periods of notice of withdrawal and/or higher sums deposited. Savings rate (20%) income tax is deducted from the interest when credited to an account. A higher rate taxpayer must account for additional tax to the Inland Revenue, and non taxpayers can claim a refund. If they are likely to remain non taxpayers they can arrange for the interest to be credited gross. Taxpayers must pay tax at 20% for interest falling in the lower rate band.

2.4 Deposit accounts are most suitable for those who want **access** to capital and they are particularly useful for an **emergency fund** which pays interest. ISAs (see later) have the same advantages with the addition of special tax treatment.

Building societies

2.5 Building societies provide the same facilities as those listed above for banks, but whereas the *prime* function of banks is to provide current account facilities, the prime function of building societies is to **lend for house purchase** and to fund that lending by means (primarily) of **deposit accounts**.

3 NATIONAL SAVINGS

3.1 There are large numbers of **National Savings investments and accounts**.

Bank accounts

3.2 National Savings has two bank accounts - **ordinary** and **investment**.

Ordinary account

3.3 The ordinary account provides an **interest paying account with instant access** to funds subject to a daily maximum. Interest is paid gross. Although the first £70 is tax free (£140 for joint accounts) the excess is taxable. The rate of interest is extremely low.

3.4 It is of prime use to **children** as practice in handling money despite low interest, and people without bank accounts who can use it for paying regular bills.

Investment account

3.5 The investment account pays a **higher rate of interest** than the ordinary account. **One month's notice** is required to withdraw funds. Interest is again paid gross but is taxable, there being no tax free sum as with the ordinary account.

3.6 Its main use is for non taxpayers such as **children** who do not need instant access to money.

Other National Savings investments

National Savings Fixed Interest Certificates

3.7 **National Savings fixed interest certificates** provide tax free growth for a period of either two or five years, but with a reduced rate on early encashment (there is no growth in the first year). The capital growth arises from the interest accruing as it cannot be withdrawn. Their principal value is for basic rate taxpayers and (even more so) for higher rate taxpayers who want a fixed rate of growth.

Index Linked Certificates

3.8 **Index linked certificates** provide similar benefits to fixed interest certificates except that their redemption value is linked to the retail prices index (RPI). This means that if the RPI falls the value of the certificates would fall, but their capital value will never be less than the purchase price. After one year additional interest is payable thus giving a real rate of return. As with fixed interest certificates, there are two-year and five-year certificates.

3.9 Their principal value is as for certificates and in addition for people who want **tax free inflation proofed investments**.

Income bonds

3.10 Income bonds pay variable monthly interest which is paid gross and is taxable. Three months' notice is required for withdrawal of funds. (Immediate withdrawal is allowed, but with loss of 90 days' interest.) Their main attraction is to investors who need **gross paid monthly income**.

Capital bonds

3.11 Capital bonds provide **guaranteed growth from reinvested interest**. The interest is taxable each year but the gross interest is reinvested. The effect of the tax treatment is that you do not receive the interest each year and yet you are taxed each year.

> **Exam focus point**
> An examination question could be based on this fact, so the wording needs to be watched carefully. You could for example be asked when the interest must be declared on your tax return, to which the answer is annually, despite the fact that interest is reinvested.

3.12 Capital bonds are primarily of value to **non taxpayers** requiring a no risk guaranteed return and who can make use of their personal allowance to cover the interest.

First option bonds

3.13 The FIRST option bond has been replaced with the **Fixed Rate Savings Bond.** This bond offers a choice of Income or Capital Growth. The rate of interest paid on the bond is determined at the outset of the bond and will depend on the initial investment amount and the term selected. There are four terms available either 6, 12, 18 or 36 months.

3.14 Interest paid with 20% tax deducted at source. The minimum purchase is £500 per bond and the maximum investment is £1 million per person in all bonds held either solely or jointly. It is available to those aged over 16. If the bond is withdrawn before the end of the term there is a 90 day interest penalty.

Pensioners guaranteed income bond

3.15 The pensioners guaranteed income bond is available only to people aged over 60. It consists of a **lump sum investment which produces a monthly income fixed for either two or five years (ie there are two year bonds and five year bonds)**. The income is taxable but paid gross. 60 days' notice is required for withdrawal which results in 60 days' loss of interest.

3.16 The main attraction is for those people over 60 who want a guaranteed income for either two or five years and can **leave their capital untouched**.

Children's bonus bonds

3.17 Children's bonus bonds have a term through to age 21, but with interest guaranteed for five years. The interest is rolled up and is tax free. The investment limit is £1,000 per child per issue.

CAT-standard cash mini ISAs and TESSA-only ISAs

3.18 These are cash mini ISAs and TESSA-only ISAs that comply with the CAT standards for charges, access and terms.

Premium bonds

3.19 These are capital protected bonds paying **no interest**. Each bond (costing £100) is entered into a monthly draw and winnings are tax free. They are attractive to higher rate taxpayers who invest the maximum sum of £20,000.

Summary of National Savings Products

		Term			Tax free	Income		Limits for investment	
	None	1 yr	2 yr	5 yrs		Gross	Net	Min £	Max £
Ordinary account	√V				£70	√		10	10,000
Investment account	√V					√		20	100,000
Income bond	√V					√		500	1,000,000
Pensioners bond			√F	√F		√		500	1,000,000
Fixed Rate Savings Bond (6, 12, 18, 36 months fixed)							√	500	1,000,000
Capital bond				√F		√		100	250,000
Fixed rate certificate				√F	√	√		100	10,000
Index linked certificate				√V	√	√		100	10,000
Children's bond				√F	√	√		25	1,000
Premium bond	√				√			100	20,000

V = Variable interest rate   F = fixed interest rate

BPP PUBLISHING

4 GOVERNMENT SECURITIES

Gilts

4.1 Gilt edged securities - gilts - are **loans to the government**. Most pay a guaranteed capital dated gilts sum (the redemption value or par value) on a specified date or within a specified period. Some are undated, in which case there is no guarantee that they will be repaid at any time.

4.2 Most of them pay a fixed rate of interest (known as the **coupon**). It is based on a guaranteed redemption value and is payable half yearly. For example if the guaranteed redemption value is £1,000 and the coupon is 10% and the gilts are issued at a discounted price of £996, the interest actually payable will be £100 pa, ie 10% of the redemption value - not 10% of the price paid for the gilts. Gilt interest used to be paid net of tax, but investors could elect to have interest paid gross. All gilts now pay interest gross. (Gilts bought through the Post Office have always paid gross.) It is important to note however that the interest is taxable.

4.3 Gilts are tradable on the stock exchange but **cannot be encashed** by asking the government to buy them back. The only promise made by the government is that they will be repaid on a specified date: before then they can only be sold to other investors. The price is then liable to fluctuate, depending as it does on supply and demand.

4.4 **Dated gilts** are divided into three categories according to the time outstanding to redemption. The categories are:

Years to redemption	*Title*
Up to 5	Short dated (shorts)
5-15	Medium dated (mediums)
Over 15	Long dated (longs)

For 2000/2001 the interest is taxable at 10% if it falls in the lower or starting rate band, 20% if it falls in the basic rate band and 40% if it falls in the higher rate band. Gilt holders can choose to receive gilt interest gross. Capital gains are tax free and losses are not allowable against gains.

4.5 The return which investors receive depends on their **outlay**. In the example below the discount is grossly exaggerated and completely unrealistic, but the sums are easier as a result. It shows a coupon of 10%, a return to the investor from the interest of 12.5%, and a final return to redemption - taking into account the guaranteed capital at maturity - of 15%.

4.6 EXAMPLE: GILTS

£10,000 nominal of a 10% gilt with ten years to maturity is bought for £8,000.

Interest payable (10% × £10,000) £1,000 pa

Return to investor	% pa
(a) Price paid = £8,000	
Interest received = £1,000 pa	
£1,000 as proportion of £8,000 = 12.5%	
Current/running yield =	12.5

		£
(b)	At redemption, guaranteed value	10,000
	Price paid	8,000
	Guaranteed capital gain	2,000

£2,000 as proportion of £8,000 = 25%

25% averaged over 10 years = 2.5

Yield to redemption 15.0

4.7 The method used in the calculation is *not* the strictly correct method which is more complicated than we need to concern ourselves with for the FPC exam. However it illustrates in principle the two yields - the **return on the interest** and the **return on interest and capital**.

4.8 The current yield or running yield is the return from the interest only, and the yield to redemption is the return from both the interest and the capital gain (or the capital loss) on redemption. There will be a capital loss on redemption if the purchase price of the gilts exceeds their face value: when this occurs, the redemption yield is lower than the current yield.

Question 1

(a) What are permanent interest bearing shares?
(b) Which National Savings investment allows instant withdrawal of cash without penalty?
(c) What is the principal difference between National Savings investments and gilts?
(d) What is a gilt running yield?

Local authority bonds

4.9 These are **loans to local authorities**. They are secure, as the local authority can use the council tax to fund repayment. They are fixed term, fixed interest securities. Interest is taxable and payable half yearly net of lower rate income tax. They are not subject to capital gains tax. They are in theory marketable but there is a very limited market in practice. They are suitable for basic rate and higher rate taxpayers who want a fixed rate of interest for a fixed period.

5 FRIENDLY SOCIETIES

5.1 Friendly societies are life assurance companies which offer a limited range of products, mostly **ten year savings plans which are either with profits or unit linked**. There is a limit on contributions for 2000/01 of £270 per annum or £25 per month. The reason for the limitation is that premiums are invested in a fund with the same special tax treatment as a pension fund.

5.2 Until April 1995 the **surrender values** under friendly society endowment policies were limited in the first ten years or (if less) three-quarters of the premium paying period to a maximum of a return of the premiums. This restriction has now been removed leaving societies to offer at any time the best possible surrender value on their qualifying policies.

5.3 They can be effected by any person (there is no minimum age) up to age 70, and each person can have one. **Annuities** can be purchased from friendly societies providing an annual income of not more than £156.

Taxation of friendly societies

5.4 Friendly societies have a life fund which is **tax exempt**. This means that the fund is not liable to any corporation tax, income tax (dividend income excepted) or capital gains tax. This compares with an ordinary life assurance fund where income and gains in the fund are liable to tax. This inevitably slows down the potential growth of the fund.

5.5 Friendly societies can also have **ordinary life funds**. This does not prejudice their ability to have a tax exempt fund provided the two funds are kept separately identifiable.

6 INVESTMENT IN LIFE ASSURANCE

6.1 **Unit linked assurance** is a relative newcomer to life assurance. It began in the late 1950s and followed from the success of unit trusts.

6.2 Term assurance, non profit and with profit life assurance, were the only forms of life assurance available for nearly 200 years. All of them gave **guaranteed benefits on death**. In the case of endowments, there was a fixed benefit at maturity for a non profit contract and, under a with profit contract, a minimum level of guaranteed benefit which was increased by bonuses.

6.3 The idea that life assurance benefits might be structured so that they were **unpredictable** was not welcomed in the early years. It was held that the principle of security which underlay life assurance would be breached if there was the possibility of the death benefit or maturity value being reduced.

How unit linked assurance works

6.4 Unit linked assurance does not provide the same kind of guarantees as with profits insurance. It works on the basis that **each policyholder's premiums buy a specific and clearly designated share of the fund** into which premiums are paid. The policyholder's benefits will depend directly on the investment performance of the fund.

6.5 The fund works on the same lines as a **unit trust**. Thus premiums buy units in the fund at a price prevailing at the time of the purchase. The fund is divided into units for the purpose of measurement of value, and is known as a unitised fund. Thus a fund with £1,000,000 in it might be divided into one million units each worth £1. As the value of the fund increases the value or price of each unit rises accordingly. Equally if the fund value falls the value of each unit will fall in the same way.

6.6 A **unit linked policy** provides that on death a sum assured will be paid which is not less than a guaranteed minimum level. This level will be fixed at the outset and in many cases will remain unchanged throughout the existence of the policy.

6.7 When the policyholder pays premiums, some part of **each premium buys investments** which are effectively allocated for the benefit of the policyholder. There is thus a fund which should be building up for two reasons.

(a) Each time a premium is paid **more investments are bought**.
(b) The **value of these investments should increase**.

6.8 Eventually the total value of the investments should be greater than the **minimum death benefit**. If the life assured dies after that point is reached it is the value of the investments which will be paid by the insurer.

6.9 If the value of the investments falls below the guaranteed minimum sum assured the death benefit will again become the **guaranteed minimum sum**. The sum assured under a unit linked life policy is therefore the greater of the sum assured and the value of the investments.

6.10 This guaranteed minimum does not apply to the **maturity value of an endowment**. In that case the sum payable will be the value of the investments - there will be no guaranteed minimum level which will apply.

Premiums

6.11 The insurance company uses some of the premiums paid by policyholders to buy units in a **unitised fund**. The number of units bought, or allocated, will depend on the price of a unit at the time of the purchase. The units allocated with the policyholder's premiums are held for the benefit of the policyholder. Thus the value of the policyholder's fund will depend on the price of units at any one time and the number of units allocated so far.

6.12 Not all of a premium paid by a policyholder to an insurance company will be used to buy units to pay out benefits. Some part of the premium will be retained by the life assurance company to help it to meet its expenses. The part that is allocated to units is known mostly as the **allocation**. How much is allocated to the units depends on the insurer and the type of policy. The higher the life cover the lower the sum that will be invested in units.

Funds

6.13 A with profits policy has only one fund into which all premiums are paid and from which all investments are made. **Unit linked investments will be kept separately in different funds** according to the type of investment. Each fund is named according to the type of investment.

6.14 Thus a fund may purchase only equities and will be known as an '**Equity Fund**'. Another fund may specialise in fixed interest securities or property and will be known as a '**Fixed Interest Fund**' or '**Property Fund**' respectively. There will also be a fund which invests in the units of other funds managed by the life company. This is usually called a '**Managed Fund**' and is normally the most popular of all the funds.

6.15 In many cases there will be other funds. Sometimes, for example, a fund **specialises** in a particular type of equity and may purchase shares only in companies in a particular market. A fund which invests only in companies involved in high technology may be called a 'High Technology Fund'. Equally a fund which invests in shares of European companies could be called a 'European Fund'. They will all be variations of an equity fund.

6.16 There is one other type of fund which does not purchase equities, fixed interest securities or property nor any other kind of asset. It places money on deposit with banks and other finance houses and is usually known as a '**Cash Fund**'. Unit prices in this fund do not vary according to the value of underlying assets as no assets are purchased. The unit price can only grow as the fund is a deposit fund to which interest is added to the premiums.

Choice of funds

6.17 We have seen that there is a **variety of unitised funds** available. The next question is, who decides which is the fund (or funds) to which premiums will be allocated? The answer is - the policyholder. At the inception of the contract the policyholder decides which fund should receive the premiums and the appropriate number of units will be purchased according to the size of premiums available for investment.

6.18 The policyholder can change his mind later if he wishes. He may decide that having chosen say, an Equity Fund, he would prefer the accumulated cash value to be transferred to the more secure Fixed Interest Fund. He can move or **switch** his accumulated cash value from the first to the second fund. There will be a small charge for doing so in most cases, although often the first one or two switches in a year will be free of charge.

The benefits

6.19 The main benefit of a unit linked policy, as with a with profits policy, is a **cash sum on maturity or death**. In the case of an endowment the maturity value, as already seen, will depend upon the number of units allocated and the unit price at maturity. Thus there can be no maturity guarantee. However if the cash value of the units is the only benefit paid on death, in the early years of either an endowment or whole life policy the protection afforded by the policy would be inadequate.

6.20 To overcome this problem, in the majority of policies there is a **guarantee of a minimum sum payable on death**. Even in the endowment, with no maturity guarantee, there is still a guaranteed minimum *death* benefit. The most common form of death benefit is a guarantee that the life company will pay the greater of the current cash value of the units and a guaranteed sum assured.

6.21 At the maturity of a unit linked endowment there will be a cash sum available which will depend on the **performance** of the relevant fund(s).

Question 2

(a) Part of the premium of a unit-linked life policy is retained by the insurer. What happens to the other part?

(b) What is the difference between an equity fund and a European fund?

Traditional life assurance

6.22 In the eighteenth century a mathematician named James Dodson revolutionised life assurance. He introduced a **new method of calculating premiums** and the insurance company he founded introduced two new types of life assurance.

6.23 Up until then only **term assurance** existed. If a term assurance policy was cancelled the policy simply lapsed. There was no payment or refund to the policy holder in such a situation. Policyholders paid premiums which increased each year with the policyholders' increasing age. Thus as the policyholders' needs became greater as they grew older, the premium became less affordable.

6.24 The innovation became possible by charging higher premiums than were necessary for pure term cover. The additional premiums created a reserve from which two further features arose. If a policyholder survived to the end of the term of a policy, it was now possible to pay him a sum of money as a kind of reward for **staying the course**.

6.25 This sum, which became known as the **maturity value**, was guaranteed from the outset of the policy on the assumption that regular premiums would be paid without fail.

Furthermore if the policy was cancelled in mid term, a sum of money was paid to the policyholder. It was not exactly a refund, and was known as the surrender value.

6.26   The expression **'surrender value'** arose because the insurers considered that the policy should run for its full term if the life assured survived the period. Any cancellation of the contract constituted a surrender of the benefits. Nowadays the expression 'surrender value' is gradually being replaced by the description 'cash value'.

6.27   The second innovation arose because the life company discovered that the premiums it was charging were far greater than were needed to provide the benefits. The profits which arose were **shared out** amongst the policyholders.

6.28   There arose a distinction between two types of policy: those which shared or participated in the profits of the insurer, and those that did not. The policies which do not share in the insurer's profits are known as **non profit, without profits or non participating contracts**. Those contracts that share in the profits are described either as **with profits or participating**.

6.29   'Traditional' life policies, as they are sometimes called, carry a guarantee of a minimum sum payable on either maturity (if they are savings plans) or death, and they do not have a direct relationship with the value of the shares or other assets in which the fund has been invested. Traditional policies are divided into the two kinds already mentioned - **non profit** and **with profits**.

Non profit policies

> **KEY TERM**
>
> The **non profit policy** does not share in any surplus produced. It is a life assurance policy which provides that a fixed sum will be payable on death. No change in that sum ever takes place, and it remains the same for as long as the policy is in force.

6.30   An **endowment** may be issued on a non profit basis. In this case the policy will have a fixed term, and a fixed sum will be paid either at the end of the term or on death within that term.

6.31   If a non profit policy is cancelled during its term a cash or surrender value will be paid, after an initial period of the policy has passed. The **amount of that cash value** will depend entirely on the insurer's judgment at the time of what is an appropriate sum.

6.32   Non profit policies are **very rare** nowadays. Their value has been eroded so much by inflation that they have been outstripped by with profits contracts.

With profits policies

6.33   At regular intervals - mostly annually - a life assurance provider values its assets and its liabilities – the **valuation**. These reveal the profits which have been made on each one of the three principal factors on which the premium is based - mortality, expenses and investment income. The total is referred to as the surplus. A decision has to be taken on how that surplus will be allocated.

6.34 If the provider is a limited company, then some of the surplus will be **allocated to the shareholders**. In all cases some part of the surplus will be **allocated to reserves**.

6.35 The **with profits or participating policy shares in the surplus**. It is customary in the case of limited companies for approximately 90% of the surplus to be allocated to policies by way of bonus, the remainder going to shareholders. In mutual companies 100% is allocated to policies. Once announced or 'declared' these bonuses are payable with the policy sum assured and they cannot be taken away. A declaration of bonus entails a public announcement of the details and the issue of bonus notices to the with profits policyholders. No cash payment is made to the assured, who is simply advised of the amount payable at the maturity of the policy.

6.36 The cash value, or surrender value, varies with age in the case of whole life policies, and **proximity of maturity date** with endowments. In all cases the surrender value will be much less than the sum assured although it will eventually at least equal the sum assured under endowment policies.

6.37 The '**reversionary bonus**' as it is called may be either 'simple' or 'compound'. A simple bonus is expressed as a percentage rate of the original sum assured at each declaration and the bonus becomes part of the policy. In the case of compound bonuses the first declaration of bonus is calculated in the same way, but the second and subsequent declarations are calculated by applying bonus percentages in one of two ways.

(a) One rate applied to the sum total of basic sum assured plus existing bonuses.

(b) One rate applied to the basic sum assured, and a different rate applied to existing bonuses.

6.38 EXAMPLE: ONE RATE FOR BASIC SUM ASSURED PLUS BONUSES

If the sum assured is £100,000 and the bonus rate is 5% compound, the bonus addition is £5,000 and the next bonus calculation will apply to the combined figure of £105,000. If therefore the next year's bonus rate is also 5%, the new bonus will be 5% of £105,000 = £5,250, making a new sum assured of £110,250.

6.39 **Once a bonus has been declared it cannot be reduced**. If a death claim were to be made on a policy just prior to the next bonus declaration it would miss the benefit of the next bonus. To overcome this an interim bonus is declared to be applied to policies becoming claims in the interim period.

6.40 Finally, there is a further kind of bonus. When a policy becomes a claim either on death or with an endowment on maturity, the sum payable, already including reversionary bonuses, will be increased by a sum usually called a **terminal bonus**. The terminal bonus is not guaranteed in advance of a claim like the reversionary bonus, nor is it always payable if a policy is surrendered. It usually reflects very favourable returns from the company's investments and can be very volatile.

Question 3

(a) Why are non-profit life policies rare?

(b) Outline the two methods of calculating reversionary bonuses on with-profits life policies.

Loans

6.41 A with profits policyholder **can borrow from the insurer** which issued the policy. The loan will be limited by the cash value and will usually be 85% - 95% of the cash value. Loans will also be available on non profit policies.

6.42 **Interest** is payable on the loan to compensate the insurer for the income lost by lending. If the loan has not been repaid by the date of death or maturity (if an endowment) of the policy, the outstanding sum will be deducted from the benefit payable.

Additional benefits

6.43 Two additional benefits are sometimes available on traditional policies: **waiver of premium** and **accidental death benefit**.

6.44 The **waiver of premium** benefit provides that, if the life assured is disabled for a period which exceeds six months, premiums will be waived during disability.

6.45 The **accidental death benefit** doubles the basic sum assured if death is caused by an accident.

Question 4

What additional benefits are available on traditional life policies?

---

7 ENDOWMENTS

7.1 The prime purpose of endowments is as **a method of long term savings**. Because of the qualifying rules for life assurance policies the overwhelming majority of endowments are for periods of ten years and over.

7.2 Their long term nature means that if they are cancelled in the early years of the term they are likely to prove a **poor alternative to short term investment**.

7.3 Their use in long term savings is primarily to fulfil two different types of objective. If the objective is to **accumulate a definite sum of money on a certain date,** then the with profits endowment is likely to prove more suitable. This will be on the grounds that bonuses can never be taken away and such endowments provide a greater certainty of maturity value than unit linked endowments. Thus they are probably most suitable as a basis for school fees planning or funding for children reaching maturity or for holiday plans.

7.4 On the other hand, where time is not as critical and where the objective is to **accumulate a lump sum** where there is no specific use other than the general desire to increase standard of living then the unit linked plan can form the basis of long term planning.

7.5 Don't forget also that with unit linked assurance if the value of units falls during the period of regular investment the effect is to enable the plan to purchase **more units** which can offset the risk of a fall in value at maturity date.

8 WHOLE LIFE ASSURANCE

8.1 Whole life assurance has two prime functions which it can perform for clients. The first is as **a method of protection on death** (discussed in the chapter on protection).

8.2 The other main function is as a means of **investment** using single premium unit linked policies, ie investment bonds.

8.3 In the same way that a **single lump sum investment** can be made in unit trusts, so precisely the same principle can be applied to life assurance funds. They are after all methods of investing money in order to produce a return for policyholders. A major market exists therefore for lump sum investment in life assurance funds.

8.4 Such investment can be made into a with profits fund and bonuses will be added to the sum invested according to the performance of the investment. Such plans are usually known as **with profits bonds**.

8.5 Much more common is a **lump sum investment in a unit linked plan**. The full name of such plans is single premium unit linked whole life assurance policies, which fortunately has been reduced to the title '**investment bonds**'.

8.6 Such bonds can be used for the same purpose as investment in a unit trust, ie the investment of a capital sum with the objective of producing a **higher capital sum** at a later stage. Such investments are open ended, ie they have no term attached to them, and there is the same choice of funds as applies to a regular premium endowment.

9 ANNUITIES

Purchased life annuities: introduction

> **KEY TERM**
>
> The purpose of an **annuity** is to provide someone with an income either:
>
> (a) for life; or
> (b) for a limited term.

9.1 Annuities are mostly issued by life assurance companies and are usually purchased by or on behalf of **individuals**. The person who receives the income is known as the **annuitant**. The title is a little confusing as the word 'annuity' is used to describe the whole arrangement and also the income which it produces. An annuity may be bought with either:

(a) A lump sum (the purchase price) *or*
(b) Regular payments.

Income payable for how long?

9.2 The two types of annuity - for life, and for a limited term - have entirely different objectives. The **objective of the lifetime annuity** is mostly to provide the annuitant with an **income in retirement**. The annuity may provide the principal retirement income or an extra income in addition to a pension. An **annuity for a limited term** is most likely to be used for a specific temporary purpose or in conjunction with another type of policy for **investment purposes**.

Payable for life

9.3 The lifetime annuities described below mostly provide for the same income to be paid every year throughout life - **a level annuity**. However other types of annuity are available (see *How much is paid?* below).

9.4 An annuity may be paid **annually**. However it is more likely to be paid more frequently than annually (see *How frequent are payments?*). In most cases, once the purchase price for an annuity has been paid it cannot be recovered. Careful thought should always be given to the purchase of any annuity for that reason.

9.5 The **amount of an annuity** will depend on a number of factors. One of them is the age of the annuitant. The payment of an annuity for life means that the older the annuitant is when the annuity begins, the lower will be the expectation of life and thus the shorter will be the likely period for the income payments. This means that the annual payments will be higher for older people.

9.6 Another factor that affects annuities is the **rate of interest** which a life assurance company can earn on its investments. The amount of the annuity - the annuity rate - will fluctuate according to other interest rates. Thus annuity rates for any given age at commencement can vary considerably, but once an annuity has commenced it will not normally change (but again, see *How much is paid?*).

9.7 Unless other arrangements have been made **annuity payments will cease when the annuitant dies.**

9.8 EXAMPLE: ANNUITIES

An annuitant pays a purchase price of £10,000 for an annuity of £120 per month but dies after having received £600 (five monthly payments). The balance of the purchase price - £9,400 - is retained by the life office.

9.9 This type of annuity is mostly suitable for an annuitant who wants the **highest possible income,** but who has no dependants nor any beneficiaries who might otherwise inherit the purchase price paid.

Extra guarantees

9.10 If an annuity provides only one guarantee, namely that it will be payable for life, then on the death of the annuitant the annuity will cease, regardless of how soon after its commencement the annuitant dies. We have just seen an example of this. However, some annuities provide **additional guarantees** as described below.

Guaranteed annuity

9.11 An annuity may provide for payments to be **guaranteed for a minimum number of years**. If the annuitant dies within that period of time then the income will be either continued for the balance of the term or commuted for a cash sum. This is a guaranteed annuity. The guarantee is an extra benefit and the price is again a reduced annuity rate.

BPP
PUBLISHING

9.12 EXAMPLE: GUARANTEED ANNUITY

An annuitant, having paid £10,000 for an annuity of £105 per month guaranteed for five years, dies after five monthly payments totalling £525. The annuity continues to be paid to the annuitant's estate for the balance of the five year guarantee period, the payments totalling £5,775 (£105 per month for 55 further months). Alternatively the monthly payments may be commuted, in which case the annuitant's estate will receive a lump sum reduced to allow for the payment being made immediately.

9.13 A guaranteed annuity is mostly used in connection with a **retirement pension**.

Joint life last survivor annuity

9.14 An annuity may continue to pay an income until the **last survivor** of a group of two or more people has died. The most common use for such an annuity is on the joint lives of husband and wife. This is a joint life and last survivor annuity, more commonly called a joint life second death annuity. On the first death the income will continue either:

(a)   unchanged; or

(b)   reduced by an agreed amount either:

    (i)   immediately; or
    (ii)   if the annuity is payable for a minimum period, as from the end of that period.

Capital protected annuity

9.15 An annuity may provide that if death occurs before the annuitant has received a sum equal to the purchase price, the balance of the purchase price will be returned to the annuitant's estate. This is a **capital protected annuity**.

9.16 The return of the balance of the purchase price is obviously an additional benefit for which a price has to be paid. That price consists of a **lower annuity rate**.

9.17 EXAMPLE: CAPITAL PROTECTED ANNUITY

The annuitant mentioned in Paragraph 9.8 above buys for £10,000 a capital protected annuity. The monthly income might be £100 instead of £120. The annuitant dies after five monthly payments totalling £500. The balance of £9,500 will be paid to the annuitant's estate. Notice that in the example the monthly income payable is less than for the immediate annuity, but the balance on death after the same number of months will be greater. Such an annuity is usually suitable for an annuitant with no dependants, but who would like any balance of the purchase price to be inherited by family beneficiaries.

When the income starts

> **KEY TERMS**
>
> - An annuity which commences within one year of payment of a purchase price and which is payable for life is known as an **immediate annuity**.
>
> - A **deferred annuity** provides for the income to commence on a specific agreed date which may be years hence. There will usually be an option for the annuitant to take a lump sum instead of an income when the annuity is due to begin. On death prior to the commencement of the annuity, premiums may be returned with or without interest.
>
> - A **reversionary annuity** provides an income to commence on the death of one person and to be payable during the lifetime of another person.

9.18 EXAMPLE: WHEN DOES INCOME START?

A husband wants to provide an income for his wife after his death. If his wife dies before him the income will no longer be needed. A reversionary annuity will be suitable for this purpose.

How much is paid?

Level

9.19 The majority of annuities - both lifetime and for a limited term - pay an income which remains the same throughout, that is a **level annuity**. The advantage of this is that the payment is guaranteed in advance.

9.20 If the annuity is for a limited term it is usually for a specific purpose for which unchanging income payments are suitable. However in the case of an annuity for life, inflationary rises in the **cost of living** will gradually wear away the value of the annuity. There are three possible ways of offsetting this problem.

Escalating

9.21 This provides for an income to increase each year by a fixed percentage of the original annuity. A 3% **escalating annuity** which starts at £300 per month will increase by 3% each year. Thus, in year 2, the annuity will have increased by £9 to £309 per month for that year. Such an annuity at the beginning of year 8, for example, will have increased from £300 per month to £369 per month.

9.22 The advantage is that the increases will help to offset the effect of inflation. The disadvantage is that the annuity payments in the first few years will be less than a level annuity for the same purchase price.

With profits

9.23 The income from a **with-profits annuity** is subject to the addition of bonuses. This is similar to the case of with-profits endowments, except that the increases take the form of income instead of a lump sum. The initial income will assume future bonuses at a level chosen by the annuitant.

The initial income will assume future bonuses at a level chosen by the annuitant. Actual bonuses will depend upon the life office's investment returns. If the actual bonus is higher than the assumed bonus, the income will rise. If it is less, the income will fall.

Unit linked

9.24 A **unit linked annuity**, like an escalating annuity, pays an income which begins lower than the level annuity income. However the payments are linked to the value of investments in a unit linked fund. On the assumption that the unit prices rise over the years (which is obviously the intention) the income from the annuity will also rise.

The fact that the annuity is unit linked means that if the price of units falls the annuity payments will also fall.

How frequent are payments?

9.25 The **frequency of payment** can be annually, half yearly, quarterly or monthly. For a given purchase price the total payments in a year will vary according to which frequency is chosen.

When are payments made?

9.26 Payment may also be made either **at the beginning or at the end of a payment period**. For example, under an immediate annuity payable annually the first payment of income may be made as soon as the purchase price has been paid, or alternatively one year after the purchase price. The former payment is know as payment 'in advance' and the latter as payment 'in arrears'.

9.27 The same can happen with **any other frequency of payment**. For example, a monthly annuity may be paid at the beginning of each monthly period - in advance - or at the end - in arrears.

9.28 The frequency of the annuity and whether it is in advance or in arrears, both affect the **amount of the payment**. An annuity in arrears will produce a better annuity rate than one in advance as the life office can earn interest on the payment during that year. Similarly, an annuity paid monthly in advance will total more in a year than if it is paid annually in advance. An annuity paid monthly in arrears will pay less each year than if it is paid annually in arrears.

How much extra is paid on death?

9.29 If an annuity is payable in arrears, then in most cases there will be a **balance of time** from the last payment before death to the date of death.

9.30 Some annuities provide for a **payment on death** in respect of that balance of time and they are known variously as with proportion or apportionable. If such an extra payment is not paid on death, the annuity is called either '**without proportion**' or '**non-apportionable**'.

9.31 EXAMPLES: ANNUITY PAYMENTS

A **lifetime annuity with proportion** pays £4,500 per year. The annuitant dies after six years and nine months. £3,375 (9/12ths of £4,500) is paid to the annuitant's estate.

A **lifetime annuity without proportion** is paying £7,000 per year. The annuitant dies after receiving payments for seven years and five months. No further payments will be made.

Underwriting

9.32 No underwriting is required in respect of annuities except in respect of **impaired lives** who ask for especially favourable terms. Long-term smokers are among those who may be able to obtain favourable terms, but there is a trend to offer enhanced annuity rates to anyone with a reduced expectation of life.

Payable for a limited term

> **KEY TERMS**
>
> - A **temporary annuity** provides for the payment of an income for a fixed term. On the death of the annuitant before the end of that term, the income ceases. A temporary annuity is usually used as part of an investment plan.
>
> - An **annuity certain** is payable for a fixed number of years irrespective of the duration of life of the annuitant. Its main use is in connection with school fees.

9.33 EXAMPLE: LIMITED TERM ANNUITIES

An annuitant dies 3½ years after a ten year annuity certain has commenced. The income continues to be paid for the remaining 6½ years.

Where does the purchase price come from?

9.34 If the purchase price comes direct from a pension fund, the annuity will usually be re-titled a **compulsory purchase annuity**, or pension, and a different set of rules will apply. If the purchase price is paid by an individual who has free choice as to whether to buy an annuity or spend the money on other things, the annuity is called a purchased life annuity. The source of the purchase money can be the tax-free cash from a pension scheme.

9.35 The rules relating to **pensions** are dealt with elsewhere in this Study Text.

Taxation of annuities

9.36 The **taxation of annuities** is determined by their nature.

(a) **Compulsory/pension annuities**. All of the annuity is taxed as earned income under PAYE rules.

(b) **Purchased annuities** (all other types of annuities). The annuity is treated as part return of capital (not subject to tax) and part interest which is subject to tax at source at the savings rate of 20%. Non taxpayers can receive the annuity gross. Lower rate tax payers cannot reclaim excess tax. Basic rate taxpayers need pay no more tax, whilst higher rate taxpayers must pay a further 20% tax.

The split between income and capital is determined by the Inland Revenue and the life insurer based upon the life expectancy of the annuitant.

FEATURES OF ANNUITIES

Feature	Detail	Title
When the income starts	At once	Immediate
	Later	Deferred
	After someone's death	Reversionary
How much is paid	The same every year	Level
	Increasing each year by a fixed percentage	Escalating
	Increasable by bonuses	With profits
	Related to unit values	Unit linked
How frequent are payments	Monthly	Monthly
	Quarterly	Quarterly
	Half yearly	Half yearly
	Annually	Annually
When are payments made	At the beginning of payment period	In advance
	At the end of payment period	In arrears
(Annuities in arrears) How much extra is paid on death	Proportion from last payment to date of death	With proportion or apportionable
	Nothing	Without proportion
Where does the purchase price come from?	Pension fund	Pension annuity
	Individual	Purchased life annuity

10 INSURANCE BASED INVESTMENTS

10.1 There are three types of insurance based contract which we consider under this heading: **bonds** (including life/unit linked investment bonds, with profits bonds and guaranteed bonds), **pensions**, and **purchased life annuities**.

Qualifying and non-qualifying life/unit linked investments

10.2 Investments by means of a life insurance product may take the following forms:

Regular premium	Single premium
Insurance based investment (eg. endowment)	Investment bond
Unit linked with profits	Unit linked with profits

In each case the funds are subject to basic rate tax on income and capital gains.

10.3 **Regular premium insurance** based investments will normally be deemed 'qualifying policies' for tax purposes. This simply means that when the policies mature no further tax is payable by the recipient.

10.4 **Single premium investments** in insurance funds will be deemed 'non-qualifying policies'. If the holder of the policy is a higher rate taxpayer at encashment/disposal, or the gain on encashment is sufficient to make the holder a higher rate taxpayer, then there will be a further tax charge of 18% (40% – 22%).

10.5 **Non-taxpayers** cannot reclaim tax suffered by the fund for either a qualifying or a non-qualifying insurance policy.

Bonds

10.6 Since the life fund into which the premiums are fed has already been taxed at the basic rate of tax on income and on capital gains, the **performance of the funds** will be affected.

10.7 If the types of investment which a basic rate taxpayer wants can be found in a unit trust, then that will probably be a more **tax efficient route** for lump sum investment.

Pensions

10.8 **Pension funds** are generally used to buy annuities which provide the pensioners' incomes. When an annuity is bought with a pension fund, ie the money comes *direct* from a pension fund, then **the entire pension is taxed as earned income**.

Purchased life annuities

10.9 Pensions and purchased life annuities perform the same function. They pay an income for life, the income may be subject to additional guarantees, they can be paid at different frequencies, and the amount payable may be level or one of the alternatives. The prime difference between them lies in the **tax treatment** described above.

10.10 If you choose to take your entire entitlement as a pension you will pay tax on all the income. If you choose to take a tax free cash sum and then use that sum to buy a purchased life annuity, **you will only be taxed on part of the annuity, the interest part**. Even if the gross payment from the annuity were to be the same as the amount of the pension you would be better off simply through being taxed on only part of the income.

Question 5

(a) What is the difference between an annuity certain and a guaranteed annuity?
(b) What option is attached to a deferred annuity?
(c) What is an annuity with proportion?
(d) When is underwriting necessary on an application for an annuity?
(e) What is the difference between the tax treatments of a purchased life annuity and a pension?

BPP PUBLISHING

11 COLLECTIVE INVESTMENTS

Investment trusts

> **KEY TERM**
>
> An **investment trust** is a means of pooling investors' resources and achieving a spread of investments in equities. It provides a level of investment management expertise which would be beyond the resources of most investors.

11.1 Investment trusts are misnamed in the sense that they are not trusts in the normal financial planning meaning of the word. They are **limited companies** like any other company, including the fact that profits are distributed by the payment to shareholders of dividends. They have a fixed number of shares which are marketable on the Stock Exchange as with other equities.

11.2 Their function is **to invest in the shares of other companies**. They will spread their investments by sectors and by a geographical spread in different countries.

Gearing

11.3 They have the advantage that they can **borrow** in order to invest larger sums in equities than they would be able to do with only the share capital of the company. This practice - known as **gearing** - is particularly valuable when share prices are rising as the larger sum available for investing means that greater capital growth and income is possible.

11.4 The disadvantage is that if share prices fall, gearing will result in much **larger losses** than would have occurred if only the company's capital had been used for investments.

Share price

11.5 Investment trusts own the equities - assets - which they have bought. However the value of the shares does not exactly reflect the **value of the underlying assets**. This is because the shares are marketed on the Stock Exchange and supply and demand has an effect on the prices.

11.6 Often investment shares are sold at a price which represents less than the value of the underlying assets. This **discount on net asset value** can vary considerably, and it is possible to make a profit on the buying and selling of investment trust shares simply because the discount has changed.

11.7 An advantage of this discount is that because it does not affect the income earned by the trust, it can lead to a **higher yield** when comparing dividends with the price paid. Don't forget, however, that while you can buy the shares at a discount to the net asset value, when you sell them you are likely again to complete the transaction at a discount.

Charges

11.8 Investment trusts incur all the normal costs of Stock Exchange dealings in equities, ie bid/offer spread and dealing commissions. In addition they themselves make an annual **management charge** on the value of the assets of the trust of (mostly) 0.5% - 1% of the value of the portfolio. This charge is deducted from the income of the trust before being distributed to shareholders.

Tax

11.9 The company's fund is free from **capital gains tax** on gains made by the fund, but the shareholder is liable for capital gains tax in exactly the same way as would happen with any other equities which showed a gain on sale.

11.10 Dividends are treated as **franked investment income**. This means the trust has no further liability for tax on them. Other incomes (interest, and dividends from foreign companies) is subject to corporation tax but can be offset by management expenses and loan interest paid. Shareholders who receive the dividend income are deemed to carry an associated tax credit of 10/90ths which discharges the liability to tax for lower and basic rate taxpayers. Higher rate taxpayers must pay 32.5% tax upon dividends. Non taxpayers cannot reclaim the tax credit.

Suitable investors

11.11 Investment trust shares are most suitable for investors who want a **reasonable spread of investments managed by professionals**. They can be used to obtain a spread of investments within particular sectors or in a variety of countries. In a rising share market gearing can boost the returns on capital, but gearing will also increase any losses arising from a falling market.

11.12 They therefore carry a **larger element of risk** than unit trusts (see below) and this is the price to be paid for potentially greater performance. As with any other equity based investment they should be regarded as a long-term investment.

Unit trusts

> **KEY TERM**
>
> A **unit trust** - like an investment trust - is a means of pooling investors' resources and achieving a spread of investments in equities. It also provides a level of expertise which would be beyond the resources of most investors.

11.13 There is a wide choice of types of trusts for the investor. Each trust will concentrate on a **different objective**. Such objectives can include investment to produce a high income, which makes them suitable for basic rate taxpayers who want income rather than capital gains. Others can aim at capital growth with low income, making them suitable for higher rate taxpayers who have not used up their capital gains tax exemption.

11.14 Other trusts will concentrate on **geographical areas**, eg UK equities, North American or Asian or European equities, or will specialise in particular sectors such as shares in energy or banking companies.

11.15 Unlike an investment trust a unit trust is an **open ended fund**, ie the more money that is invested in it the larger the number of units that are issued, and vice versa. In contrast, the price of an investment trust's shares, because they are limited in number, is affected by supply and demand. The units of a unit trust are not affected by supply and demand because a demand for investment in a unit trust simply leads to the creation of more units to meet the demand.

Unit prices

11.16 The price of units directly **reflects the value of the underlying assets** without the intervention of any demand and supply influence. A unit trust cannot take advantage of gearing as it is not allowed to borrow. Consequently the risk associated with gearing in a falling market does not exist in a unit trust.

11.17 Regular monthly savings plans are available for unit trusts with many of them being linked to **ISAs**.

11.18 Unit holders do not own a unit trust in the same way as investment trusts are owned by their shareholders. Units are encashable with the managers of the trust at the current price which, as we have seen, is not dependent on supply and demand of units, although the value of the **underlying investments** is dependent on supply and demand. It is easy to buy or sell through the managers.

Tax

11.19 The tax treatment is the same as for investment trusts: **capital gains** in the fund are not taxed but investors are taxed on gains arising from selling units. The trust's dividend income is passed to the unit holders with no further tax on the trust. Interest and foreign share dividends are taxable income within the trust, but these will often be minimal. Management expenses can be offset against taxable income before corporation tax is charged. Distributions by the fund are deemed to carry an associated tax credit which discharges the liability to tax for lower and basic rate taxpayers. Higher rate taxpayers must pay 32.5% tax upon distributions. Non taxpayers cannot reclaim the tax credit.

Charges

11.20 Unit trusts make an **annual management charge** of (mostly) 0.5% - 1.5%. There is also a **bid/offer spread** on units which can be of the order of 5% - 7%. If investors have large sums to invest it may be possible to negotiate a discount on the bid/offer spread.

Suitable investors

11.21 They are useful for investors who have funds to invest but who want **a larger spread of risk** than is possible for most investors. They are an inexpensive method of retaining professional investment expertise and there is a wide choice of trusts available.

OEICs

KEY TERM

Open ended investment companies (OEICs) are collective investment schemes and are a hybrid of unit trusts and investment trusts. The OEIC issues shares (normally preference shares) to investors in much the same way as a unit trust issues units, that is investors deal exclusively with the OEIC manager. OEIC's are open ended by nature like unit trusts, hence the fund manager may issue new shares or cancel shares.

11.22 OEICs were introduced in 1997, primarily to comply with EU legislation requirements for investment schemes. One key distinguishing feature is that OEICs are quoted on a **single pricing basis** instead of the dual pricing bid/offer basis employed by unit trusts and investment trusts.

11.23 OEICs can issue **different classes of share** (income, capital) and moving between them is not deemed to be a disposal under capital gains tax rules. In most other respects OEICs are **taxed** in the same way as unit trusts.

Insurance bonds

11.24 We have already dealt with the principles of an **insurance (investment) bond**. Such bonds may specialise in specific types of investment, in which case the name of the fund reflects the type of investment, eg fixed interest fund, property fund. The bond itself may be named after the type of investment, eg property bond, managed bond.

11.25 Each type of investment can suit the requirements of investors with **different objectives**. A managed bond (an insurance bond invested in a managed fund) gives a spread of risk among equity funds, fixed interest funds, property funds and cash funds.

11.26 A **money fund** is another name for a cash fund in which money is placed on deposit with financial institutions and earns interest. It is thus a safe fund as the price of units cannot fall. Remember that despite this an investor can still make a loss - albeit a small one - as a result of the operation of the bid/offer spread.

11.27 **Gilt funds** offer some safety in that the maturity value of a dated gilt is guaranteed. There is nevertheless the risk of loss arising from trading gilts in the market and this can be reflected in the performance of a gilt fund.

Planning factors

11.28 The **tax treatment** of the different funds is highly relevant to different investors. Insurance bonds are of greatest interest to higher rate taxpayers as basic rate tax and capital gains tax liability has already been met by the fund. This is especially useful for the investor who is already using the annual capital gains tax exemption regularly. Switching between funds is easy and cheap in insurance bonds, which produce no taxable income until encashment.

Offshore bonds

11.29 **Offshore bonds** are funds investing in equities or foreign currencies or foreign government stock usually as a tax haven. They operate either as investment companies or as unit trusts.

11.30 The income of the fund attributable to UK domiciled residents is **payable gross and is taxable**. Capital gains by the investor are also taxable. Whilst there is a tax liability to UK domiciled residents, there is no actual tax chargeable until the invested funds or gains or income from them are brought back onshore. Thus the investments can roll up without deduction of tax provided they remain offshore.

Charges

11.31 There will be **initial charges** on purchase and **annual charges for management** of the funds which will vary considerably from one fund to another.

Planning factors

11.32 Their main advantage for UK taxpayers lies in the fact that the fund will increase faster **without taxation**.

11.33 Their main disadvantages are that they are **not subject to UK financial controls**, and exchange rate movements can adversely affect the performance of the investment.

Question 6

(a) Explain the effect of gearing.
(b) What is the difference between a unit trust and an investment trust?

12 ISAs, TESSAS AND PEPS

ISAs

12.1 ISAs (**Individual Savings Accounts**) are packaged investments which became available from 6 April 1999. They consist of up to three components:

(a) cash;
(b) life insurance;
(c) stocks and shares.

12.2 They are available to individuals who are over 18 and either **UK resident** or **ordinarily resident**. They are scheduled to be available for ten years, although a review will begin after seven years.

12.3 An individual can invest a **maximum of £7,000** in the 2000/2001 tax year (same as in 1999/2000) but only £5,000 pa in subsequent tax years. There are annual **sub-limits** for each component:

(a) Cash: £1,000 (£3,000 in 1999/2000 and 2000/2001)
(b) Life insurance: £1,000
(c) Stocks and shares: £5,000 (£7,000 in 1999/2000 and 2000/2001)

12.4 Each year, the individual can choose *either* a '**maxi ISA**' *or* a '**mini ISA**'. Once the individual has made his choice, he must stay with it for that year, although he may choose a difference type of ISA in a subsequent year.

12.5 With a **maxi ISA** all the money invested goes into one ISA. It can consist of:

(a) entirely stocks and shares (demutualisation shares are not allowed) - £7,000 in 1999/2000 and 2000/2001, £5,000 each year thereafter.

(b) stocks and shares *plus* either life insurance (£1,000 in any year) *or* cash (£3,000 in each of 1999/2000 and 2000/2001, £1,000 thereafter) *or* both, but always subject to the overall annual limit of £7,000 in 1999/2000 and 2000/2001, and £500 in subsequent years.

Each maxi ISA has one ISA manager.

12.6 A **mini ISA** is restricted to any one of the three 'components' specified above: cash; life insurance; or stocks and shares. An individual can open up mini-ISAs with different ISA managers. The component and overall limits are the same as for maxi ISAs, except that a limit of £3,000 pa applies to a stocks and shares mini ISA. Thus, the maximum an individual can invest in total overall is £5,000 in one tax year, or £7,000 in both 1999/2000 and 2000/2001.

12.7 There is **no minimum investment level** other than that imposed by the provider. The provider may set a **minimum withdrawal level,** but this minimum must not be set above £10. Withdrawals can be made without loss of tax relief.

CAT standards

12.8 Certain restrictions apply to each component part of an ISA. These restrictions are intended to provide **uniformity of charges, access and terms**: the initials of these three provide the title 'CAT standards'.

	Charges	**Access**	**Terms**
Cash	There should be no one-off or regular charges except for replacing lost documents.	Minimum transaction sizes must be no greater than £10, and withdrawals must be effected within 7 working days or less.	The interest rate should be no lower than 2% below base rate; upward interest rate changes must follow base rate changes within one calendar month; downward changes may be slower; no other conditions are allowed (an example being no limits on the frequency of withdrawals).
Life assurance	The annual charge must be no more than 3% a year of the value of the fund. There can be no other charges, eg no separate charge for the guarantee on surrender values.	Minimum premiums must be no more than £250 lump sum pa, or £25 per month.	Surrender values should reflect the value of the underlying assets. After three years, surrender values should return at least the premium.
Stocks and shares	Annual charges can be no more than 1% of net asset value.	The minimum saving can be no more than £500 lump sum, or £50 per month.	The fund must be at least 50% invested in shares and securities listed on EU stock exchanges; units must be single priced at mid-market price; the investment risk must be highlighted in literature.

12.9 ISAs are **free from income tax and capital gains tax**. As with PEPs, the tax credit on dividends from UK equities was reduced to 10% from April 1999 and will disappear from April 2004.

TESSAs

12.10 A **Tax Exempt Special Savings Account** - TESSA - is a deposit account, just like any other. The prime difference between a TESSA and any other deposit account is that the interest on a TESSA is tax free.

12.11 In return for the **tax advantage** the government placed limitations on investment in a TESSA. The account had to be held for five years and the limit on investment was £1,800 in each year except for the first year when the limit is £3,000. Only £9,000 could be invested in total.

12.12 **No new TESSAs** could be started after 5 April 1999. Existing TESSAs could continue, and these have no effect on the ISA allowance. At maturity of a current TESSA at the end of five years, the proceeds can either be taken tax-free or the original capital can be transferred into the cash component of an ISA and is known as a TESSA-only ISA. Such a transfer does not affect that year's ISA allowance.

PEPs

12.13 A **personal equity plan** (PEP) is a package of equities and companies' bonds with special tax advantages.

12.14 Both the income and any capital gains in a PEP are **totally free from tax**. This can make them quite attractive to basic rate taxpayers but it made them even more attractive to higher rate taxpayers.

12.15 In order to obtain the special tax treatment, PEPs must be administered by plan managers who are **approved and authorised under the Financial Services Act**.

12.16 The shares purchased by a PEP fund manager are **restricted** to ordinary and preference shares and some corporate bonds in UK and European Union companies, investment trusts and unit trusts provided the trusts invest at least 50% in UK or EU equities.

12.17 The **limit on the investment** in PEPs in any one year was £6,000 but within that limit it was possible to invest in units of an unauthorised unit trust up to £1,500.

12.18 In addition to the PEP described (known as a general PEP) it was also possible to invest an additional sum in a PEP which invested in the shares of just **one company**. Such 'single company' PEPs were open to all investors but employees of the company whose shares make up the single company PEP were especially interested in purchasing their own company's shares in this way. The limit for a single company PEP was £3,000 a year.

12.19 Both the limits of £6,000 for a general PEP and £3,000 for a single company PEP were **annual limits** and it was therefore possible to build up a substantial portfolio of tax free share ownership over a number of years.

12.20 **No new investment could be put into PEPs** after 5 April 1999, but existing PEPs can continue and will not affect the ISA allowance. They will therefore have no effect on ISAs, nor will ISAs have any effect on PEPs. PEPs can remain as a tax-advantaged investment in addition to any investment in ISAs.

13 CHARGING STRUCTURE

Unit linked assurance

13.1 All life assurance companies must make some allowance somewhere for their expenses of administration and the cost of providing the benefits. In the case of a unit linked policy the life company's income takes the form of very clear **charges** which are visible and which have a clear basis of calculation.

13.2   We have already seen one of those charges: that part of the premium which is retained for life cover. We now examine the **other charges**.

Unit price

> **KEY TERM**
>
> The **unit price** is the fund value divided by the number of units into which the fund has been split. In practice, where the initial allocation of units takes place a life company adds a charge to the unit price. There is no such addition when units are cashed in order to provide benefits.

13.3   There is thus a difference in the price of units when they are allocated from the price at which they are cashed. The higher of the two prices is known as the **offer price** and the lower is known as the **bid price**. The difference between the two, usually around 5%, is known as the **bid/offer spread**.

Annual management fee

13.4   The life company makes an **annual charge** on each of its funds. The charge varies with different insurance companies but is mostly between 0.5% and 1% per annum, with the majority standing at 0.75% or 1%.

13.5   In practice, if the charge was made once a year and the fund **varied considerably** in value, the company would withdraw a large sum if the fund value happened to be high at charging time, and conversely would have a low income if the fund value was down at the relevant time.

13.6   In order to achieve fairness between the policyholders and the life company, the company makes a **proportionate charge** at more frequent intervals. Thus if the annual fee is 0.75%, a monthly charge might be made of 1/12th of 0.75%. Alternatively a charge of 1/365th of 0.75% might be made each day. In order to know the value of the fund on which the charge can be based, the fund must be valued as frequently as the charge is made. In practice most funds are now valued daily.

Additional management charge

13.7   Sometimes the low allocation of units described earlier is not the method used to pay for the life cover. There is an alternative method which consists of making an **additional charge** throughout the term of the policy. That additional charge is not made on all the units allocated but is confined to those allocated during the early period of the policy. How long that period will be depends on the policy and the age of the policyholder, but it is likely to be between 12 and 30 months.

13.8   In order to make this charge, units allocated during that **initial period** must be segregated from other units allocated subsequently. They are also given a separate name. Units allocated during the initial period are known either as **initial units** or **capital units**. Units allocated during the remainder of the policy or units allocated throughout a policy term if there are no capital units, are known as accumulation units.

Policy fee

13.9 Sometimes **a flat fee** may be charged on a policy. This is likely to be relatively small, usually up to £12 per annum or £1 per month. The policy fee may be applied in one of two ways.

 (a) It may be **added to the basic premium**.
 (b) It may be **deducted from the part of the premium used to allocate units**.

Cancellation fee

13.10 If a regular premium policy is cancelled, after an initial period there will be a cash or surrender value payable to the policyholder. This will consist of the cash value of the units. However a **surrender charge** will usually be made if the policy is cancelled within ten years, and in practice may be greater than the cash value in the early years of the policy.

Lump sum investment

13.11 The additional management charge, the policy fee and the cancellation fee are charges which will apply only to **regular premium contracts investing in unit linked funds**.

With profits assurance

13.12 The charges relating to with profits assurance are **not as transparent** as those relating to unit linked assurance. The administration costs are incurred by the company in respect of management and investment but there is no specific charge which is related directly to any one of the expenses.

13.13 The nearest that a with profits policy comes to making specific administration charges is a **policy fee** which is charged on some contracts and added to the premium. As an alternative to a policy fee it is possible that rates of premium are reduced for higher levels of premium.

13.14 Ultimately the effect of costs of administration which are higher than anticipated when premium levels were set will impact on the **bonus rates** declared.

14 RISK AND RETURNS

14.1 When you put a sum of money in any form of investment there are a number of factors which have to be taken into account. These have been mentioned earlier, eg the **business risk** of a company failing, the risk that inflation will reduce the value of investments, the **interest rate risks** and possible **exchange rate risks**.

14.2 In general, **risk** and **return** can be regarded as two factors on opposite ends of a pair of scales. The lower the risk, the lower the possibility of losing money, but almost certainly the lower is the possible return on the investment.

14.3 An extreme example of this is between **deposit accounts** and **traded options**. A deposit account is relatively safe and there is little risk of losing your money. However the return is likely to be relatively low especially over a long period of time. On the other hand if you buy and sell traded options the potential return can be quite considerable but equally the possibility of loss is high.

14.4 With any equity based investment there is an element of risk. Dividends may produce a fairly steady income but it is the assumption that dividends will increase over the years together with the capital value of the shares that is attractive to many investors. However, as we have sometimes seen, the safest of companies can collapse for quite unexpected reasons and it is not possible to **ignore the element of risk with equities** in any financial advice.

14.5 There is a greater chance however that the rate of return on an asset-based investment will match the **rate of inflation** over the years than interest on a deposit account. An investor should always have reasonable expectations regarding the rate of interest. The greater the expectations the less possibility that they will be matched by the return of an investment.

15 EARLY ENCASHMENT

15.1 With some investments such as regular investment in unit trusts there is little risk of incurring a loss solely on the grounds that the investment has been **encashed early**. There may well be a loss simply because the price of units in a unit trust for example are low at the time of encashment, and this can result in an investor receiving less encashment value than has been invested. However, that is purely a question of timing.

15.2 It is primarily in the area of life assurance policies that there are likely to be **penalties** on early encashment. These penalties will apply irrespective of the value of investments.

15.3 For example with a unit linked contract there could be an encashment penalty of **a percentage of one year's contributions**. In the early years it is possible for the total cash value of a unit linked plan to be outweighed by the size of the surrender charge and for there to be no return due to the investor.

15.4 In the case of with profits contracts the **low surrender value in the early years** (nil in the very early years) can lead to an investor suffering financial loss.

15.5 It is therefore essential with such investments to accept that the objective is to provide **long term benefits** and that early encashment should take place only as a last resort.

16 INVESTMENT CRITERIA

16.1 There are a number of factors which need to be taken into account in assessing the **investment record** of a product provider. They include the following.

- Past performance of investments within the group divided into the **overall investment record** and the **record of particular funds**
- The number of years that a fund has been in the **top quartile** of an investment range
- The **selection of funds** that is available
- The **charges** that are made on investments - both initial and annual
- The **flexibility** of a contract, in particular where there is a fixed term or where it is advisable for tax reasons to divide an investment into smaller units
- The **safety and strength** of the product provider
- The **charging structure** of the product
- The **period of time over which an investment record is available**

16.2 All of the above will need to be matched with the **investor's own needs**. These will include the period of time over which an investment is required, the individual's attitude to risk and the need for access to both capital and income as well as the investor's own tax position.

Question 7

(a) What are offshore bonds?

(b) What are the charges on a regular-premium unit-linked life assurance policy?

(c) What is an investment bond?

(d) What is the difference between the tax treatments of the two types of National Savings Bank accounts?

(e) What is the difference between the tax treatments of purchased life annuities and pensions?

Chapter roundup

- *High and low risk.* Risk covers: losing capital; poor return. Low risk savings: deposits; National Savings; Gilts. Capital high risk: unit trusts; investment trusts; investment bonds; new companies; PIBS; futures and options.

- *Savings accounts*
  - *Banks.* Prime function: current accounts for cash; deposit accounts for interest; accessible.
  - *Building societies.* Prime function: lending for house purchase; cash and deposit accounts as for banks.

- *National Savings.* Two bank accounts for gross interest: limited amount tax free; useful for non taxpayers, including children. Other investments - various features: short term or long term capital growth; fixed or index linked; income producing for all or specific groups; regular saving.

- *Government securities and local authority bonds.* Gilts: most promise fixed capital payment after fixed/flexible term; all are interest bearing; most interest rates are fixed.

- *Friendly societies.* Mostly ten year tax exempt savings plans. Also have ordinary life funds.

- *Investment in life assurance.* Unit Linked Life Assurance. Benefits depend directly on performance of units in fund subject to guaranteed life cover. Specific part of premiums: retained by life office; buy units. Policyholders' choice of funds gives choice of investment risk. Can be changed by switching. Benefits: cash on death; (endowment) maturity directly linked to investment performance.

- *Traditional life assurance*
  - *Non profit policies.* Fixed sum on death and maturity. Inflation has eroded value.
  - *With profits policies.* Bonuses. Annual valuations produce surplus: surplus allocated to reserves, shareholders (if any) and with profits policyholders. Method of surplus allocation: increase in sum assured - reversionary bonuses (simple or compound) on total sum assured, or different rates for basic sum assured and accumulated bonuses; terminal bonus reflects favourable investment returns.
  - *Loans.* Available on surrender value.
  - *Additional benefits.* Waiver of premium. Accidental death benefit.

- Endowments. Long-term savings mostly for ten years or more. Early cancellation produces loss. Purpose: build up specific sum on specific date; with profits produces guarantees; build up capital without specific time scale; unit linked gives direct performance related results.

- Whole life assurance. Purpose: regular premium; protection on death; single premium; investment by with profits bonds or investment bonds.

- Annuities provide income for life or limited term. Issued by life assurance companies.
  - For life: provide retirement income; income depends on mortality and life company's investment returns; income (annuity rate) depends on those factors when annuity purchased.
    - Annuity may be guaranteed: for minimum period (guaranteed); until second death (joint life second death); may repay balance of purchase price (capital protected).

- Annuity may start: when price paid (immediate); later (deferred); when someone dies (reversionary).
  - Amount may be: level; escalating; with profits; unit linked.
  - Frequency may be: monthly; quarterly; half yearly; annually.
  - May be paid at beginning or end of payment period - in advance or in arrears.
  - If in arrears, may be with or without proportion.
  - ° *For limited term:* until earlier death - temporary; fixed - annuity certain.

- *Insurance based investment bonds*: single premium non qualifying contracts. Life fund is taxed on income and gains - affects performance of fund. Policyholder liable to higher rate tax if gain on bonds creates or increases higher rate taxable income. Non taxpayers cannot recover tax paid by fund.

- *Pensions and purchased life annuities*

  ° *Pensions.* All taxed as earned income if purchase comes direct from pension fund.

  ° *Purchased life annuities.* Part treated as non taxable return of capital (amount is decided by Inland Revenue), part treated as interest and taxed as income. PLA can be bought with free capital including tax free cash from pension fund, tax advantage as only part is taxable.

- *Collective investments*

  ° *Investment trusts.* Pooled investments through limited company. Provide spread of investments by sectors and geographical distribution. Gearing is borrowing in order to have more to invest: useful if share prices rise, produces bigger losses if prices fall. Share price influenced by supply and demand, shares may sell at discount on net asset value - can lead to higher yield. Charges are normal ones of Stock Exchange dealings plus management charge. Fund gains are free from capital gains tax, shareholder liable to tax on dividends and gains. Suitable for investors wanting spread and expertise. Gearing increases potential for profit and loss.

  ° *Unit trusts.* Pooled investments through open ended funds. Provide spread of investments by sectors and geographical distribution and income producing capacity. Cannot borrow. Share price based directly on asset value and not influenced by supply and demand. Units encashable by unit trust managers at current price. Tax same as for investment trusts. Charges: annual management charge and bid/offer spread. Suitable for investors wanting spread and expertise.

  ° *OEICs.* Pooled investments through open ended funds but differing from unit trusts in that shares, not units, are issued to investors. Characteristics are very similar to unit trusts except for single pricing and wide range of types of share in issuance.

- Insurance bonds. Bonds invested in life fund, including managed funds and cash funds. Tax treatment makes them more relevant to higher rate taxpayers, especially if investor is using CGT allowance regularly. Switching is cheap and easy. Tax deferrable until encashment.

- Offshore funds. Funds investing in overseas equities - operate as investment companies or unit trusts. Income distributed to UK domiciled residents is paid gross and taxable. Gains taxable. Charges on purchase and annual management charges. Fund increases faster without taxation. Disadvantage: not subject to UK controls, affected by exchange rate movements.

- TESSAs. Deposit account with tax free interest. Limits: 5 year term; investment year 1 £3,000; years 2-5 £1,800; overall £9,000. No new issues of TESSAs from 5 April 1999.

- PEPs. Package of equities and bonds with no tax on income (until 6.4.99) or capital gains. Must be administered by approved PEP fund manager. Limits on types of equities: cash limit of £6,000 pa plus £3,000 pa in single company PEP. No new issues of PEPs from 5 April 1999.

- *ISAs*. Package of deposit account, insurance and equity investment with no tax on income or capital gains. Must be issued by Inland Revenue authorised provider. Three annual sub-limits, cash £1,000 (£3,000 in 1999/00 and 2000/2001) life insurance £1,000 and equities £5,000 (£7,000 in 1999/00 and 2000/2001). Maxi ISA, all monies go into either equity or split across equities, plus either life assurance or cash. Mini ISAs restricted to any one of the three components. May or may not comply with CAT standard (charges, access, terms).

- *Charging structure: unit linked assurance*. Charges consist of: retained premium; bid/offer spread; annual management fee; capital units; policy fee and cancellation fee not applicable to single premium investments.

- *Charging structure: with profits assurance*. Charges not transparent. No specific charges except for policy fee. Effect of charges ultimately revealed in bonus rates.

- *Risk*. Factors: failed company; inflation; interest rate and (for overseas investment) exchange rate risks. Safety and high risk conflict, high risk usually means low security and vice versa. Dividends depend on company performance. Safe companies can collapse. Equities likely to match inflation over reasonable period.

- *Early encashment*. Unit trusts: little risk of loss solely through early encashment. Life assurance: great risk of loss through penalties or low surrender values.

- *Investment criteria*. Factors - Performance. Regularity of good performance. Funds available. Charges. Flexibility. Strength of provider.

- *Taxes on investments*

  - *Deposits*. Variable interest taxable on individuals. 20% rate income tax deducted at source; recovery: non taxpayers - all; additional 20% payable by higher rate taxpayers. Non taxpayers may pay gross. ISAs (TESSAs) are tax free deposits.

  - *Government investments*. National Savings bank accounts taxable (except first £70 interest on ordinary account) and interest paid gross. Other National Savings investments have variable tax treatment. Gilts - tradable assets paying taxable interest, mostly at fixed rate: no CGT on gains or allowance on losses.

  - *Equities*. Dividends taxable: have tax credit of 10/90ths of dividend paid; non taxpayer cannot recover; basic rate and lower rate taxpayer pays no extra; high rate taxpayer pays 32.5%. Gains taxable.

  - *Property as investment*. Rent taxable. Mortgage interest deductible. Gains taxable.

  - *Purchased life annuities*. Interest taxable as investment income. Lower rate deducted at source.

  - *Pensions*. Pensions taxable. Pensions subject to PAYE.

  - *Life assurance policies*. Gains subject to higher rate tax except for qualifying policy. Fund subject to income tax and capital gains tax. Gains subject to capital gains tax if policy has been purchased. Unit Trust CGT free: investor treated as shareholder on income and gains.

Quick quiz

1   The maximum sum which an individual can invest in the fifth year of a TESSA is:

A   £600;
B   £1,800;
C   £3,000;
D   £9,000.

2   Angus and Alice Cooper have been retired for several years and have a substantial amount of capital in a bank current account. They want to know how to produce an income from it while retaining instant access to their capital. An appropriate means would be to invest it in:

A   a deposit account;
B   an investment bond;
C   a temporary annuity;
D   a with profits bond.

3   Why is the cash element of an ISA of no special benefit to non-taxpayers?

A   Basic rate tax is deducted from interest at source and is not recoverable.
B   The account pays non-recoverable tax on its income.
C   The interest is taxed irrespective of the personal allowance.
D   A non-taxpayer can receive a gross rate of interest on any deposit account.

4   Janet Jackson wants to save money, but wants to be able to have immediate access to it at any time without loss. She will be able to achieve this with a:

A   building society deposit account;
B   flexible whole life policy;
C   guaranteed bond;
D   with profit endowment.

5   How is the income taxed on an annuity bought with the proceeds of a pension contract?

A   As earned income on the entire annuity.
B   As earned income on part of the annuity.
C   As investment income on the entire annuity.
D   As investment income on part of the annuity.

6   What is the effect of bonuses under a with profits policy?

A   The sum assured increases annually by terminal bonuses.
B   Bonuses increase the sum assured by a fixed annual percentage.
C   Terminal bonuses may be paid on death or maturity.
D   Annual bonuses are used to reduce the net annual premium.

7   One of the features of unit linked life assurance policies is that they:

A   are invariably linked to the value of units in a unit trust;
B   are subject to an annual charge known as the bid/offer spread;
C   invest premiums in units at the offer price;
D   do not allow a policyholder to switch accumulated investments.

8   What are capital units under a unit linked regular premium policy?

A   Units allocated to single premium bonds.
B   Units which do not have a bid/offer spread.
C   Units allocated following an initial period of allocation of accumulation units.
D   Units subject to an additional management charge.

9   Giles Booker has just bought an immediate annuity with money deposited in a building society. How will he be affected by tax?

  A   He will receive tax relief on the purchase price.
  B   The income will be taxed as earnings.
  C   The income will be tax free if he is a basic rate taxpayer.
  D   Part of the income is treated as interest and taxed.

10 The most suitable investment from the following for an adult who needs regular income and is a non-taxpayer is:

  A   a building society deposit account;
  B   an investment bond;
  C   a low coupon gilt;
  D   the National Savings Index-linked Certificates.

11 One group of individuals who will benefit from a high rate of inflation are those who:

  A   are receiving a fixed occupational pension;
  B   have bought an annuity escalating at 3% per annum;
  C   are receiving fixed social security benefits;
  D   possess index linked National Savings certificates.

12 A feature of a fixed interest gilt with a flexible redemption period of 4 - 7 years is:

  A   it is redeemable automatically in the earlier year;
  B   it cannot be redeemed by the Government in less than 7 years;
  C   it can be redeemed by the investor at any time between 4 and 7 years;
  D   it is classified as a medium dated stock.

13 The price of units in a unit trust depends on:

  A   supply of and demand for units;
  B   the amount of money available for investment;
  C   the price at which the existing owners are willing to sell;
  D   the stock market valuation of the underlying investments.

14 Jill has saved £1,000 and wants to invest it in such a way that she has access to the capital without any risk at any time of losing it or forgoing any tax advantages. Which investment will achieve the objective?

  A   Gilt edged securities.
  B   Guaranteed growth bonds.
  C   Index linked savings certificates.
  D   Tax exempt special savings accounts.

15 Which of the following investments would normally carry the lowest risk (if any) of capital loss?
  A   Equities.
  B   Investment trusts.
  C   National Savings.
  D   Works of art.

The solutions to the questions in the quiz can be found at the end of this Study Text. Before checking your answers against those solutions, you should look back at this chapter and use the information in it to correct your answers.

Answers to questions

1   (a)   Undated shares with a fixed rate of interest issued by building societies.

     (b)   Ordinary account.

     (c)   National Savings are easily encashed without loss; gilts are marketable securities with risk of loss other than at maturity for dated gilts.

     (d)   The return on cost produced by the coupon.

2   (a)   It buys units in a unitised fund.

        (b)   They are both equity funds, but the European fund is more specialised.

3   (a)   Their value has been eroded by inflation.

        (b)   Percentage of total sum assured; one percentage of the basic sum assured and a different percentage of allocated bonuses.

4   Waiver of premium and accidental death benefit.

5   (a)   An annuity certain pays an income for a fixed term, even if the annuitant dies within that term or lives for many more years; a guaranteed annuity is payable for life but subject to a minimum number of years.

        (b)   To take a lump sum when the annuity is due to begin.

        (c)   An annuity payable in arrears: income due between date of death and the next payment date will be paid as a lump sum.

        (d)   When favourable terms for an impaired life are required.

        (e)   A purchased life annuity is only partly taxed; a pension is fully taxed.

6   (a)   A loan provides greater sums for investment; gains and losses will be greater as a result.

        (b)   A unit trust is an open-ended fund; an investment trust is a limited company.

7   (a)   Unit trusts or investment companies based outside the UK.

        (b)   Uninvested premium; bid/offer spread; annual management fee; capital/initial units; switching charge; cancellation fee.

        (c)   A single-premium unit-linked whole life assurance policy with investment growth as its principal objective.

        (d)   The first £70 of interest on an ordinary account is tax-free; all investment account interest is taxable.

        (e)   Part of each purchased life annuity payment is tax-free; all of a pension is taxable.

Updates for this Study Text are available on the BPP website at:

www.bpp.com

See page (v) of this Study Text for further details.

Appendix
Tax tables

A   INCOME TAX

1   *Rates*

1999/00				2000/2001		
£		%		£		%
1 - 1,500		10	Lower rate/starting rate	1 - 1,520		10
1,501 - 28,000		23	Basic rate	1,521	28,400	22
Above 28,000		40	Higher rate	Above 28,400		40

2   *Allowances*

	1999/00	2000/01
	£	£
Personal allowance	4,335	4,385
Personal allowance (65 - 74)	5,720	5,790
Personal allowance (75 and over)	5,980	6,050
Married couple's allowance*	1,970	abolished
Married couple's allowance (65 - 74)*	5,125	5,185
Married couple's allowance (75 and over)*	5,195	5,255
Income limit for age-related allowances	16,800	17,000
Additional allowance for children *	1,970	abolished
Widow's bereavement allowance*	1,970	2,000**
Blind person's allowance	1,380	1,400

* Relief restricted to 10%

** For those widowed during 1999/2000 who have not remarried before 6 April 2000

B   INHERITANCE TAX

1   *Rates*

6.4.97-5.4.98	6.4.98 -5.4.99	6.4.99-5.4.00	6.4.00 onwards	Rate on death	Rate on discretionary trusts
£1 - £215,000	£1 - £223,000	£1 - £231,000	£1 - £234,000	Nil	Nil
Excess	Excess	Excess	Excess	40%	20%

2   *Tapering relief on death within seven years of a potentially exempt transfer*

Time to death (years)	% of tax payable
Up to 3	100
Over 3, up to 4	80
Over 4, up to 5	60
Over 5, up to 6	40
Over 6, under 7	20

3   *Exemptions*

	£
Annual exemption	3,000
Small gifts to one person	250
Gifts on marriage: from parent	5,000
from remoter ancestor or from one party	2,500
other	1,000

4   *Business property relief*

Unincorporated businesses and unquoted/AIM holdings   100%

Controlling holdings in quoted companies   50%

5   *Agricultural property relief*

Vacant possession, right to vacant possession within   100%
12 months or a tenancy starting after 31 August 1995

Otherwise   50%

C   CAPITAL GAINS TAX

1   *Annual exemption*

	Individuals £	Most trusts £
1993/94	5,800	2,900
1994/95	5,800	2,900
1995/96	6,000	3,000
1996/97	6,300	3,150
1997/98	6,500	3,250
1998/99	6,800	3,400
1999/00	7,100	3,550
2000/01	7,200	3,600

2   *Rates of tax*

Individuals	(2000/01)	10%, 20% and 40%
	(1999/00)	20% and 40%

3   *Retirement relief*

Available from age 50, on gift or sale of a business. (This is being phased out from 6.4.99 until eventual abolition on 5 April 2003)

Exempt gain: first £150,000 (1999/00: £200,000)
Gain 50% exempt: next £600,000 (1999/00: £800,000)

D   PERSONAL PENSION CONTRIBUTIONS

1   *Limits*

Age at start of tax year	Maximum percentage %
Up to 35	17.5
36 - 45	20.0
46 - 50	25.0
51 - 55	30.0
56 - 60	35.0
61 or more	40.0

2   *Earnings cap*

Year	Cap £
1993/94	75,000
1994/95	76,800
1995/96	78,600
1996/97	82,200
1997/98	84,000
1998/99	87,600
1999/00	90,600
2000/01	91,800

E   RETIREMENT ANNUITY CONTRIBUTION LIMITS

Age at start of tax year	*Maximum percentage* %
Up to 50	17.5
51 - 55	20.0
56 - 60	22.5
61 or more	27.5

F   NATIONAL INSURANCE CONTRIBUTIONS 2000/2001

2000/01 Rates

Class I (employed)	*Weekly*	*Monthly*	*Yearly*
Lower Earnings Limit (LEL)	£67.00	£290	£3,484.00
Primary threshold (employees)	£76.00	£329	£3,952.00
Upper Earnings Limit (UEL)★	£535.00	£2,318	£27,820.00

★ UEL for employee only - No UEL for employer

	Employees contributions	
Total earnings £ per week	*Contracted In Rate*	*Contracted Out Rate*
Below £76.00	Nil	Nil
£76.00 - £535.00	Nil on first £76.00 plus 10% between £76.00 and £535.00	Nil on first £76.00 plus 8.4% between £76.00 and £535.00
£535.00 and over	£46.80	£39.31

Class II (self employed)	flat rate per week £2.00 where earnings exceed £3,825 pa
Class III (voluntary)	flat rate per week £6.55
Class IV (self-employed)	7.0% on profits £4,385 to £27,820

G   RETIREMENT PENSION 2000/2001

Basic pension

Single   £67.50 per week

A woman aged over 60 is entitled to a full pension provided she has paid enough NICs in the past. Otherwise, she is entitled to a pension based on the husband's contributions, provided the husband is himself receiving a pension and equal to 60% of the basic single pension.

Practice examination 1

Time allowed: 2 hours

Read each question carefully and decide which ONE of the four answers is correct or best.

1   You are an IFA and general insurance broker whose firm has seven authorised advisers. You have taken the actions listed below. Which action is a breach of the financial services regulatory rules?

   A   You have dismissed an appointed representative without notice within two weeks of his appointment.

   B   You have cleared out and destroyed your firm's financial records within four years.

   C   Neither you nor your four partners - all authorised advisers - have made any locum arrangements.

   D   You have failed to create a written record of your compliance procedures.

2   A correct description of inflation is one of the following.

   A   It is measured by the rise in the national average earnings index.
   B   It is the rate at which the wholesale prices index increases.
   C   Pay rises faster than prices.
   D   It is the increase in the price of goods and services over a period of time.

3   An investment trust is:

   A   An open ended investment fund;

   B   A private company limited by guarantee;

   C   A public company which invests solely in unit trusts to give a spread of investment risk;

   D   A public limited company which is closed-ended.

4   A periodic inspection visit is intended to ensure that an authorised company has:

   A   Adequate records of staff salaries;
   B   Adequate staff to deal with administrative needs;
   C   Invested assets that are not less than its liabilities;
   D   Adequate and effective compliance procedures.

5   On which of the following National Savings products is interest taxable annually, but is not available to the investor for five years?

   A   National Savings certificates.
   B   Investment accounts.
   C   Capital bonds.
   D   Ordinary account.

6   Who pays Class 1A National Insurance contributions?

   A   Only employers in respect of employees who have taxable benefits in kind.
   B   Employers and employees in respect of taxable car benefits.
   C   Employers on all an employee's earnings and employees up to the upper earnings limit.
   D   The self-employed in respect of inducements received from suppliers.

7   Which of the following criteria will a Recognised Professional Body operate in deciding whether or not to authorise a member to give investment advice?

   A   At least 50% of the member firm's staff is qualified to give financial advice.
   B   No more than 10% of the firm's income arises from investment advice.
   C   The investment business is incidental to the member's normal activities.
   D   Investment advice forms a substantial part of a member's business.

8   Benefits in kind are normally taxable, but an employee will *not* be taxed on:

    A   Private use of a company car;
    B   An employer's contribution to a personal pension;
    C   An interest free mortgage for house purchase;
    D   A loan at a preferential rate of interest.

9   Which one of the following is exempt from income tax?

    A   Dividends from shares.
    B   Premium Bond winnings.
    C   Interest from gilts.
    D   Rent from property.

10   What is the effect of withdrawal of capital from a TESSA before the end of the term?

    A   It has no effect on the account nor any of the investment's tax treatment.
    B   A special penalty tax is imposed on the sum withdrawn.
    C   Interest will be paid net of 20% tax.
    D   Both income and the capital become subject to tax.

11   Redundancy payments above what amount will be subject to income tax?

    A   £4, 385
    B   £28,400
    C   £30,000
    D   £32,785

12   Jim is a sole trader who is an IFA. In the same town as his office is the head office of a national firm of IFAs with several registered advisers in each branch. What additional responsibility falls on Jim which does not apply to the national IFA?

    A   He must choose from a wider range of product providers when giving investment advice.

    B   He must keep both hard copy and computerised records of his activities.

    C   He must ensure that another IFA is available in his absence to give advice to clients.

    D   He is required to have a dedicated telephone line for his fax machine.

13   A low cost endowment consists of two contracts. These are:

    A   Personal pension plus level term assurance;
    B   Unit linked endowment plus level term assurance;
    C   With profits endowment plus decreasing term assurance;
    D   Whole life assurance plus decreasing term assurance.

14   Which of the following state benefits is tax free?

    A   Retirement pension.
    B   Working Families Tax Credit.
    C   Jobseekers' allowance.
    D   Widow's pension.

15   If an individual dies while domiciled in the UK, inheritance tax is potentially chargeable on asscts situated:

    A   Only in the United Kingdom;

    B   Only in European Union countries;

    C   Only in Great Britain;

    D   Anywhere in the world.

16   National Savings Bank Ordinary Account interest for each year is exempt from income tax on interest up to:

    A   £50

    B   £60

    C   £70

    D   £100

17   The second tier core conduct of business rules applies to which of the following regulatory bodies?

    A   Recognised Professional Bodies.

    B   Recognised Investment Exchanges.

    C   Securities and Futures Authority.

    D   Financial Services Authority.

18   Amy is a self employed fashion designer who started to trade on 1 June 1994 and whose financial year ends on 31 May. Her tax for her 2000/01 fiscal year is £10,000. When must she pay the tax?

    A   £10,000 on 6 April 2001.

    B   £10,000 on 1 January 2002.

    C   £5,000 on 6 April 2001 and £5,000 on 6 October 2001.

    D   On 31 January 2002, with interim payments on 31 January 2001 and 31 July 2001.

19   Herman is a businessman who normally lives in Germany and has German domicile. He has visited this country on business for an average of two months a year for the last 20 years. The effect on his tax status in the UK is that he is:

    A   Non-resident and non-domiciled for all tax purposes;

    B   Ordinarily resident for income and capital gains tax purposes;

    C   Ordinarily resident for the purposes of inheritance tax liability;

    D   Deemed domiciled for the purposes of inheritance tax.

20   Peter is married with two grown up children. He and his wife want to accumulate some capital over a period of at least ten years. Which contract will achieve this objective?

    A   An endowment.

    B   A family income benefit contract.

    C   An investment bond.

    D   A level term assurance.

21   Which of the following contracts is the most suitable for providing long term savings directly related to investment performance?

    A   Convertible term assurance.

    B   Family income benefit.

    C   Unit-linked endowment.

    D   With profits endowment.

22 Andrew has received a net dividend of £80 together with a tax credit of £8.89. He is retired, and his total taxable income after all allowances and deductions in 2000/01 before taking account of the net dividend will be £4,300. What will be his tax liability in respect of the dividend?

A   He will be liable to pay a further £1.89 in tax.
B   He will be neither liable for further tax nor entitled to a refund.
C   He is unable to use the tax credit, and will be liable to pay £22.56 tax.
D   He will be able to claim a refund of £3.50 for overpayment of tax.

23 The second tier core conduct of business rules must be observed by which one of the following individuals?

A   The administration manager of a firm of chartered accountants.

B   An authorised representative giving investment advice on behalf of an independent financial adviser.

C   The manager of a computer department of a product provider who advises IFAs on information technology.

D   A tax specialist employed by a firm of solicitors to advise clients on inheritance tax mitigation.

24 What is a standard condition on which Permanent Health Insurance income protection benefit is payable to someone who is unemployed?

A   They must not be claiming any state benefits.
B   They must be confined to their house.
C   Payment continues only during overnight hospital stays.
D   Payment is limited to a percentage of expenditure.

25 The maximum possible compensation payable under the Investors' Compensation Scheme is:

A   £20,000
B   £30,000
C   £48,000
D   £50,000

26 If a married couple divorce, the effect of the rules of insurable interest is that they:

A   Enable the wife subsequently to insure her ex-husband's life without limit;

B   Require the husband to maintain adequate life assurance for the wife until she remarries;

C   Oblige the husband to surrender any whole life policies on the wife's life;

D   Allow the wife to maintain on the husband's life a policy effected before they divorced.

27 Non-disclosure of relevant information on a proposal form for life assurance has the effect of:

A   Making a policy automatically void;
B   Rendering an intermediary liable for non-payment of a claim;
C   Prejudicing the payment of any claim;
D   Creating a breach of the regulatory requirements.

28   Your client has been paralysed from the waist down following an industrial accident. He will be confined to a wheelchair for the rest of his life, and major structural alterations will be needed to his house to accommodate his new way of life. The insurance which would have been most appropriate to cope with the heavy expenditure he now faces is:

A   Critical illness;
B   Family income benefit;
C   Permanent health insurance;
D   Whole life with waiver of premium benefit.

29   Walter is arranging a deal for a client but, as a result of that client's actions, is not under any duty of care to the client. A possible reason for this is that:

A   The client has been referred to Walter by an existing client for whom Walter has carried out a similar transaction;

B   Walter and the client have signed a discretionary fund management agreement;

C   Walter has already produced a written report for the client stating clearly the investment options available to the client;

D   The client does not wish to act on Walter's advice, and has instructed Walter to arrange the deal.

30   Retirement benefits under a personal pension must include:

A   A tax free cash sum;
B   A pension guaranteed for five years;
C   A pension for life;
D   A pension guaranteed for ten years.

31   Early retirement (other than on the grounds of ill health) may be permitted by the Inland Revenue under any occupational pension scheme from age:

A   45
B   50
C   55
D   60

32   In life assurance, what constitutes an offer?

A   An insurer's acknowledgement of receipt of a proposal form.
B   An advertisement in an insurer's shop window.
C   A postal offer of life assurance with a free gift.
D   A completed proposal form.

33   What is one of the effects of a client agreement permitting cold calling?

A   It absolves the adviser from subsequently confirming in writing the details of an investment deal.

B   It prohibits the adviser from acting in an execution only capacity.

C   It maintains the client's right to treat an ensuing life or pensions agreement as unenforceable.

D   It removes any previous limitation on the investment authority of an investment adviser.

34   Jane (25) and John (30) are getting married next month. They want to know the current level of the Married Couples' Allowance for income tax. Which of the following is correct?

    A   £1,920
    B   £4,385
    C   £2,000
    D   It has been abolished.

35   What authority do enforcement officers possess when they are making a periodic inspection visit?

    A   To declare the compliance officer as not a fit and proper person.
    B   To inspect any records and question staff.
    C   To instruct a firm to cease conducting a particular class of business.
    D   To withdraw authorisation of a member.

36   The maximum period for which payment is made under a personal accident and sickness insurance contract is:

    A   26 weeks
    B   48 weeks
    C   52 weeks
    D   104 weeks

37   When an employee is liable for Class 1 National Insurance contributions, the employer is automatically liable to pay:

    A   Secondary class 1 contributions;
    B   Class 2 contributions;
    C   Class 3 contributions;
    D   Secondary class 4 contributions.

38   What acts as security for a mortgage?

    A   A property.
    B   A life assurance contract.
    C   A mortgage deed.
    D   A mortgage indemnity guarantee.

39   The term 'best execution' applies to advisers in conjunction with:

    A   Advising on unit trusts;
    B   Arranging term assurance;
    C   Carrying out client instructions without giving advice;
    D   Purchase and sale of shares.

40   The social security fund pays which of the following benefits?

    A   A lump sum of four times earnings following the death of an employee.
    B   An index linked pension of two thirds of an employee's final salary.
    C   A basic pension which is not dependent on National Insurance contributions.
    D   A contribution related pension linked to the retail prices index.

41   A lifetime gift cannot be treated as a potentially exempt transfer if it is made to:

    A   A donee from his father;
    B   An interest in possession trust;
    C   A donee from her grandson;
    D   A discretionary trust with named beneficiaries.

42 Policies which pay benefits if an insured person is made redundant are mostly available only in connection with:

A   Disability insurance;
B   Funding for school fees;
C   Term assurance;
D   A mortgage or loan.

43 Income support is payable to individuals whose income is inadequate on condition that they are:

A   Over 16 and totally unemployed;
B   Over 16 and taking part in community work;
C   Over 18 and working less than 16 hours per week;
D   Over 18 and working less than 20 hours per week.

44 Independent Financial Transactions Ltd - a firm of IFAs - publish a quarterly newsletter for their clients. When they make a recommendation in the newsletter, they are prohibited from:

A   Including any investment advice in the recommendation;
B   Dealing on their own account until a reasonable time after publication;
C   Giving advice to any client who is affected by a topic covered in the newsletter;
D   Discretionary dealing with any client's assets without specific client instructions.

45 Charles has a personal pension fund of £10,000 with which to buy a single life compulsory purchase level annuity guaranteed for five years. He will obtain the highest income in each year from an annuity payable:

A   Monthly in advance;
B   Quarterly in arrears;
C   Half yearly in advance;
D   Annually in arrears.

46 Mrs Brown dies without leaving a will. Her estate will be distributed:

A   Entirely to her husband or their children;
B   Equally between husband and children;
C   According to the law of succession;
D   According to the wishes of her husband.

47 What is the maximum number of weeks after which incapacity benefit at the highest rate becomes payable?

A   26
B   28
C   40
D   52

48 Firms must produce a formal written compliance manual if their advisers number not less than:

A   5
B   10
C   12
D   15

49   In order to be eligible for statutory sick pay, a person must be:

    A   An employee;
    B   A housewife;
    C   Self employed;
    D   Unemployed.

50   Capital gains tax will be potentially chargeable on gains made by individuals from the sale of:

    A   Chattels valued at less than £6,000;
    B   Gilt edged securities;
    C   Stocks and shares;
    D   A private car.

51   The higher allowance for individuals aged 65 and over is known as the:

    A   Age allowance;
    B   Pension allowance;
    C   Retired allowance;
    D   Supplementary allowance.

52   An employee who started work in 1992 may contribute to an occupational pension scheme up to a maximum in 2000/01 of:

    A   15% of earnings up to £91,800;
    B   15% of any earnings;
    C   15% of earnings including employer's contributions;
    D   17.5% of Schedule E earnings up to £91,800.

53   The maximum amount which can be invested in the cash element of an ISA in 2000/01 is: (excluding transfers from a TESSA)

    A   £1,000
    B   £3,000
    C   £2,000
    D   £5,000

54   Martin is an IFA who has obtained a referral from a client to approach Andrew. He takes the action detailed below. Which action is against the cold calling rules?

    A   He calls on Andrew without warning in the middle of the afternoon.

    B   He telephones Andrew at 9 am to arrange an appointment one hour later.

    C   He gives Andrew his business address but declines to give him his private telephone number.

    D   He declines to give to Andrew the name of the person who gave the referral.

55   What pension contributions are paid net of basic rate income tax?

    A   Employee's AVCs to an in-house scheme.
    B   Employee's personal pension contributions.
    C   Self-employed contributions.
    D   Employers' occupational pension scheme contributions.

56   A capped mortgage is one where the rate of interest is:

    A   Fixed for an unlimited period;
    B   Limited to a maximum rate for a fixed period;
    C   Directly linked to the London inter-bank offered rate;
    D   Linked to the European Currency Unit for a fixed term.

57   Premiums paid will be entitled to tax relief for which of the following products?

    A   Private medical insurance.
    B   Low cost endowment.
    C   Personal pension term assurance.
    D   Permanent health insurance.

58   Which one of the following is not eligible to be a member of an occupational pension scheme?

    A   A Schedule E taxpayer.
    B   A company director.
    C   A part-time employee.
    D   A self-employed painter.

59   The best execution rule applies to:

    A   Business investors;
    B   Experienced investors;
    C   Private investors;
    D   Professional investors.

60   The life company investment product listed below which pays an income to a person for a fixed period in return for a lump sum investment is known as:

    A   A family income benefit;
    B   A lifetime annuity;
    C   A term assurance;
    D   An annuity certain.

61   Ranjit and Aziza are getting married and they receive £5,000 from each one of their parents. It is the first time their parents have ever made any transfers of any kind. How much of the total sum given by all four parents to Ranjit and Aziza could be chargeable to inheritance tax?

    A   None
    B   £8,000
    C   £20,000
    D   £28,000

62   One of the conditions which applies to a tax-exempt Friendly Society savings plan which does not apply to ordinary life assurance policies is that:

    A   Life cover must not be included;
    B   There is a legal limit on contributions;
    C   Only single contributions can be made;
    D   Only whole life policies can be issued.

63   A non-taxpayer is entitled to reclaim tax in respect of income from:

    A   A building society deposit account;
    B   Gilts bought through the post office;
    C   National Savings investment account;
    D   Personal Equity Plans.

64   An advantage of a with profits endowment is that:

    A   Reversionary bonuses are added at a rate guaranteed from inception;
    B   Surrender values are guaranteed for every year of the contract;
    C   Reversionary bonuses increase the guaranteed maturity value;
    D   Surrender values are index linked from inception.

65   What is a life assurance company's consideration?

    A   Acceptance of the payment of a first premium.

    B   Payment of a death claim on production of a death certificate.

    C   Confirmation that a proposal for life assurance has been accepted.

    D   A promise to pay when a specified event occurs.

66   Susan was born in Uruguay of English parents, both of whom were UK domiciled. She returned to this country, married, and has two adult children. She has continued to live in this country, but has not changed her country of domicile. Her current tax status is that she is:

    A   UK domiciled for the purposes of inheritance tax liability;

    B   Uruguayan domiciled for inheritance tax purposes but UK domiciled for income tax;

    C   UK resident for income tax purposes and Uruguayan resident for receipt of overseas investment income;

    D   Uruguayan resident for inheritance tax and UK resident for income tax purposes.

67   The definition 'Disability means that the insured is totally unable to follow his occupation as stated in the policy and is not following any other occupation' is found in:

    A   Critical illness insurance;

    B   Level term assurance;

    C   Long term care insurance;

    D   Permanent health insurance.

68   Benjamin has asked his insurance company to lend him £5,000 based on the surrender value of his with profits endowment. The insurance company has agreed. The fact that the loan is not more than £25,000 means that the transaction will be regulated by:

    A   The Consumer Credit Act 1974;

    B   The Data Protection Act 1984;

    C   The Insurance Companies' Act 1982;

    D   The Policyholders' Protection Act 1975.

69   A single taxpayer with no dependants has taxable income after all allowances and deductions of £35,000. How much tax will he pay at the higher rate of tax in 2000/01?

    A   None

    B   £886

    C   £2,640

    D   £4,250

70   Which of the following is free from income tax?

    A   Salary paid Civil Servants.

    B   The capital element of income from a PLA.

    C   Coupons paid on a Gilt.

    D   Statutory Maternity Pay.

71   If one of two joint tenants dies, the property will automatically:

    A   Belong to the deceased's estate;

    B   Be inherited by any children;

    C   Be held in trust until the death of the survivor;

    D   Belong to the survivor.

72   The main advantage of a building society deposit account is that:

   A   It offers high liquidity;
   B   It is an open ended fixed interest investment;
   C   It requires investment for a fixed period;
   D   It offers guaranteed capital gains.

73   If a client refuses to supply relevant information, the action that must be taken by a
       financial adviser is to:

   A   Decline to act for the client;
   B   Notify the adviser's regulatory body;
   C   Recommend the client to seek advice elsewhere;
   D   Record the fact that data was not supplied.

74   The 'know your customer' rule requires investment advisers to:

   A   Declare their status;
   B   Follow the best execution rule;
   C   Give execution only advice;
   D   Obtain adequate information about a prospective client.

75   A life policy where the policyholder can change the balance towards either life cover or
       towards savings or a mixture of both is known as:

   A   A flexible whole life policy;
   B   A flexible endowment;
   C   A variable endowment;
   D   A variable whole life policy.

76   The condition which must be fulfilled in *all* cases where employees are contracted out of
       SERPS is that:

   A   The employer must undertake to provide a guaranteed minimum pension;
   B   An alternative pension scheme for the employees must be arranged;
   C   Contributions must be paid to an appropriate personal pension scheme;
   D   A minimum lump sum death benefit must be provided for the employees.

77   Which method of mortgage repayment carries the greatest risk of a shortfall in capital at the
       end of a mortgage period?

   A   A low-start endowment.
   B   A single-company PEP.
   C   A unit-linked endowment.
   D   A with-profits endowment.

78   Carl has approached Colin to discuss pensions following a referral from Carl's client Peter.
       Colin asks who suggested that he might be interested in pensions? What should Carl do?

   A   Decline to answer, as he has been requested not to divulge Peter's name.
   B   Give Peter's name having obtained his permission at the outset to do so.
   C   Give Peter's name and explain briefly the nature of Peter's business with the company.
   D   State that he must first obtain his client's permission to reveal his name.

79   The personal allowance can be claimed by:

   A   Employees only;
   B   Married couples on a joint basis;
   C   Married men only;
   D   All UK residents.

80   John does not have any income but has made a capital gain of £1,000 after taking into account the annual exemption and loss relief. What rate of tax will he pay on this gain, if any?

    A   Nil, as it is below the personal allowance.

    B   10%

    C   20%

    D   22%

81   Placing a life policy under trust will:

    A   Delay the settlement of the claim while inheritance tax is settled;

    B   Ensure the proceeds are not part of the deceased's estate for inheritance tax purposes;

    C   Defer the payment of any inheritance tax on the policy;

    D   Ensure that the proceeds must be subject to probate.

82   What is 'better than best' advice?

    A   Advice which shows a product to be better than any other.

    B   Advice for which an adviser shares his remuneration.

    C   A recommendation by a tied agent that a client should consult an IFA.

    D   Extra careful advice arising from a conflict of interest.

83   The rate of mortgage interest relief at source for 2000/01 for existing home income planholders is:

    A   15%

    B   20%

    C   22%

    D   40%

84   What is the effect on the tax liability and allowance entitlement of a single woman aged 70 when her gross income exceeds the income limit?

    A   Her personal allowance will reduce by 50% of the excess over her taxable income.

    B   She will be unable to offset pension contributions against her gross income.

    C   She can mitigate the reduction by investing in National Savings income bonds.

    D   Her age allowance reduces by £1 for every £2 over the income limit.

85   Which of the following is totally exempt from income tax?

    A   The first £70 of interest on a National Savings Bank ordinary account.

    B   Investment returns in an ordinary friendly society fund.

    C   Income paid under a compulsory purchase annuity.

    D   Income from a gilt edged security.

86   The income chargeable under Schedule E is:

    A   Earnings from self employment;

    B   Interest from deposit accounts;

    C   Earnings from employment;

    D   Interest from gilts.

87   A client acknowledges his prime need is for protection, which is best provided by a twenty-year level term assurance for £100,000. However, he wants a ten-year endowment for £2,000 which he can afford. Your correct recommendation should be:

    A   A ten-year level term assurance for £50,000 for a lower premium;

    B   A twenty-year level term assurance for £100,000;

C A ten-year endowment for £2,000;

D A whole of life policy for £2,000.

88 Anthony Barker is paid a salary of £50,000 by his employer. In 2000/01 he has made a net capital gain after indexation of £18,365. His only allowances are the personal allowance for income tax and the annual exemption for CGT. He is liable for capital gains tax of:

A £4,040

B £4,466

C £7,200

D £7,346

89 Alexander Duffy needs protection which provides that, if he dies while his children are still financially dependent on him, his wife with be able to meet the day to day expenses of looking after herself and them. A suitable contract would be a:

A Family income benefit policy;

B Permanent health insurance;

C Whole life assurance policy;

D With profits endowment.

90 The basic condition on which employees can be contracted out of SERPS is which one of the following.

A They must be entitled to a guaranteed minimum pension.

B Contributions must be made to an alternative pension arrangement.

C Guaranteed minimum contributions must be paid to a private pension.

D The employer must contribute to a contracted out pension.

91 You are a designated individual and have given advice as a result of which your client has suffered financial loss. Her first steps to recover her loss should be made to which of the following?

A Regulator.

B Investors Compensation Scheme.

C Company that employs you.

D Treasury.

92 How long may the unused part of an inheritance tax annual exemption be carried forward?

A One year.

B Two years.

C Three years.

D Four years.

93 Part of a policyholder's premiums for a unit linked endowment are used to:

A Enable reversionary bonuses to be paid;

B Purchase units in a life fund;

C Make direct investment in equities;

D Purchase units in a unit trust.

94 A surrender value is not available under a:

A Decreasing term assurance;

B Non-profit endowment;

C Non-profit whole life policy;

D Unit linked whole life policy.

95   What is the maximum award that may be made by the Regulators Ombudsman Bureau in respect of a regulated complaint?

A   £20,000
B   £30,000
C   £48,000
D   £50,000

96   For how many years can personal pension contributions be carried back for an individual who has been abroad for a year?

A   One
B   Two
C   Three
D   Four

97   What are surrender values under a unit linked endowment based on?

A   Bid price and number of units.
B   Investment performance throughout the term.
C   Number of premiums paid.
D   Offer price of accumulation units.

98   What is the objective of Permanent Health Insurance?

A   Enable a policyholder to receive an income for not more than 104 weeks following disability.

B   Pay a fixed income to a policyholder while he is confined to hospital.

C   Replace earnings lost through long term disability.

D   Provide an income for life following an accident.

99   Which description applies to a low start low cost endowment?

A   An endowment to which reversionary bonuses are allocated at a reduced rate for the first five years.

B   A life policy which requires increasing premiums to be paid usually during the first five or ten years.

C   An endowment which has a reduced surrender value during the first five or ten years.

D   A life policy which provides an increasing death benefit for the first ten years.

100   A pension purchased for an employee after the employee has retired is known as what?

A   A capital protected annuity.
B   A Hancock annuity.
C   An occupational annuity.
D   A retirement annuity.

Practice examination 2

Time allowed: 2 hours

Read each question carefully and decide which ONE of the four answers is correct or best.

1　The Investors' Compensation Scheme is liable to make payments when investors have:

　A　Incurred losses in excess of £50,000;

　B　Received advice from an authorised adviser who has no professional indemnity insurance;

　C　Suffered loss from an authorised firm which has ceased business or is likely to do so;

　D　Suffered financial loss through adverse movement in market prices.

2　Enforcement officers possess certain powers when they are making a periodic inspection visit. Those powers include which of the following rights?

　A　Declare the compliance officer as not a fit and proper person.
　B　Inspect any records and question staff.
　C　Instruct a firm to cease conducting a particular class of business.
　D　Withdraw authorisation of a member.

3　When a life assurance policy is assigned by way of sale, ownership of the policy passes to which of the following people?

　A　Assignee.
　B　Assignor.
　C　Borrower.
　D　Insurer.

4　Which of the following is a consequence of the rules of insurable interest?

　A　An employer can insure the life of an employee.
　B　The sum assured under an own life policy is limited.
　C　A creditor can insure a debtor for an unlimited sum.
　D　The sum for which a husband can insure his wife is limited.

5　The requirement to be authorised by a regulatory body applies to:

　A　Management accountants;
　B　Independent financial advisers;
　C　Recognised investment exchanges;
　D　Official receivers.

6　Which of the following is used to determine eligibility for the married couples age allowance?

　A　The age of the husband.
　B　The age of his wife.
　C　The age of the oldest partner.
　D　The age of the youngest partner.

7　A cancellation notice must be sent to a client in every case involving a recommendation to put into effect:

　A　A recommendation under a discretionary management agreement;
　B　A non-profit endowment assurance;
　C　Non-unit-linked permanent health insurance;
　D　Term assurance for five years.

8   A compliance action plan must be reviewed at least every:

A   6 months;

B   12 months;

C   18 months;

D   2 years.

9   Bloggs is about to retire. He has sufficient investment income to be liable for higher rate tax, even before taking account of his forthcoming pension of £10,000 a year. If he takes the maximum tax free cash from his pension fund, he will then receive a pension of £7,000. If he uses the tax free cash to buy a Purchased Life Annuity paying £2,500 a year gross and having a capital content of £2,100, by how much will his annual net income increase or decrease compared to taking the £10,000 a year pension?

A   Reduce by £1052.90.

B   Increase by £80.

C   Increase by £472.90.

D   Reduce by £500.

10   A discretionary investment management agreement is required in order to give advice to a client on:

A   Investment-linked permanent health insurance;

B   A portfolio of investments;

C   Small self-administered pension schemes;

D   Unit-linked term assurance.

11   An individual dies in 2000/01 leaving an estate of £431,000, before deduction of the nil rate band. What will be the inheritance tax payable on the balance?

A   £93,600

B   £91,800

C   £78,800

D   £172,400

12   An individual incurs in the year 2000/01 net chargeable gains after indexation of £6,300, £7,600 and £9,800, and net allowable losses of £9,400. What will be the total taxable gain?

A   £7,100

B   £14,300

C   £16,600

D   £23,700

13   Angela Askew is a tied agent and has a client whose need is for a product which Angela's company does not have in its range. What course of action can she take?

A   Arrange for the client to effect one of the other products in her company's range.

B   Recommend the product of a competitor which Angela considers suitable advice for her client's needs.

C   Refer the client to an independent financial adviser and receive remuneration for the referral.

D   Refer the client to another provider on condition that she does not make a specific recommendation regarding any of its products.

14   Who pays Class 1 National Insurance contributions?

A   Employers and employees.
B   Employers only.
C   The self employed.
D   The self employed and employees only.

15   An IFA is not required to supply a reason why letter to a client if:

A   The client has been introduced to the IFA by another client;
B   The IFA is acting on a fee basis;
C   The client acts on an execution only basis;
D   The IFA is regulated by the Financial Services Authority.

16   Philip is 31, single and wants a long-term savings contract to boost his retirement pension. An appropriate savings vehicle would be a:

A   Guaranteed income bond;
B   Purchased life annuity;
C   Tax exempt special savings accounts;
D   With profits endowment.

17   If an insured under a permanent health policy resides for six months outside the free limits, the effect on the payment of a claim is that:

A   The policy is automatically cancelled;
B   Benefit payments will be limited until the insured returns to the free limits;
C   The policy is suspended until the insured re-enters the free limits;
D   The insured becomes ineligible as a non-resident to tax relief on the premiums.

18   Which with profits bonus is guaranteed from inception to be payable?

A   None.
B   Compound.
C   Interim.
D   Terminal.

19   The amount of interest which is tax free on a joint National Savings ordinary account in a year is:

A   £50
B   £70
C   £100
D   £140

20   When an investment adviser advertises an investment which may fluctuate in value, a warning must be given on the advertisement of the possibility of a fall in value. This is a requirement of the:

A   Ten FSA Principles;
B   Advertising Standards Authority;
C   Department of Trade and Industry;
D   Financial Services Authority.

21   At the end of the first review period of a flexible whole of life policy, if there are insufficient units to pay for life cover, the policyholder will be given two options, one of which is:

    A   To reduce the level of life cover;
    B   To borrow the premium from the policy;
    C   To cancel the policy;
    D   To reduce the premium.

22   Brenda has just borrowed £25,000 under a repayment mortgage and needs the cheapest possible life assurance to repay the loan on her death. A suitable policy would be a:

    A   Convertible term assurance;
    B   Decreasing term assurance;
    C   Flexible life policy;
    D   Low cost endowment.

23   The earliest allowable age for early retirement under an occupational pension scheme set up in 2000/01, other than on serious ill health, is:

    A   40
    B   45
    C   50
    D   55

24   In order to be able to invest in an ISA, Joseph must satisfy one of the following criteria.

    A   Be aged 18 or over and resident in the UK (or a crown employee).
    B   Be aged over 16, domiciled and resident in the UK.
    C   Be aged over 18, domiciled resident and a taxpayer.
    D   Be aged over 16 resident and a taxpayer.

25   Employees who wish to improve on their occupational pension scheme independently of the scheme can do so by which method?

    A   Making additional voluntary contributions.
    B   Contributing to a personal pension plan.
    C   Contributing to a temporary annuity.
    D   Paying a contributions equivalent premium.

26   A cancellation notice must be sent to clients regardless of the advice you have given. One of the exceptions to this rule is when:

    A   You have advised the client on term assurance which expires before age 70;

    B   You have a cold calling arrangement under a discretionary investment management agreement;

    C   You have recommended a convertible term assurance to your client;

    D   Your client is effecting a personal accident and sickness plan.

27   The pension benefits to which an employee who has personally contracted out of SERPS is entitled are known as:

    A   Protected rights;
    B   Appropriate benefits;
    C   Contracted out rights;
    D   Segregated benefits.

28 One of the additional factors required in an insurance contract which does not exist in a commercial contract is:

A   Unrevoked offer and acceptance;
B   An intention to create a legally binding contract;
C   The existence of utmost good faith;
D   The existence of consideration.

29 One of the effects of the Consumer Credit Act 1974 is that:

A   The rate of interest on any agreement must be limited to within an upper and lower limit;

B   A consumer must be allowed to sign an unreasonable agreement if he wants to;

C   Life assurance companies do not need a licence to grant credit to policyholders;

D   There is no control over the method of calculating the annual percentage rate.

30 Which one of the following can be assigned to a lender as security for repayment of loan capital?

A   Bank deposit account.
B   Building society share account.
C   Low cost endowment.
D   Personal pension.

31 A building society deposit account differs from an equity in that:

A   It enables non-taxpayers to receive interest gross;
B   It can provide a regular tax free income;
C   It can provide tax free growth;
D   It provides capital growth independently of interest earned.

32 National Broking Advisers Ltd are planning to appoint a new director. When must the appointment be notified to the Regulators?

A   At least 14 days in advance.
B   At least 28 days in advance.
C   Not later than 10 business days after the appointment.
D   Not later than 15 business days after the appointment.

33 The maximum amount one may invest into the equity element of an ISA in 2000/01 is:

A   £7,000
B   £3,000
C   £5,000
D   £1,000

34 Withdrawals from an ISA can be made as follows:

A   Subject to no minum but subject to tax if withdrawn within one year of investing;
B   Subject to a minimum and subject to tax if withdrawn within one year of investing;
C   Subject to a minimum but not subject to tax if withdrawn within one year of investing;
D   Not subject to a minimum nor subject to tax.

35 The sum assured under a unit linked regular premium whole life assurance policy will normally be the greater of a guaranteed sum or:

A   The bid value of units at the date of death;
B   The offer price of the capital units plus the offer price of accumulation units;
C   The offer price of accumulation units only;
D   The bid value of accumulation plus the offer price of capital units.

36   Hugh has just retired and wants to know how he and his wife Elizabeth can maximise their income. They are prepared to accept the total loss of capital after they have both died. A suitable product would be:

A   An immediate annuity;

B   A family income policy;

C   A guaranteed income bond;

D   A gilt edged security.

37   FSA has the power to investigate complaints against firms who are:

A   Members of a recognised investment exchange;

B   Directly authorised by one of the Regulators;

C   Members of the Chartered Institute of Management Accountants;

D   Members of the Institute of Chartered Accountants in England and Wales.

38   Which of the following investments guarantees an inflation proofed return?

A   Guaranteed income bond.

B   National Savings income bond.

C   National Savings index linked certificate.

D   Unit trust.

39   If employees are made redundant and have insufficient income on which to live, they can apply for additional income from:

A   A family income benefit policy;

B   A life assurance policy;

C   The social security system;

D   A premium bond.

40   The executor of a will is the person who:

A   Receives a bequest from a will;

B   Is nominated to administer an estate;

C   Draws up a will;

D   Witnesses signatures in a will.

41   Which statement applies to the capital content of an immediate annuity?

A   It is fixed by the life company making the payments.

B   It is treated as investment income in the hands of the annuitant.

C   It increases by the amount of the bonuses under a with profit policy.

D   It is fixed by the Inland Revenue and based upon mortality tables.

42   Brenda is an IFA who has just advised a client not to transfer pension rights from an employer from whose employ he has just resigned. What is one of the reasons that Brenda should keep a careful record of her advice and why she gave it?

A   To protect herself if the client later says he was not given reasons for the recommendation.

B   Because the completion of a fact find is a specific FSA requirement.

C   To demonstrate that there was no alternative of obtaining control over his pension investment decisions.

D   To show that FSAVC contributions were considered as a suitable alternative to taking a transfer value.

43 What is a personal equity plan?

A A unit linked endowment where premiums are allocated to an equity fund.
B An equity linked mortgage.
C A package of equities subject to special tax treatment.
D An investment eligible for tax relief on the sum invested.

44 Bruce is officially described for tax purposes as 'ordinarily resident' in the UK. This means that he is in the UK:

A For a period exceeding 7 days in a tax year;
B On a sufficiently regular basis;
C For a period exceeding 6 months in a tax year;
D Because it is his permanent home.

45 Jane Butcher and Kenneth Bachelor live in and own a house as joint tenants. Kenneth dies without leaving a will. What will happen to his half of the house?

A Its ownership will automatically be inherited by Jane Butcher.
B Its value will be exempt from inheritance tax.
C It will be inherited by their children.
D It will be treated as part of his estate.

46 National Insurance contributions are payable by:

A Employees on eligible earnings between the earnings threshold and upper earnings limit;
B Employees on total taxable earnings;
C Employers on an employee's earnings up to an upper earnings limit;
D Employers on an employee's total taxable earnings, including benefits in kind.

47 Which action could lead to a liability for capital gains tax?

A Encashment of units in a personal equity plan.
B The sale of ordinary shares in a quoted company.
C Proceeds of sale of government stock.
D Sale of your home.

48 In unit linked policies, the bid/offer spread is the difference between:

A The amount paid in premiums and the surrender value;
B The gross and net premiums;
C The highest and lowest price during the financial year;
D The unit buying and selling price.

49 A deceased person who was not born in the UK but who had lived there for at least 17 out of the last 20 years before death (but not in the year of death), may consequently be described at death as:

A Deemed domiciled;
B Domiciled;
C Ordinarily resident;
D Resident.

50 Inflation is measured by:

A The Financial Times Ordinary Share Index;
B The FT-SE 100 Index;
C The National Average Earnings Index;
D The Retail Prices Index.

51 An employer establishes a final salary occupational pension scheme which is contracted out. What effect will this have on the employer's and employees' National Insurance contributions?

   A The contributions will continue to be payable without change.

   B The employer and employee will pay the same rates of contributions on smaller amounts.

   C The employer and employees will pay reduced rates.

   D A contributions rebate will be paid to the scheme by the Department of Social Security.

52 Clive is an IFA who obtains complete information from all his clients on the grounds that they are all:

   A Business investors;
   B Execution only clients;
   C Market counterparties;
   D Private investors.

53 A fact find must be completed by an investment adviser before giving advice or making recommendations except when the client:

   A Has been referred by an existing client;

   B Has bought an investment product within the previous six months from another adviser;

   C Is an existing client of the investment adviser;

   D Wants an investment regardless of advice.

54 Mrs Johnson wants to save through a small endowment policy in a tax free fund. Which of these would be able to offer her the nearest suitable investment environment?

   A A friendly society.
   B A building society.
   C A mutual company.
   D A proprietary company.

55 Which of the following is true regarding the payment of the State Earnings Related Pension to people retiring in 2000/01?

   A It will be paid at 65 for males and 60 for females.
   B It will be paid at 60 for both sexes.
   C Everybody is entitled to the State Earnings Related Pension.
   D It is paid as an alternative to the basic state pension.

56 Which of the following contracts could *not* be used to help repay the capital under an interest only mortgage?

   A Mortgage protection plan.
   B Personal pension plan.
   C Personal equity plan.
   D Unit linked endowment policy.

57 Jane is married, self employed and has investment income. For tax purposes her investment income will be:

A Added to her husband's income;
B Taxed at her marginal rate of tax;
C Free from basic rate income tax;
D Subject to capital gains tax.

58 What is an additional disclosure requirement in a life assurance contract which does not apply in a normal commercial contract?

A To give information that has not been specifically requested.
B To disclose the terms on which the contract becomes effective.
C To agree a date on which the agreement comes into force.
D To agree the date on which the consideration becomes payable.

59 The right of an employee to withdraw from his employer's pension scheme is known as:

A Contracting out;
B The open market option;
C Opting out;
D Scheme withdrawal.

60 Which one of the following is not a requirement of the Data Protection Act 1998?

A Data must be kept only for as long as necessary for its original purpose.
B The person whose information is registered must be allowed to see the information.
C Individuals must be given a copy of any agreement which they sign.
D The Data Protection Register must reveal who is entitled to see data held on file.

61 One of the essentials of a valid will is that:

A The beneficiaries must be notified that they will have legal rights when the testator dies;

B The witnesses to the testator's signature must not themselves be beneficiaries;

C The will is stated to be valid in all circumstances unless the testator changes it;

D It can ensure that an estate is distributed in the manner laid down by the rules of succession.

62 What is an advantage of a free-standing additional voluntary contribution scheme?

A The employer will pay the scheme charges.
B A self-employed person can use it to top up a personal pension.
C It can be arranged on a final salary basis.
D An employee can choose the pension fund provider.

63 When selecting a product provider, which of the following factors is an IFA not required to take into account?

A Capitalisation.
B Claims service.
C Efficiency of service.
D Financial strength.

BPP PUBLISHING

64   The effective marginal rate of income tax in 2000/01 for a basic rate taxpayer over 65 whose level of income has begun to reduce the age allowance is:

    A   22%
    B   20%
    C   33%
    D   40%

65   Joan is the assured under a policy on the life of Roland, whom she has never met, and with whom she has no financial relationship. Why is it possible for her to receive benefit on Roland's death?

    A   Insurable interest is not essential after a policy comes into force.
    B   A life policy is subject to the same rules as any other commercial contract.
    C   She effected the policy on the understanding that he would be a surety for a loan.
    D   The rules on insurable interest can be waived if both parties agree.

66   Oliver is a tied agent for the Alpha Insurance Company. The company's with-profit endowment is suitable for the long-term saving needs of his client, but has been at the bottom of the performance tables for the last three years. What should Oliver do?

    A   Advise the client to divide the savings between the with-profit and the unit-linked endowments.

    B   Recommend to the client an alternative product in the Alpha range.

    C   Suggest that the client approach the Omega Insurance Company whose endowments have a consistently good performance.

    D   Recommend that the client effects the endowment.

67   Anthony started work as a barrister in July 1994 and has the status of a self-employed person for income tax purposes. His earnings for his financial year ending 30 June 2000 are taxed as the earnings of which fiscal year?

    A   1999/00
    B   2000/01
    C   2001/02
    D   1999/00 and 2000/01

68   What is an Executive Pension Plan?

    A   A self-administered final salary scheme.
    B   A pension plan restricted to senior employees.
    C   A method by which an employer insures against an employee's death.
    D   An Occupational Pension Scheme.

69   Why does a low-start low-cost mortgage endowment premium increase by no more than 100% during the increase period?

    A   To maintain entitlement to MIRAS on the interest.
    B   To obtain tax relief on the premium.
    C   To retain the qualifying status of the policy.
    D   To maintain entitlement to tax relief on capital repayments.

70 Mr Jones, a single parent, requires high life cover for at least 15 years at low cost. Which of the following is most likely to be suitable?

    A   Decreasing term assurance.
    B   Level term assurance.
    C   Low cost endowment.
    D   Whole life assurance.

71 Caroline is a senior secretary with an international company. She is single, earning £21,675 a year and paying £1,000 a year in pension contributions. She pays £2,000 a year in rail fares for travel between home and her office. Her tax liability in 2000/01 will be:

    A   £3,621
    B   £3,803
    C   £3,401
    D   £4,385

72 Income from which of the following sources is paid always on a gross basis?

    A   Purchased life annuities.
    B   Gilts.
    C   Occupational pensions.
    D   Building society interest.

73 Which of the following is NOT a term available on National Savings Fixed Interest Savings Bond?

    A   6 months
    B   1 year
    C   18 months
    D   5 years

74 What circumstances will enable a widow to claim the Widow's Pension in the current tax year?

    A   She is over 45 but under 65 and her widowed mother's allowance has ended.

    B   She is under state retirement age and her husband was not receiving state pension.

    C   She has children under the age of 16 (or 19 if in full time education).

    D   She has paid full national insurance contributions and has children under the age of 16 (or 19 if in full time education).

75 Mr James has refused to accept your advice to effect a protection plan for his family, and insists that he wants you to arrange a savings plan for himself. The correct course of action for you to take is to:

    A   Refer the matter to the Regulator for authorisation;
    B   Refer the matter to the general manager of your company or society;
    C   Refuse to have any further dealings with him;
    D   Carry out his instructions and record the fact.

BPP PUBLISHING

76   MIRAS at basic rate is available on condition that:

   A   A borrower is over 65 and is taking advantage of the special tax treatment of existing home income plans begun before 9ᵗʰ March 1999;

   B   A borrower is buying either their own home or a second home for holidays but not rental;

   C   A borrower is UK resident and is paying sufficient tax to benefit from MIRAS;

   D   A borrower is buying their own home or they are over 65 and using free equity in their house as security.

77   The effect of tapering relief in inheritance tax is that it reduces:

   A   The level of tax on lifetime transfers made more than three years before death;

   B   The level of inheritance tax when someone dies within a year of receiving a tax inheritance;

   C   The value of a lifetime gift made more than three years before death;

   D   The value of business assets if the deceased person had a substantial interest in them.

78   National Insurance contributions are payable on which of the following National Insurance benefits?

   A   Child benefit.
   B   Incapacity benefit.
   C   Statutory Maternity Pay.
   D   Unemployment benefit.

79   Mrs Bassett has suffered a loss of £7,000 as a result of poor advice received from an authorised independent adviser who is now insolvent. In order to recover her loss, she can make a claim against the:

   A   The Regulator;
   B   Investors' Compensation Scheme;
   C   Policyholders' Protection Board;
   D   Financial Services Authority.

80   A widow's pension is payable to a widow whose age is within what range?

   A   40 - 50
   B   45 - 60
   C   45 - 65
   D   50 - 60

81   Mr Hoffnung has complained that he effected a flexible whole life contract, on your advice as a company representative, but he now feels that a with-profit endowment would have been more suitable. What is the first step you should take in investigating his complaint?

   A   Advise him that he must take his complaint to the Regulator.
   B   Notify the Regulator that a complaint has been made.
   C   Ensure the complaint is investigated by someone not connected with the sale.
   D   Notify the Investors' Compensation Scheme of a potential claim.

82   Which of the following social security benefits is not taxable?

   A   Incapacity Benefit.
   B   Statutory Maternity Pay.
   C   Family Allowance.
   D   Widowed Mother's Allowance.

83   Mark has been made redundant from his company. He has received total redundancy pay of £37,150, of which £6,150 is his minimum statutory entitlement. On how much of the total payment will he be liable for income tax?

    A   None
    B   £1,000
    C   £6,150
    D   £7,150

84   A life time 10 year guaranteed annuity costing £200,000 (with proportion) is payable at a rate of £10,000 per annum annually in arrears. The annuitant dies after 10 years 6 months. The estate will receive

    A   Nothing
    B   £10,000
    C   £5,000
    D   £100,000

85   What is the tax treatment of local authority bonds?

    A   Interest is taxable but there is no capital gains tax.
    B   Interest is paid gross and interest and gains are taxable.
    C   Interest is paid net and gains are taxable.
    D   There is no tax on either interest or gains.

86   One of the advantages of convertible term assurance is that it can be changed - without medical evidence - into:

    A   Permanent health insurance;
    B   Critical illness insurance;
    C   Medical expenses insurance;
    D   Whole life assurance.

87   Some life assurance policies include a guaranteed insurability option which entitles the assured, without medical evidence, to increase the sum assured. An example of the circumstances when such an option can be exercised is when the assured:

    A   Increases a mortgage;
    B   Reaches the age of 60;
    C   Becomes self-employed;
    D   Effects critical illness cover.

88   Which of the following is a chargeable transfer?

    A   A lifetime transfer into an interest in possession trust.
    B   A transfer on the death of a donor to the donor's daughter.
    C   A lifetime transfer from father to son.
    D   A death transfer to the donor's spouse.

89   What income is deducted from permanent health insurance benefit payments?

    A   Company dividends.
    B   Bank deposit interest.
    C   Family income benefit.
    D   Statutory sick pay.

90 Joanna has received money in the 2000/01 tax year from the four sources listed below. The one on which she cannot be liable for any tax under any circumstances is:

A Interest on National Savings certificates;
B Interest on a building society deposit account;
C The interest portion of a purchased life annuity;
D Her profit on the sale of a painting.

91 Morbidity is the risk of:

A Dying;
B Suffering from depression;
C Becoming disabled;
D Contracting Alzheimer's disease.

92 Which of the following pension arrangements is not set up under trust?

A Occupational Pension Plan.
B Hancock annuity.
C Executive Pension Plan.
D Self-administered Pension scheme.

93 On what condition can an employee take a tax-free lump sum from an Occupational Pension Scheme?

A The scheme must be in trust.
B The employee must have contributed to the scheme.
C The employee must be over 60 at retirement.
D The pension is reduced (commuted).

94 Which of the following earnings can be used as a basis only for Personal Pension Contributions and not for Occupational Pension Plan benefits?

A Salary.
B Bonuses.
C Profits.
D Directors fees.

95 What is the maximum investment in National Savings Childrens' bonds per Issue of bond?

A £500
B £1,000
C £5,000
D £10,000

96 What is the minimum type of life cover which should protect a repayment mortgage?

A Decreasing term.
B Level term.
C Whole life assurance.
D Low-cost endowment.

97 What is a feature of an escalating annuity?

A Increases through the addition of bonuses.
B Increases through a direct link with investments.
C Increases at the discretion of the insurer.
D Increases by a fixed percentage each year.

98 Which of the following National Savings investments is of particular value to higher rate taxpayers?

    A   National Savings certificates.
    B   Income bonds.
    C   Ordinary bank account.
    D   Pensioners' Guaranteed income bond.

99 An employee has worked for an employer for 40 years, and retires on a salary of £48,000. He has no other remuneration. What is the maximum pension that the Inland Revenue will permit the employee to receive?

    A   £32,000 p.a.
    B   £48,000 p.a.
    C   £36,000 p.a.
    D   £24,000 p.a.

100 Which of the following falls into a business category which requires authorisation?

    A   Advising a client on the benefits of private medical insurance.
    B   Referring a client to an insurance company for advice.
    C   Selling shares purchased for your own benefit.
    D   A satisfied policyholder refers a business colleague to his insurer.

Answers

ANSWERS TO QUIZ QUESTIONS

Chapter 1

1   A

2   A

3   D

4   C

5   A

6   B

Chapter 2

1   C

2   D

3   C

4   A

5   B

6   D

7   D

8   A

9   A

Chapter 3

1   A

2   B

3   D

4   A

5   C

6   A

Chapter 4

1   D

2   A

3   A

4   D

Chapter 5

1   B

2   C

3   C

Chapter 6

1   A

2   B

3   D

4   B

5   A

6   C

7   D

8   D

Chapter 7

1   B

2   D

3   A (10% of £1,520 plus 22% of £15,480)

4   B

5   C

6   B

Chapter 8

1   D

2   C

3   D

4   D

5   B

6   C

Chapter 9

1	D
2	B
3	C
4	D
5	B
6	D

Chapter 10

1	A
2	C
3	B
4	A
5	D

Chapter 11

1	C
2	C
3	B
4	B

Chapter 12

1	C
2	D
3	B
4	B
5	C
6	C
7	D
8	B
9	D

Chapter 13

1	C
2	D
3	C
4	B
5	C
6	D
7	A

Chapter 14

1	A
2	B
3	A
4	C

Chapter 15

1	B
2	A
3	D
4	A
5	A
6	C
7	C
8	D
9	D
10	A
11	D
12	D
13	D
14	C
15	C

ANSWERS TO PRACTICE EXAMINATION 1

1. B   Records should be kept for a period of six years at least

2. D   Inflation is the increase of prices over time

3. D   An Investment Trust is closed-ended and is a PLC

4. D   The PIV is the regulators spot check on the company's compliance procedures

5. C   The interest paid on a Capital Bond is gross but is taxable. The term of the investment is five years

6. A   Class 1A is now paid on all taxable benefits in kind by employers (although there are some small exceptions)

7. C   The investment business should be incidental to the main purpose of the business

8. B   Personal pension contributions by the employer are not taxable. This makes this benefit in kind very attractive to the employee

9. B   Premium bond prizes are completely exempt from income tax

10. C   If the capital is withdrawn then tax will be paid on the interest from the TESSA

11. C   Redundancy payments above £30,000 are subject to income tax

12. C   Locum arrangements have to be in place to cover the absence of a sole trader from the business

13. C   It is a with profit endowment and a decreasing term assurance

14. B   The Working Families Tax Credit is free from any tax liability. It is designed to increase the income of low paid families who have children and are working at least 16 hours per week.

15. D   Inheritance tax from a UK domiciled individual relates to their assets anywhere in the world

16. C   £70 per person is the exemption from income tax on Ordinary Account Interest

17. C   The second tier rules apply to SROs

18. D   Under self-assessment the tax will be paid on the 31 January during the tax year (based on 50% of the previous years assessment) and a further 50% on 31 July in the tax year following the current tax year and then the final payment known as the 'balancing payment' will be due on 31 January following the current tax year.

19. A   As he is in the the UK for less than 90 days per year on average he is not considered UK resident. He would also have to be UK resident for 17 out of the last 20 years to be deemed domiciled for IHT purposes. So Herman is neither resident nor domiciled

20. A   An endowment is the only regular savings plan in the list which will provide a tax efficient lump sum after ten years. An investment bond would be used to invest an existing capital sum for growth

21. C   Unit linked endowment is aimed at long term savings because the fund is unit linked it is directly related to investment performance

22.	B	As Andrew is a basic rate taxpayer there will be no further tax liability as the tax credit of 10% satisfies the liability in full
23.	B	The second tier rules relate to people giving regulated investment advice under the Financial Services Act 1986
24.	B	They must not be capable of work
25.	C	Maximum compensation is £48,000, maximum *claim* is £50,000
26.	D	The insurable interest only has to exist at the start of the policy
27.	C	The payment of a claim will be at the discretion of the life company
28.	A	Critical Illness insurance would have provided a lump sum which could have been used to meet the conversion costs and ongoing living expenses
29.	D	The client has decided to act on an execution only basis
30.	C	At the present time a pension for life must be bought. There may be an *option* to take a five or ten year guarantee period or tax-free cash
31.	B	The Pension Scheme Office will allow early retirement from age 50
32.	D	A completed proposal form constitutes offer in the legal contractual sense
33.	C	Cold calling is strictly regulated to ensure that the client may not be subject to undue influence
34.	D	The Married Couples allowance has been abolished for those under the age of 65 on 6th April 2000
35.	B	They have the authority to look at any type of record and ask questions of any staff they wish
36.	D	It will run for a maximum of 104 weeks
37.	A	Secondary Class 1 National Insurance Contributions will be paid by the employer
38.	A	The property is secured under a mortgage by a legal charge in favour of the lender. The property will be released from the charge when the mortgage is repaid
39.	D	Best execution is the duty of the broker to purchase the shares at the best possible price in the market
40.	D	The basic state pension is linked to National Insurance Contributions or Credits throughout the individuals working life and is linked to the Retail Prices Index. Pensions are increased every April by the change in RPI to the previous September
41.	D	Lifetime gifts to discretionary trusts are treated as Chargeable Lifetime Transfers and would be subject to tax immediately if the transfer is in excess of the nil rate band exemption
42.	D	They are usually sold as an ancillary product to a mortgage
43.	C	Income Support is only available to those over 18 and who are not working full time
44.	B	They must not deal as the effect of the letter could be to increase the share price. If the company already held the stock this could be a clear conflict of interest
45.	D	Annually in arrears would give the highest pension as the life company gets to hold the money for longer so the investor wishes to be

compensated accordingly

46.	C	If an individual dies intestate then their estate will be distribution in accordance with the laws of succession under the Administration of Estates Act 1925 and subsequent statutes
47.	D	The maximum number of weeks before the payment of the higher rate is 52
48.	B	The firm must have a compliance manual if there are 10 or more advisers
49.	A	Statutory Sick Pay is only available to employees
50.	C	Capital gains tax will be payable on stocks and shares not in an ISA or a PEP, the other items listed are specifically exempt from CGT
51.	A	The age allowance is given to individuals aged over 65 before 6th April 2000. It applies to income up to £17,000 and will be reduced by £1 for every £2 over this amount thereafter.
52.	A	An employee in an Occupational Pension Scheme may contribution up to 15% of their total remuneration up to a maximum of the current level of the earnings cap (£91,800 in 2000/01)
53.	B	The 1999/2000 limit was retained under the March 2000 Budget so the investor may still contribution £3,000 under the plan
54.	D	If a client has been referred the name of the person giving the referral should be disclosed (with their permission)
55.	B	Pension contributions made by an employee are paid net of tax at the basic rate. A self-employed person would be paid gross
56.	B	There is a maximum rate set for the mortgage but the rate can vary below this rate. At the end of a fixed period it is usual for the mortgage to revert to the Standard Variable Rate
57.	C	Personal Pension Term Assurance will have premiums subject to tax relief
58.	D	A self-employed painter, as you have to be subject to Schedule E tax (an employee) to belong to an Occupational Pension Scheme
59.	C	Private investors benefit from the best execution rules as they are less likely to have access to up to date market information
60.	D	The key words here are a 'fixed period'. An annuity certain will pay out an income in return for a capital sum for a fixed period. A lifetime annuity would payout for as long as the individual survived and not a fixed period
61.	A	This will be covered by the marriage exemption under the IHT rules. Each parent may give up to £5,000. If the annual exemption of £3,000 has not been utilised, it is possible to combine the gift to make use of this in addition to the existing exemption
62.	B	Contributions are limited because of the tax relief given to the fund
63.	A	Tax can be reclaimed if deducted from a savings account. It is possible to complete a form R85 to have interest paid without the deduction of tax
64.	C	The reversionary bonus is added to the basic sum assured. Once added the reversionary bonus cannot be removed

65.   D   Consideration from the life company is the provision of life cover on the payment of a premium.

66.   A   She acquires her domicile of origin from her father so would be British domiciled. In any case if she lived in the UK for 17 out of the last 20 years she would be deemed domiciled here.

67.   D   This would be a term found in a PHI/Income Protection Policy

68.   A   The Consumer Credit Act 1974 applies to non-home loans below £25,000

69.   C   £35,000
                (£28,400)
                  £6,600   taxable at 40%
                £6,600 @ 40% = £2,640

         The question states that all allowances have been given

70.   B   The capital element of income from a Purchased Life Annuity will be free of income tax

71.   D   Joint Tenancy means that the survivor inherits the deceased's share of the property rather like a joint bank account

72.   D   The building society will return your capital in full without risk of loss (unless it goes bust)

73.   D   The refusal has to be recorded on the fact-find in the appropriate section

74.   D   The adviser needs to obtain adequate information regarding the clients circumstances before making a recommendation

75.   A   Whole of life policies can be written to aim towards investment or life cover or a combination of the two

76.   B   If employees are contracted out of SERPS the employer must provide an adequate alternative. If the employee contracts herself out of SERPS then an Appropriate Personal Pension is used as a replacement for the SERPS forgone

77.   B   High-risk because the single-company PEP is invested in one stock and therefore volatile. It was only possible to use this method up to 5th April 1999

78.   B   The name of the person making the referral must be given to the client.

79.   D   Everyone resident in the UK is allowed to claim the personal allowance (even a new-born baby)

80.   B   Capital gains can from 2000/01 be subject to tax at 10% in so far as the starting rate limit has not been utilised by other income.

81.   B   The proceeds of the policy will not form part of the estate of the individual on death and the executors will not have to wait

82.   D   Where the adviser has a conflict of interest with a product it must be shown that the product recommended is 'better than best' advice

83.   C   Existing home income plans will continue to receive relief at the basic rate of tax

84.   D   When income is over £17,000 (2000/01) the personal allowance is reduced by £1 for every £2 that income is over this figure. However, the personal allowance given cannot fall below the £4,385 that everybody else gets. This is why answer A is incorrect

85.	A	The first £70 of National Savings Ordinary Account interest is exempt from income tax
86.	C	Earnings from employment are taxed under Schedule E
87.	B	Your recommendation should fulfil the clients needs

88. B   £18,365

(£7,200) Annual Exemption (2000/01)

£11,165

Anthony is a 40% taxpayer so the tax due would be £4,466

89.	A	Family Income Benefit would provide his wife with a regular income which is free from income tax
90.	B	Contributions have to be made into an alternative arrangement for the employee
91.	C	Complaints should be addressed in the first instance to the firm concerned to try and reach resolution.
92.	A	The unused annual exemption may be carried forward for one year only and can be utilised only once the current year's exemption has been used
93.	B	The Unit Linked endowment premium is used to buy units in a life fund
94.	A	Decreasing term assurance does not offer a surrender value at anytime as it is a pure insurance contract
95.	D	The ombudsman bureau can only award up to £50,000 at present
96.	B	If there are no earnings in the carry back year, the regulations allow carry back to be stretched for a further year making two as a maximum
97.	A	Current bid price is used to determine the value of the Unit Linked endowment
98.	C	The Income Protection/PHI policy is designed to protect income lost through inability to work
99.	B	The policy is designed for people who have a low income at the start of their mortgage but expect to have a higher income in the years following eg a young doctor, lawyer or other such professional
100.	B	A Hancock annuity is a pension provided by an employer usually for a long serving employee and is purchased after the employee has retired. It will be taxed as a Pension annuity

ANSWERS TO PRACTICE EXAMINATION 2

1. C   It is for customers of firms that are or are about to be insolvent

2. B   They have the power to look at any record in any form and talk to any member of staff they wish to

3. A   The person who has security is the assignee and is often the mortgagee of a property

4. A   An employer has insurable interest if the death of the employee could mean the loss of profits

5. B   As they are giving advice to the general public they are deemed to be conducting investment business under the Financial Services Act 1986

6. C   It is the age of the eldest partner that is used to determine eligibility for the Married Couples Age Allowance. To claim this one partner had to bc at least 65 by the 6th April 2000.

7. B   Endowment insurance has an investment content and therefore must come under the cancellation notice rules

8. B   12 monthly reviews must take place of the compliance plan

9. B   Maths time.

   If take £10,000 pension it will all be taxed to income tax.

   £10,000
   (£4,385) Personal Allowance (2000/01)
   £5,615

   £1,520 @ 10% = £152.00

   £4,095 @ 22% = £900.90

   Total tax = £1,052.90

   If take £7,000 pension this will be taxed as income. Of the £2,500 from the Purchased Life Annuity £2,100 will be exempt from tax. So only £400 will be taxed and as savings income not as earned income.

   £7,000
   (£4,385) Personal allowance (2000/01)
   £2,615

   £1,520 @ 10% = £152.00

   £1,095 @ 22% = £240.90

   £400 @ 20% = £80.00

   Total Tax = £472.90

   First option would give an income of £10,000 less £1,052.90 tax = £8,947.10

   Second option would give an income of £9,500 less £472.90 tax = £9,027.10

   The second option is an **increase in income of £80**

10. B   When a client has a portfolio, a discretionary management agreement is normally required

11.	C	£431,000 less £234,000 = £197000 taxed at 40% is £78,800
12.	A	Total of gains less the losses and the annual exemption of £7,200
13.	C	She may refer the client to an IFA and receive commission. The key fact is that her company does not have a product which is suitable for the clients needs.
14.	A	Employers and employees have to pay class 1
15.	C	A Reason Why letter is not supplied if the client is making the transaction on an 'execution only basis' as advice is 'neither being sought nor given'.
16.	D	With-profit endowment is a long term savings contract
17.	B	The insurance company would limit benefits until the policy-holder returns to an appropriate area.
18.	A	With profit bonus is not guaranteed it is discretionary
19.	D	£70 per person
20.	D	It is an FSA rule
21.	A	Reduce the life cover or increase the premium to keep the life cover constant
22.	B	Decreasing term assurance would be used, as the capital on the mortgage is being repaid through the repayment loan
23.	C	50 is the lowest age allowed for early retirement
24.	A	To be eligible for an ISA an individual has to be 18 or over, UK resident or a crown employee working abroad eg a soldier
25.	A	AVCs can be made to boost the pension entitlement under an occupational pension scheme
26.	D	A cancellation notice is not required for accident and sickness insurance
27.	A	Protected Rights are the benefits from contracting out. They are not guaranteed
28.	C	Utmost Good Faith is the requirement that you must disclose all material facts to the insurer as you are in a position of greater knowledge
29.	B	
30.	C	Endowments can be assigned, but Pensions, ISAs, Bank and Building Society Accounts cannot
31.	A	Equity tax credits cannot be reclaimed by a non-taxpayer
32.	B	28 days notice is the current requirement to the regulator
33.	A	£7,000 is the maximum in the equity component of a Maxi-ISA for 2000/01
34.	D	Withdrawals from an ISA are not limited and are not taxed in any way
35.	A	Greater of death sum assured or the bid value of units
36.	A	Income will be maximised via an immediate annuity as part of the return is a return of capital in addition to an investment payment from the life company
37.	B	FSA can investigate the members of any regulator

38.	C	Index-linked National Savings Certificates provide inflation proofing plus a return on top
39.	C	Social security may be available but is means-tested
40.	B	An executor is the person who winds up the estate and follows the wishes laid down in the will by the deceased person
41.	D	The capital content is laid down by the Inland Revenue based on how long the individual should live
42.	A	Records should be kept to protect both the adviser and the client, as it provides an audit trail for regulators
43.	C	It is a wrapper around equity investments or some types of bonds. The income from the investments and gains are free from income and capital gains tax
44.	B	At least 90 days on average over a four year period
45.	A	Joint tenancy means that the survivor inherits the property outright
46.	A	Earnings between the earnings threshold and the upper earnings limit are subject to NICs on the employee
47.	B	The sale of shares could lead to a chargeable gain for CGT
48.	D	Bid price is the selling price and the offer is the buying price for the client
49.	A	If resident in UK for 17 out of the last 20 years, it would mean deemed domicile
50.	D	RPI is used in the UK to measure the current rate of inflation
51.	C	The employer pays 3% less NICs in a final salary scheme and the employee will pay 1.6% less
52.	D	Private investors are required to complete a fact find
53.	D	The client wishes to act on an execution only basis
54.	A	A Friendly Society policy is a tax-free fund
55.	A	It is paid at the state retirement age which is currently 65 for men and 60 for women
56.	A	A Mortgage Protection Plan provides life cover on a decreasing term basis and has no surrender value or investment content so cannot be used to repay the capital on the mortgage
57.	B	Investment is taxed at the marginal rate. Although if it falls in the 22% band, then it is taxed at 20%
58.	A	Duty of Utmost Good Faith
59.	C	Opting out. Not normally good advice!
60.	C	A copy of all agreements is not normally required
61.	B	Witnesses are excluded from benefiting under the will
62.	D	The employee chooses the provider under the FSAVC but this need not be the case under the AVC
63.	A	Capitalisation is not normally covered. The requirement is to look at the financial strength of the company
64.	C	33% as there is an additional 50% tax to pay on the income over £17,000 (50% of 22% is 11%)
65.	A	Insurable interest only has to exist at the start of the policy

66.	D	A tied agent does not consider the performance in the market. The tied adviser should only recommend those products considered suitable
67.	B	Profits are taxed in the tax year in which the accounting year end falls
68.	D	An EPP is a type of Occupational Pension Scheme
69.	C	If the premium increased any more the policy would cease to be qualifying
70.	B	Family income benefit would be ideal but level term assurance is the best response to meet the need for a specific period and is cheap

71.   C   Tax liability is £21,675 less pension £1,000 less £4,385 = £16,290

£1,520 @ 10% = £152.00

14,770 @ 22% = £3,249.40

Total tax is £3,401.40

72.	B	Gilts are always paid gross
73.	D	The terms available on the National Savings Fixed Interest Savings Bond are 6, 12, 18 and 36 months. Five years is one of the terms offered on the Fixed Rate Savings *Certificate*
74.	A	The Widows' Pension is paid to women over 45. If she is under 45 and has children for whom she is still receiving Family Allowance, she will be entitled to claim the Widowed Mothers Allowance which is a basic amount plus an addition for each dependent child
75.	D	If the client does not wish to act on your advice you should note the file accordingly and replay the fact that he/she is acting contrary to your instructions in correspondence with the client. This will protect the adviser against future claims
76.	A	MIRAS relief is still available at basic rate (22% in 2000/01) for those who had taken out a Home Income Plan before 9th March 1999
77.	A	Taper relief reduces the tax liability on gifts made during the lifetime of the individual concerned. The effect will be to reduce tax on gifts made more than three years before death and there will be no tax on gifts made more than seven years before death
78.	C	Statutory Maternity Pay is subject to both income tax and National Insurance
79.	B	The Investor Compensation Scheme will provide compensation in cases like this were the adviser has subsequently gone insolvent.
80.	C	A Widows' Pension is paid from age 45 and she has the option to swap this for a Retirement Pension at 60 but she may alternatively continue her Widows' Pension to age 65 should she wish to do so
81.	C	In the first instance, an Independent individual in the firm concerned should investigate the complaint.
82.	C	Family Allowance is not subject to income tax
83.	D	Redundancy payments are free of tax up to a statutory maximum of £30,000
84.	C	The key here is with-proportion. This means that the annuitant's estate will receive payment for the period that the annuitant lived since the last payment. In this case, the annuitant died six months

after the last payment, so six months worth of annuity is payable (half of £10,000 is £5,000)

85.	A	They are taxed to income tax on the interest but in common with gilts they are free from capital gains tax on any gains made
86.	D	It is convertible into a long term policy such as an endowment or a whole of life assurance at the option of the policyholder
87.	A	Increase in a mortgage, marriage etc are examples of situations where the sum assured may be increased by the policyholder
88.	B	Transfers on death to children of the deceased are not exempt transfers
89.	D	Statutory Sick Pay and benefits from other PHI/Accident and Sickness policies would have to be taken into account
90.	A	National Savings Certificates are completely free of all UK income and capital gains tax
91.	C	Morbidity is the risk of illness as opposed to the risk of death which is mortality. In this case the best answer is the risk of disability because this covers all of the other illnesses mentioned
92.	B	A Hancock Annuity is an ex-gratia payment made to a pension provider for a long serving employee to receive a pension
93.	D	It is not normally possible to have both the tax free cash and the full pension. Where the tax-free cash is taken the pension must be commuted to a lower figure. (The Civil Service and other public sector schemes do provide full tax-free cash and an unreduced pension, this is the only exception)
94.	C	Profits are taxed under Schedule D. Occupational Pension contributions are made with reference to earnings taxed under Schedule E
95.	B	£1,000 is the maximum investment per Issue of Childrens' Bonds
96.	A	Decreasing term has life cover which reduces in line with the capital repayments on a mortgage
97.	D	An escalating annuity is one in which the payment to the annuitant increases over time
98.	A	National Savings Certificates would be most valuable to higher rate taxpayers because they are free from income and capital gains tax
99.	A	Two thirds of final remuneration (2/3 x £48,000 = £32,000 per annum)
100.	B	If you are providing financial advice to clients you must be authorised. You may if you are a tied adviser refer the client to another company if you do not have a product in your range that meets the clients needs. This activity still requires authorisation as you are being paid for your investment advice

List of key terms and index

BPP
PUBLISHING

BPP PUBLISHING

ORDER FORM

BPP publish Study Texts and Practice & Revision Kits for papers of the Financial Planning Certificate, the Advanced Financial Planning Certificate. Each Study Text is, like this one, tailored precisely to the syllabus. Practice and Revision Kits contain banks of questions and answers, plus full Mock Exams.

To order Study Texts and Kits, telephone us on 020 8740 2211. Alternatively, complete the order details below and send your order to us at the address shown or by fax on 020 8740 1184.

We aim to deliver to all UK addresses inside 5 working days; a signature will be required. Orders to all EU addresses should be delivered within 6 working days. all other orders to overseas addresses should be delivered within 8 working days.

To: BPP Publishing Ltd, Aldine House, Aldine Place, London W12 8AW
Tel: 020 8740 2211   **Fax: 020 8740 1184**   **Email: publishing@bpp.com**

Full name (Mr/Ms): _____

Daytime delivery address: _____

_____ Postcode: _____

Please send me the following books:

Financial Planning Certificate		Quantity	Total (£)
Study Texts (5/00)			
FP1: Financial Services and their Regulation	£25.95		
FP2: Protection, Savings and Investment Products	£25.95		
FP3: Identifying and Satisfying Client Needs	£25.95		
Practice & Revision Kits (6/00)			
FP1: Financial Services and their Regulation	£15.95		
FP2: Protection, Savings and Investment Products	£15.95		
FP3: Identifying and Satisfying Client Needs	£15.95		
Advanced Financial Planning Certificate			
Study Texts (7/00)			
G10: Taxation and Trusts	£32.95		
G20: Personal Investment Planning	£32.95		
G30: Business Financial Planning	£32.95		
G60: Pensions	£32.95		
G70: Investment Portfolio Management	£35.95		
G80: Long-term Care, Life and Health Protection	£35.95		
H15: Supervision and Sales Management	£35.95		
H25: Holistic Financial Planning	£35.95		
Practice and Revision Kits			
G10: Taxation and Trusts	£19.95		
G60: Pensions	£19.95		
		Subtotal	

Postage and packaging
UK: £3 for first book, £2 for each extra   **p & p** [ ]
Europe (inc ROI & CI): £5 for first book, £4 for each extra
Rest of the world: £20 for first books, £10 for each extra

Total [ ]

I enclose a cheque for £_____ **(Cheques to BPP Publishing Ltd) or charge to my Access/Visa/Switch**

Card number [ ][ ][ ][ ][ ][ ][ ][ ][ ][ ][ ][ ][ ][ ][ ][ ]

Start date (Switch only) _____ **Expiry date** _____ **Issue no. (Switch only)** _____

Signature _____ **Daytime Tel. (for queries only)** _____

For Updates, visit our website: www.bpp.com

REVIEW FORM & FREE PRIZE DRAW

All original review forms from the entire BPP range, completed with genuine comments, will be entered into one of two draws on 31 January 2001 and 31 July 2001. The names on the first four forms picked out on each occasion will be sent a cheque for £50.

Name: _____   Address: _____

_____

Date: _____   _____

How have you used this Text?
(Tick one box only)

☐ home study (book only)

☐ on a course: at _____

☐ with 'correspondence' package

☐ other _____

Why did you decide to purchase this Text?
(Tick one box only)

☐ recommended by training department

☐ recommendation by friend/colleague

☐ recommendation by a lecturer at college

☐ saw advertising

☐ have used BPP Texts in the past

☐ Other _____

During the past six months do you recall *(Tick as many boxes as are relevant)*

☐ seeing our advertisement in *Financial Adviser*

☐ seeing our advertisement in *Money Management*

☐ seeing our advertisement in *IFA Contact*

Which (if any) aspects of our advertising do you find useful?
(Tick as many boxes as are relevant)

☐ prices and publication dates of new editions

☐ checklist of contents

☐ facility to order books off-the-page

☐ none of the above

Your ratings, comments and suggestions would be appreciated on the following areas.

	Very useful	*Useful*	*Not useful*
Introductory section	☐	☐	☐
Main text	☐	☐	☐
Questions in chapters	☐	☐	☐
Chapter roundups	☐	☐	☐
Quizzes at ends of chapters	☐	☐	☐
Practice examination	☐	☐	☐
Structure and presentation	☐	☐	☐
Availability of Updates on website	☐	☐	☐

	Excellent	*Good*	*Adequate*	*Poor*
Overall opinion of this Study Text	☐	☐	☐	☐

Do you intend to continue using BPP Study Texts?   ☐ Yes   ☐ No

Please note any further comments, suggestions and apparent errors on the reverse of this page, or write by e-mail to rogerpeskett@bpp.com

Please return this form to: Roger Peskett, BPP Publishing Ltd, FREEPOST, London, W12 8BR

REVIEW FORM & FREE PRIZE DRAW (continued)

Please note any further comments, suggestions and apparent errors below.

FREE PRIZE DRAW RULES

1 Closing date for 31 January 2001 draw is 31 December 2000. Closing date for 31 July 2001 draw is 30 June 2001.

2 Restricted to entries with UK and Eire addresses only. BPP employees, their families and business associates are excluded.

3 No purchase necessary. Entry forms are available upon request from BPP Publishing. No more than one entry per title, per person. Draw restricted to persons aged 16 and over.

4 Winners will be notified by post and receive their cheques not later than 6 weeks after the relevant draw date. Lists of winners will be published in BPP's *focus* newsletter following the relevant draw.

5 The decision of the promoter in all matters is final and binding. No correspondence will be entered into.